Contemporary Critical
Theory and M

Contemporary critical theory's methodology is currently taking shape under the impact both of transformative internal developments within the discipline, and of external pressures and incentives arising from a series of international debates.

In this book Piet Strydom presents a groundbreaking treatment of critical theory's methodology, using as a base the reconstruction of the left-Hegelian tradition, the relation between critical theory and pragmatism, and the associated metatheoretical implications. He assesses extant positions, presents a detailed yet comprehensive restatement and development of critical theory's methodology, compares it with a wide range of current concepts of social criticism and critique, and analyses leading critical theorists' exemplary applications of it. Besides immanent transcendence and the sign-mediated epistemology common to the left-Hegelian tradition, special attention is given to the abductive imagination, reconstruction, normative and causal explanation, explanatory mechanisms and the communicative framework which enables critical theory to link up with its addressees and the public.

Contemporary Critical Theory and Methodology is recommended reading for senior undergraduate and postgraduate students, as well as professionals working within disciplines such as sociology, philosophy, political science, critical theory and cultural studies.

Piet Strydom is Senior Lecturer in the Department of Sociology, School of Sociology and Philosophy, at University College Cork, Ireland. His research interests include areas such as critical theory, the history and philosophy of the social sciences, and cognitive social science, in which he has noted publications.

Social Research Today

Edited by Martin Bulmer

The *Social Research Today* series provides concise and contemporary introductions to significant methodological topics in the social sciences. Covering both quantitative and qualitative methods, this series features readable and accessible books from some of the leading names in the field and is aimed at students and professional researchers alike. This series also brings together for the first time the best titles from the old *Social Research Today* and *Contemporary Social Research* series edited by Martin Bulmer for UCL Press and Routledge.

Other series titles include:

Principles of Research Design in the Social Sciences
Frank Bechhofer and Lindsay Paterson

Social Impact Assessment
Henk Becker

The Turn to Biographical Methods in Social Science
Edited by Prue Chamberlayne, Joanna Bornat and Tom Wengraf

Quantity and Quality in Social Research
Alan Bryman

Field Research
A sourcebook and field manual
Robert G. Burgess

In the Field
An introduction to field research
Robert G. Burgess

Qualitative Analysis
Thinking, doing, writing
Douglas Ezzy

Research Design (second edition)
Catherine Hakim

Measuring Health and Medical Outcomes
Edited by Crispin Jenkinson

Methods of Criminological Research
Victor Jupp

Information Technology for the Social Scientist
Edited by Raymond M. Lee

An Introduction to the Philosophy of Social Research
Tim May and Malcolm Williams

Research Social and Economic Change
The uses of household panel studies
Edited by David Rose

Introduction to Longitudinal Research
Elisabetta Ruspini

Surveys in Social Research (fifth edition)
David de Vaus

Researching the Powerful in Education
Edited by Geoffrey Walford

Researching Race and Racism
Edited by Martin Bulmer and John Solomos

Statistical Modelling for Social Researchers
Principles and practice
Roger Tarling

The International Social Survey Program 1984–2009
Charting the globe
Edited by Max Haller, Roger Jowell and Tom W. Smith

Models in Statistical Social Research
Götz Rohwer

Managing Social Research
A practical guide
Roger Tarling

Martin Bulmer is Professor of Sociology at the University of Surrey. He is Director of the Question Bank (a WWW resource based at Surrey) in the ESRC Centre for Applied Social Surveys (CASS), a collaboration between the National Centre for Social Research (NatCen), the University of Southampton and the University of Surrey. He is also a Director of the department's Institute of Social Research, and an Academician of the Academy of Learned Societies for the Social Sciences.

Contemporary Critical Theory and Methodology

Piet Strydom

Routledge
Taylor & Francis Group

LONDON AND NEW YORK

First published 2011
by Routledge
2 Park Square, Milton Park, Abingdon, Oxon, OX14 4RN

Simultaneously published in the USA and Canada
by Routledge 270 Madison Avenue, New York, NY 10016

Routledge is an imprint of the Taylor & Francis Group, an informa business

First issued in paperback 2013

© 2011 Piet Strydom

Typeset in Baskerville by Prepress Projects Ltd, Perth, UK

British Library Cataloguing in Publication Data
A catalogue record for this book is available from the British Library

Library of Congress Cataloging in Publication Data
Strydom, Piet
Contemporary critical theory and methodology / by Piet Strydom.
p. cm.
Includes bibliographical references.
1. Critical theory. 2. Critical theory–Methodology. I. Title.
HM480.S77 2011
301.01–dc22
2010035713

ISBN: 978-0-415-54827-4 (hbk)
ISBN: 978-0-415-71495-2 (pbk)
ISBN: 978-0-203-87556-8 (ebk)

I dedicate this book in gratitude to

Frederik van Zyl Slabbert (1940–2010),

who first introduced me to the philosophy of social
science,

and to

Karl-Otto Apel,

who shaped my understanding of the field like no other

Contents

Figures and tables

Figures

Tables

Preface and acknowledgements

The central argument advanced in this book owes its inspiration to a remark of Karl-Otto Apel to the effect that the young Marx understood knowledge in terms of a process of mediation which approached the *medium quo* or sign-mediated theory of knowledge developed in fine detail by his younger contemporary, the founder of pragmatism, Charles S. Peirce. The inspirational meaning of this remark was progressively brought home to me by a series of debates of the past three decades or so. The urgency of exploring it is signalled by the fact that these debates in some way all grapple with the current problem situation that arose in the wake of the late twentieth-century return of historicism: how to resolve the relation between transcendental foundationalism and hermeneutic circularism. The first debate concerns the revitalization of left-Hegelianism, which both Marx and Peirce represent, and the recovery of its concept of 'immanent transcendence'; the second is what has become known as 'the renaissance of pragmatism'; and the third is the debate about social criticism and critique. I should mention also my interest in the cognitive revolution and its implications for the social sciences, Critical Theory in particular, which allowed me to appreciate a certain connection among these three debates. The concept of immanent transcendence, Peirce's emphasis on the clarifying and unifying function of general concepts, and the possibility of critique all turn on the most basic cognitive phenomenon: that something belonging to the world is nevertheless able to distinguish itself from the world and to develop a perspective on and relation to the world.

The idea of the book, however, arose in connection with a paper I presented on immanent transcendence and the left-Hegelian heritage of Critical Theory at the tenth anniversary conference of the *European Journal of Social Theory* held in June 2008 at the University of Sussex, organized by Gerard Delanty, editor of the journal. I have been intrigued by the concept of immanent transcendence for a long time and for many years prior to the conference I have been working on the methodology of the social sciences, including Critical Theory. However, it is this event that crystallized the vision of a book project that would bring these various concerns together in a systematic way. I owe a debt of gratitude to Gerard Delanty for helping me to see the goal as well as the path towards it more clearly. My thanks for comments and discussions in this context are also due to Klaus

Eder, Krishan Kumar, Larry Ray, Chris Rumford, Göran Therborn and Laurent Thévenot.

Over many years, some of the ideas in the book were flagged in undergraduate courses and graduate seminars dealing with Critical Theory and the philosophy of social science. A stimulus to investigate certain relevant matters a little more closely was provided by an invitation in 2007 which came via the International Sociological Association to contribute an extensive article – published in 2009 – on philosophies of the social sciences to UNESCO's massive online *Encyclopedia of Life Support Systems*, which seeks to bring together all relevant knowledge to confront the civilizational crisis we are facing today. I am indebted to Charles Crothers, secretary of the Research Committee on the History of Sociology, for this opportunity. Also in 2007, I had the opportunity to explore the relation between Critical Theory and critical realism in the context of a conference, 'Critical turns in Critical Theory: *Festschrift* in honour of Piet Strydom', the proceedings of which were published in 2009. In this context, I wish to express my deepest gratitude to Seamus O'Tuama, who organized the event and edited the publication, as well as to Gerard Delanty, Mauricio Domingues, Ananta Kumar Giri, Gerard Mullally, Patrick O'Mahony, Tracey Skillington, Andrea Pontual and other participants. In 2009, various contexts lent themselves to the development and presentation of ideas related to the concept of immanent transcendence and the methodological issues central to this book. On two different occasions, in March and June, in the framework of a visiting professorship at the Université de Provence, Aix-en-Provence, France, I was able to present papers centred on the concept of immanent transcendence and its implications for critical social science and for a cognitive approach. In this case, I wish to thank above all Alban Bouvier, but for a variety of comments and discussions also Yves Gingras, Paul Roth and Jesús Zamora-Bonilla. In May, the Sociology and Philosophy Summer School organized by members of the School of Sociology and Philosophy at University College Cork, in particular Kieran Keohane and Partick O'Mahony, and held at Blackwater Castle, Castletownroche, Ireland, offered another opportunity to focus on the methodology of Critical Theory with specific reference to the concept of immanent transcendence. It allowed attention to be given specifically to the epistemological and ontological presuppositions of Critical Theory. In this context, my thanks go to Kieran Bonner, Maeve Cooke, John O'Neill and Tony O'Connor. I am also grateful to Ananta Kumar Giri, Madras Institute for Development Studies in Chennai, India, who has regularly issued invitations over the past several years for material on relevant topics such as Critical Theory, cognitive sociological analysis, creative social research, ontology, philosophical anthropology and knowledge for publication in a variety of works. More recently, in May 2010, some of the ideas in this book were presented and discussed at the second Blackwater Castle Summer School on 'Evaluation, Judgement and Critique' organized under the auspices of the School of Sociology and Philosophy, University College Cork. In this case, my thanks are due to Julia Jansen, Kieran Keohane and Patrick O'Mahony as well as other participants. Here at University College Cork, I have become dependent on regular discussions with Patrick O'Mahony and, equally, discussions with Gerard

Mullally, Seamus O'Tuama and Tracey Skillington – not to mention the sustaining encouragement and support I receive from them.

My hope is that this book contributes not only to a better understanding and thus the advancement of Critical Theory, but also to the consolidation of the new School of Sociology and Philosophy at UCC.

Piet Strydom
Kinsale, May 2010

Introduction

The principal argument of this book, the argument regarding contemporary Critical Theory's methodology, is a response to a significant development internal to Critical Theory as well as to demanding contextual pressures exerted upon it. Both the internal development and the contextual change can be dated to roughly the same period. From the late 1980s, it became increasingly evident that a new concept, the concept of 'immanent transcendence', has emerged to take the place of Critical Theory's key concept. It brought Critical Theory's left-Hegelian heritage into much sharper focus than ever before, highlighting in particular the relation between Critical Theory and pragmatism. At about the same time, the international debate about critique, which was earlier marked by the clash between Habermas and Gadamer, was rekindled by a wave of both direct and indirect assaults on Critical Theory from a variety of vantage points, some of an interpretative kind and others representing concepts of critique differing from that of Critical Theory. These attacks did not just call forth predictable defensive reactions from Critical Theory, but more productively also stimulated reflection, self-examination and efforts aimed at self-clarification and elaboration. The confluence of the internal development and contextual pressures pointed towards the need for the specification of Critical Theory's methodology in terms of its left-Hegelian heritage as encapsulated by the new concept of immanent transcendence.

This task was taken up first in the early 1990s, but it has gained momentum only in the new millennium. Although a number of significant milestones have been erected along the way, much still remains to be done. The aim of this book, therefore, is to make a contribution to this task by taking the elaboration of Critical Theory's methodology a step farther in terms of the currently prevailing internal requirements of its own tradition and external demands emanating from the wider intellectual context in which it is embedded. In Part I, the internal development of Critical Theory is traced from the perspective of the new concept of immanent transcendence, with due regard for those elements of the left-Hegelian tradition which have been rendered visible by this novel vision. In Part II, the methodology of contemporary Critical Theory is developed and illustrated in terms of this new concept and its metatheoretical and theoretical implications, based on recent achievements and located within the context of the international debate about critique.

Internal development of Critical Theory

The development that eventually culminated in the recognition of immanent transcendence as the key concept of Critical Theory was initiated by Karl-Otto Apel and Jürgen Habermas in the post-war period. In the 1960s, they were faced with making sense of the relations among hermeneutics, the tradition which continued uninterrupted through the Nazi era, and the two traditions which returned from exile after the war, namely Critical Theory and positivism, in a way that critically salvaged the defensible elements of the core German tradition. Besides a critique of science and a critique of hermeneutics, which bloomed into the well-known positivist dispute and Habermas–Gadamer debate, they found vital support in pragmatism, particularly on the basis of Apel's groundbreaking studies of its founder, Charles S. Peirce. Pragmatism resonated with various trends in the broader intellectual milieu, such as the linguistic-pragmatic turn, the cognitive revolution and the structuralist revolution, yet more important still was that, like Critical Theory, it not only maintained a relation between theory and practice but also formed part of the left-Hegelian tradition. Both the two leading second-generation critical theorists – to resort to the somewhat arbitrary device of generations for expository purposes – returned again and again to left-Hegelianism and its classical roots in Kant and Hegel and on that basis identified, besides Marx, also Peirce and Kierkegaard as its authentic representatives. Although for them this tradition, as these three names suggest, was concerned with world constitution and transformation, problem-solving knowledge production and subject formation, they saw Peirce as having provided the necessary means to think through this whole complex of relations. It took the form of his semiotic theory of signs and the associated sign-mediated theory of knowledge with its multilevel conception of reality.

Habermas and Apel drew out a variety of implications of this fuller understanding of the left-Hegelian tradition, including for example a pluralist philosophy of social science, a communication theory of society, the normative foundations of critique, the concept of immanent transcendence, the threefold theory of signs and the relation between Critical Theory and pragmatism, but partial emphases, incomplete developments and gaps remained. In addition to continuing the major lines such as the normative foundations of critique and the communication theory of society, the third generation of critical theorists became attentive to some of these inadequacies and introduced a series of diversions and qualifications. Among these were the appeal to praxis philosophy to overcome the dualism of lifeworld and system (McCarthy, Honneth); the shift from language to recognition (Honneth); the introduction of feminism (Benhabib, Fraser); the pragmatization of Critical Theory to do justice both to the impurity of the historical realization of reason (McCarthy) and to the democratic social organization of critical social research and knowledge production (Bohman); the placing of the concept of immanent transcendence on the agenda and pursuit of methodology to some degree (McCarthy, Honneth); and, finally, the development of a theory of structure formation to fill a conspicuous gap in the theory of the process constitution of society (Eder). As the international debate about critique inter fied, the third generation gradually increased the attention paid to methodolc (McCarthy, Honneth), but it is remarkable that this methodology's link with immanent transcendence was not adequately substantiated and that its episte-mological underpinnings rooted in the semiotic theory of signs were virtually completely ignored. A consequence of this twofold deficiency was that Critical Theory's explanatory function remained below the required level of explication.

The relative neglect of Critical Theory's methodology was highlighted by the intensifying international debate about critique and, in fact, awareness of it became so acute that, besides efforts on the part of Honneth, the emerging younger generation of critical theorists overwhelmingly tends towards addressing this problem. They do so from different angles, stretching from a rehabilitation of ideology critique (Jaeggi), through an elaboration of reconstructive critique beyond Habermas's communication-theoretical and Honneth's recognition-theoretical versions (Iser, Celikates) as well as putting in place and appropriating Foucault's genealogical critique (McCarthy, Honneth, Saar, Basaure), to a rehabilitation of the psychoanalytical model (Basaure, Celikates) and rethinking the relation between Critical Theory and its addressees (Celikates). What is remarkable despite this level of response, however, is the continuing methodological deficit. Various aspects are indeed fruitfully addressed, but appreciation for the left-Hegelian tradition and thus the relation between Critical Theory and pragmatism is too low for its metatheoretical, epistemological and ontological significance to receive sufficient recognition. Occasionally, the key concept of immanent transcendence is mentioned, yet is afforded little elaboration, whereas the sign-mediated theory of cognition, knowledge production and action disappears from sight and is no longer available as a source for the systematic development of Critical Theory's methodology. As a consequence, the latest phase in the development of Critical Theory tends to reproduce, despite the oft-repeated demand that it must be able to provide causal explanations, the explanatory deficit from which it has been suffering for some time. Not only do the critical theorists need to go beyond a preponderant emphasis on normative critique, yet without surrendering it, but they are also required to come to grips with the advances and demands of the post-empiricist phase in the development of the social sciences.

It is against this background of the internal development and failures of contemporary Critical Theory that the aim of this book and the thrust of its principal argument become comprehensible. In Part I, it first seeks to recoup left-Hegelianism in a way that highlights the relation between Critical Theory and pragmatism as two related strands of this tradition and to bring out the core they have in common.[1] Although the concept of immanent transcendence is cen-tral here, this core also embraces the semiotic theory of signs and the associated epistemological and ontological assumptions. On this basis, Part II is devoted to providing a systematic and coherent development, presentation and illustration of contemporary Critical Theory's methodology. This is done with due regard for the international debate and the competing concepts of critique in relation to which this methodology is taking shape.

International debate about critique

The debate which most immediately impinged and still impinges on contemporary Critical Theory, the international debate about critique, is intelligible only against the background of the profound intellectual changes of the late twentieth century such as the linguistic-pragmatic, the interpretative and the cultural turns. For their part, these events were themselves borne by a series of epistemological-methodological debates (Strydom 2008a) which left the philosophy and practice of social science in a transfigured form by the dawn of the new millennium. These transformative events of the 1950s to the 1970s included, for example, the functionalist debate, the methodological individualist debate, the cognitive revolution, the rationality debate, the Popper–Kuhn debate, the positivist dispute, the structuralist revolution, the Habermas–Gadamer debate, the post-structuralist debate and the realist debate. It is in this broad framework that the debate about critique took off with Critical Theory's rise from obscurity in the 1960s in the specific context of the positivist dispute and Habermas–Gadamer debate. Over the following years and decades, it was periodically reinvigorated by new developments and participants with competing views. This has generated a proliferation of positions and approaches claiming either to represent some form of critique or to have a bearing on the concept of critique. In recent years, the debate is once again becoming more intense, particularly around Critical Theory. Considering the context-setting role the debate plays in Part II, a brief retracing of its trajectory and dynamics could help prepare for an understanding of contemporary Critical Theory.

Against the background of the confrontation between Adorno and Popper in 1961, the debate about critique was launched in all earnest by Habermas's contributions to the Positivist Dispute (e.g. Habermas 1972), supported by Apel's (Apel et al. 1971) comparable position on ideology critique and its emancipatory potential. The debate obtained not only a remarkable momentum due to Habermas's appropriation of hermeneutics for the purposes of renewing Critical Theory, but it also opened a field of contestation between two distinct directions. The name of this cross-section of the debate, the 'hermeneutics-dialectics' or more popularly the 'Habermas–Gadamer debate' (Bubner, Cramer and Wiehl 1970; Apel et al. 1971; Misgeld 1977), indicates unmistakably the directions henceforth involved in contestation. From here runs a line of development not only of Critical Theory, but also of the interpretative turn. Whereas the reception of the initial formulation of critique in terms of the exposure of ideology bloomed into a broad wave of popularization of Critical Theory internationally, Habermas's own understanding underwent a relatively drastic transformation with the differentiation of the central concept of reflection into 'self-reflection' and 'rational reconstruction' (1974: 22). His adoption of the concept of reconstruction leading to the idea of Critical Theory as a 'critical-reconstructive social science' (1990) took place against the foil of the convergence of the cognitive and the structuralist revolutions. Taking cues from John Searle's Berkeley approach to cognition in terms of a linguistic theory forming part of a theory of action, on the one hand, and from Piaget's cognitive psychology and Chomsky's generative linguistics, on the other, he arrived at a genetic-structuralist, reconstructive view of social science. Although reconstruction became his central concept, Habermas (1979) emphasized its implied realist moment, which makes possible theoretical explanatory knowledge vital to Critical Theory. The theory of communicative action was developed according to the model of reconstructive science and was complemented by an explanatory and critical moment with reference to distorted communication and systems imperatives which infringe on and deform the communicative infrastructure of the lifeworld (1984/87).

In France, during the same period and also under the impact of the cognitive and structuralist revolutions, Pierre Bourdieu and Michel Foucault developed competing ideas of a critical social science. By the late 1970s, Bourdieu's (1986) demonstration of his conception of critique confirmed the strength of his voice in the debate. The social critique of the judgement of taste exhibited by the different social classes in France, reinforced by his 'vulgar critique' of the 'pure critiques' to be found in Kant and Derrida's works on aesthetics, profiled his type of objective sociological critique. Its focus is the distinct practical uses different classes make of their shared cognitive-symbolic forms in their classification struggles, in which language serves as the medium of symbolic violence for the establishment of social boundaries of distinction. As in Habermas's transformation of Critical Theory in the medium of the linguistic turn, Bourdieu's focus on a plurality of different uses or practices accounts for his surrendering of the semantic concept of ideology in favour of a pragmatic one. Foucault's (1986a) decisive signalling of his unique presence with the publication in early 1984 of his assessment of the Enlightenment and the legacy of its concept of critique indicated that the twist he gave to the debate was a challenge Critical Theory could not ignore. While appreciating Kant's innovative contribution, he pursued the original left-Hegelian transformation of critique in a practical yet situational emancipatory direction in the Nietzschean spirit of genealogical critique. Its aim was to highlight paradoxical reversals or relapses of social ideals or norms into disciplinary and normalization practices requiring the development of a new sensitivity for ambiguity. Contemporary critical theorists' considered appropriation of Foucault's basic insights has reached a decisive point with the recent conference in Frankfurt on the relevance of his contribution (Honneth and Saar 2003).

The 1970s also saw an innovation in Britain against the background of the emerging post-empiricist situation and the work of the philosopher of science Rom Harré, the structuralist revolution and Marxism. This innovation introduced a new conception of critique into the debate: Roy Bhaskar's realist or naturalist philosophy of social science with its concept of 'explanatory critique' (Bhaskar 1989; Bhaskar and Collier 1998). Although this position has a following in Britain as well as some support in Scandinavia, thus far it has entered the debate around Critical Theory only through William Outhwaite (1987, 2000) and lately also

Danermark et al. (2002), who have argued for a certain realist overlap of the respective positions of Habermas and Bhaskar.

Michael Walzer (1987, 1988) and Richard Rorty (1989) intervened in the debate in the late 1980s with conceptions of social criticism that opened what seems to be the second phase in the debate. On account of their comparable tendencies to emphasize the intertwined relation of the critic to the criticized community, a major motif of the interpretative turn since Gadamer (1975), they became stylized in the debate as representing similar conceptions. A closer look shows, however, that this prima facie reading of Rorty from an internal perspective is incomplete. It holds as long as one focuses on his contextualist account of 'the contingency of community' (Rorty 1989: 44–69), but once one considers his epistemologically inspired account of the role of different 'vocabularies' (1989: 3–22), especially ones opening up new goals inspiring changes in self-understanding, it is clear that he adds a world-disclosing dimension to his situated, internal or immanent criticism. For this he appeals to Heidegger. What Walzer and Rorty do share, however, is a denial of the relevance of a theory of society and the explanatory perspective it makes possible. The pragmatist elements in Rorty found a stronger pragmatist and, indeed, Critical Theory-friendly articulation in the work of James Bohman (1991, 1999) in the course of the 1990s. Perceiving clearly a common concern with a new democratically organized way of searching for problem-solving alternatives based on self-transformative capacities, he argued for a merging of Critical Theory and pragmatism to provide a basis for a positively reformulated conception of critique instead of the orthodox negative one.

From the early 1990s, Honneth's (1985, 1992) anthropologically based recognition theory representing a reconstruction-oriented yet alternative position to Habermas's language-based theory came to play an increasingly important role in redirecting the debate about critique. An important step in the renewal of Critical Theory was his emphasis on the left-Hegelian principle of immanent transcendence. Honneth filled out his Hegelian departure precisely during the period when Habermas (1996) turned increasingly strongly to Kant and Kantian-inspired political philosophy, which adopts a constructivist orientation in the sense of giving centre stage to the process of the generation of norms. For instance, Rawls's (1985: 57–65) allowance of 'criticism' of institutions which do not meet the normative principles of justice guiding such norm creation left a certain mark on his concept of critique. From the late 1980s, a number of American authors maintaining close relations with Habermas began to figure in the debate. Seyla Benhabib (1986) brought Critical Theory forward through a consideration of questions of difference which have been opened up by the cultural turn in general and feminism in particular. Nancy Fraser's (1989, 1997) understanding of critique eventually gained high visibility in the context of the debate with Honneth about the relation of redistribution to recognition (Fraser and Honneth 2003). In both his assessment of Foucault's genealogical approach and dispute with the Foucauldian David Hoy from the viewpoint of Critical Theory in the early 1990s, Thomas McCarthy (1993, 1994a) simultaneously sought to reassert the left-Hegelian tradition while giving prominence to its Kantian moment in such a way that critique was attributed the sense of a practically relevant socio-historical analysis of the situated or 'impure' realization of ideas of reason. Along similar lines, McCarthy (2001a, 2004) later also engaged in a demonstration of the limits of Rawlsian constructivism.

Although Luc Boltanski and Laurent Thévenot (1991) launched their new departure in pragmatic sociology in the early 1990s, it started to have an impact on the debate in a way that drew Critical Theory in only relatively recently. The definitive moment of mutual engagement is marked by Boltanski's Adorno lectures in Frankfurt and his interview and discussion with representatives of the Institute for Social Research (Boltanski 2008; Boltanski and Honneth 2009). At the centre of the confrontation is Boltanski and Thévenot's turn against Bourdieu's critical sociology towards a 'sociology of critique' and the question this shift gives rise to, namely whether a sociology focused on the reflexive and critical capacities of ordinary social actors alone is able to fulfil the requirements of critique. The latest round in the debate is characterized by Honneth's response as well as that of the emerging generation of critical theorists in Frankfurt to the new configuration of concepts of critique. Following on earlier pieces which started from the debate concerning internal social criticism and external critique (Honneth 2000a, 2007a), Honneth produced a series of articles which explicitly focus on the central issue raised by the debate and their implication for Critical Theory (2004a, 2007b,c,d). Each in his own way, the younger authors Mattias Iser and Robin Celikates seek to mediate between the counterposed forms of 'internal' and 'external' critique and thus to go beyond both towards 'reconstructive critique'. Iser (2008) sees both Habermas's theory of understanding and Honneth's theory of recognition as forms of reconstructive critique which are able in some way to accommodate the internal and external poles, but he undertakes to eliminate the one-sidedness of each of these by proposing their integration into a theory of 'communicative rec-ognition' as a new version of Critical Theory. Celikates (2009) envisages a solution in the development of Critical Theory as a form of reconstructive critique based on the psychoanalytical model which is focused on social pathologies as structural reflexivity deficits.

Besides being a crucial part of the context of contemporary Critical Theory, this debate is of interest from the perspective of this book for various reasons. The book is conceived as a contribution to the renewed concern with the concept of critique in general and the renovation of Critical Theory's concept of critique in particular. What it is more specifically aimed at, however, is to recast the percep-tion of the debate as an antinomic field in which internal social criticism and external critique confront each other in an irresolvable contradiction. This is done by showing that, once the multidimensional nature of Critical Theory's concept of critique is appreciated, it becomes evident that the parameters of the debate are too complex to be confined to the conventionally accepted internal–external distinction. Critical Theory goes beyond it by mediating reconstructively between the immanent and the transcendent moments, on the one hand, and by engaging in explanatory critique from the viewpoint of the observer and excluded, on the other.

/ on methodology in this book begs the question of its meaning as well as
in Critical Theory. In the scientistic or, more specifically, the positivistic
ɔn which dominated the social sciences until the onset of post-empiricism,
odology was reductively interpreted in keeping with the then prevailing
ʮ trine of the 'unity of science'. Since the scientific method was accordingly
regarded as the one and only method, the need for any reflection on methodology
was jettisoned in favour of shifting the emphasis to methods instead. Beyond such
sheer methodologism, however, the etymology of the word – that is, *methodos* + *logos*
or the logic of the way, or direction and steps, to be followed for the purposes of
reaching a goal – suggests that the meaning of methodology is in the first instance
determined by the suffix '-logy'. Rather than methods and related procedures and
techniques, therefore, the term refers to the systematicity of methods in a certain
domain, the logic or theory governing methods for the purposes of knowledge and
theory production. Needless to say, there is of course a wide range of quantitative or extensive, qualitative or intensive and critical methods from which Critical
Theory could select for the purposes of critical social research. As Adorno et al.
(1976: 72) insisted, any such methods must be appropriate to the object of study,
but this by no means excludes the requirement that both their selection and use
be subject to more general methodological considerations beyond and above mere
methods. Methodological reflection in the broad sense accepted in this book has in
any case always been regarded as an integral part of Critical Theory.

Critical Theory as an intellectual tradition articulated in terms of a social
scientific theoretical and research programme provides the context within
which methodology finds its place. The overall architectonic of this programme
embraces a number of different yet closely interrelated aspects which are indicated in Table 0.1.

Table 0.1 Architectonic structure of Critical Theory

Dimension	Focal concern
Transcendental	Conditions of possibility
Dialectical	Goal pursued
Normative	Guiding moral-ethical-political principles
Ontological	Character and scope of social reality and its relation to nature
Theoretical	Core components and features of social reality and their relations
Epistemological	Cognitive and knowledge production process, the interest guiding its pursuit, kind of knowledge, modes of inference, and context of intersubjective justification
Methodological	Logic of knowledge and theory production, social scientific employment, intersubjective testing, justification and practical use

Transcendental dimension

The first constitutive aspect, the transcendental dimension, concerns the most basic set of assumptions regarding the conditions making Critical Theory possible as distinct from other types of social science: empirical, realist and interpretative. Most basically, it is assumed that humans are practical, corporeal beings who engage with the world in a restricted number of ways which allow the opening up of different perspectives, interests in knowledge, categorical lines of questioning and constitution of corresponding objects of knowledge as well as intersubjective reflection in the form of argumentation or discourse (Apel 1984; Strydom 2008a). Rather than adopting an instrumental orientation, as in the case of empiricism, or an ontological one, as in realism, or a hermeneutic one, as in interpretativism, Critical Theory is based on a type of engagement with reality which is geared towards exposure for the benefit of learning and the enhancement of human socio-cultural existence within the limits of the natural order. As regards the practical, corporeal existence of human beings, it should be noted that the left-Hegelian tradition from Marx and Kierkegaard, through Horkheimer, Adorno and Marcuse supported by Freud, to Habermas and Honneth, stresses the subject's vulnerability and propensity for suffering, which is a vital condition for the possibility of critique as well as receptivity of the critical message.

Dialectical and normative dimension

Critical Theory's characteristic normative orientation becomes clearer when these transcendental conditions of possibility are dialectically modulated to give rise to the question of the corresponding goal of Critical Theory in distinction to the other types of social science. Whereas empiricism potentially serves control, governance, planning and social engineering, and interpretativism the clarification of meaning and furthering of understanding, Critical Theory aims at enlightenment, emancipation and transformation, including self-transformation. Its goal is to clarify the process of the constitution of society by accounting for the mechanisms at play in the process and, particularly, in its deformation or blockage, and to do so in a way that facilitates problem solving and world creation. The pursuit of this goal is normatively guided by its moral-ethical and related political concern – a concern that is denied any relevance in empiricism in the name of objectivistic 'value-freedom', and is represented in a severely truncated conventionalist and hence relativist form in interpretativism under the title either of what Weber, following Heinrich Rickert, called 'value-relatedness' or of communitarianism.

For Critical Theory, by contrast, the normative dimension concerns how morality and ethics figure in both social life and in the practice of social science. Social reality embracing both of these is regarded as being structured by ideas of reason or regulative ideas that operate simultaneously as immanent moral obligations and transcendent guidelines or critical standards for autonomous agents' ethically informed orientations and actions. Critical Theory's key concept of immanent transcendence captures precisely the factual role in situated social life of per-formatively presupposed counterfactual assumptions in the form of normatively pregnant guiding ideas. What is crucial for its normative orientation and, by the same token, its critical function is the fact that the factual role of counterfactual ideas of reason can be either norm-setting or concealing and misleading, or pos-sibly even both at the same time.

Ontology

Ontologically, Critical Theory assumes that social reality is socio-culturally consti-tuted in an open-ended process of constitution, organization, transformation and evolution. This active, processual and temporal conception entails that society cannot simply be regarded as an empirical phenomenon made up, for instance, of regularities, as in empiricism, or of intentions and their expressions, as in interpre-tativism, but is to be treated as a complex that is dynamically structured by sets of rules and relations which are partly real yet hidden, non-empirical, unobservable and partly counterfactual. These rules and relations cannot be confined to func-tionally emerging reflexive instances recursively regulating social subsystems, as in functionalist objectivism, since society as a self-substitutive order consists, over and above functional structures, also of normative structures or good reasons. Accordingly, Critical Theory focuses on the dynamics of structure formation in terms of stability and transformation or change, while privileging those moments of tension, contradiction or conflict in which structure formation, due to whatever forces, factors or processes, becomes a problem or crisis-stricken and therefore an at least potential issue with a moral, ethical or political significance which, if resolved through acceptable reasons or grounds, could have a more or less signifi-cant impact on the continuing process of constitution in a normatively adequate manner.

According to Critical Theory's ontology of 'weak naturalism' (Strydom 2002; Habermas 2003, 2005), it is assumed, furthermore, that social reality is not a purely socio-cultural phenomenon since, ontologically, there is continuity between nature and the socio-cultural form of life. This relation, however, is not interpreted in a strong determinative sense which could lead to an epistemologi-cal reduction of society to nature. Although indeed forming part of nature, the socio-cultural form of life is relatively independent and epistemically primary for Critical Theory, yet it is appreciated as still being open to the impact or inter-ference of nature – an example being the ecological crisis, which is recursively impacting on the socio-cultural form of life in a way that compels societal and subjective self-transformation.

Theory

As a theoretical undertaking, Critical Theory adopts the form of a theory of soci-ety or social theory which articulates the previously mentioned common set of basic ontological assumptions. Corresponding to the complexity of this ontology, however, this theory is of a multidimensional kind.

Since any particular major critical theorist represents but a selective and stylized take on these ontological assumptions, different theoretical versions of Critical Theory can be distinguished. This shows first on the deepest theoretical level: the process of the constitution, reproduction, organization, transformation and evolution of society. This is the level of reconstructive theory, as Habermas (1990; Habermas and Luhmann 1971) proposed to call it, on which philosophical and substantive types of theory – in line with the concept of immanent transcendence – stand in a complementary relation to one another. For instance, Marx chose labour as his perspective, whereas Marcuse, Habermas and Honneth adopted the human drives, language and recognition as their respective prisms through which to refract Critical Theory's ontology in both a concrete situational and a situation-transcendent direction.[2]

The second major level houses the substantive historical-sociological or materialist theory of society. This type involves theoretical knowledge of those interfering forces, factors or processes which allow the intrusion of an element of distorting or blocking violence into social relations and the process of the factual realization of the potential of counterfactual socio-cultural ideas of reason. Such theoretical knowledge is focused on the explanation of the vehicles, structures or mechanisms carrying the offending interference and intrusion. Second, this critical type of theory is required to make this knowledge amenable to the critique of problematic, crisis-stricken or pathological social states of affairs in a way that provides enlightening – both negative and positive – situational interpretations which impact on the self-understanding of those involved as well as the broader public and have the potential to direct and guide problem solving and world creation. The reference to self-understanding and situational interpretation, which imply self-transformation, suggests that this theory is by no means a purely macro-theory. On the contrary, it is multidimensional so as to include also a theory of the subject.

Epistemology

Of all the aspects of Critical Theory, besides methodology, most attention is given in this book to its epistemological dimension, which concerns assumptions regarding access to reality, the process of cognition and knowledge production, the kind of knowledge sought of reality, the interest in knowledge guiding that search, the inferential modes at play in the acquisition of knowledge, and the intersubjective context in which knowledge is developed and justified. It is indeed one of the principal aims of this book to bring into view the *medium quo* or sign-mediated theory of cognition, knowledge and action shared by Marx and Peirce, the latter of whom worked it out in detail. It was promoted by Apel in particular as well as by Habermas, but is neglected by contemporary critical theorists – with negative consequences for their ability to clarify Critical Theory's methodology. Rejecting the subject–object dualism, whether in the guise of objectivism or of subjectivism, this epistemological position regards knowledge as being generated in a process mediated by signs or sign-bearers that refer to objects, whether natural or social, and are interpreted in the at once real and counterfactual communication community represented by both science and society in the present and future. Besides the traditionally emphasized inductive and deductive modes of inference, special significance is assigned to abduction in the sense of the imaginative or creative forging of relations between felt qualities, objective givens and conceptual or theoretical insights. Further, every act of knowing and therefore the process of the generation of knowledge are regarded as being part of reality itself in the sense not only of the knowers themselves belonging to the world, but more profoundly still also of the actual knowledge acquired in turn feeding back into and thus impacting on the further development of reality itself. Forming part of reality, Critical Theory is epistemologically underpinned by the constant awareness that every act of cognition, knowledge production and their practical employment for the purposes of problem solving and meaning or world creation represents a moment of participation in the evolution of reality – that is, of society and nature – which demands responsible sign interpretation and engagement with reality. Shouldering such responsibility, Critical Theory focuses by way of its cognitive interest in particular on problems or crises with a moral, ethical and political significance whose treatment could potentially lead to problem solving or crisis resolution as well as to world creation. The latter would involve the improvement or transformation of the world, for instance, a lasting or at least long-term enhancement of the moral quality of the constitution and organization of society or of the degree of sustainability of the relation of society to nature.

In terms of theoretical philosophy, Critical Theory's overall epistemological position can be called 'pragmatic epistemic realism' (Strydom 2002; Habermas 2003, 2005). It accepts that reality is knowable in principle but becomes visible only to the extent that we engage with it through confrontation with problems, threats or challenges, or impact on it through our activities or practices in such a way that we are compelled by the consequences to take it into account. Reality is not an objective world whose workings we want to gain complete knowledge of, as empiricism assumes, nor is it an ineffable complex independent of us whose being we desire to fully grasp, as ontological realism holds, and even less is it a purely symbolically structured complex whose meaning calls for understanding, as interpretativism maintains. Instead, Critical Theory proceeds from the pragmatic-realist assumption that reality is something external to and independent of us which we experience through its real generative mechanisms when we run up against it under particular circumstances and are compelled to form a concept or theory of it which could guide appropriate action; thus reality exposes us and we expose ourselves for the benefit of learning, problem solving and world creation.

Methodology

Methodology refers to the complex set of assumptions underpinning the carrying out of social research. From the perspective of Critical Theory, these assumptions concern not just the systematicity or logic of knowledge production and theory construction, but also what follows from that regarding the social scientific employment of the theoretical knowledge and its intersubjective testing, justification and practical use. Theoretical knowledge developed by Critical Theory is employed for explanatory purposes, for instance, accounting for mechanisms such as social-structural and cultural-structural forces and factors or related processes which interfere in and thereby distort or block the realization in concrete social life of the potential harboured by counterfactual cultural models or socio-practical ideas. An explanation of this type provides the basis for the critique of a problematic, crisis-stricken or pathological social state of affairs in a way that has a practical effect. Such an effect takes the general form of the creation of resonance, stimulation or the acceptance of relevant insights by those concerned and instigation of learning processes geared towards solving problems and creating a world. The intersubjective testing and justification of theoretical knowledge and the explanation and critique made possible by it cannot be limited to the traditional positivistically conceived 'context of justification' confined to the scientific community alone since, as both critical theorists (Horkheimer 1970) and pragmatists (Dewey 1938) understand, we are not dealing here with a purely intra-scientific process, but one which is social as well. The immanent realization of situation-transcendent ideas of reason through critique depends on both the communication and the communicative monitoring of the results beyond the social scientific context.

If it is a matter of testing or verification in the medium of public communication, however, then the process cannot be confined to Critical Theory and the agents directly addressed or those directly involved, since the communicative structure of the process is in an important sense constituted also by the broader anonymous audience or public. It is for this reason that the neglected structure of the three-dimensional communicative framework embracing the relations filling out the public sphere must be incorporated into the methodological reflections and assumptions of Critical Theory. These relations are those among the active participants, that is, Critical Theory (ego) and the agents involved and directly addressed (alter), and the non-participating yet observing, evaluating, judging, monitoring and commenting public, which ethically represents the third point of view, the collective will, common good or moral point of view (the other) in the situation.[3] The communicative monitoring of the results is of particular importance, over and above its constitutive significance for public communication, on account of its situation-defining, regulative and disclosing role in relation to the active agents. What is most remarkable, despite its importance, is that this third moment of communicative contingency is as a rule not pursued, even by those critical theorists and pragmatists who insist on the indispensability of public testing or verification or the third point of view. The full structure of communication as the medium not only of the development but also of the application of knowledge must explicitly be reflected upon in Critical Theory's methodology.

In the wake of the methodological disputes of the 1960s, Critical Theory was given a number of different names to distinguish it methodologically from the competitors on its extremes: the naturalistic scientist paradigm, on the one hand, and the idealistic interpretative paradigm, on the other. They included 'hermeneutic-dialectics' (Radnitzky 1970), 'dialectical-hermeneutics' (Bleicher 1980) and 'critical-hermeneutics' (Thompson 1981). That these designations are not entirely adequate and indeed potentially misleading, however, is borne out by the effect they have had on the understanding of Critical Theory: namely the mistaken assignment of Critical Theory to the hermeneutic tradition (e.g. Bhaskar 1989). At least two things are wrong with this imputation. First, it overlooks the distinct historical sources of the three paradigms (Strydom 2008a): the modern reactivation of hermeneutics in the dispute over the interpretation of the Bible in the Reformation and its consolidation in the Romantic and conservative reaction against science and positivism in the nineteenth century; the establishment of mechanical-experimental explanatory science by royal edict in the wake of the early modern scientific movement in the so-called 'Great Instauration' of the mid-seventeenth century; and finally the introduction of critique in the Enlightenment and its consolidation by the left-Hegelians in the mid-nineteenth century and their followers in the early twentieth. Second, the two-barrel nature of the designations is dangerously close to, if not complicit in, reproducing the dominant yet inadequate dualistic epistemology of modern times rather than evoking the three-place sign-mediated epistemology which Critical Theory actually presupposes. The terms 'dialectical' and 'critical' indeed contain the possibility of going beyond a dualistic understanding, but the reference to 'hermeneutics' means that it remains opaque due to being caught in the antinomic field of interpretation and critique.

A more appropriate indication of the methodological nature of Critical Theory is offered by the designation 'critical-reconstructive' (Apel 1977, 1984) or, more fully, a 'critical . . . theoretical . . . objective . . . explanatory . . . hermeneutic reconstructionism' (Habermas 1990: 32, 28). It is specifically designed to suggest, not simply the critical interpretation of meaning, but rather the critical, interpretative reconstruction of real mechanisms in the context of the development of social structures in socio-historical processes. Such a critical genetic-reconstructive methodology not only picks up on Marx's pithy methodological suggestion, 'we have to make these petrified social relations dance by singing their own tune' (Marx (1967a: 253), but also provides the platform from which the leading and emerging critical theorists have been proceeding in recent times. This methodological understanding is moreover in keeping with contemporary Critical Theory's key concept of immanent transcendence as well as with its – at least implied – sign-mediated epistemology.

The core chapters of the book – particularly Chapter 4 on immanent transcendence and Chapter 6 on methodology – contain detailed clarification of all the pertinent issues regarding Critical Theory's methodology as well as its epistemological, ontological and normative assumptions. The remainder of the book provides the necessary contextual, philosophical, meta-theoretical, theoretical and illustrative backup for these arguments. The first three chapters trace the line of development from Kant and Hegel, via left-Hegelianism and the Frankfurt School, to the relation between Critical Theory and pragmatism up to the point of the emergence of the concept of immanent transcendence which is dealt with systematically in the fourth, closing, chapter of Part I. A review of contemporary critical theorists on methodology opens Part II, setting the scene for Chapters 6, 7 and 8, which are devoted to the analysis of respectively Critical Theory's methodology, its comparison with competing approaches and finally its illustration by means of a series of concrete examples from the research of Habermas, Honneth, McCarthy and Eder.

Part I

Metatheoretical foundations

It seems as though reason and history are mutually exclusive, yet they belong together in our identity for we are simultaneously rational and historical beings.

Herbert Schnädelbach

1   Classical foundations

Introduction

Debates in and around Critical Theory during the past three to four decades highlighted the need to take a new look at its classical foundations. Developments in both continental and analytic philosophy, for instance the linguistic and pragmatic turns, which recast the question of knowledge in the mould of language and action in keeping with transformations in social life, made available a new philosophical basis. This prompted a clarification of the subterranean connection between Critical Theory and pragmatism, which in turn led to an elaboration of this relation. Charles S. Peirce emerged here as the central figure, the 'American Kant', who kept alive enough potential contact points to allow a fruitful articulation of Critical Theory and pragmatism. From here the attention then shifted towards Critical Theory's own classical tradition in which questions were raised about the taken-for-granted understanding of these roots. Most immediately, the focus fell on the left-Hegelians, the first generation after Hegel, among whom the towering figure of Marx remained in his dominant position but was now joined by two others from the same generation who had not often been recognized as belonging to this same tradition, namely Peirce and Kierkegaard. By the mid-1980s, this debate about the Hegelian left, the most characteristic heritage of Critical Theory, forced the discussants to take yet a further step back in order to re-investigate the question of the relation between Kant and Hegel as well as the relation of Critical Theory to Kant and Hegel. Like the linguistic and pragmatic turns, like the relation with pragmatism and like the status of the left-Hegelian heritage, the question of the theoretical sense of the relation between and to Kant and Hegel has remained a matter of reflection, debate and elaboration into the twenty-first century.

Considering that contemporary Critical Theory's methodology cannot be clarified without drawing some lessons from its reflexive self-examinations of the past three to four decades, this chapter is devoted to a re-engagement with its classical foundations with the specific aim of ferreting out anchor points for the concept of immanent transcendence to be discussed later. The chapter opens with a crucial section on Kant in whose philosophy the structure of thinking informing critique is extrapolated and formalized in an unprecedented way. Hegel's exceptionally important criticism and simultaneous transformation of Kant which prepared the ground for the succeeding generation, particularly the left-Hegelians, is the theme of the next section. The final section is then devoted to a consideration of the three major figures who embody the left-Hegelian heritage of contemporary Critical Theory, namely Marx, Peirce and Kierkegaard.

Kant

Immanuel Kant's (1724–1803) pre-eminence in the philosophical canon is justified by his creative, judicious and fruitful bringing together of the different concerns and motives of the Enlightenment: from knowledge, science and reason, through freedom, morality and law, to publicity, the improvement of political and social conditions and, of course, critique. Although his peculiar significance derived from the way in which he was able to marshal elements from these various strands to resolve the problem of knowledge in his great epistemological work, *Critique of Pure Reason*, the compelling power his philosophy exercised subsequently over hearts and minds largely depended on the conviction with which he advanced his moral vision of the world as well as its broad scope. He certainly appreciated the Enlightenment in cultural historical terms as an event that would never be forgotten since it revealed a latent human capacity for civilizational advancement, but he understood it specifically in moral terms as pinpointing 'the freedom to make public use of one's reason at every point' (1957a: 4–5). Rather than focusing his critical vision on the losses accompanying the early modern gains in freedom and the resulting social heteronomy, as did for instance Rousseau, he drew attention to the question of justice. Fittingly for someone who was aware that he lived in 'the very age of critique', Kant concentrated at the core of his work on the development of a method of critique that he initially applied in the epistemological field of thinking or knowledge, but then progressively extended to other areas of human activity such as willing or morality, law and politics as well as feeling or aesthetics. It was designed to investigate the form in which the principles of reason emerge with a view to determining their validity, particularly the extent to which they are necessary and universally applicable, and the kind of judgement associated with them. Accordingly, his work was divided into a theoretical, a practical and an aesthetic part to which he devoted his three critiques respectively – *Critique of Pure Reason*, *Critique of Practical Reason* and *Critique of Judgement* – which were paralleled by a career-long investigation culminating in 1798 in *Anthropology from a Pragmatic Point of View*. Although Kant hated all orthodoxy and was convinced that 'to critique everything . . . [including] religion . . . and . . . law-giving . . . must submit' in the sense of a 'test of free and open examination' in order to gain 'the sincere respect which reason accords' (1968: 9), these works are all cautious formal statements exhibiting his awareness of the threat of the prohibition of his philosophy emanating from the rule of Frederick William II.

The aim of the *Critique of Pure Reason* was to determine through mature judgement how knowledge that is able to make an authoritative claim to validity is established and, by the same means, to draw the limits of knowledge by exposing the human propensity toward groundless pretensions, illusions and delusions. Such a critical investigation of knowledge required the bringing together of his own rationalist tradition, with which he had become partially disillusioned, and the psychology-based British empiricist tradition, which he likewise regarded as inadequate if left standing on its own. He found the answer to the problem of the articulation of these two positions in a complex mode of 'synthesis' at the centre of which is his unique achievement of having transformed the lingering Greek theory, according to which the object of knowledge is given, by the radically new theory according to which the understanding constitutes the object of possible experience and knowledge. This synthesis involves three different levels of elements and stages in the formation of valid knowledge. First, sensation had to be consolidated into perception, a process of formation that required and was made possible by the forms of space and time which are available in the human mind. Second, perception needed to be shaped into experience that was made possible by concepts or categories which, through schematization, were linked to concrete features of the world and thus made available an object of knowledge. Finally, through judgement experience required to be transformed into knowledge. Over and above the forms and categories, this crucial step depended on general principles or 'ideas of pure reason' which were necessarily and unavoidably presupposed in any and every cognitive process. Without the presuppositions that there is a reality ('world'), that there is a knowing subject ('soul') and that validity ('God') can be attained, knowledge can achieve no unity and extension – indeed it is simply impossible. In the later *Critique of Judgement*, however, Kant drastically modified his argumentation by identifying the faculty of judgement as the source of ideas of reason and thus obviating the need for a reference to a sense-transcendent intelligence.

Of particular importance for Kant's critical method as one designed to discriminate between 'lawful claims' to knowledge, on the one hand, and 'illusory knowledge', 'groundless pretensions' or 'delusive' reasoning, on the other, are what he discusses in the 'Transcendental dialectic' under the title of 'ideas of pure reason' (1968: 318–19). These general ideas have a number of characteristics. They are transcendental in that they are necessary and unavoidable conditions which make knowledge possible; they are formal structures in that they operate in all cognitive processes, which means also that they have universal application; they are regulative in that they are principles which guide and give direction to cognitive processes by providing them with a goal or *focus imaginarius*; and they are transcendent in that they point beyond all given experience. Kant insists that these ideas of reason have no objective reality. Neither actually existing, nor being concepts of objects, they are at best only capable of lending systematic unity and extension to the conceptual basis of knowledge. For this reason, in the *Critique of Judgement* he relates ideas of reason to what he calls the 'reflective judgement' rather than the 'determinant judgement' (1972: 15–6). It is because of this feature that, besides their positive function, ideas of pure reason can also induce illusory, pretentious and delusive usages by misleading reason to claim that they refer to actually existing objects or states of affairs. Ideas of pure reason thus also indicate the necessary limits of knowledge. In fact, he is emphatic about the twofold role of these ideas, which, although not real, nevertheless are by no means merely figments of the imagination. On the one hand, they provide the standards for critique and, on the other, they are fertile soil for the nurturing of misleading transcendental illusions.

It is interesting that Kant, rather than waiting for the opportunity created later by his moral philosophy presented in the *Critique of Practical Reason* (1956), claims already in the *Critique of Pure Reason*, particularly the 'Transcendental dialectic', that the ideas of pure reason are not just ideas, but at the same time also ideals. Whereas ideas lay down rules, ideals serve as archetypes or examples which can be followed. Ideas of reason are indeed not constitutive like Platonic ideas, yet they do possess '*practical* power (as regulative ideas)' and 'have their own good, proper and therefore *immanent* use' in that they 'form the basis of the possible perfection of certain actions' by providing a 'standard for our actions . . . with which we compare and judge ourselves, and so reform ourselves, although we can never attain to the perfection thereby prescribed' (1968: 486, 532). In fact, despite the fact that they are 'not completely pure concepts', he nevertheless regards 'moral concepts' as good examples of ideas of reason. The shift from epistemology or theoretical philosophy to morality or practical philosophy entails, of course, that it is no longer objects of knowledge that are at the centre of attention, but rather objects of the will. That this shift is an important one for Kant is borne out by his reversal in the *Critique of Practical Reason* (1956: 124) of the primacy accorded to theoretical reason over practical reason in all previous philosophy. In so far as theoretical reason points beyond itself by way of ideas of pure reason, it is determined by the needs of practical reason. This step beyond the theoretical is finally consolidated in his *Anthropology from a Pragmatic Point of View* (1996) where the question of the human being is posed.

The same critical method he applied to theoretical reason Kant also brought to bear on practical reason. His so-called 'Copernican revolution' in epistemology involving a shift from an emphasis on things to a manner of acting is thus also carried out in morality. Inspired by Rousseau's pregnant statement regarding 'obedience to a law which we prescribe to ourselves in liberty' (1966: 16), he therefore avoided the traditional approach of starting from a definition of some material good and instead took the experience of obligation as his point of departure from which to derive the moral law. The basic moral principle in the *Critique of Practical Reason*, accordingly, is the 'categorical imperative', which theoretically formulates the formal conditions of obligation as being the freedom of the will and at the same time the necessary relation of the good to it: 'So to act that the maxim of your will could always hold at the same time as a principle establishing universal law' (1956: 30). Autonomy or freedom of the will is morally paramount, yet it requires an object to guide moral action to which it stands in a necessary relation that, nevertheless, does not destroy the moral agent's freedom. It must be an unconditioned object that it gives itself, and this object can only be autonomous or free willing itself, which by implication is thus universalized.

By contrast with its pure version, Kant also speaks of finite practical reason, in which case autonomous or free willing becomes manifest as a practical ideal in the form of the good will. It is 'a model . . . [which all] . . . finite rational beings . . .

[can be expected] . . . to strive towards even though they cannot reach it . . . The utmost that finite practical reason can accomplish is to make sure of the unending progress of its maxims towards this model and of the constancy of the finite rational being in making continuous progress' (1956: 33). Although generally Kant extended his practical philosophy, of which morality is the centre piece, to the philosophy of the state, law, international politics and history, this very insight is also employed in these writings – for instance, where he deals with possible human progress through such topics as cosmopolitanism and perpetual peace. As regards the apparent contradiction in these writings, one has to disregard his older dogmatic-metaphysical view that nature has an intention which guarantees progress in human history (1957b: 24) in favour of his critical position on the role of ideas of reason or regulative ideas and, further, on practical reason's priority over theoretical reason. It is on this basis that the regulative idea and moral postulate or practical ideal of good will can be regarded as morally and politically 'making it our duty to work toward this end, which is not just a chimerical one' but a task (1957b: 32), namely a just cosmopolitan order characterized by perpetual peace.

The absolutely crucial point that Kant thus established is that reason, through ideas of pure reason and moral postulates, has a world-creating or world-forming force.

Hegel

Georg Wilhelm Friedrich Hegel's (1770–1831) philosophy consummated the idealistic movement to which Kant's thought gave rise and which Johann Gottlieb Fichte (Schulz 1962) fundamentally and systematically shaped by emphatically making self-consciousness – subjectively reflection and objectively the world as a system of reason – the principle of idealism. On the one hand, Fichte jettisoned Kant's highly problematic conception of the unknowable reality behind every object of knowledge and, on the other, he focused exclusively on elaborating his conception of reason's spontaneous and creative production of its objects of experience and thought. This latter transcendental-logical dimension provided the starting point for Fichte's development in fine detail of the dialectical method which Hegel so profusely applied in all spheres and at all levels. If, for Fichte, the essential nature of the mind was to divide itself and then from that state of internal division to recreate its original unity under new conditions, Hegel turned to the historical process as the medium of 'mind', 'spirit' or the 'idea', whether the history of consciousness or universal history, including the history of society or 'objective spirit'. It is a process driven by mind, spirit or the idea as the self-determining and self-reflective subject representing the whole, which unfolds itself in such a way that its particular forms at each of its different stages of thesis, antithesis and synthesis possess significance as links in this self-creative process. In its objective development, which is relevant here, spirit shapes for itself successively the rational, reason-filled or mindful forms of family life, civil society and finally the state as the realization of consciousness in general or the ethical idea. Traditional ethical life centred on family and political life had to make room at the beginning of modern times for civil society centred on

civil and economic interests whose dialectic generated competition, class formation, conflict and internal division, which could be overcome and reconciled only
by the state as the realization of an ethical totality. This conception of society or
objective spirit as an essentially normative reality was determined by the impact
of Kant's towering moral vision of the world and Fichte's endorsement of it by
making moral science his principal concern.

Hegel's acute sensibility for focusing in on the historically specific – for 'philosophy to apprehend its own time in thoughts' (1967: 11) – while never losing sight
of the larger context, not only distinguished him rather sharply from Kant, but at
the same time also allowed him to develop a penetrating and multifaceted yet by
no means unproblematic criticism of his predecessor. Although he accepted with
Kant that the 'principle of the modern world is freedom of subjectivity' (1967:
addition 165), which had to be protected at all costs, he nevertheless directed his
scalpel especially at Kant's partial account of morality, particularly the categorical
imperative, but this criticism had implications also for the latter's views of the
subject, society and history as well as knowledge.

In his famous criticism of Kant's practical philosophy in his *Philosophy of
Right* (1967), Hegel made essentially four points (Kuhlmann 1986). Kant's moral
doctrine is formalistic and thus devoid of any content; second, its universalistic
reach is abstract and thus unhistorical; third, the individualistic moral demand
it articulates is nothing but a mere ought and therefore without any consequence
whatsoever; and, finally, its emphasis on pure conviction of the need to fulfil one's
duty harbours the danger of repression. The source of these formalistic, abstract
universalistic, subjectivistic and terroristic weaknesses Hegel traced back to the
fact that Kant fundamentally misconceived not only the individual, but also the
world to which the individual belongs as well as the relation between the two. On
the one hand, the individual is indeed seen as a free subject capable of rationally
giving itself and maintaining the moral point of view, yet only at the cost of being
reduced to the pure internality of a rational subject cut off from its world and thus
unable to give any effect to moral claims and demands. On the other hand, the
individual's world, embracing the natural and social environment including the
individual, its actions and their consequences, is an unhistorical and unchanging
reality, devoid of any rationality and closed to any demands of reason. From this
gulf between a morally impotent subject and an indifferent world Hegel drew the
influential conclusion that Kant's position allowed no possibility for the realization
of reason in reality.

Hegel's answer to these deficiencies was encapsulated by his concept of
Sittlichkeit or 'concrete ethical life' which was strongly influenced by Aristotle and
his criticism of Plato. From this standpoint, by contrast with Kant, moral autonomy or freedom cannot simply be something subjective, confined to the individual
mind, a practically inconsequential demand and opposed to an indifferent world.
Rather, ethical life manifests the fact that reason has already been incorporated
in the real world and continues to be effective there. Social reality is shot through
with concretized moral rules or rational reasons so that it becomes 'immanently
rational' (1967: paragraph 29). They have entered habits, mores, institutions and

forms of life and have become effective in structuring social life by regulating orientations, actions and relations. Having taken concrete and objective form, moral considerations have been generalized and obtained universal validity. This objective ethical reality not only makes possible and throughout supports individual self-consciousness, but provides the individual with identity and a feeling of self-worth and confidence. Indeed, Hegel argues that ethical life is emancipatory. It makes possible 'liberation' from the demands of 'natural impulse' and 'indeterminate subjectivity', thus allowing the individual to obtain 'substantive freedom' (1967: paragraph 149).

The reference to substantive freedom gained in a real ethical community is a reminder that Hegel is not just criticizing Kant's narrow focus on 'the standpoint of morality', but is actually engaged in a critical diagnosis of his own time (Honneth 2001). As made clear in the introduction to the *Philosophy of Right*, he is concerned about two closely related matters. On the one hand, he views critically the widely accepted yet confusedly one-sided concepts of freedom which arose and became diffused in the early modern period, such as individual moral freedom and legal freedom secured by rights. On the other, he draws critical attention to the social pathological consequences of the orientations and actions inspired by those concepts, such as the 'fanaticism' and 'destructiveness' (1967: paragraph 5) accompanying individualization, the indeterminacy of subjectivity such as feelings of emptiness and 'depression' (1967: paragraph 149), and in civil society an inner dialectic which leads to 'class divisions' (1967: paragraph 201) resulting in 'the creation of a rabble of paupers . . . [and] . . . at the other end of the social scale . . . the concentration of disproportionate wealth in a few hands' (1967: paragraph 244). Social pathologies such as these can be mitigated or resolved, according the Hegel, only if concrete ethical life contextualizes individual freedom in a way that prioritizes substantive freedom – which presupposes that all individuals ethically actualize the idea of freedom in mutual recognition of each other in their social world.

Hegel's criticism of Kant is of course not free from its own difficulties. Although the criticism of the latter's individualistic subjectivism is to the point, the objections to formalism and abstract universalism cannot be sustained in the form in which Hegel presented them, and the point regarding totalitarianism is simply false. In fact, the undemocratic tone he strikes from time to time in the *Philosophy of Right*, which inspired the Hegelian right, points to the real weakness of his position. The most basic problem is his ontologization of mind or spirit, and the central problem of the *Philosophy of Right* is his substantialist or over-institutionalized concept of the state as the ethical realization of the idea of freedom. Yet, whatever the problems with his criticism of Kant and more generally of his position, Hegel raised the serious question of how the interrelation of the formal, abstract and general principle of morality, on the one hand, and the material, concrete, historically specific situation, on the other, could be conceived and achieved. Indeed, this issue may be regarded as the kernel of his work as a whole.

In Hegel's view, the subject matter of philosophy is 'the Idea' (e.g. freedom), which means the concept together with the actualization of that concept. The

idea is 'the rational factor' which is investigated in terms of its 'immanent development' or the shapes it assumes in the course of the process of its actualization
(1967: paragraph 1). What Kant referred to as 'mediation' (1968: 181) in his
epistemological discussion of schematization, in the sense of linking a concept
to concrete features of the world and thus making available an object of knowledge, became the key for Hegel in thinking through how different dimensions
in diverse historical domains are brought together in the actualization of an
idea. Mediation is the mechanism which in the course of the process, whether
the process of generation of civil society or of the state, brings about a concrete
unity of explicit differences – unique individuals, particularity such as members or
citizens, and universality such as institutions, government, the law – so as to realize
the whole: the concept of civil society or the state. For Hegel, civil society itself
can be regarded as a process of mediation in which a variety of differences are
continually being played out against and related to one another. He conceived of
this mechanism as operating through different media, for instance language, social
labour and social interaction, which were treated in varying ways in the different
phases of the development of his thought (Habermas 1974).

By thus focusing the attention on the 'rational factor' and its 'immanent'
actualization and development through mediation, Hegel opened the door for
the deliberate and concerted detranscendentalization of the Kantian concept of
reason after his death in 1831 – a step which became the characteristic feature of
the left-Hegelian tradition. Rather than fixing on the rational subject and pure
reason, as did Kant, those following in Hegel's wake clearly sensed that reason is
impure in so far as it is embedded in culture and society and borne by embodied,
engaged and situated beings. None other than Hegel himself set the stage for
a transformation of the critique of pure reason into a 'sociocultural critique of
impure reason . . . [with] . . . practical intent' (McCarthy 1994a: 8). Where he
failed to appreciate the significance of this achievement of his, however, was in
his role as the philosopher of the Restoration who insisted in the preface to the
Philosophy of Right that '*What is rational is real and what is real is rational*' (1967: 10).

The left-Hegelians

Hegel's philosophy of history was both the fulcrum and the acid test of his thought.
Not surprisingly, as a result, it provoked extreme reactions among his pupils and
followers. It turned on Hegel's innovative emphasis on the unity of philosophy
and time by way of his statement that philosophy is its own time apprehended in
thought. The ambiguity of this proposition allowed him to give it a past-oriented,
reactionary interpretation which denied every possibility of transcending the
present and rejected every imperative containing a reference to what should
be. However, the proposition left open also the possibility of an interpretation
drawing on the future as a resource and focusing on what could and even should
be brought into being in opposition to the status quo by the active engagement
of the new generation. Hegel's pupils and followers divided accordingly. On the
one hand, the right-wing 'Old Hegelians' sought to preserve Hegel's philosophy,

both its conservative political animus and its philosophical Christianity. On the other, the left-wing 'Young Hegelians' not only undertook a radical critique of its religious and political assumptions, but also claimed to pursue the realization of its true core. This categorization into Old and Young or right and left was first proposed and more generally accepted in the first decade after Hegel's death (Löwith 1964), and since then it has become part of conventional wisdom that Ludwig Feuerbach, Arnold Ruge, Max Stirner, Bruno Bauer and Karl Marx belonged to the original left-Hegelian group from which a strand runs to Georg Lukács and the Frankfurt School. Marx's consistently developed material or practical viewpoint of course differentiated him from the other Young Hegelians and provided the basis for his distinction as the outstanding left-Hegelian figure.

It is interesting that recently Axel Honneth, while associating Critical Theory's characteristic form of normative critique with left-Hegelianism, described 'the left-Hegelian tradition as a whole' as running from 'Marx to Lukács' (2000b: 88). It is of course the case that this tradition actually has a much wider scope, incorporating a number of strands other than the one stretching from the original group directly to Lukács and beyond. In the course of the twentieth century, various authors explored the proliferation of directions in the post-Hegelian period with different intentions. For instance, Karl Löwith (1964) in his classical study of the radical shift from Hegel to Nietzsche in the late 1930s added Søren Kierkegaard and contrasted him with his contemporary Marx within the context of left-Hegelianism; the young Habermas (1954; also 1987) in his doctoral thesis of the early 1950s on Schelling, who himself had a close relation with the original left-Hegelians, painted a comparable background; and Karl-Otto Apel (1967, 1970; translated 1981, reprinted 1995) in a groundbreaking study of American pragmatism in the 1960s brought Charles S. Peirce into this constellation. Taking this decisive step, Apel argued that, in addition to Marxism and existentialism, there is only one more philosophy that can claim to partake of the left-Hegelian heritage and thus function in the sense of mediating theory and practice in social life, namely pragmatism. Subsequently, Habermas took this evaluation on board in a series of works (1972, 1991a, 2001, 2002), most recently referring to pragmatism as 'the American branch of Young-Hegelianism' (2001: 167–8). The US critical theorist Thomas McCarthy likewise takes the view that American pragmatism in its heyday was a variant of this innovative and today still relevant nineteenth-century departure. Thus three left-Hegelians need to be considered more closely: Marx and Peirce in particular, but also Kierkegaard.

Marx

By bringing Hegel's philosophy into line with the times, the Young Hegelians prepared the ground and opened the way for Karl Marx (1818–83), notwithstanding his more or less severe criticism of various aspects of their positions. He himself referred to this group as the representatives of 'Young-Hegelian philosophy' and, ironically if not scathingly, as the 'Critical School'. Feuerbach was the first to criticize Hegel's philosophical Christianity as well as religion, and he was also instrumental in transforming philosophy anthropologically so that human beings, corporeal existence, sensuousness and social relations took philosophical centre stage. Ruge relentlessly historicized philosophy, focusing it on the changing spirit of the age and searching for the reason of the age, which at times is borne by public opinion, yet under different circumstance is a public secret that needs to be ferreted out by means of critique in the name of the progress of humankind. Both the radical critics Bauer and Stirner each in his own way proclaimed the end of philosophy and focused on their own time as a transitional phase engulfed in crisis, but embraced a reductive individualism and finally ended in nihilism. Assisted by a rather critical and selective appropriation of insights from his fellow Young Hegelians, Marx was able to proceed to a serious critique of politics and of society with a view to the formation of a political subject.

The central problem for Marx was the relationship between ideas and the material dimension, whether in the guise of the conditions of human existence, the active life process, the way of life, society, the economy or socio-cultural reality. This problem is the one to which Kant originally gave rise and which then came to occupy a significant place in Hegel's thought, from where it trickled down into Young-Hegelian thinking. It arose from Kant's conception of ideas of reason, his establishment of a connection between reason and interest through the notion of regulative ideas, and his insistence on the primacy of reason's practical over its theoretical capacity. As for Hegel, it found expression in that famous assertion of his which created so much controversy during the 1830s and 1840s, especially among the Young Hegelians, to the effect that what is rational is real and what is real is rational. Marx shared with Hegel this very principle of the unity of reason and reality and, by extension, the principle that reality is the unity of essence and existence, but they interpreted it in contrary ways. For Marx, ideas have consequences since they at least imply some striving towards a practical goal. They should be judged not on their manifest content, therefore, but on the practical consequences of their propagation. Whereas Hegel sought to reconcile reason and reality, Marx by contrast manifested a determined will to realize the potential of ideas in reality and thus change the world. What takes the place of Hegel's philosophy in the new era succeeding his must stand in the service of history. For this reason, Marx focused not on the identity of reason and reality, but on the discrepancy between the two instead. By contrast with the older Hegel, who felt he had to accommodate to the post-Napoleonic Restoration, the young Hegel indeed provided a pointer in this direction in his assessment of the French Revolution: whereas the French practically realized the idea of freedom in a reality for which they have a particular feeling, conditions and orientations across the border were such that the Germans kept the idea and all the activity surrounding it in their heads protected by their sleeping caps.

Given his understanding of the consequences of Hegel's conciliatory position in light of his own more differentiated interpretation of the relation between idea and reality, Marx adopted a twofold strategy. On the one hand, the previous era's predominant interpretation of the world, the prevalent conception of the present, had to be combated with a view to transforming the consciousness of the time. To begin with, it was a matter of Hegel's philosophy and the religious and political consciousness shaped by it that needed to be attacked and transformed. Then the attention shifted to the 'German ideology' of his fellow Young Hegelians, those 'sheep who take themselves and are taken as wolves', who are fighting 'a philosophic struggle with the shadows of reality, which appeals to the dreamy and muddled German nation' (Marx and Engels 1969: 1–2). At the mature stage of his project, it was a matter of the liberal-capitalist theory put forward by the British and French political economists, 'political economy', and its consequences as wrought by its leading idea of the 'commodity form' (Marx 1954). On the other hand, a meticulous and penetrating analysis of reality itself, whether a backward Germany which needed to be dragged into the present already occupied by its neighbours or a conflict-ridden bourgeois-capitalist society, was required which could provide the necessary basis for whatever action was appropriate and required to bring about the envisaged change. Critique in the proper sense of the word, for Marx, thus included both a critical uncloaking and dissolution of the prevailing consciousness and its leading cultural models as well as a critical analysis of the concrete situation in terms of operative ideas with some footing in reality which have the potential of contributing to the formation of a political subject capable of transformative action.

When Engels published Marx's 'Theses on Feuerbach' (1967b) in 1888, he put it forward as 'the brilliant germ of a new worldview'. Considering the irresolvable theoretical and political problems Marx generated by transposing Hegel's philosophy of the unfolding of spirit into a causal and teleological, speculative-dialectical, dogmatic historical determinism, however, it is more meaningful and fruitful to approach this brilliant germ from an epistemological angle while also having regard for its ontological and normative implications than to treat it as a worldview. The epistemologically revealing critical evaluation that Marx developed of Feuerbach's materialism and Kant and Hegel's idealism is of particular importance in conjunction with his understanding of the relationship between ideas and society. The innovative theory of knowledge he thus suggestively outlined is moreover ontologically supported by a complementary theory of society.

Marx's ontology is outlined in five of the eleven theses (3, 4, 6, 7, 10),[1] and two more (1, 8) also contain relevant material. His most basic assumption is that the object of knowledge is 'the historical process' (6), which becomes accessible in the form of 'a particular society' (7). The latter consists of 'an ensemble of social relationships' (6) that embraces the 'human individual' who appears as abstract and isolated only as long as it is conceived anthropologically rather than as a social being (6, 7). Social reality or 'society' (3) itself is characterized by 'cleavage and self-contradictoriness' that divide it in two, a 'basis' and 'an independent realm in the clouds' (4) that are accompanied by 'mysteries' or obfuscating ideologies which often mislead theoretical thinking (8). Since 'social life is essentially *practical*' (8), the transformation evidenced by the form that society takes in the course of the historical process must be regarded as the result of 'human activity' (3) or 'human practice' (8). Although the latter gives rise to all sorts of 'mysteries' (8), it also takes the form of 'practical-critical' as well as 'revolutionary' activity (1). These productive forms of activity not only bring about 'the change of circumstances' but also entail 'self-change' (3). Forming part of a temporal process as it does, social reality is not simply manifested in the present, but already contains future possibilities or potentialities which have a shaping effect on the present. Far from being exhausted by the actually existing 'bourgeois society', therefore, social reality contains ideas of reason such as 'human society or socialized humanity' which go beyond the present yet are nevertheless effectively operative in it (10).

As regards his theory of knowledge applicable to the object delimited above, Marx outlines his position in five of the theses on Feuerbach (1, 2, 5, 8, 9), with another (4) adding some valuable clarity. This epistemological statement, even more than his ontological statement, is of particular importance in the present context of clarifying the methodology of contemporary Critical Theory. Most basically, Marx assumes that knowledge is not a property of the consciousness of an abstract, isolated, separate individual, but rather forms part of the historical process of the transformation of society. As such, it involves a number of distinct moments which require to be brought together through being mediated with one another in the course of the process. Accordingly, he insists as against older forms of materialism, including Feuerbach's, that knowledge is not simply the 'perception' or contemplation of an object (1). The object is not given in the external world only to impact on consciousness by leaving an impression through being perceived. By its emphasis on 'the active side', Marx counters, idealism in the persons of Kant and Hegel cogently argued that the subject of knowledge makes an important contribution to knowledge (1). Rather than passively observing a given object, the subject actively takes part in the constitution of every object of knowledge – which was precisely the point of Kant's transcendental logic. The problem with idealism, however, is that it subscribes to a very limited understanding of activity and, by extension, of the object. Rather than 'actual, sensuous activity' of the sort involved in the process of the production and organization of society, idealism limits itself to thinking and, therefore, to 'thought objects' to the exclusion of objects of human practices and human will. It is not enough to take the 'theoretical attitude' as definitive and thus to conceive of knowledge in a purely abstract way, but the practical attitude must be acknowledged so that knowledge is understood as being developed not only through thinking, but also through related practical activity: 'practical-critical' and even 'revolutionary' activity (1). 'Objective truth' cannot be established purely theoretically, but requires to be acquired through 'practice' with reference to 'reality' and the mechanisms or 'power' inherent in it as well as to the practical goal (2). The reality in question is the particular form of society as it becomes manifest in the historical process of its production and organization, and its pertinent features include internal differentiation, the emergence within it of independent realms, and concurrent modes of obfuscation – features that need to be critically 'understood' with reference to human practices and their goals (8) and 'explained' in terms of the mechanisms generating cleavages and internal contradictions (4). On this basis, Marx rejects Feuerbach's contemplative or 'perceptual materialism' (5, 9) in favour of a new form of materialism.

Marx's new epistemology learns from idealism regarding the constitution of the object and directing general ideas, but then goes materialistically beyond it by both taking reality into account and locating the active development of knowledge as a social activity in the context of the historical process of society's production and organization. As part of the process, the knowledge produced contributes to the furtherance of the historical process through practices of various kinds led by particular goals which, in turn, confirm or disconfirm the objective truth of such knowledge. Underpinning this theory of knowledge are not only presupposed general concepts regarding a social world that can be known, a subject that can gain knowledge, and the possibility of valid knowledge – what Kant considered theoretical 'ideas of reason' necessary for the unity of knowledge. Guiding the potential employment of such knowledge, there are also practical ideas of reason or moral postulates – one that Marx mentions in the tenth thesis on Feuerbach being 'human society' or 'socialized humanity' as the overriding normative idea which transcends liberal-capitalist society and provides a standard for its critique and potential improvement.

In summary, then, Marx epistemologically conceives of a process of the development of knowledge in the course of which a number of distinct moments require to be brought together through being mediated with one another in such a way that the historical process to which it belongs is redirected by the achievement of a practical end. A perception is stimulated by an aspect of reality (e.g. a cleavage in society) that has to be constituted as an object of knowledge which, in turn, calls for the production of knowledge. Such production is accomplished through interpretation, understanding and explanation (e.g. by a cultural-ideological and an economic mechanism), and the produced knowledge is given practical effect through critique (e.g. of existing cultural and social arrangements) which relates it to practices (e.g. the formation of a political subject) directly relevant to the creation and organization of society (e.g. the resolution of the cleavage and the furtherance of 'socialized humanity'). Whether the knowledge is objectively valid is decided by its relevance for the continuation of the historical process in terms of its regulative idea.

Although Marx does not give attention to the precise nature of the process of knowledge development and the medium in which it transpires, it does represent – as Apel (1974) has pointed out – what has come to be called a semiotic process that presupposes that the mediation of its different moments is enabled by the sign medium. In any event, there can be no doubt about the fact that what Marx presents here is a *medium quo* theory of knowledge. This is borne out by his direct and explicit criticism of all the presuppositions of the opposite type of theory of knowledge, a *medium quod* theory for which there is no process and hence no mediation. This innovative epistemology of his, important to note, is complementary to and thus accommodates the central left-Hegelian idea inherited from Kant and Hegel that there is a historically accumulated potential which reflection could make apparent so that it becomes amenable to being realized through social practice.

Peirce

Recognizing and including Charles Sanders Peirce (1839–1914) among the left-Hegelians, as Apel did and both Habermas and McCarthy acknowledged, is a vital step in acquiring an adequate understanding of the classical foundations of Critical Theory. The left-Hegelian strand he represents, particularly its explicitly elaborated semiotic or sign-mediated theory of knowledge, is of the utmost importance in the present context. Peirce is sometimes regarded as 'the American Kant' not only because he founded the most characteristic American philosophy – pragmatism – in 1868, but also because he drew the very core of his thinking and hence of this philosophy from Kant. Having studied Hegel very closely indeed from his sixteenth through to his sixty-fourth year, however, Kant's famous successor also left an indelible mark on Peirce's thought. The combination of Kant's concern with knowledge, ideas of reason, the priority of practical reason and pragmatic anthropology, on the one hand, and Hegel's concern with the process of development in the course of which its distinct elements are mediated with one another so as to result in an outcome, on the other, became characteristic of Peirce's pragmatism or 'pragmaticism', as he preferred to call it, and at the same time confirmed him as a rightful member of the left-Hegelians. The circumstance of having Kant and especially Hegel in their wings accounts for the remarkable similarities between Peirce and his famous German contemporary, Marx, who was only twenty-one years his senior. It will be necessary, at a later stage, to consider also the differences between the two of them which bear directly on the nature of contemporary Critical Theory as being dependent on the full range of the left-Hegelian tradition.

In the formulation of the ideas which later were named pragmatism, Peirce started from Kant's use of the word 'pragmatic', deriving from the Greek *pragma* meaning action, to designate the practical, moral-ethical or normative domain and the relationship between our knowledge and ultimate normative concerns. His core idea is what he called the 'pragmatic maxim' (5.2),[2] which, he admitted, was inspired by Kant's *Anthropology from a Pragmatic Point of View*. According to this maxim, one can grasp the meaning of any concept by engaging in a 'practical consideration' in the sense of regarding it in connection with a possible practically relevant situation and corresponding action and, thus, the 'upshot', 'effects' or 'practical consequences' which might conceivably result from it. In criticism of followers of his such as James and Dewey who tended to portray pragmatism straightforwardly in terms of action or instrumentalism, however, Peirce stressed that what counts are rather 'the ends of action' or – with an oblique reference to Kant's theoretical and practical ideas of reason – 'general ideas as the interpreters of our thought' and guides of our actions. All concepts, then, have a normative sense, and that sense resides in general directive ideas. In extending this maxim into wide-ranging epistemologically relevant investigations, Peirce went well beyond Kant and drew on Hegel, with the latter's impact clearly visible in the conceptualization of knowledge in terms of process and, particularly, in the tripartite structuring of the process.

Emphasizing human beings as agents and their practical relations to the world, Peirce was obliged to reject – just like Marx – the traditional and still widely accepted view of the subject of knowledge as a lone spectator who adopts a reference orientation and engages in a contemplative or perceptual attitude to observe externally given objects with a view to obtaining eternal knowledge about them. He supported this rejection by a critical demonstration of the untenability of the dualistic Cartesian thinking presupposed by so much Western philosophy and thinking – from subject and object, mind and body, conceptualization and perception, through theory and fact, fact and value, deduction and induction, copy and reality, to individual and society, culture and nature, signifier and signified, and so forth. By contrast, he – in principle by no means dissimilarly to Marx – regarded the subject of knowledge as a member of a community of investigators, interpreters and deliberators who adopt a practical or use orientation and engage in the creative employment of language and knowledge to disclose and open up possibilities, some of which could be realized in the service of resolving common problems and improving the quality of the world in which we live. In line with these assumptions, knowledge for Peirce is something social that is anchored in a process of reasoning dealing with actual collective problems in an effort, not simply to accumulate knowledge, but to overcome those problems to the benefit of the collectivity whose problems they are and the enhancement of the relations among all those involved as well as between them and nature. The process is a semiotic one in that it produces a meaningful outcome and, as such, it is mediated by signs which make possible the fruitful bringing together of three constitutive moments (5.6): feeling ('firstness' or spontaneity) generated by perception of the situation, experience ('secondness' or confrontation with actuality) of the objects involved, and finally the interpretation, clarification and 'communication' of meaning ('thirdness' or possibility). Such a meaningful outcome allows those involved to grasp not only the possible practical consequences of their ideas and actions, but also how they could fit their ideas and actions into a larger pattern so as to contribute to a more appropriate and reasonable organization of the world.

Given that the process of the development of knowledge is conceived on the model of the pragmatic maxim, it is itself interpreted and guided by a general idea which makes the end and hence the meaning of the process clear. Indeed, Peirce identified at least three relevant general ideas playing this role. The first pertains to the goal of knowledge in the sense of our understanding of the object of knowledge, namely reality: 'The real . . . is that (more exactly: the object of the opinion) which, sooner or later, information and reasoning would finally result in, and which is therefore independent of the vagaries of me and you' (5.311). The second concerns the presupposition of this conception of reality, namely the subject of knowledge: 'a *Community*, without definite limits, and capable of a definite increase of knowledge' (5.311). The third, finally, relates to the practical effect of knowledge and the securing of the indefinite community in its world: the furtherance of 'the development of concrete reasonableness' (5.3), which means to say, making a contribution to 'the evolutionary process in some way' (5.4).

Kierkegaard

That Søren Kierkegaard (1813–55), who was barely five years older than Marx, can rightly be regarded as a member of the Young or left-Hegelians is borne out by his relation to Kant and Hegel. Like his fellow travellers, he had Kant's prioritization of practical reason behind him, with the result that he, comparably to Marx and Peirce, was alive to the practical consequences of ideas. For instance, he denounced Hegel's speculative way of thinking as having ruined the possibility of an authentic existence in the nineteenth century – and, by extension, he rejected the proposals of the other Young Hegelians as exacerbating this unfortunate outcome even further. He thus critically responded to Hegel's termination of theoretical metaphysics in historical metaphysics and developed his own answer to Hegel and the problematic situation of the time. His contribution was by no means confined to a criticism of Hegel, with whom he studied, and Hegelian philosophy alone. In much of his writing he was preoccupied with a critique of the events of his time and, more generally, of the quality of his age. Although he belonged to the movement of the time, his characteristic concern and focus was the individual.

Basic to his thought in various areas was the same Hegelian principle that exercised so many others. However, whereas he regarded Hegel as having reconciled reason and reality or essence and existence only in thought, he interpreted it along Young Hegelian lines with an emphasis on real existence. The issue for him was not what exists, but rather that it exists. By contrast with Marx, for whom real existence was social, political and economic, however, Kierkegaard stressed ethical and religious existence. Whereas Marx wanted to realize reason or essence in real historical human existence through a revolutionary political subject, Kierkegaard evaluated Hegel's identification of reason and reality as allowing the universal to snuff out the individual who alone is capable of incarnating and realizing the universal in a way possessing existential meaning. This is the viewpoint from which he criticized his time as an age of crisis and dissolution, an age that was 'sick unto death' (Kierkegaard 1980) and urgently required the stabilizing corrective of the individuality of existence. The vehicle of such an existence is the individual who is capable of self-examination and the nurturing of self-being, has self-understanding in relation to the age, and has the courage to decide 'either/or' (Kierkegaard 1992), to live in 'irony' with paradox and to maintain an ethical existence. The demand of the time for groups to be formed who could instigate social reform and influence the course of history was exactly the wrong solution to the problem. The individual was the sole salvation of the age, for how could the crisis be overcome if individuals failed to prepare for such an eventuality and seriously nurtured their self-realization as subjects of the new arrangement? In opting for the individual, Kierkegaard took a cue from another of the Young Hegelians, namely Stirner, but by contrast with the latter's individualistic nihilism he adopted the diametrically opposite stance of the ethical individual – particularly the individual who, faced with the question of 'either/or', chose true Christianity, not official Christianity, which he regarded as a major force responsible for the sickness of the age.

It is ironic that, although Kierkegaard in anti-Hegelian mode wholeheartedly embraced the individual and stylized himself as the exemplar of what is urgently needed in a transitional phase, he nevertheless could not escape the Hegelian speculative tendency. For Marx, the solution to the problem of existence was equally speculatively the social realization of the unity of reason and reality under conditions of communism. For Kierkegaard, a theocracy established on the blood of individual martyrs and ruled by sacred ministers who knew how to separate the crowd into individuals was the only answer. That both thus ultimately capitulated before the Hegelian propensity for dogmatism – thus falling foul of Kant's stricture against hypostatizing ideas of reason – is borne out by the *Communist Manifesto* (Marx and Engels 1978) and *A Literary Review* (Kierkegaard 2001), which were both written about the same time just before the great yet failed convulsion of 1848. In spite of this gross failure, however, Kierkegaard has an undeniable claim to a unique and significant achievement. It is that he was the first to have articulated the formal requirement for every individual henceforth to pursue self-realization through a responsible and authentic life made possible by a particular kind of reflexivity. He thus contributed a concern with subject-formation which, by way of Nietzsche and Freud, entered Critical Theory.

Conclusion

This chapter revisited the classical foundations of contemporary Critical Theory from the viewpoint of identifying anchor points for its key concept of immanent transcendence. It covered from Kant's critical theoretical and practical philosophy and Hegel's historically oriented philosophy of mediation, to the left-Hegelians Marx, Peirce and Kierkegaard. Normatively, the investigation shed some light on the moral-ethical assumptions underpinning critique and, ontologically, it began to make visible the basis of a processual and transformative theory of society. The central gain, however, is a first step towards a better understanding of the epistemological foundations of Critical Theory. This *medium quo* theory of knowledge, which is absolutely crucial for clearly working out the methodology of contemporary Critical Theory, is pursued in more detail in the next chapter in terms of the relation between Critical Theory and pragmatism.

2 Appropriation of the classical foundations

Introduction

The aim of this chapter is to highlight the approximate similarities between the pragmatist and critical theoretical understanding of the epistemological, ontological and normative presuppositions deriving from their creative appropriation of the classical sources. Of particular importance, accordingly, are the *medium quo* theory of knowledge, processual theory of society and counterfactual ideas of reason. Of interest is also the interaction between Critical Theory and pragmatism, however minimal it was at this early stage.

Accordingly, the following paragraphs present an overview of the initial appropriation of the classical presuppositions via left-Hegelianism by the pragmatists and the critical theorists. It covers the early phase from the late nineteenth to the mid-twentieth century during which, on the one hand, pragmatism gained a public profile and impacted on social science and, on the other, the Frankfurt School was established and gained wider influence. Considering that pragmatism seriously started to take shape in the 1890s and attracted worldwide attention by 1907, well before Critical Theory, it is dealt with first. Its development is traced from Royce and James through Dewey and Mead to C. Wright Mills. The Institute for Social Research was formally founded in 1923 in Frankfurt, but Critical Theory was given its proper form only when Horkheimer became the third director of the Institute in 1931. Critical Theory's development is followed from Korsch and Lukács to the Frankfurt School represented by the main figures Horkheimer, Adorno and Marcuse. Considering that Critical Theory is the focus of this book, more detailed attention is given to the relevant work of its representatives.

Pragmatism

The appropriation of Peirce's ideas by his followers and hence the development of pragmatism in his wake tended in two different yet intertwined directions. In a sense, Peirce himself laid the tracks for this division by a certain ambivalence exhibited by his by no means systematically unified writings. On the one hand, on the basis of his highly consequential semiotic transformation of Kant's philosophy in his early period, he adopted a position that retained a transcendental element through a concern with general ideas which regulated, guided and thus allowed the control of thinking, relating to reality and action. In the presentation of his pragmatist ideas after the late 1870s, on the other hand, certain formulations regarding the fixation of belief seemed to weaken this position by shifting the emphasis to the formation of habits which supposedly make action possible. One of his followers, Royce, pursued a course which, in certain respects very different from Peirce, took up and innovatively elaborated on the former, more transcendental, line of argumentation. James and Dewey, by contrast, focused more consistently on the latter, more action-oriented, strand and succeeded in working it up into the widely accepted understanding of American pragmatism. During his late years, Peirce defended a position closer to his earlier one under the title of 'pragmaticism' against James and Dewey. It was left to Mead to once again bring about a convergence of the two separate directions in the historical development of pragmatism after Peirce. Later, C. Wright Mills's thinking benefited from this more considered and complex position, which was strengthened by his familiarity with the work of the critical theorists in exile in the United States.

Royce

Josiah Royce (1855–1916) took a significant yet by no means completely defensible step in appropriating Peirce's philosophy from the perspective of the late nineteenth-century neo-Hegelian movement. He innovatively went beyond Peirce by elaborating the insight encapsulated in the pragmatic maxim in terms of interaction (Royce 2001; Apel 1980). Instead of regarding the process of clarifying a concept with reference to its conceivable consequences, he highlighted the process of social interaction through which meaning is constituted in the human community. Developing Peirce's semiotics with Hegel in mind, he presented social interaction as a process of interpretation and translation which takes place in the medium of communication and has a triadic structure of perception, conceptualisation and interpretation. A human being perceives something, conceives a concept in confrontation with reality, and interprets and re-interprets it in the mediating stream of communication borne by the historical human community.

On this basis, Royce was able to extend and, indeed, transform his predecessor's idea of the community of investigators and interpreters beyond the logical and scientific context to which it was confined into the human community of interpretation as such. For Peirce, the community of investigators and interpreters was a 'general idea' along the lines of Kant's 'ideas of reason' in the sense of a regulative principle. It is a normative idea which invokes the ultimate goal of all investigation and interpretation and thus exercises both a directing and a guiding role in relation to actual processes of the development of knowledge. Royce's innovative shift to the human community of interpretation meant a significant broadening of the horizon of this regulative principle. Yet Royce, the neo-Hegelian absolute idealist, was not content to treat the human community of interpretation simply as such a regulative principle, but instead was given to hypostatizing it in a bout of delusive reasoning, as Kant would have said. For him, the realization of this ideal community was guaranteed by the absolute system and teleological process of the human being reflexively representing itself and attaining self-knowledge. Peirce

(8.45–54) himself subjected the Hegelian and religious presuppositions underpinning Royce's position here to penetrating criticism.

James

Interested above all in psychology, William James (1842–1910) focused on subjective experience in particular contexts of situated action in which practical events pose a test for ideas. This emphasis on the situated practical problem context of the individual, action and ideas, which was not always presented with the necessary care, called forth a spate of criticism internationally when his lectures were collected in 1907 in *Pragmatism* (1978). The objections were to a perceived reduction of truth to utility. Indeed, Peirce himself felt obliged to take distance from James both formally in publication (5.3) and personally. Already a decade before the furore, in a letter dated 13 March 1897, he pointed out to James that, although it is a basic pragmatist assumption to test everything in terms of its practical consequences, for him this means that the goal is not sheer action but rather the generalization of such action with a view to regulation or control of action as the realization of thought (8.249). James tended to translate Peirce's pragmatic maxim too directly into the practice of everyday life and, thus, to foreshorten not only generalized ideas or rules to particular situated actions, but also conceivable practical consequences to subjectively experienced psychological effects. Over and above whatever flaws there may be in his conception of pragmatism, James's role in pragmatism can be compared, perhaps, to that of Kierkegaard in Young Hegelianism. Considering his abiding concern with the relation between truth – for him particularly religious truth – and the individual facing problems in everyday life, he can rightly be considered one of the precursors of existential philosophy (Joas 1993: 58–9). His undoubted positive contribution is to be found at the level of the theory of the subject.

Dewey and Mead

Both John Dewey (1859–1952) and George Herbert Mead (1863–1931), the two authors who brought pragmatism to bear on the social sciences, developed into pragmatists in a context shaped by Darwinism and late nineteenth- and early twentieth-century idealism. While natural evolution retained its relevance for both, Dewey shed his Hegelianism in favour of a naturalistic pragmatism and Mead sought to reconstruct his Kantian–Hegelian baggage from a pragmatist viewpoint. This difference explains Mead's closer relation to Peirce's most basic concerns and Dewey's greater distance. They of course shared the general pragmatist presuppositions, such as anti-Cartesianism and the views that action is constitutive and that cognition and knowledge are mediated by signs, and from relatively early on both appreciated the need for developing a psychological approach suited to the pragmatist theory of action. Directed against both the stimulus–response model and the pre-set goals model, it was designed to clarify the function of consciousness in the different phases of the process of action as

the latter constitutively moves from resistances encountered though self-re:
to creatively opening possibilities and setting goals.

Owing to a predilection to confine his view to everyday life and the (
intelligent mediation of means and goals arising immanently from the si_____ ,
Dewey tended to question the necessity of ultimate ends and, hence, to overlook
the ethical-moral problem of establishing general ends, especially in view of the
presence of less than normal situations. Nevertheless he was able to identify and
criticize limitations and blockages to rational communication required, say, for
converting 'a problematic situation into a set of conditions forming a definite
problem' (1938: 493).

Mead (1959, 1974) did not just develop an innovative pragmatist account
of communicatively mediated situations in which the actors, as qualitatively
peculiar signs themselves for their partners, have to acquire self-consciousness
and exercise self-control throughout the process by means of self-reflection. To
this classic theory of symbolically mediated social interaction and the cognitive
self belonged, moreover, not only the concept of 'the generalized other' (1974:
90, 154), but more generally still also the idea of reason and normative ideal of
'human society', which itself presupposes the ideas of 'democracy' in the sense
of communicatively organized social relations and of a community of 'universal
discourse' (1974: 327–8). That even the generalized other is a regulative idea, like
the previously mentioned more general ones, is borne out by Mead's oblique reference to Kant's ideas of reason – and, indeed, Hegel's *Sittlichkeit* – when he writes:
'The organized community or social group which gives to the individual his unity
of self may be called "the generalized other"' (1974: 154). Mead moreover sees
this general idea as 'enter[ing]' (ibid.) the experience, thinking and action of the
members and thus as a structuring factor in the process of the organization of the
community.

Dewey, like Mead, did not remain unaffected by the classical republican tradition which infused the American context with its ideal of democratic communal
self-organization. In works from the late 1920s and 1930s, we see him taking up
the question of democracy and analysing the communicative organization and
self-control or self-governance of the community. *The Public and Its Problems* (1927)
presented his political philosophy – and sociology – which traces the process of
the collective encounter of common problems and their cooperative processing
in a way that does not just solve the problems, but at the same time also enhances
democracy. The process which draws in all those concerned about the problem
as well as those affected by its consequences, individuals and institutions alike,
meanders along a communicatively mediated course from the construction of the
problem, through its collective interpretation, assessment and decision making,
to its resolution by appropriate action. The collective engagement sustaining the
process is subject to self-regulation in terms of collective standards generated
immanently, yet invoking the idea of communicatively enabled cooperative self-
governance. In *Logic, the Theory of Inquiry* (1938), Dewey offered a parallel account
in which he critically analyses the impediments to a rational and democratic construction of problems, for instance a too practically oriented attitude which takes

problems as already clearly defined, and outlined what contribution the social sciences could make to the resolution of collective problems and the strengthening of the principles of cooperation and hence democracy.

Mills

C. Wright Mills (1916–62) offers an interesting example of the early interaction between pragmatism and Critical Theory. From early in his studies he was influenced by his pragmatist mentors and entered an academic career on the basis of a thesis submitted at the University of Wisconsin which was posthumously published under the title of *Sociology and Pragmatism* (1964). However, in the graduate programme he was following there, he also worked closely with Hans Gerth, a German émigré very knowledgeable about the Frankfurt School, as a result of which his work right up to *The Sociological Imagination* (1970) was shot through with insights and ideas deriving from Critical Theory. Significantly in the present context, his work could be regarded as a combination of these two American and German traditions.

Against the background of Pierce's pragmatic maxim and Dewey's work on social inquiry and the relation of freedom and culture, Mills not only offered a sociological account of the institutionalization of pragmatism as shaped by Pierce, James and particularly Dewey, but actually translated pragmatism into a philosophically informed sociological approach. As *The Sociological Imagination* attests, he adhered to the end to this general orientation. His employment for this purpose of Dewey's conception of language and vocabulary as collective action combined with insights drawn from German thought, is reflected also in an interesting and today still relevant early essay, 'Situated actions and vocabularies of motive' (1940), in which his critically oriented sociological pragmatism speaks loudly. Remarkable is the centrality given to language and the pervasive understanding of the mediated nature of both social reality and the process of the development of knowledge. Although strongly influenced by Dewey, Mills nevertheless attacked his nakedly utilitarian scheme and proposed to sociologically correct its lack of understanding of the intrinsically social character of motives. In keeping with his later emphasis on the importance of the use of models, Mills outlined a metatheoretical framework for the analysis and explanation of social actions and their coordination in social situations. He regarded this approach as being applicable to different historical epochs and societal structures, but his focus was on delimited problem or crisis situations.

Within the much broader horizon and wider sweep of *The Sociological Imagination*, which was strongly influenced by work Mills did together with Gerth and contains references to members of the Institute for Social Research in exile in the United States, the impact of the left-Hegelian connection is clearly visible. In his criticism, one could say ideology critique, of the major trends in mid-twentieth-century social science he followed a pattern reminiscent of the 'Theses on Feuerbach'. One the one hand, 'everyday empiricism' (1970: 138) and 'abstracted empiricism' (1970: 61) were exposed as respectively naïve and methodologically inhibited; this

naïveté and inhibition lead to a fixation on isolated facts and a consequent failu
to come to grips with real problems of any significance. On the other, the forma
ism of 'grand theory' (1970: 33) was explicitly exposed following the model of th
young Marx's critique of Hegel, eventuating in the evaluation that it suffers from
a 'fetishism of the Concept' (1970: 60). In his own alternative approach, Mills
insisted on taking historical reality, including the historically specific situation and
historical change, seriously. In this respect, he adopted the historical understanding
of the dialectical method which is characteristic of Critical Theory. Emphasizing
both history and structure, the historical trajectory of the genesis of the object
must be followed and the structures which formed in the course of the process
must be extracted with reference to the real conditions as well as the salient trends
and the possible future state serving as its goal – for instance securing 'reason and
freedom' (1970: 192) in society. While stressing that the framework of society,
the social structure as a whole, must always be kept in mind, he is nevertheless
acutely aware of the dangers of thinking in terms of the 'whole' (1970: 170),
for example dogmatically hypostatizing it. In this context, the coordinates within
which analysis proceeds are biography, society and history, with the task of the
social scientist being to identify socially and politically significant problems which
are manifested both as 'personal troubles of milieu' and as 'public issues of social
structure' (1970: 14). Since such problems have a moral substance, their identification and analysis unavoidably involves evaluation – that is, taking a stance on the
values at stake, the threat to them and alternative ways of advancing the positive
aspect of those values under the newly emerging conditions.

Mills's work represents an important example of the pragmatist appropriation
of the classical foundations of social science and in this respect the most interesting aspect of *The Sociological Imagination* is his treatment of the classical notion of
ideas of reason. It opens with a critique of Parsons's conception of the normative
structure or order of society, which he presents in terms of his general sociological
theory as being universal in a sense that excludes disagreement, legitimacy problems and conflict. In Mills's view, normative structure has to do with what he
calls 'master symbols of legitimation' (1970: 46) – a phenomenon which has or
should have a central place in social science. Parsons's dealings with it, however,
parallel Hegel's presentation of the Idea as self-determining and self-moving, and
therefore the purported autonomous status and causal weight he ascribes to it calls
for a critique similar to that of left-Hegelianism. The ideas should be related to the
people and strata who make use of them. Indeed, Mills very significantly stresses
that 'the relations of such symbols to the structure of institutions are among the
most important problems of social science' (1970: 46) – a relation which cannot
be fixed beforehand by some general theory, but must be empirically investigated
in historically specific situations rooted in the historical process of transformation
and change. Since these master symbols do not merely define situations but are at
the same time also yardsticks for the evaluation of practices, leaders and followers,
it is necessary to recognize that they have a dual social and motivational relevance.
They are used for both the justification and the questioning of the organization of
power and related positions, and thus they motivate either adherence to the status

quo or opposition to it. Focusing exclusively on justification, therefore, is one-sided and unacceptable. Where conflict arises over the use of these master symbols, it is the task of social science to contribute to the 'enlarge[ment] of freedom and reason' (1970: 193) in society so that the conflict is mediated through argumentation rather than let it fester into an apparently irresolvable conflict which calls power and repression onto the scene.

At this juncture, Mills's view of the proper understanding of ideas of reason in their regulative function becomes clear, including also the particular one he regarded as most relevant to his own time. Not only do the ideas of freedom and reason play a role in reality by providing direction and guidance to the 'individual life', the arrangement of 'human affairs' and 'the making of history', but they also make possible the serious, consistent and imaginative 'formulation of problems' in social science (1970: 192, 193). Mills was particularly disturbed by the decline he observed in mid-twentieth-century American society of free individuality and of reason in society – a twofold decline that posed a challenge which required giving central importance to the idea of a free and rational society.

Critical Theory

Critical Theory started explicitly as a renaissance of left-Hegelianism. Requiring the critical and creative recovery under new conditions of the roots of Marx's thought in German idealism and its aftermath, it was necessitated by several interrupting factors. They included the ossification of Marxism into a scientistic and ideological system, a whole series of competing philosophical ideas launched by Schopenhauer, Liebmann, Nietzsche, Dilthey, Husserl and Simmel, and finally the drastically changed historical circumstances in the early twentieth century compared with the 1840s. What needed to be recovered were the radical innovations of Kant and Hegel and, in particular, the model of critique made possible by those innovations but given effect first by the left-Hegelian transformation of philosophy. This renaissance was inspired by Korsch and Lukács; the former through his involvement in the early years of the Institute of Social Research in Frankfurt and then his publication of *Marxism and Philosophy*, and the latter through his seminal book *History and Class Consciousness*. Another decisive factor which confirmed the direction in which Korsch and Lukács were pointing was the publication for the first time in 1932 of Marx's so-called 'Paris Manuscripts of 1844'. The activation of the left-Hegelian heritage in a manner commensurate with the changed conditions in the second and third decades of the twentieth century was confidently taken up and carried out by the core members of the Frankfurt School, namely Horkheimer, Adorno and Marcuse. The overwhelming historical event that started unfolding with Hitler's rise to power as well as the experience of exile interfered with their effort at a critical creative appropriation of the classic foundations and delineated a context in which these theorists tended to increasingly emphasize a latent aspect of their thinking which took them in a different direction. Under these new conditions, paradoxically, the very sources of inspiration of the renaissance – both Korsch's and Lukács's insistence on a theory that tightly integrates all the dimensions of society – also provided starting points for the debilitating Marxist functionalism which then came to dominate Horkheimer's, Adorno's and Marcuse's thinking. This theoretical model, according to which society is a totality unified by the economy in a way that turned culture, politics, democracy and all else into functional components of capitalism, which is regarded as developing from a competitive to a totalitarian system, starkly contradicted or rendered ineffective their acute insights into the social significance of the idealizing content of culture. By contrast with Mills's combination of ideas stemming from both pragmatism and Critical Theory, it is this same theoretical stance that also stood in the way of the critical theorists in exile in the United States and kept them from learning from pragmatism. Saddled with misleading presuppositions, misguided interpretations and unsustainable criticisms and rejections, they seemed unable to engage in a constructive way with this important line of thinking and investigation. After a close investigation of the relevant texts, Joas came to the following reasonable conclusion (in a not altogether balanced essay, which ignores, for instance, the fact that in the late 1930 and 1940s Americans themselves turned their backs on pragmatism): 'the relationship between "Critical Theory" and America and its intellectual traditions remained unproductive throughout the various fields of thought' (1993: 89). As will become apparent in the next chapter, this would drastically change only in the 1960s.

Korsch

In the early 1920s, Karl Korsch (1886–1961) took a decisive step in preparing the ground for Critical Theory through discussion of his ideas in the run-up to the establishment of the Institute for Social Research and their eventual publication in *Marxism and Philosophy* (1966: 116). Prompted by the crisis of Marxism stemming from its official ossification and more general vulgarization, he took aim at the misguided treatment meted out to the ideational dimension of social reality, whether through exclusion or trivialization, which indicated that Marx's 'materialistic-dialectical principle' (ibid.) originally advanced in his early writings was not grasped in its full scope and depth. This deficiency entailed not only that the constitutive subject of historical practice was overlooked, but also that all societal forms of consciousness which form a crucial objectified practical dimension of social reality, including philosophy, religion, art, law and aspects of the state, were demoted to a ghostly appearance not worthy of attention. In order to correct this deficit, he insisted that every trace of naïve realism, positivism, one-dimensional materialism and strong naturalism must be rejected in favour of the restitution of Marx's model of critique, which takes into account all the different levels of social reality. This 'societal critique' (1966: 124) embraced not only a critique of political economy, production relations and economic forms of consciousness, but importantly also the critique of all other societal forms of consciousness, whether pre-scientific, extra-scientific or scientific – what Korsch called 'critique of ideologies' (1966: 125).

Korsch regarded it as necessary to recover the epistemological and methodological sense of the shift from the classical transcendental approach to the dialectical approach. This required taking seriously Marx's aphorism: 'The form has no value if it is not the form of the content' (Korsch 1966: 129–30).[1] Whereas the transcendental standpoint is unable to grasp this intimate relation, since it regards the content as empirical and historical and the form as universally valid and necessary, the dialectical approach by contrast incorporates the form in the mutable and transitory empirical-historical reality and thus in the very thick of the struggle. On the basis of this detranscendentalizing dialectical understanding, Korsch reconstructed Marx's 'real methodological standpoint' (1966: 130) in three statements: all thinking is the processing of perceptions and representations into concepts; all categories of thinking, even the most general, are but the abstract and one-sided relations of a concrete and living whole; and the object grasped by thought is something real which remains independent outside the head. However, because he shared the assumption of the philosophy of consciousness predominant at the time and was not aware of available alternatives put forward by, for instance, Peirce or Frege, Korsch was not able to spell out the full implications of this epistemological-methodological position.

Lukács

Georg Lukács's (1885–1971) most famous book, *History and Class Consciousness* (1968), consists of two new essays and a number of previously published pieces dating from the period 1919 to 1922, which apparently impacted on Korsch. Shortly after its publication in 1923, followed by Korsch's book, both authors were attacked as so-called revisionists by the representatives of orthodox Marxism, Lukács particularly severely from the highest echelons of the Communist party. Although he publicly recanted under pressure, the various criticisms, also from other than party sources, led him to distance himself intellectually from a number of the ideas in the book. Members of the early Frankfurt School were also among his critics, yet their Critical Theory is inconceivable without this seminal work of his.

A major flaw in Lukács's argumentation, acknowledged by himself as an abortive attempt to 'out-Hegel Hegel' (1968: xxii–xxiii), goes back to his too strong a Hegelian recovery of left-Hegelianism in his enthusiasm to bring revolutionary praxis back into Marxist theory in the context of crisis after the First World War when a world revolution seemed to be on the cards. Given that it was a matter of left-Hegelianism, however, it is also here that the strength of his recuperation of the tradition lies. The flaw hinges on his acceptance of identity theory, by which he regarded the proletariat as both subject and object which realizes itself in the process as 'the identical subject-object' of history and society (1968: 149). It is on this basis that he built his standpoint epistemology according to which the self-understanding of the proletariat is not only the objective knowledge of society, but by the same token also the objective possibility that transcends the present and towards the full realization of which the historical process is inexorably moving. Lukács's later self-criticism targeted the implied idealism of envisaging the fulfilment of the objective possibility projected by proletarian class consciousness through revolutionary praxis from the viewpoint of Engels and Lenin's materialist theory of nature, which purportedly would bring the communist society into being. Besides the fact that he, in addition, came to accept also the untenable dogma that the Communist party was the vanguard leading this process, the identification of the objective possibility of societal development with the class consciousness of one single class, irrespective of whether conceived in terms of idealized praxis or a materialistic party, entailed the hypostatization – as Kant would have said – of an idea of reason or general concept. What he nevertheless positively yet by no means faultlessly achieved was to draw attention in analytical detail to the historical process of the socio-cultural construction, formation and transformation of society, including obstacles interfering in it, and to clarify the epistemological and methodological requirements for gaining potentially practically meaningful knowledge of it.

As against positivism and neo-Kantianism, Lukács drew on left-Hegelianism to present the view that reality is reducible neither to individual objects nor to an irrational manifold, but is rather dialectically a matter of the forms of objects that are transformed into a process in the course of which they become concretely realized. The concept of 'mediation' (1968: 156, 203), referring to the mechanism allowing the establishment, maintenance and concretization of flexible relations, is central to the transformative interrelation of the various elements in the process. From the priority ascribed to dynamics it follows that what counts are not the phenomena or objects as such but rather the 'tendencies' (1968: 155, 162, 181) exhibited by those phenomena or objects in the context of the process. Not what they are but rather what they are becoming is important. As the key concept of 'totality' (1968: 50, 170) demands, this whole processual set of relations must at all times be kept in mind. From these basic ontological assumptions Lukács drew significant epistemological and methodological conclusions, but a consideration first of his very influential more concrete application of this dialectical view to society – deriving from left-Hegelianism but significantly influenced by Weber, Simmel and Kierkegaard – would assist in better understanding these conclusions.

Society is a totality in the sense of a constructive 'socialising process' which has its roots in the past, takes a particular form in the present and reaches – according to Lukács's moral-ethical and political view – towards the future objective possibility of 'the socialisation of the whole human society' (1968: 176). Under conditions of capitalism, however, a process of 'rationalisation' has led to the predominance of the 'commodity form' which has penetrated all spheres of life, inducing the widespread negative phenomenon of 'reification' (1968: 83, 176, 197) in the sense of the transformation of direct human social relations into something akin to abstract relations between things. This reification is moreover accompanied by deeply damaging human 'estrangement' (1968: 87, 89, 91) which locks large numbers of people into the present. Yet it simultaneously also forces those suffering most from this condition to gain a sense of the future possibility of a socialized human society. This contradiction in the way capitalist relations are actually experienced is a factor in making society a self-activating totality. Since the contradiction operates as an impetus in the ongoing process involving engagement in the mediation of form and content or essence and existence, the proletariat can be looked upon as possessing the potential to continually 'disrupt the reified structure of existence' and eventually to 'overcome' (1968: 197) it through a revolutionary act, thus transforming the world. But this requires that the proletariat's consciousness of both the contemporary conditions as well as the larger process be nurtured and awakened. For Lukács, recouping the characteristic motif of left-Hegelianism, this is the task of critique. It involves the critique of society, the unmasking of reification, the exposure of illusions, and in particular the development of critical awareness of progressive potentials, the degree already realized and what is practicable under existing conditions (1968: 205). In turn, critique is conducted on the basis of 'painstaking historical analysis . . . [guided by] . . . the category of objective possibility' (1968: 52) – that is, a counterfactual projection which makes it 'possible to infer the thoughts and feelings which people would have in a particular situation if they were able to assess . . . their objective situation' (1968: 51).

The core of *History and Class Consciousness*, contained in the essay on reification, is an incisive epistemological-methodological analysis which, quite astonishingly, confirms the similarities between Marx and Peirce at this particular level. In keeping with his ontological emphasis on process, mediation and totality, Lukacs rejects the widely accepted dualisms or 'antinomies' of Western thought, such as subject and object, freedom and necessity, individual and society, and form and content. However, the main task is to clarify, both structurally and temporally, how social reality can be approached in order to make possible a type of cognition and the generation of a kind of knowledge that lends itself to the achievement of practical purposes. Structurally, it is a question of the different depth dimensions of reality that are brought together or mediated in the course of the process of cognition and knowledge production; and, temporally, it is a question of how cognition can come to terms with social reality as a process with simultaneous references to the present, the past and the future.

Lukács's first step is to identify three distinct dimensions which represent essential elements of an adequate position (1968: 153–6). The first is the immediately available empirical dimension, which, essential as it is, can be taken as the sole level of interest only at the cost of being able to provide at best only a superficial description. Thus he severely criticizes an empiricist or positivist fixation on 'objects' or 'immediacy' and being content with 'first sight'. A shift from 'the immediacy of empirical reality' to the second dimension requires 'rationalist reflection' in the sense of conceptualization and theorization which makes possible the identification of 'relations' between the objects and thus a 'system of relations' beyond the objects yet allowing them to interrelate. However indispensable such relationalism is, however, he immediately insists on the inherent limits of 'formal, rational and abstract conceptual systems', which are incapable of leading beyond the purely factual level. What is necessary, third, therefore, is for cognition to penetrate through to 'reality'. Only in this way can it achieve 'greater concreteness'. This is done by approaching the 'totality of the empirical' or understanding 'the objects of the empirical world . . . as aspects of a totality, i.e. as the aspects of a total social situation caught up in the process of historical change'. It is at this point that not only the category of mediation becomes relevant, but also the temporal dimension. Mediation concerns the dynamic whole that encompasses both the first and second dimensions, but at issue here is also the process of development and transformation of social reality of which the knowledge producing act forms a part. Beyond facts, even social facts rendered more meaningful through theorization, therefore, Lukács stresses here 'the real tendencies of the objects themselves', but at the same time also 'the "critical movement" . . . of the "creation" of the object' (1968: 155). Cognition is an inherent part of the process of transformation and by producing knowledge the cognitive act contributes to the shaping of reality and the direction in which it is going. This third dimension, then, concerns reality in the proper sense of the word: 'reality is not, it becomes – and to become the participation of thought is needed' (1968: 204).

Whatever disagreements the major representatives of the early Frankfurt School had with Lukács, it is this innovative recovery of left-Hegelianism and its incisive ontological and epistemological-methodological articulation that became the most direct important source of inspiration for their Critical Theory.

Horkheimer

For Max Horkheimer (1895–1973), Critical Theory was a materialistic theory of society with an explicit practical intent in the sense of an inbuilt striving on the part of the theory and associated research to contribute to the realization of a core of leading normative ideas; that is, not 'mere ideas' drawn from eternity and idealistically opposed to existing reality, but ones which have a 'foothold in the present' (1970: 62). His establishment of Critical Theory thus conceived in the 1930s, especially in the tradition-founding *Traditional and Critical Theory* and its 'Postscript' (1970: 12–56, 57–64), unmistakably indicates his adoption of the left-Hegelian legacy in the wake of the redirection of Marxism introduced by Lukács and Korsch. Like these two authors, he fought against the orthodox and vulgar Marxist stance according to which classical German idealism could be treated like a dead dog since, purportedly, it had been definitively overcome and rendered redundant. Indeed, Kant pervaded his thinking, especially the latter's practical or moral philosophy, but of course by no means without critical reception, and he was to a large extent yet equally critically also in agreement with Hegel's critique of Kant. Rejecting their turn to irrationalism, he regarded both Schopenhauer's and Nietzsche's criticism of idealism and morality in particular as helpful in clarifying reason. What the continuation of the left-Hegelian tradition allowed him to do, however, was to present not only a critical theory of morality and ethical life under modern capitalist conditions, but also to place this whole normative complex within the framework of Marx's dialectic of sublation and realization in which, nevertheless, Kantian ideas of reason continued to play an important role. Horkheimer accepted that Kant's philosophy opened up a dynamic normative perspective which could only be redeemed by political means, and in this respect he was convinced that Kant pointed beyond the limits of the existing society, morality and ethical relations. From the materialistic viewpoint, he could of course not accept the Kantian distinction between theoretical and practical reason. Critical Theory formed part and parcel of the project to improve human relations, which means that it incorporates practical philosophy rather than leaving it standing as an independent intellectual endeavour. This entails that, through the left-Hegelian appropriation of German Idealism, Critical Theory as an interdisciplinary programme retained a philosophical moment. It task was to 'expose . . . harmonistic illusions', to reveal the dark side of dominant conceptions – for instance showing up 'injustice', 'domination', 'restriction on human relations' and 'destitution of peoples' – and to point to 'the interests of real people' and the ends presupposed by them, but in principle to do so with reference to 'the basic relation of the epoch' in the context of the real historical process of the transformation of society (1970: 59–60).

In Horkheimer's programmatic presentation of Critical Theory by contrast with what he called 'traditional theory' – including positivism, neo-Kantianism, hermeneutics, the sociology of knowledge and even orthodox and vulgar Marxism as well as generally the Cartesian-inspired disciplinary division of labour – one can clearly see the left-Hegelian model of critique at work. It bears close comparison with the position Lukács put forward earlier. For Horkheimer, Critical Theory is the intellectual side of real as well as possible historical transformations which emanate from the living social life process itself – not the process positivistically hypostatized in isolated facts or data, idealistically elevated to a self-activating concept, sociologically cut and dried into isolated complexes of ideas rooted in social positions, or tied to the perspective of a particular class, and even less fragmented by the academic division of labour. The fulfilment of this task requires the interdisciplinary generation of knowledge of different kinds, from historical and empirical to diagnostic and pragmatic knowledge, by means of the employment of whatever techniques, especially advanced ones, are available. However, characteristic of Critical Theory is a critical mode of thinking which itself possesses a number of distinct yet dialectically interrelated dimensions. It is exhibited, for example, by the very way in which Horkheimer incorporated moral philosophy shorn of its idealistic baggage into Critical Theory as its practical cutting edge. With some assistance from Hegel, Schopenhauer, Nietzsche and Freud, first, he subjects the claim to the effect that morality can be regarded as deontological, universal and rational to a devastating ideology critique (Schnädelbach 1987: 213–7). Being absolutely averse to reductionism as are Lukács and Korsch, however, in a second step he redeems from the ruins the universalistic import of morality and, together with it, also its rational quality understood in a non-metaphysical sense. The vehicle for this is politics. The ideas and ideals of freedom, equality and solidarity have their seat in the concrete historical and social context of life where they arise from human praxis and, hence, are subject to possible change in the course of attempts at their realization. These ideas and ideals are therefore not so much moral as they are political and therefore social principles of the organization of collective life. The reference to the political and social already entails a shift to the third dimension of Horkheimer's model of critique. He is insistent that Critical Theory belongs to the very object domain it investigates. It is part of the real historical process of social transformation and thus an element in the project and practical attempt to go beyond the current situation by improving conditions regarding the relations among human beings, collective life and nature. Far from being an isolated activity engaged in for its own sake, therefore, ideology critique, in both its negative destructive and its positive redeeming sense, makes sense only in so far as it contributes to the advancement of the historical process and the organization of society by clarifying the current situation and serving as grist for the practical mill.

The orientation of Critical Theory to rational action of this kind is rooted in a defining 'interest'. The manner in which Horkheimer conceives of this guiding and directing interest by contrast with other options, such as emotion and voli-tion, throws further light on the structure of his epistemological-methodological position. Both emotion and volition as a basis for an orientation towards, say, a problematic situation, are accompanied by doubt about the efficacy of reason and, as a result, eventuate in the dramatization either of an emotional response or of the urgent need to make a decision. An interest-based approach, by con-trast, while by no means denying the role of the emotions and decision making, represents a much calmer and considered assessment and engagement with the situation. Interest for him is therefore a category of mediation which embraces and thus allows the integration of the other two moments. It is interesting that this understanding invites comparison with Peirce's semiotics based on the tri-adic sign-relation. Emotion is the one-dimensional qualitative moment, volition the two-dimensional establishment of a relation with the object or situation, and interest the three-dimensional medium allowing the interrelation of all the differ-ent moments. More concretely, Horkheimer conceives of interest in terms linked to the historical process of the development, transformation and organization of society through human practices guided and directed by an idea and ideal of reason.

As regards its content, Horkheimer offered a variety of different descriptions of the particular interest underpinning Critical Theory. According to the leading for-mulation, it is 'an interest in the overcoming of social injustice' (1970: 56). However, he also filled out this negative formulation, which encapsulates the materialistic content of the idealistic concept of reason, more positively by specifying it as 'an interest in transformation . . . which strives after a situation devoid of exploitation and repression' (1970: 55) or as 'an interest in rational conditions' (1970: 21) or 'a rationally organized future society' (1970: 49). In a number of comparable most interesting statements, Horkheimer submits that Critical Theory's perspective, the goal of a rational society, which under current conditions may well seem like no more than pure fantasy, is actually immanently grounded in every human being and in human activities, especially labour (1970: 63, 32).

Here Horkheimer raises two very serious problems which remain undeveloped in his work. The first concerns the normative foundations of his Critical Theory, which is signalled by the concept of interest and, more specifically, by the appeal to every human being and to human activities as the basic anchor point. Although he insisted that it is part of Critical Theory's task to clarify and legitimize its defining interest, and although he located it in its proper place, the problem of normative foundations remained a systematic gap which he never filled. Besides this basic justificatory deficit, a theoretical problem is also apparent. It concerns the relation between normative ideas and ideals such as a rational society which, on the one hand, transcend the existing state of affairs but, on the other, are simultaneously immanent in concrete social givens or practices. Despite the obvious centrality of this problem and the fact that it crops up regularly in his writings, he did not take time to explicate it as such.

Adorno

Theodor Adorno's (1903–69) major epistemological-methodological work is *Negative Dialektik* (1970) which was written between 1959 and 1966 yet contained parts going back as far as 1932 and 1937. Representing his particular appropriation of the left-Hegelian tradition in the wake of Lukács, the title refers to the 'logic of critique' (Schnädelbach 1987: 194) and, accordingly, he presented it as the very 'organon' (Adorno 1970: 25) of Critical Theory. By contrast with both Kant and Hegel's idealistic dialectics and Marx's materialistic dialectics, he understood the logic of critique as open to history and the future, yet not without a goal or regulative principle. The openness and the goal, which is impossible to specify in terms of content, are indicated by the adjective 'negative' and the basic concept of 'the non-identical' used throughout the book. His insistence on openness was played out against Hegel's absolutism, and the unspecifiable idea of reason paid homage to Kant, who was of great importance to Adorno but whose contribution was in turn critically strengthened by transforming it in terms of Hegelian–Marxian dialectics. It is from this perspective, which stresses that experience is from the start and throughout saturated in thought, that he engaged in a wide-ranging criticism of different philosophical and social scientific directions of his time as a foil against which to profile his own negative dialectical Critical Theory.

   Adorno opened his criticism by launching in against the modern disciplinary system, which under the auspices of the patriarchs of modernity, Descartes and Bacon, dehistoricized and compartmentalized thought in order to focus in traditionless *tabula rasa* fashion on the directly given, the pure present and the eternal object. In this context, he then attacked a whole range of diverse positions for their fixation on immediacy – from empiricist positions that are predisposed to hypostatize isolated elements of the present as facts or problems, to intuitionist positions that wallow in the contemplation of essences or the non-conceptual. In opposition to such approaches, he is adamant that, irrespective of whether it is a matter of sense impressions or perceptions or of noeses or intuitions, in so far as experience is at stake conceptual thought is necessarily and unavoidably implicated. It is not simply that experience is always already shaped by thought, however; dialectically understood, thought always has an ideational goal which directs and guides the operational working out of thought. This is all the more the case where responsibility has to be taken for cognition and knowledge. There is an element of 'utopia', of something coming into being that is not yet, in thought, and there is an element of 'hope' of breaking through existing barriers attached to it. These elements are captured by the concept of 'idea', which, considered closely, is 'a negative sign' (1970: 151), for instance Kant's 'ideas of reason' or Adorno's own 'the non-identical'. On the other hand, Adorno rejects the widespread prioritization of deduction in the sense of the subsumption of something under a concept and the classificatory approach of fitting something into a conceptual framework. Indeed, one of the most, if not the most, characteristic features of Adorno's work is his acute awareness, despite his emphasis on conception as such, of the liabilities and limits of conceptual thought.

Characteristically, therefore, Adorno struggled with what he experienced as the dilemma of the concept. Of reality he says 'What is, is more than it is' (1970: 162), and, in so far as the concept is but a 'moment' (1970: 22) of this reality in process, it is capable of capturing only a part of it. Indeed, he speaks of the concept as 'cutting away' part of the 'internality' (1970: 162) of reality. What falls out of the grasp of the concept is 'the non-conceptual' dimension, which has two aspects in that its import is both 'immanent' and 'transcendent' (1970: 21). The first concerns the 'specificity', 'quality' or 'deictic' aspect of reality or the object (1970: 162, 51, 22), and the second the tendency of reality or the direction of transformation of 'the real historical process' (1970: 166) and, hence, also the idea directing and guiding the cognitive process, what he generally calls 'the non-identical' (1970: 22). The keywords in the compensation of the problems inherent in conceptualization are 'mimesis' (1970: 24, 53) and 'conceptual reflection' (1970: 23). Conceptual mimesis, which Adorno distinguished from both artistic imitation and intellectual contemplation, refers to the incorporation of the quality of experience as the starting point of conceptual thought into the concept through 'nestling up to and clinging onto' (1970: 22, 51) the internal core of something. Only in this way can the particular or individual be included in its qualitative significance. Simultaneously, the non-identical in the sense of the end or vanishing point must also be granted its sway in the cognitive process. Critical thought must always and throughout keep in mind and relate to its goal or end. Adorno referred to it in different ways, calling it 'reconciliation' (1970: 16), a condition in which 'dialectics is shorn of its power' (1970: 16), 'the hope of the name' (1970: 60), 'the condition in which no subject is sacrificed' (1970: 275), a 'society that guarantees the freedom of individuals' (1970: 217) or a 'totally socialized society' (1970: 307). This twofold accomplishment of incorporation of both origin and end allows the mediation of the concept through the non-conceptual and thus the establishment of non-reductive experience in the medium of conceptual reflection. To redirect conceptual thought in order to take the non-conceptual into account is, according to Adorno, the very step on which 'negative dialectics hinges' (1970: 22) – which means to say, it is characteristic of Critical Theory. It should be obvious at this stage that Adorno's position, like the similar ones of Lukács and Horkheimer, is basically comparable to Peirce's triadic framework. The immediate qualitative experience of an aspect of reality is conceptualized and theorized with reference to the potential collective understanding of reality in the long run.

Adorno offered a more precise account of what these epistemological-methodological suggestions entail under the rubric of a 'collection of concepts' or, more properly, a 'constellation' (1970: 166, 60, 162) in the social scientific context. It includes more specific indications that bear on his own methodological practice. Negative dialectics and hence Critical Theory approach the hardened objects of a reified society with the suspicion that they do not correspond to their own reality and, accordingly, seek to penetrate them with reference to both their specificity and directional tendencies. This is what a constellation or a collection of concepts surrounding the object of knowledge is designed to accomplish. It locates the object in a set of conceptually mediated relations which captures the object's unique quality, including both its negative or ideological and its positive sides, as well as its possibilities or what it could become given the fact that it is only a single moment in a more encompassing reality which is in a process of transformation.

Methodologically, negative dialectics and hence Critical Theory conduct this constellational type of analysis by means of models. Indeed, critical thinking takes the form of 'an ensemble of model analyses' (1970: 37). Adorno mentioned two of these models, namely language (1970: 27, 59–60, 162, 166) and reading (1970: 60, 163, 165), the first methodologically more general and the second more specific. The analysis generally follows the structure suggested by language with a view to gaining a coherent and dynamic grasp of the whole set of relations in which the object of knowledge is situated. As a 'sign system' (1970: 162) serving cognitive functions, it is perfectly suited to conveying these relations, but, above and beyond that, language as a medium also generates meaning not only by retaining the unique qualities of what is being referred to, but also through its capacity to name what is only in the process of coming into being, even if at best in the form of distant and unclear primitive images. The sign-mediated medium of language is the necessary and unavoidable means through which negative dialectical thinking expresses itself and is able to attain critical theoretical representation, description and explanation. With this particular understanding of the medium of thinking, cognition and knowledge, Adorno places himself unequivocally and indisputably in the company of Peirce and his *medium quo* theory and confirms its presence also in the left-Hegelian tradition. It is particularly interesting that, whereas Peirce went back to medieval language theory against the background of his Kant and Hegel studies, Adorno severely criticized the persistent modern attempt to pursue the ideal of method at the expense of language. In addition to the appreciation of language as medium, his depiction of his own practice in terms of constellational analysis also implies, despite his notorious strictures against communication (1970: 49–50), that negative dialectics and hence Critical Theory follow a 'discursive logic' and thus represent a 'discursive practice' (Schnädelbach 1987: 196) in which the depiction of reality is constantly being subjected to revision in keeping with the process of transformation.

Adorno's more specific methodological approach to analysis according to the model of reading follows the semiotic logical of language and is thus attuned to the temporal process of the transformation of reality and the way it is experienced. His guideline is to 'read the elements of reality as a text of its becoming' (1970: 60), which means that the objects are regarded as holding the sedimented history of their historical development and transformation and, therefore, that parallel to it analysis must make sense of the history and penetrate the sedimentations to unearth the structures they contain. Through reading the signs, how something has come to incorporate its own history must be deciphered. Adorno conceives of this kind of negative dialectical or critical theoretical analysis in terms of a combination of idealist and materialist dialectics, thus resulting in something like an interpretative-critical procedure. Whereas idealism narratively and interpretatively follows the internal history of the immediately given objects, the materialist approach exposes the untruth of those objects and locates them within the larger transforming reality to which they belong. To this, negative dialectics adds depth by concerning itself with the incorporation with the non-conceptual and non-identical aspects, the qualitative and the sense of a guiding vanishing point.

The basic error Adorno committed in his presentation of negative dialectics as the logic of critique is the one he inherited from Hegel and Marx and was strengthened by the decisive impact Lukács had on him: namely the hypostatization of an idea of reason, which led, in Kant's cautionary words, to 'delusive reasoning' and hence dogmatism. On the one hand, Adorno saw clearly that Kant's idea of a state in which the freedom of each is able to coexist with the freedom of all represents a counterfactual 'cipher' (1970: 277) which makes visible not only the compulsion operative in various parts of society, together with the pathological individuality it breeds, but also the possibility of working towards the transformation of both for the better. On the other, however, he self-contradictorily adopted a holistic, Marxist functionalist ontology and, based on it, a totalizing theory of society. Not unlike Lukács's erroneous treatment of all objectifying processes as reification, and his compounding of the error by identifying reification and alienation, this totalization found expression in the unsustainable concept of a society, a closed system based on exchange, in which every individual and everything is mediated by the commodity form. This 'exchange society' (*Tauschgesellschaft*) casts a 'spell' (*Bann*) like a mythical force over the whole without distinction and without exception and thus 'blinds' (*Verblendung*) all and everyone to reality (1970: 335–41). Adorno criticized Weber's concept of ideal-type, which is a version of the Kantian idea of reason, for expressing only the subjective side of the cognitive procedure and for being nominalist and thus failing to capture the proper sense of the concept, but the non-identical, as his own version, was, in Hegelian manner, pursued to the unacceptable extreme of conceptual realism. Instead of a regulative idea, indeed one a good deal stronger than the ideal-type, this predilection for totalization transformed his key concept of the non-identical into an exclusive and intolerant dogma.

Marcuse

Both in his foundational essay 'Philosophy and Critical Theory' (1972: 134–58) and more extensively in the book *Reason and Revolution* (1973), Herbert Marcuse (1898–1979) located the origin of Critical Theory in the 1830s and 1840s, yet he was not happy with linking it to left-Hegelianism as such since Marxian social theory alone continued the critical tendencies of Hegelian philosophy, unlike the other representatives, who fought against Hegel. Besides Marx, who got a lengthy treatment, he discussed Feuerbach and, as a contrast, Kierkegaard as well – the last of whom is given an exclusively critical if not scathing treatment. Over and above the nineteenth-century materialist theory of society, however, the appropriation of the left-Hegelian tradition and, through it, classical idealism was necessitated by the need to return to the past. This necessity was not only due to the defeat of the proletariat as the envisaged agent of transformation, but also because of the destruction of culture and its inherent ideas of reason by the wave of Fascist barbarism which swept Europe. He regarded the new situation of the 1930s as compelling the Critical Theory to prevent the loss of truths which past generations have laboured to attain and to focus more sharply its concern with human potentialities.

The justification for the turn to the past is that an essential characteristic of Critical Theory are ideas of reason – a characteristic implying an abiding orientation to the future and a defining interest in transformation for the better. As in the cases of Horkheimer and Adorno, Kant is of central importance to Marcuse in this respect, although treated critically in many other contexts. It is not only the concept of interest as anchor point that attracted attention, but also and especially the emphasis on reason as something to be pursued in an interested and committed way. Through his three famous questions – What can I know? What should I do? What may I hope? – Kant focused and concentrated what he called 'the interest of reason' (1968: 430, see also 630), thus shifting the emphasis to human potentialities and pointing beyond the existing order. Among the ideas of reason Marcuse includes freedom, rights, a liberated humankind and a rational society, and in his *Eros and Civilization* (1969a) on the basis of a critical appropriation of Freud he speaks of a 'non-repressive civilization' based on a 'polymorphous sexuality'. Reference is frequently made also to happiness, although it is at best only what could be hoped for. Not only are these ideas part of Critical Theory, in his view, but together with the latter they form part of the historical process of the transformation of society in which their role is to bring to awareness potentialities under new conditions and to exert a progressive impetus towards their concrete realization.

Although he at times seems to regard philosophy as having become redundant and therefore something to be ignored, Marcuse's position is actually that the shift from idealism to left-Hegelianism entails that a philosophical element has migrated into Critical Theory and forms an inalienable part of it. Refusing to make facticity the criterion, great philosophy has always concerned itself with human potentialities and thus looked beyond the existing order. It has been the repository of universal ideas which Critical Theory seeks to preserve, yet it at the same time relates more strongly to the future with a view to the transformation of the existing social structure. On the one hand, Critical Theory shares with philosophy its capacity for 'imagination' or 'phantasy', which makes possible the retention of 'what is not yet present as a goal in the present' (1972: 154). On the other, however, it goes well beyond philosophy in so far as its 'constructive character' (1972: 143) and employment of 'constructive concepts' (1972: 153) are oriented not purely towards the generation of knowledge, but rather towards actually bringing into being a 'new form of the world' (1972: 151). Even though Critical Theory is basically a materialist theory of society, Marcuse stressed that it is characterized by the fact that it is underpinned by idealism in a particular sense. It is given direction and guided by the rational idea of a 'reality' that is contained in 'the concrete social situation' as a set of 'potentialities' which is 'not yet given' but represents a 'progressive impetus' pressing towards its concrete realization (1972: 153, 142, 152).

Marcuse stressed that the critique of ideology is an essential medium in which Critical Theory manifests its interest in and relation to philosophy. In its examination of philosophical doctrines with a view to extracting the ideas of reason deposited in them, it deals first with the misunderstanding and camouflage present in them by explaining these negative features by the material conditions of life. Both Kant and Hegel, for instance, recognized that reason is freedom and pointed to the outstanding need to realize freedom, but given the conditions of the time they internalized idealism, putting forward the individual as having the capacity to realize freedom internally without any impact on the concrete situation. Freud is regarded as a philosopher and receives the same ideology-critical treatment (1969a). More generally, culture is treated in a similar way. The prevailing culture, 'affirmative culture' (1972: 95), segregates an independent mental and spiritual realm of value from the conditions of life and holds it up as realizable by the solitary individual from within regardless of the conditions. It thus affirms the existing state of affairs and simultaneously conceals the new conditions demanding realization, yet far from being merely ideology it has positive progressive content worthy of redemption. For Marcuse, this suggests an alternative concept of culture which is suitable as a research instrument for Critical Theory: namely, a concept that gives centre stage to 'the implication of the mind in the historical process of society' (1972: 94). There is a historically accumulated potential marked by an idea of reason which through reflection could be made available for realization under concrete conditions which, in turn, would entail the transformation of the present state of affairs and the bringing into being of a new world.

Critical Theory does not confine itself, however, to the ideology critique of culture. Marcuse is absolutely unequivocal that reality is of central concern to it. Assuming reality as a 'process' that passes through 'phases of realization', the focus is on the existing state of affairs, which is regarded as possessing immanently both negative and positive aspects. On the one hand, the negative aspect is treated as being in the process of 'disappearing' and is therefore subjected to a negative critique. On the other, the positive aspect is identified with reference to the 'ultimate goal' of Critical Theory, the transcendent guiding idea of a 'liberated humankind', as well as the real 'potentialities' and directional 'tendencies' of the historical process, as being in the process of emerging as a potential 'element of the coming society'. For this reason, the positive aspect is 'liberated' by a saving critique which makes it available to be 'transformed' so as to be appropriate to the newly emerging societal arrangement (1972: 145–6; 1973: 315). In later work conceiving society in terms of Freudian theory as rooted in the biological necessity of the instincts, Marcuse (1969a) likewise critiqued advanced industrial or 'overdeveloped' society for being organized through alienated labour and military mobilization in such a way that it socially exploits the destructive energy of the aggressive instinct to fuel growth and war. By contrast, he saw potential for a transformation to non-alienated labour and the social prioritization of libidinal energy generated by the erotic instinct, which favours the protection, preservation and amelioration of life instead.

Although ideology critique is a characteristic feature of Critical Theory, the latter's method is more encompassing. The left-Hegelians, particularly Feuerbach and Marx extending him, transformed Hegel's dialectical method, which had already been a critical method, into a 'genetico-critical' method which, as against Hegel, basically assumes that 'nature is the primary and thought the secondary reality', but in addition is then given the form of a 'historical method' (1973: 268, 314). Rather than simply starting with the object to demonstrate and understand it, this method consists of tracing the origin, formation and emergence of the object in the course of a long historical process and then, instead of being satisfied with the result so far, pressing on by subjecting the object to both a negative and positive critique. The coming into being of the object is constructivistically followed and the structures which formed in the course of the process are reconstructed with reference to the real conditions as well as the direction of development or tendency and the possible future state serving as its goal. Marcuse shared this understanding with Adorno, which Marx in his inimitable style captured with the phrase: 'we have to make these petrified social relations dance by singing their own tune' (Marx 1967a: 253).

Marcuse's Critical Theory exhibits problems similar to those of his fellow critical theorists, and here too signs of Lukács's impact on the thinking of the Frankfurt School are visible. It concerns in particular the tendency towards a totalizing ontology inspired by the Hegelian–Marxist concept of totality. As in the case of Horkheimer and Adorno, the adherence to the shift from Hegel's conception of the totality of reason to the notion of society as a totality also led Marcuse to operate with a kind of thinking that has been called Marxist functionalism. Earlier on, it found expression in his endorsement of Marxian theory as 'an integral and integrating theory of society . . . [in which] . . . the economic process of capitalism exercises a totalitarian influence' (1973: 320) and, later, in the very idea of *One Dimensional Man* (1968). But the real problem involves more than just totalizing the existing society. It consists of the closely related predilection to hypostatize the direction-giving, guiding and regulating ideas of reason, which are invoked as the ultimate goal of Critical Theory. As against idealism, these ideas were quite correctly shorn of their purely transcendental character by being brought down from heaven, as still presupposed by both Kant and Hegel, to the ground of historically changing society. Despite their having thus been identified as 'impure . . . transcendent truths' (1972: 141), the counterfactual character of these ideas was overlooked and instead absolutized into utopia. By being separated from existing reality as utopian ideas requiring a one-off total transformation of society, they lost the defining feature of ideas that have a foothold in everyday life and society, yet point beyond existing reality in a way that works back in a regulative and structuring way on that reality.

Conclusion

In this chapter, the appropriation of the classical foundations of contemporary Critical Theory as represented by Kant, Hegel and the left-Hegelians by both the pragmatists – Royce, James, Dewey, Mead and Mills – and the critical theorists – Korsch, Lukács, Horkheimer, Adorno and Marcuse – were traced. With reference to the work of the authors mentioned, it filled in essential background regarding the normative, ontological and epistemological presuppositions of contemporary Critical Theory required for the clarification in Part II of the latter's methodology. It also provides the necessary basis for considering the current relation between Critical Theory and pragmatism in the next chapter.

3 Contemporary Critical Theory and pragmatism

Introduction

A drastic change dating from the 1960s led to the remarkable rise of an intellectual trend in the 1990s which has come to be referred to as 'the renaissance of pragmatism' (Joas 1993: 56,75; Sandbothe 2000; Böhler et al. 2003: 172). Whereas the mutual criticism of Habermas and Rorty is a central feature of the recent phase of the renaissance, the debate has intensified in the past decade or two around the issue of regulative ideas, centring in particular on the position of Apel, the philosopher who has played a vital role in laying the groundwork for the upsurge of interest in pragmatism and of seeing it in relation to Critical Theory.[1] Although the renaissance and the developments that led up to it form the background of the account offered here, the aim of the chapter is to clarify the relationship between Critical Theory and pragmatism since the drastic redirection of the 1960s. The leading interest is in the nature and character of contemporary Critical Theory as it has been taking new shape under the impact of its incorporation of a range of pragmatist ideas.

The analysis of the interaction between Critical Theory and pragmatism has to start from Apel's seminal contribution, particularly his recovery of Peirce's sign-mediated theory of knowledge and conception of regulative ideas, which made possible an unprecedented and most fruitful articulation of Critical Theory and pragmatism. From there the development is followed through Habermas to younger critical theorists such as Wellmer, Eder and Honneth, who have actively incorporated pragmatist elements into Critical Theory. Aspects of the internal debate in Critical Theory regarding pragmatism and regulative ideas are touched on in the course of the account. The overview of Critical Theory is then complemented by a parallel treatment of pragmatism, which is traced from Bernstein and Rorty to McCarthy and Bohman, the last two of whom have both actively engaged in pragmatizing Critical Theory.

Critical Theory

The second generation

Apel: dialectic of the real and ideal communication community

In his earliest work, his doctoral thesis, Karl-Otto Apel (1922–) developed an assessment of Heidegger's transformative impact on the epistemology of Cartesian–Kantian provenance, the results of which he recapitulated in the introduction to the original publication of his important two-volume collection of essays on the transformation of philosophy. In sum, by transforming Kant's unhistorical transcendental presuppositions of knowledge into fundamental ontological *existentialia* or temporal principles of human existence, including 'being-in-the-world', 'being-with-others', 'being-alongside', 'ready-to-hand', 'being-ahead-of-itself' and 'care', Heidegger (1967) founded hermeneutic phenomenology, which demonstrated that basic human structures are what Apel calls 'quasi-transcendental' (Apel 1973, I: 24) conditions of cognition and knowledge. The core of Heidegger's achievement in Apel's view, however, lay in his conception of human existence as 'understanding' or 'interpretation', which presupposes the priority of possibility over actuality and thus focuses the attention on the 'fore-structure' guiding the relation to the world: human existence, which is always already situated in the world, is oriented towards the future, which must continually be interpreted in a way relevant to the present, entailing that through embodiment, working on the environment and language, it is characterized by an all-pervasive pre-understanding allowing it to live forwards in a self-correcting mode. This spiral process of the projection of a transcendent meaningful future, which is then in a feedback movement allowed to work in upon the immanent arrangement of actual existence, is captured by the model of the so-called hermeneutic circle.

Since Heidegger did not give adequate attention to language, Apel (1962) subsequently undertook a study of the Western tradition of language philosophy. However, it was in particularly in view of Heidegger's complete neglect of the problem of justification or validity, which moreover had to be seen in a morally and politically relevant context, that Apel returned to Kant and the left-Hegelian strands. Rather than the hermeneutic circle, therefore, Apel focused on the broader problem of the relation between theory and practice, of which Marx and Peirce, as well as Kierkegaard, proposed different versions. His reassessment of the left-Hegelian tradition, focusing principally on the young Marx but also mentioning Peirce, dates from the late 1950s to the early 1960s and was originally published in 1962 titled 'Reflexion und materielle Praxis' (1973, II: 9–27). It deals with the problem of dialectics between Hegel and Marx. From this point on, Peirce moved increasingly to the centre of his attention, culminating in his two-volume edition of a selection of Peirce's writings accompanied by one of the best available analyses of and introductions to (Apel 1967, 1970) the American philosopher's pragmatism, which was also published as a separate book in both German in 1975 and English (1981, 1995).

In his re-appropriation of the young Marx, Apel (1973, II: 9–27) focused on the manifestation of the effective history of Hegelianism in the post-war intellectual situation with its opposite trends of idealist and materialist dialectics, beyond which, in his view, it was necessary to go. Marx's 'Theses on Feuerbach' served as his basic reference point. This is a monument to the genius of Marx's approach, but simultaneously also a source of ambiguity. Positively, Marx regarded materialism and hence the objective development towards the future as having to be mediated through an active moment of praxis, but negatively his historical materialism tended to objectify this moment without leaving so much as a trace of it. As regards the mid-twentieth-century intellectual situation, on the one hand, the idealist strain of dialectics was represented by Gadamer, who, in extension of Heidegger, innovatively renewed Hegel by conceiving of the substantive dialectical disclosure of the meaning of history as a continuous conversation. The problem with it, however, was that, while giving effect to the idealist moment of reflection, it excluded Hegel's critical dialectics, which Marx transformed into ideology critique, and, by extension, it also lost sight of the normative basis of such critique. As a consequence, Gadamerian hermeneutics fell into a new form of relativist historicism. On the other hand, orthodox Marxism represented the materialist strain of dialectics with its metaphysical emphasis on the objective dialectical process of nature, which, indeed, preserved the materialist moment, yet did so in a way that sacrificed not only the idealist moment of reflection but also the subjective moment or praxis. In this case, the problem is the endemic dogmatism of Marxism, and even of neo-Marxism, which results from an unacceptable totalization of only one aspect of dialectics. In totalizing the opposite subjective aspect of dialectics, the tradition of existentialism going back to Kierkegaard is, in Apel's estimation, equally plagued by a resulting problem, namely irrationalism.

The dual critique of idealism and materialism allowed Apel to clarify the more complex relations pertaining to what he called 'the dialectics of the situation' (1973, II: 23). What must be appreciated is that the basic elements of ideal reflection and material praxis are mediated through a substantive interpretation of the world as a historical situation which, on the one hand, obtains universalistic import through reflection and, on the other, is rooted in embodied existence through praxis. For Apel, his third, broader interpretation of dialectics corresponds to language as the medium of the interpretation of the world, which makes possible not only reflection with a universalistic thrust but also contact between meaning intentions and forms of articulation, on the one hand, and embodied, situated existence, on the other. Referring to *The German Ideology* and *The Phenomenology of Mind*, he produced evidence that this corresponds precisely to the conception of language which Marx shared with Hegel. In this way, Apel showed that the re-appropriation of left-Hegelianism in a contemporarily relevant manner required the bringing back in of an underplayed and even excluded third dialectical dimension represented by the medium of language.

According to Apel's own account, his initial familiarity with pragmatism was confined to James and Dewey and it is from there that in the 1960s he embarked on an intensive study of Peirce, the still unknown so-called precursor. It could be pointed out that his initial interest was stimulated by the fact that there is a certain similarity between Heidegger's hermeneutic phenomenology and Wittgenstein's linguistic-pragmatic departure, of which Apel was acutely aware, which resonated with pragmatism. However, the more specific force which drove his search leading to Peirce's work derived from both the strengths and weaknesses of Heideggerian–Gadamerian hermeneutics and Marxism. On the one hand, the hermeneutic highlighting of the historical process of interpretation as conversation and the young Marx's appreciation of language as the immediate reality of thought needed to be clarified and worked out in detail and, on the other, hermeneutics' historicism and Marxism's dogmatism had to be avoided by giving full sway to the problem of validity and justification. Proposals for approaches to both matters were to be found in Peirce. Indeed, Apel's (1973, 1980) own philosophical project, namely the transformation of philosophy which eventuated in his characteristic 'transcendental pragmatics' (1998), was fundamentally shaped by his study of Peirce, and various of its component parts were directly inspired by him. Apel's principal line of argument was that Peirce succeeded in transforming Kant in a significant and far-reaching way. More specifically, he showed that in doing so Peirce not only made available a *medium quo*, sign-mediated or semiotic theory of knowledge that is more adequate than widely accepted competing theories, but through clarification of the status of regulative ideas basic to Peirce's version of pragmatism also provided a starting point for making progress on the normative question of validity and justification.

In opposition to the psychological conditions emphasized by British empiricism, Kant clarified in the *Critique of Pure Reason* the deep-seated, abstract, metadimensional conditions which make scientific knowledge possible: so-called 'transcendental' conditions represented by such presupposed faculties as intuition, imagination, understanding and reason, which allow the synthetic unity of consciousness as the point where the cognitive process culminates in knowledge. On the basis of the displacement of consciousness by language due to the linguistic turn in philosophy since the late nineteenth century, however, twentieth-century analytical theorists of scientific knowledge claim that not only Kant's dependence on consciousness has become irrelevant, but by the same token also his conception of transcendental conditions. What takes the place of his transcendental dimension, the subject of knowledge, is the language of science conceived in terms of its structural or syntactic dimension expressed in logical consistency and its meaningful or semantic dimension involving reference to things or objects. Beyond this there is no need for a subject of scientific knowledge, as the early Wittgenstein asserted. Contrary to this position, however, Apel (1973, 1980) argued that a development inaugurated by Heidegger, the later Wittgenstein, Charles Morris, John Searle and others, the so-called 'pragmatic turn', has brought the pragmatic dimension of language – relating to action and practice in ordinary everyday life – into view. This calls into question the assumptions of the analytic logic of science. Not only can hypotheses or theories not be directly confronted with brute facts without the mediation of basic statements on which scientists as pragmatic interpreters agree, but the formalized syntactic–semantic language of science can be introduced and rendered acceptable or legitimate as a conventional framework only through the medium of a pragmatic interpretation in ordinary language.

In Apel's view, this pragmatic dimension involves the level of the interpretation of signs, which is a metadimensional condition of science and, as such, can be regarded as the semiotic equivalent of Kant's transcendental synthesis – now no longer a matter of consciousness, but rather of language or, better, interpretation. Apel was adamant that this semiotic dimension, this transcendental-pragmatic dimension in the form of a community of communication and interpretation which stretches through time, represents the subject of science and of knowledge excluded and ignored by the mainstream theory of science. He was able to argue this on the basis of the achievement of Peirce, whom he regarded as having taken the first innovative and decisive steps towards such a position. Peirce's principal achievement, in Apel's terminology, lies in his semiotic transformation of Kant's transcendental logic and hence of classical epistemology.

Peirce's overall transcendental or metadimensional semiotic position, according to Apel, implies a *medium quo* or sign-mediated theory, which accounts for his persistent criticism of the *medium quod* or unmediated theory of cognition and knowledge dominating modern philosophy in the form of Cartesian dualism and nominalist empiricism. Foreshortening knowledge by identifying it with immediate observation, the *medium quod* theory focuses on the effect of things on consciousness. The *medium quo* theory, by contrast, is a theory of the mediation of immediate experience of the real external world through a conclusion in the face of an uncertain future about the consequences for the community at large and its world – something that is possible only in and through the medium of signs and sign-interpretation. Central to Peirce's transformation of Kant, according to Apel's interpretation, was the introduction of his theory of the sign-relation or sign-function, which articulates closely with his doctrine of categories and modes of inference – all based on a basic triadic scheme which should in principle be regarded in terms of a semiotic process. It is of the utmost importance not only for the interface between pragmatism and Critical Theory, but also for the form the methodology of contemporary Critical Theory takes.

The threefold sign-relation rests on the circumstance that a sign refers to something real for a sign-interpreter. The semiotic process in which these different dimensions are interrelated takes place through three kinds of signs, namely icons, indices and symbols, which correspondingly bring the different ontological aspects involved into play in the form of three universal categories. Icons capture 'firstness' or the singular quality of reality experienced, indices 'secondness' or the dyadically confronted and identified object, and symbols 'thirdness' or the triadic representative interpretation which interrelates and renders consistent these various moments. This process happens for an investigator-interpreter who, belonging to an investigation and interpretation community, engages with reality through three inferential modes, namely deduction, induction and, above all, abduction. Deduction, corresponding to thirdness, is a logically correct or necessary inference establishing a generality which could play a guiding role, yet under particular conditions such a logical relation could turn out to be false. Induction, aligned with secondness, has the role of allowing particulars to assert their authority in relation to purported generalities under specific spatial and temporal conditions, either confirming or falsifying such deductions. Abduction, paralleled with firstness, is of the utmost significance for Peirce since it opens up possible experience and is thus the only kind of inference by which new knowledge is produced. It comes about through a sudden insight, a flash or, more often, a surprising change of circumstances which makes us see something in a new light, overcoming a previous blind spot, or even discloses the world in an entirely new way. It is the key since it supplies the substance required by both deduction and induction. Abduction involves the synthetic cognition of new qualities of something, bringing together a sense impression and feeling about something and allowing it to be mediated through the remaining kinds of inference. Sign-users employ these different kinds of inference in an intermediated manner to come to a consistent judgement in the face of an uncertain future about the practical consequences of accepting the outcome of this process – that is, it is a matter neither simply of instrumentalism nor merely of happiness, but rather of the long-term meaningfulness for the community at large regarding both its human and the natural world. For this reason, Apel also refers to Peirce's semiotic approach as a 'meaning critical approach' (Apel 1981, 1995): it is not simply a critique of knowledge, like Kant's, but much more broadly a critique of the meaning of such knowledge.

The three dimensions of the sign-function – the sign, the signified reality and the sign-user – are irreducible to each other and, therefore, each presupposes the others. Methodologically, this means that the exclusion of either one or two of these semiotic moments would result in a 'reductive fallacy' (Apel 1974: 287) of some kind which fractures the mediated nature of the cognitive process and the resulting knowledge. Similarly, negative consequences also follow from an inadequate conception of each. First, the sign possesses its own material aspect in the sense that it is not merely a figment of the imagination but rather, as part of the process of the constitution of the universe in which the sign-users participate, has a foothold in reality. Second, the investigating and interpreting sign-user is not the individual, but rather the community to which he or she belongs, which itself is dependent on a continuous process of communicative interpretation of reality stretching into the future. Third, the signified reality is real and not merely something like sense-data, an intentional object, a phenomenon or a fiction. That this reality is independent of the sign-users is confirmed by the fact that contact with it is achieved only to the extent that conventional iconic signs link up with natural indications – 'sin-signs' – and expressive signs – 'quali-signs' – which refer to causal relations, discovered resemblances and so forth. As Apel (1995: 165–6) stresses, it is at such a point of contact that abductive inference plays its paradigmatic role. It brings together a sensation, a feeling, an experience and a signification of a comprehensible and communicable causal nexus, a *Gestalt* resemblance or analogy, and thus secures the identity of an external thing and the knowledge object. To be actually taken up into knowledge production, this experiential process and its abductive result must be mediated with other signs and inferences in a process of discussion, interpretation and reasoning whereby the status of reality is established and, indeed, goes on to be established. It is in this sense that reality, for Peirce, is something both factually known and not yet known but in principle knowable. It is something with which we have contact and come to know in a particular situation in a way that keeps open the possibility that we may be proven wrong and be able to improve our knowledge, so that reality is that which we could come to know in the long run. On the one hand, we have Peirce's theory of pragmatic realism or what Apel called 'meaning critical realism' and, on the other, his theory of reality as the object of the ultimate opinion of the interpretation community, to which Apel related 'the consensus theory of truth'.

Against this transcendental semiotic background, Peirce focused on working out the logic of research or the process of knowledge production borne by the scientific community. Given the nature of the process as conceived by Peirce, as Apel made clear, this logic had not only a semiotic dimension, but very importantly also a normative one. Semiotically, the development of knowledge taking place through the mediation of three-dimensional signs is driven by creative abductive inference or hypothesis formulation, which, in the first instance, is embedded in the process of communication and interpretation of the scientific community and, in the second instance, forms part of the evolution of the universe. In accordance with the normative logic of sign-interpretation, therefore, this process is directed and guided by unifying goals or regulative ideas and normative postulates not only bearing on the adequacy of the hypothesis to reality, but also arriving at consensus and hence truth in the scientific community (Peirce's 'ultimate opinion'), and finally fulfilling the demands of sign-interpretation – arriving at an interpretation representing a proper stance towards the world (Peirce's 'ultimate logical interpretant') and engaging in responsible practices in relation to it (Peirce's 'habit').

Apel ascribed particular significance to what he regarded as Peirce's core innovative contribution on the normative level, namely his idea of the infinite community of investigators, even though it remained limited to the scientific community. Inspired by hermeneutic philosophy and capitalizing on the pragmatist broadening of Peirce's idea by Royce's community of interpreters and Mead's community of universal discourse, he put forward his own idea of the ideal communication community as the regulative ideal not only of the social sciences, particularly Critical Theory, but also more generally of ethics. From the viewpoint of the articulation of the relation between Critical Theory and pragmatism, this proved to be nothing less than a seminal departure. Already at the end of his project to introduce Peirce to the German intellectual world in 1970, Apel (1970: 210–11, 1995: 196) offered a sharp and challenging diagnosis of this relationship: Critical Theory will have to learn from pragmatism to drop its dogmatism in favour of adopting a sense of history as open and mediated by communication, while pragmatism will have to learn from Marxism that the constitution and organization of society requires more than just problem solving. A year or two later, he concretized this proposal regarding the historical mediation of theory and practice by way of the idea of 'the dialectic of the real and ideal communication community' (1973, II: 429, 1980: 139–40, 280–2). On the one hand, human beings find themselves in a real world mediated by communication, a real communication community in which they are socialized as members embedded in social relations and caught up in conflicts of interest; on the other, they not only presuppose an ideal communication community which endows the real one meaning, but even counterfactually anticipate the possibility of its realizatio the real communication community.

Apel regarded this principle of the dialectical mediation of idealism and materialism, which is his mature restatement of the core left-Hegelian insight, as the basic framework not only of Critical Theory, but also as the minimal inter-subjectively binding normative ethic that sets the standard for Critical Theory's normative evaluations and value judgements. First, Critical Theory's object of study, the real historical society, must accordingly be regarded as manifested on two dialectically interrelated dimensions: the concrete dimension where a mate-rialist theory of society and realism are in place, and the ideal dimension of the presupposed and counterfactually anticipated ideal communication community that calls for critical normative reconstruction and potentially could be realized through historical practice. Second, Apel's minimal normative ethics, which was initially referred to as the 'ethics of communication' (1973, II: 426, 1980: 278) and later renamed 'discourse ethics', was seen as not only providing a standard for Critical Theory, but also representing more generally the framework for demo-cratic will-formation through agreement. Although it is indeed a deontological ethics in the sense of being based on idealized principles, Apel acknowledged the spectre of a substantive vacuum in Kant's formalistic categorical imperative and thus supplemented it by an ethics of moral responsibility which takes into account the difficulties and risks entailed by every morally self-regarding attempt to institutionalize ideal presuppositions in a concrete historical situation. From this normative ethical framework it was then possible to derive two fundamental regu-lative principles for the long-term strategic orientation of moral action in general and hence for a non-dogmatic Critical Theory in particular. Whereas the first demands that all actions and omissions should be oriented towards 'ensuring the survival of the human species qua *real* communication community', the second specifies the goal of the first by requiring 'realizing the *ideal* communication com-munity in the real one' (1980: 282).

The framework that Apel thus established for Critical Theory rests not only on an unprecedented understanding of both Critical Theory and pragmatism, but also on an innovative, penetrating, critical and self-critical, indeed, seminal articulation of the relationship between these two highly intellectual yet practi-cally oriented traditions.[2]

Habermas: between facts and norms

Although Apel's Peirce studies and the conclusions he drew from them had a tre-mendous impact on Jürgen Habermas (1929–), Apel's understanding of Marxism and Critical Theory was in turn conditioned by Habermas's re-appropriation of left-Hegelianism in the early 1960s (1974: 195–252).[3] Whereas the young Marx's response had been solicited by the falsity and political consequences of idealist phi-losophy, Habermas understood the mid-twentieth-century need for a restatement of the basic left-Hegelian principles in continuity with Horkheimer's founding of

Critical Theory as being necessitated by the sciences' effective reproduction of idealism through the positivistic and unreflective division of labour and ignorance of their own consequences for the process of reproduction and transformation of the society of which they formed a part. Required instead was the revitaliza- tion of Critical Theory in the form of a theory that, on the one hand, proceeds from a pre-understanding or 'anticipatory interpretation of society as a whole' (1974: 210) 'which has come to be historically' (1974: 205) and, on the other, cultivates 'practical . . . [or] . . . political intentions' (1974: 201, 205). Only on the adoption of such a unifying interest could the key left-Hegelian principle, that is, Marx's materialist transformation of Hegel's demand for a substantive mediation of Kant's distinction between the transcendental and the empirical, be preserved under the new conditions in a way that keeps the transcendent moment within the bounds of the immanent rather than elevating it idealistically.

In an essay on the relation of Critical Theory to American thought, Joas (1993: 90) wrote that Habermas never took a clear stance on pragmatism. There is some truth in this, considering that for some three decades Habermas at best made but selective use of pragmatist ideas before clarifying his particular position in the late 1990s and early 2000s. First, Peirce was introduced in 1968, and then in the 1970s certain pragmatist ideas served as a means of developing his universal pragmatics and consensus theory of truth and of appropriating Piaget's genetic structuralism, following which Habermas shifted his attention to Mead in the 1980s and again to Peirce in the late 1980s and early 1990s. Criticism of Rorty's neo-pragmatism pre- ceded Habermas's (2003) attempt finally to state his position – so-called 'Kantian pragmatism' – more systematically in 1999. In the context of an anthology on his relation to pragmatism (Aboulafia et al. 2002), he recently offered some clarify- ing autobiographical remarks. Most basically, his receptivity was sharpened by having discovered that pragmatism was originally the outcome of 'an earlier and overwhelmingly productive American–German encounter' (Habermas 2002: 227). Of the pragmatists, Peirce had the most formative impact on him in epis- temology, especially regarding the conception of 'the internal relations between forms of knowledge and types of action', but also regarding the reconciliation of a transcendental with an evolutionary perspective and thus the adoption of a ' "soft", non-scientistic naturalism' (Habermas 2002: 227). Mead, whom he taught in Frankfurt in the 1960s, provided him with a conceptual framework which, sup- ported by hermeneutics and the Humboldt tradition of language and dialogue, served as a guide in the development of the theory of communicative action. The convergence between his own theory of the public sphere and that of Dewey he discovered only in the late 1980s. In addition, the anti-elitist, democratic and egalitarian attitude of all the pragmatists also benefited him greatly. Overall, in his evaluation: 'Pragmatism constitutes, besides Marx and Kierkegaard, the third Young Hegelian tradition, and the only one that convincingly develops the liberal spirit of radical democracy' (Habermas 2002: 228).

Whereas *Knowledge and Human Interests* (1972) started from a critical re-appropri- ation of the young Marx's metacritique of Hegel's critique of Kant, Habermas was able to achieve his aim of broadening the concept of knowledge beyond its scientistic and methodological reduction by positivism and the analytic philosophy

of science only by adding pragmatist ideas to those Kantian ones prese
transformed guise in Marx's left-Hegelianism. Although Peirce – who after
been a philosophizing natural scientist – was here at some length discusse
in relation to the development of the philosophy of the natural sciences, his basic
pragmatist insight pervaded Habermas's book by helping to structure his principal
argument throughout. Kant uncovered the framework of transcendental conditions making scientific knowledge possible, Hegel demonstrated that scientific
knowledge is embedded in the genetic development of consciousness through the
mechanism of reflection, and Marx materialistically translated this developmental
process into the history of society and the reflexive mechanism of progress into
social labour. Although Habermas took Marx to task for having reduced reflection
purely to labour, he regarded the theory of knowledge implicitly contained in
the latter's materialized Kantian conception of synthesis through labour as corresponding to the transcendental-pragmatist theory of natural science which Peirce
inaugurated and Dewey later elaborated. It is this theory, in terms of which knowledge production depends on and is structured by a framework consisting of an
experientially related goal and its corresponding practices serving some aspect of
the social life process, that Habermas then employed to distinguish the categories
of natural, cultural and critical social science from one another. It is noteworthy
that it is Peirce's idea of the unlimited community of investigators in the enriched
form Apel gave it that enabled Habermas to specify the nature of cultural science
and, by extension, also of critical social science.

Peirce's name appeared a few times in Habermas's Gauss lectures of 1972,
which laid the groundwork for his consensus or discourse theory of truth of 1973
and universal or formal pragmatics of 1976, both of which were fundamentally
shaped by Apel's Peirce studies. The very idea of a consensus theory of truth was
inspired by Peirce's theory of reality, according to which the real is that which the
ultimate opinion of the community of investigators in the long run would coincide
with. If one regards it from the angle of discourse, that is, as a discourse theory
of theoretical truth and of practical correctness, then the formal properties of
discourse as the medium in which alone any truth or correctness claim could be
vindicated provide the necessary conditions for arriving at a rational agreement
regarding the claim – conditions Habermas called 'the ideal speech situation'
(1984: 174–82). This idea of a consensus established under ideal conditions, which
Habermas regards as a necessary and unavoidable presupposition that is counterfactually anticipated in any discourse and, as an anticipated normative principle,
nevertheless has a structuring effect on the discourse, likewise owes much to Peirce's
pragmatic maxim, normative logic and community of interpretation. The closely
related analysis of 'the validity basis of speech' or, more particularly, the four
'validity claims' – *uttering* something understandably; giving the hearer *something*
to understand; making *himself* thereby understandable; and coming to an understanding *with another person* – at the centre of Habermas's (1979: 1–68) universal
or formal pragmatics clearly corresponds to the structure of the semiotic process
as conceived by Peirce. More generally, the basic theoretical distinction between
action and discourse which pervades Habermas's thinking since his embrace of
the linguistic turn in the years after the publication and widespread criticism of

Knowledge and Human Interests, including his discourse theory of truth and formal pragmatics, depends on a basic pragmatist idea – as he himself confirmed (1984: 108). It is the notion of problematic situations which fracture previously taken-for-granted assumptions and thus have disillusioning effects which compel those involved to undergo learning processes so as to be able to take corrective action.

Habermas (1984/87, II) saw Mead as innovatively bringing together under the title of 'social behaviourist' two lines of development, the separation of which marked the decomposition of the complex problematic that Peirce had still held together in his opposition to the philosophy of consciousness, namely language analysis and behavioural psychology. Mead simultaneously took into account the process of evolution in the wake of Darwin, on the one hand, and the socio-cultural world which emerged from it when language and the symbolic forms it generates took shape, on the other – although in certain respects confining his investigations to the ontogenetic level rather than broadening out to include the phylogenetic one. In his interpretation, Habermas focused on Mead's account of the medium of propositionally differentiated language which emerged from gestures and signal language in the course of evolution and thanks to its complex and structure-forming nature makes available a principle of organization allowing the constitution of a sophisticated socio-cultural world characterized by linguistically mediated intersubjectivity as well as a corresponding psychological type with an autonomous and flexible ego-identity. He capitalized on this achievement of Mead's as providing him with a set of concepts to guide his development of the theory of communicative action, but over and above that he regarded Mead as significantly having furnished social science as such with an indispensable communication theoretical foundation. Habermas's (1992: 149–204) finely grained analysis of language, social interaction, the self, taking the attitude of the other and the generalized other led him to his core interest in Mead. This is the normative problematic associated with the communication-theoretical approach that Mead, moreover, developed explicitly in a critical appropriation of Kant's ethics.

With Kant, Mead accepted a universalistic morality which assumes that the authority of norms rests on the general interest. For him, the 'ought' quality of norms is not merely a matter of philosophy or idealism, but has consequences for social integration. Mead's understanding could be summarized by saying that, when language becomes the medium of socialization, the generation of intersubjectivity and social integration, then the binding force of norms becomes effective as validity claims carried in communication. Any norm then ultimately has validity only on the condition that it could be accepted with good reasons by everyone affected. Correspondingly, individuals develop in such a way that they become individuated as unique but autonomous and accountable persons who are capable of opposing their contemporaries' moral judgements – Mead's 'I' – at the very same time as they are socialized into social human beings – Mead's 'me'. On this basis, he transformed Kant's categorical imperative communicatively into what he himself called a 'rational procedure' whereby, say in the case of the need to resolve a conflict, those involved engage in 'discourse' guided by the formal ideal of 'universal discourse' to come to an agreement about how to go forward and thus to bring about and participate in 'a higher and better society' (Habermas 1984/87, II: 94, 95, 96, 98, quoting Mead). The conceptual structure or theoretical model characterizing Mead's Kantian-pragmatist mode of argumentation played a crucial structuring role in *The Theory of Communicative Action* despite the fact that in this role it remained below the level of thematization. For instance, it animated Habermas's concern with the problem of how culture, say in the form of validity claims, becomes incorporated into spatio-temporally identifiable contexts and situations of action and is effective as a social fact in structuring orientations and actions – a problem that, by extension, includes also the question of blockages to such incorporation and structural violence involving the distortion of the formal conditions of communication as well as of barriers internal to culture itself against distorting intrusions of different kinds. Habermas's return once again to Peirce in the late 1980s provided the prompt to begin to articulate this basic figure of thought in its own right.

A conference paper of 1989 on 'Peirce and communication' (1992: 88–112), originally published in 1991, represents Habermas's first systematic attempt to come to grips with the American philosopher. A few years later, he drew on this achievement for the purposes of his major work, *Between Facts and Norms* (1996). In general, his assessment was that, although Peirce had made a seminal semiotic contribution, he tended towards a cosmological interpretation of general impersonal sign-mediated processes in nature to the detriment of his lesser interest in intersubjective processes involving human speakers, listeners, audiences and interpreters. As regards this second level, on which Habermas obviously came to focus, he followed Apel's lead by regarding Peirce as having inaugurated the linguistic-pragmatic turn before Frege and Wittgenstein. This engagement with Peirce's semiotics inspired Habermas to return to questions of theoretical philosophy – that is, epistemology and ontology – in the 1990s and, very importantly, to give more detailed attention to the concept of truth, which led to the revision of his strictly epistemic justificatory or 'consensus theory of truth' by the inclusion of a non-epistemic concept incorporating a theory of reference to objects forming part of an independent external world (Habermas 2003). However, what is of particular interest is that in this conference paper he emphatically connected to Peirce a new formulation of the core Kantian insight in its transformed left-Hegelian guise, at which he had arrived in the late 1980s: the new concept of 'transcendence from within' or 'immanent transcendence'. This concept not only came to form the very core of the title of *Between Facts and Norms*, referring to the tension-laden problem of the immanent realization of transcendent normative structures which from the start in any case have a foothold in ordinary everyday practices, but in the subsequent fifteen years attained a central position in Critical Theory.

Peirce's semiotic transformation of epistemology required, as Habermas saw it, the substitution of six characteristic assumptions of the philosophy of consciousness with more adequate principles: introspection relying on private evidence had to be replaced by generally accessible evidence that is open to public assessment; intuitionism emphasizing either immediately given objects or absolutely certain ideas had to make way for the acknowledgement that mediation through signs renders an absolute starting point impossible; foundationalism that privileges self-consciousness needed to be rejected in face of the fact that mental states and psychic events depend on interchange with the external world; phenomenalism, which assumes that there is a hidden reality behind appearances, had to be corrected by a conception of reality as imposing restriction on knowledge yet is in principle knowable in the long run; the assumption of a worldless subject separate from the world as a whole had to be done away with in favour of the understanding of the subject who, as part of the world, is nevertheless under certain circumstances able to develop a questioning perspective on some aspect of the world; and, finally, the privileging of the knowing subject had to be relativized by the recognition that knowledge is interwoven with practices and, further, that both of these involve the symbolic medium of language – which means that the place of the subject is taken by the intersubjective process of communication and practice. By accomplishing all of this, Peirce succeeded in rethinking representation in three-place semiotic instead of two-place mentalistic terms, thus stressing a third dimension of mediating symbolic forms: an object does not appear as a mental picture in the mind, but becomes interpreted, understood and agreed upon in a process taking place in a communication and interpretation community. For instance, a predicative sentence in language not only refers to an object in the world, but through the predicate ascribes a property to the object, which is a general or universal concept making sense only in the larger community of interpretation. Peirce's third symbolic dimension is thus made up of not static symbolic structures but ones possessing illocutionary force in the sense of admitting of being communicated, convincing, agreed upon, accepted and more generally regarded as true. Objectivity, or the objective property of the object, is maintained in such a process by the concrete anchorage of a sequence of signs in the course of perceptual judgement through an icon (a *Gestalt*) and conventional index (denotation) linking with a quali-sign (preexisting quality or similarity) and a natural sin-sign (causal mechanism). Such anchorage, which it is the task of a 'language-independent . . . theory of reference' (Habermas 2003: 34–5) to clarify, typically becomes habitual so that we conventionally see something as something, but in problem situations or under new conditions it is abduction, in the sense of a lightening insight, a world-disclosing new perspective or a creative hypothesis, that makes possible the forging of such linkages. Once forged, such linkages are made sense of and possibly agreed on at the symbolic level through the discursive or reflexive semiotic process of communication and interpretation. Considering the tripartite nature of the sign and more generally of the semiotic process, Habermas (1992: 102–3; 2003: 36–42) argued in accord with Peirce that a simple agreement here and now among those immediately involved is not sufficient to secure the objectivity of the object and thus to rationally assert something in a generally acceptable way approximating the truth regarding its reality. Against the background of a problematized certainty or unconditional truth operative in everyday life, a truth claim asserted in the form of a fact needs to pass through a justificatory discursive process, on the one hand to test if the asserted fact is indeed

supported by conventional and natural signs rooted in the object in questio
on the other to have recourse to the transcendent counterfactual instanc
consensus arrived at under ideal conditions, what Peirce called the 'final o
. . . [in the] . . . *Community* without definite limits . . . [regarding] . . . the mal
object' (5.311). Over and above the mere 'existence' or actuality (*Wirklichkeit*) of
the object, therefore, a projection regarding its 'reality' (*Realität*) requires a moment
of 'transcendence from within' (Habermas 1992: 103). The paradoxical state in
which we are convinced by good reasons, yet assent under the proviso of fallibility,
marks the gap between justification or rational assertibility and truth – a gap that
in principle can never be completely bridged, but can nevertheless be reduced by
collective 'learning processes' which eliminate previous errors without protecting
against future ones (Habermas 2003: 41).

As regards immanent transcendence, the concept was anticipated by a number
of essays included in *Postmetaphysical Thinking* (1992) which contain different formulations of the implied problematic that, in Habermas's view, emerged in the
wake of nineteenth-century attempts to 'detranscendentalize reason' (1992: 43).
The paradigmatic example is of course the left-Hegelian focus on the possible
practical realization of ideas of reason obfuscated by philosophy. Needless to say,
references to left-Hegelianism abound in his writings, and as a rule it is mentioned
in conjunction with the immanent-transcendence problematic. From references
it is clear that Habermas was sensitized to a sharpened perspective on the problem at least partly by authors who were associated in some sense or another with
pragmatism. Whereas Rorty prompted him to detranscendentalize his own position, which he would of course never fully do since he represents not pragmatism
pure and simple but a transcendental or Kantian pragmatism, Putnam apparently
provided him with a formulation that hit the point home: 'Reason is . . . both
immanent (not to be found outside of concrete language games) and transcendent
(a regulative idea that we use to criticize the conduct of all activities and institutions)' (Putnam 1982: 228, cited by Habermas 1992: 139). Accordingly, Habermas
proposed to treat reason as 'situated reason' (1992: 139); 'pragmatic yet unavoidable idealizing presuppositions' such as truth, justice, sincerity, accountability and
so forth permeate everyday practices representing demands toward 'unity and
organization' (1992: 143) and thus structure such practices. By functioning in this
manner, he significantly stressed, such ideas transfer a 'tension' (1992: 142) into
the social world, often in the guise of situations of disagreement, legitimation
struggle and even conflict, which the actors themselves have to deal with and try
to resolve. These insights formed the basis for the original explicit introduction of
the concept in 1988 (1991a: 127, 142, 155–6) and 1989 (1991a: 25; 1992: 103),
which was then followed by an increasing fascination with it. A whole series of
subsequent writings, from *Between Facts and Norms* (1996) to *The Inclusion of the Other*
(1998a), gave prominence in one way or another to the concept and thus helped
spawn a wider interest in it. In Chapter 4, a detailed discussion of immanent
transcendence as the key concept of contemporary Critical Theory is offered.

In the late 1990s, under the rubric of 'Kantian pragmatism', which is a
variation on Apel's original 'transcendental pragmatics', Habermas returned

in *Truth and Justification* (2003) to theoretical philosophy in order to pick up the epistemological and ontological threads he had left in abeyance since *Knowledge and Human Interests*. Although it elaborated on the pragmatic, epistemic, realist epistemology and the naturalistic ontology he had adopted already in the 1960s, the renewed focus on these assumptions in terms of a pragmatist conception of cognition and knowledge tempered by the linguistic-pragmatic turn brought with it some significant repositioning. As indicated earlier, this involved especially a shift from the purely epistemic concept of truth implied by his consensus theory to a more complex position that includes a non-epistemic concept of truth related to the representational function of language. Instead of the tendency to present truth as something achieved by discursive justification alone, the reference to an object or state of affairs actually existing and hence forming part of an objective world independent of the mind and language was now given due emphasis. Habermas achieved the recuperation of this representational dimension within the framework of the pragmatist conception of cognition and knowledge, which owes something not only to Peirce and Dewey but also to Marx. By contrast with the traditional model of the two-place relation between picture and copy and between static proposition and object, it presupposes a dynamic understanding of the accumulation of knowledge through problem solving and justification on the basis of learning. As framework for its conceptualization served Peirce's tripartite sign-relation and, by extension, its rendering in the language mould by means of speech act theory, which is likewise to be understood in terms of the threefold relation between expression of an intent, representation of an object and communication of import to others. In the face of a problem situation, whether the experience of success-oriented failure or socially significant disagreement, the cognitive process mindfully and creatively works towards an appropriate solution that makes possible learning, correcting errors, meeting objections, achieving agreement and going forward. Knowledge is thus the outcome of the cognitive contributions of a passive moment of experiencing breakdown or failure and an active constructive moment of projecting, interpreting and justifying, which through their mediation leads to learning, an agreement on a resolution, a positive experience and a new mode of conduct. The cognitive and active overcoming of problems and the resulting spurts of conduct-changing learning are thus together the defining feature of the pragmatist conception of cognition and knowledge. In Habermas's view, it has important consequences, both epistemologically and ontologically – pragmatic epistemic realism and weak or soft naturalism respectively – which are characteristic of his own Kantian pragmatism.

From the perspective of 'pragmatic epistemic realism' (Habermas 2003: 7), reality is regarded not as something to be mirrored, but rather as something manifested only through the constraints and resistances it subjects our position taking, activities and learning processes to. We meet reality not through contemplation, but performatively through engaging with it and running up against its walls – whether an objective problem or a morally significant social conflict. Such natively manifested reality presupposes a reference to an object or state of affairs about which a propositional assertion is made, the validity of which can itself be rendered acceptable only through discursive justification with an orientation to the regulative idea of truth. Complementing this pragmatic epistemic realism, Habermas ontologically opted for 'weak naturalism' (2003: 22). It proceeds from the assumption that there is continuity between nature and culture or an analogy between the natural historical processes giving rise to *Homo sapiens* and human social cultural forms of life. In turn, this relation is conceived as involving a scale of learning processes, from the solution to evolutionary problems in the course of natural historical development that gives rise to naturally formed structures possessing cognitive import, to socio-cultural forms of life emerging on that basis, in the context of which humans are enabled to learn, develop knowledge and to construct an ever more inclusive social world. Notwithstanding the assumption of continuity, Habermas insisted on ascribing ontological priority to nature and epistemological priority to the socio-cultural world. We are able to obtain knowledge only from our human point of view from within our socio-cultural world, yet nature in so far as it possesses genetic primacy can at any time give rise to an intrusive event or structure that changes the conditions of the socio-cultural world, which the latter is then compelled to process. Epistemologically, therefore, it is important to distinguish between the different corresponding methodological approaches, one based on the participant's perspective and the other on the observer's, yet without reifying them.

Habermas's Kantian pragmatism represents a 'detranscendentalization' (2003: 17) or pragmatic deflation of Kant's transcendental philosophy, yet it still retains a weak or quasi version of the transcendental frame. It rejects Kant's strict separation of the empirical (the world) and the transcendental (beyond the world) in favour of a relation of tension that is relocated in the world such that the actors involved themselves have to cope with it and try to resolve it in a way favourable to them and their world. The crucial distinction for Habermas, therefore, is between the world in the sense of presuppositions such as the pre-understanding of the rules to follow in conduct or projected idealization to realize, on the one hand, and inner-worldly practices and processes that are given direction and guided by such transcendental structures as rules and idealizations, on the other. In the wake of Hegel and Marx, Kant's ideas of reason have been brought down to earth precisely as 'desublimated pragmatic forms' (2003: 83) such as these. Conceptual realism pragmatically understood is of great importance here since it allows the acknowledgement of pragmatic forms as 'existing universalities' (2003: 31) belonging to the in principle normatively structured human social world. However, Habermas stressed in particular the transcendental distinction between the world and the inner-worldly, which he critically played out against Heidegger's transcendental idealism and Quine's strong reductionist naturalism. This distinction ultimately lies at the bottom of his Kantian pragmatism and, therefore, also informs the concept of immanent transcendence, which has moved to the centre of contemporary Critical Theory. Had it not been for pragmatism, it would have remained virtually impossible to articulate this position.

The younger generation of critical theorists

In one way or another, a number of the third generation of German critical theorists have followed Apel and Habermas's lead in seeking to enrich Critical Theory by calling on pragmatism to help clarify some of its own assumptions and transforming it through the incorporation of new attitudes and ideas. Central to their respective contributions, although not always explicitly mentioned, is the concept of immanent transcendence. Among these younger representatives of Critical Theory Wellmer, Eder and Honneth are the most important from the current point of view.

Wellmer: anti-idealistic universalism

Albrecht Wellmer (1933–)[4] originally came to prominence on the basis of his *Critical Theory of Society* (1971), in which he offered a succinct presentation of Habermas's new beginning in Critical Theory, but from the perspective of the contemporary relationship between Critical Theory and pragmatism his role as internal critic looms larger. In *Ethik und Dialog* (1986), he used the opportunity offered by a contrast and comparison of Kant's ethics and Apel and Habermas's discourse ethics to develop a detailed and penetrating criticism of Apel and Habermas's adoption of Kantian style regulative ideas. Subsequently, this criticism of idealization theory became a standard feature of Wellmer's (1998) position as against Apel and Habermas. As late as 1998, Habermas (2003) still found it necessary to defend his position against Wellmer's attack, and both Apel's seventy-fifth and eightieth birthday conferences were the scene of yet further rounds of debate between Apel and Wellmer (Böhler et al. 2003).

   Although drawing inspiration from the later Wittgenstein's pragmatic philosophy, Wellmer (1986: 202) initially took as model for his criticism Merleau-Ponty's analysis of the problematic structure of the Marxist idea of a classless society – problematic, because the idea paradoxically refers to the end of history or an unattainable fixed point beyond history, while it is simultaneously supposed to be the historically locatable successor to the capitalist system. Since the idea cannot function as a realizable ideal which we could gradually approximate ever more closely, the only possibility remaining is the 'elimination' or 'determinate negation' (1986: 126) of negative instances, of inequality, discrimination, a democratic deficit and so forth. Wellmer by no means denied that the presupposition of an ideal communication community accepted by both Apel and Habermas is cogent. On the contrary, he affirmed that it is a necessary and unavoidable pragmatic presupposition which is constitutive for real discursive situations. What he objected to was what he regarded as the misleading metaphysical or utopian interpretation of this presupposition as the anticipation of an ideal state that could be realized in the real communication community – an interpretation suggested by various misleading yet subsequently modified formulations to be found in both Apel and Habermas's writings. The presence of the ideal communication community in the
   ꭓne is indeed an indication of an incontrovertible orientation towards validity,

yet it neither provides a final foundation for morality nor is a glimpse c
reconciliation. By contrast with a position which depends on an ideal keyst
perspective *sub specie aeternitatis*, therefore, Wellmer insisted that the real issu
the problem of the mediation of the general and the particular. This comp
be approached by surrendering an orientation towards 'the completion of s
favour of 'eliminating nonsense' or, differently, replacing a concern with the 'rational
meaning' of normative obligation by the 'rationalizable core' of normativity built
into the reciprocity structure of social relations (1986: 124, 139). An example
would be collective moral learning processes, such as the inclusion of women or
gay people, whereby relations of mutual recognition are expanded through the
critical elimination of narrow, transmitted, cultural interpretative models, social
practices and individual orientations that supported forms of inequality. A critical
question that could be directed at Wellmer's strategy of playing 'determinate negation' off against the notion of 'the approximation of an ideal' (1986: 127) guided
by a regulative idea, however, arises if there is historical evidence for the structuring
effect of the idea of equality just as there is for the elimination of inequality. Does
reflexivity in relation to cultural ideals not also play a role under certain circumstances in historically situated, concrete action sequences?

In his recent criticism of Apel, Wellmer (2003) maintained his anti-idealistic
universalism in addressing the theme of 'pragmatism without regulative ideas'.
Critically drawing on Rorty, he argued on the one hand with Apel that a concept
such as truth involves a grammatically based pragmatic or performative idealization, but on the other he objected against the transcendental-pragmatic position
that such idealization is relative to context and dependent on the interplay of the
distinct perspectives of speaker and listener. Although his argument was based on
the assumption that idealizations should be confined strictly to the performative level
of the participants to the exclusion of any context-transcending metatheory, Apel
(2003) in response pointed out that Wellmer himself in formulating his own theory
of truth was in actual fact operating at the very metalevel he portrayed as being inco-
herent and untenable and thus obviously lacked an adequate reflexive theory.

It would be fair to conclude that with his relentless penetrating questioning
Wellmer not only compelled both Apel and Habermas to attempt to formulate their
positions more stringently, but also problematized the relation between the ideal
and the real in a way that helped to focus the problem encapsulated by the concept
of immanent transcendence. There is reason to believe that Wellmer's probing was
one factor in Habermas's introduction of this concept in the late 1980s.

Eder: situations and counterfactuals

Rather than philosophically, Klaus Eder (1946–) approaches the dimension of idealization in Habermas from a social-theoretical angle.[5] Although he was initially
Habermas's right-hand man in developing the theory of social evolution in terms
of Piaget's model of ontogenetic developmental logic, his position underwent
such a drastic transformation in the second half of the 1980s that he was able to
focus rather critically on the normative structures Habermas saw developing in

the course of social evolution as well as on the developmental model employed to theorize evolution (Eder 1988; Strydom 1992, 1993, 2009a).

Although ontogenesis refers to individual developmental processes, Habermas transferred this model to the level of society, with the result that society is portrayed, on the one hand, as the embodiment of individual competences and, on the other, as passing through parallel stages of development. Regarding normative structures as central to social evolution, he focused, at the individual level, on the development of moral consciousness from a pre-conventional through a conventional to a post-conventional stage and, at the societal level, on the development of law and its legitimation foundations from tribal through traditional to modern society. Objecting that only the effects of evolutionary mechanisms thus come into view rather than the generative process itself and its particular conditions, Eder insisted on the redirection of attention to the preceding process of the self-production of society – with reference to Alain Touraine – and associated collective learning processes – with reference to Max Miller – which give rise to knowledge and moral representations and thus make evolution possible. Such a correction of Habermas's ontogenetic fallacy not only pulls the rug from under the reduction of the theory of evolution to a classification of societies guided by an aprioristically projected end state, but also exposes the treatment of ethical systems as though they mark the proper achievement of evolution, particularly at the modern stage, as idealistic and even ideological. What is shared is not some morality, but rather the discursive framework established by the defence or questioning of normative stipulations. What is crucial is not the level of learning achieved as reflected in a sequence of structural models of society, but rather the manner in which learning takes place and use is made of what has been learned, which depends on structures of practice. Such situationally structured learning and use of its results in the first instance potentially provide starting points for evolution in the sense of the institutionalization of macro-cultural structures interrelating situations or contexts of generation and utilization. In Eder's (1988) view, it is only such a theory of the social evolution of practical reason, which to be sure does not completely give up communicative reason in favour of practical reason, that could serve the purposes of a critical theory of society.

At times it seems as though Eder adopts a position comparable to Wellmer's proposal of the elimination of negative instances to the exclusion of any positive reference point, for instance as when he writes that:

> Habermas . . . attempts to anchor the critique of modern rationality in a counterfactual discursive (and therefore implicit) form of rationality that is seen as constitutive of modern culture. Whether this model is sufficient to serve this function is open to debate . . . We can fulfil the critical task only by deconstructing the illusions of rationality, or its substitutes, ascribed to a society or to a social class or to a social group.
>
> (1993: 133, 139)

Yet, in his appropriation of the theory of the public sphere, Eder is emphatic that the inclusion of the counterfactual moment, which he appreciates stems from the

Kantian tradition (Eder 2007), is what elevates Habermas's position head and shoulders above those of his critics:

> In terms of empirical evidence, this does not imply that we look for instances of this as opposed to instances of its opposite. It requires nothing but the account of highly particular and decisive events in which the counterfactual force really entered historical processes.
>
> (2006: 336)

His empirical work is thus replete with examples contrary to the negative procedure. In research on the construction of environmental issues (Eder 1996), he shows how the process of discursive conflict and competition among social movement, industrial and political actors gave rise to the ecological master frame, which, by replacing the previous industrial master frame, became not only the new stake in legitimation struggles, but at the same time also efficacious in structuring institutions, ethical orientations and identities. Additionally, in research on Europeanization (Eder 2001), discussed in Chapter 8, he analyses the role of sustainability as a cultural device in the construction of a European society by focusing on the different uses that the European Union elite as well as other groups make of the idea, thus revealing its diverse structuring effects on the emerging complex of social relations and the reflexive rules to which it gives rise in terms of which critique becomes possible.

Eder's approach is designed to compensate for the structural deficit in Habermas due to his tendency to overemphasize universals and, correspondingly, to neglect the process of structure formation and the structural properties of practice that set the situational parameters of the process. Here Miller (1986) hovers in the background with his demonstration that, although Habermas did assume that whoever engages in communicative action necessarily enters a social relationship possessing structural features that are presupposed by the participants, he did not take the time to clarify the nature of those structures. However, Eder (2007) also appeals directly to American thought, symbolic interactionism and Goffman, to indicate the sense of the structural model of practice with reference of the concept of interaction order. The important concept of the lifeworld is not sensitive enough to bring fully into view the structured intersubjective experiential contexts within which collective learning takes place and use is made of its outcomes. This accounts for Eder's adoption of what he calls a 'situation-theoretical perspective' (Eder and Schmidtke 1998; Eder et al. 2002), which brings into its purview also the scripts followed narratively by social actors (Eder 2000, 2009), as a component of the much broader framework of the critical theory of society.

Honneth: immanent transcendence

In any attempt to grasp the nature of contemporary Critical Theory, Axel Honneth's (1949–) contribution is of central importance. Of the critical theorists, he is the one who explicitly highlighted the core concept of immanent transcendence. The initial background was the popularization and virtually boundless diversification of the critical approach since the 1960s and 1970s as well as the acrimonious debate internal to Critical Theory itself (Dubiel 1988), which pitted the 'theory of pure domination' of *The Dialectic of Enlightenment* (Horkheimer and Adorno 1972) against the 'theory of pure emancipation' advanced in *The Theory of Communicative Action* (Habermas 1984/87). The urgency of reinforcing the proper understanding of contemporary Critical Theory was then underlined by the attack Nancy Fraser launched from a more orthodox position against Honneth's own version (Fraser and Honneth 2003). In this context, he saw as the main problem the identification and spelling out of the authentic core shared by the different versions of Critical Theory and thus providing a basis for the most appropriate contemporary approach. The core he had in mind is represented by Critical Theory's 'left-Hegelian legacy' of 'immanent transcendence' (2007b: 64; 2003: 238–9).

The trajectory of Honneth's (1985) thought took off from a criticism of the dualistic structure of Habermas's system–lifeworld model, which confined communication to the latter level, to the normative impoverishment of the former. His corrective measure against this lopsided model was a return to an alternative version of the critical theory of society which did not merely restore the mediating function of communication, but also located it in the substance of human activities. In its light, social order is the institutionally mediated communicative relation of different culturally integrated groups which unfolds in the medium of conflict as long as social power resources are asymmetrically distributed. Included in this relational complex is the material production of society, which is likewise communicatively organized. The implied notion of the social as at one and the same time a network of communication and a field of conflict served as the basis for Honneth's next step: the development of the alternative communication approach in the form of the theory of a morally motivated 'struggle for recognition' (1992) at the core of the normative development of society.

It is noteworthy that Honneth accomplished this by way of a re-appropriation of the left-Hegelian problematic of a historically accumulated potential that presses towards realization under concrete conditions – which explains why the mantle of leading third-generation critical theorist has fallen on his shoulders. He started from the young Hegel's concept of the struggle for recognition, but in order to allow proper identification and theoretical articulation of the three individual, social and political forms of recognition, he reverted to Mead, who naturalized the Hegelian approach. As one would expect, Honneth (1992) treated Mead as a true left-Hegelian, a pragmatist continuing the innovative and fruitful line running from Peirce to Dewey. The Hegelian–Meadian struggle for recognition refers to the motor of directed social transformation in which subjects permanently seek to expand intersubjectively backed rights and thus to enhance their own personal freedom and autonomy. In keeping with the Hegelian, left-Hegelian and especially pragmatist emphasis on the fecundity of problematic situations, developments of this kind are best observed in historical situations of transformation where broadened moral ideas or normative innovations become the motivational core of collective mobilization and social movements which lead to the expansion of social norms and formal rights as well as the inclusion of more persons who have gained a higher degree of freedom for self-realization. The expansion of such media or forms of recognition as 'love' at the personal level and 'rights' at the legal level in turn feeds into 'solidarity', making possible mutual recognition at the level of the concrete form of life of a community (Honneth 1992: 146). In this last case, collectively shared existential challenges, threats or risks encapsulated in goals and values provide a motivating experiential context in which those involved are able to enter relations of mutual recognition.

There can be no doubt that Honneth's extrapolation from Hegel and Mead of the three forms of recognition which make social integration and thus society possible is conceived in keeping with the post-Hegelian notion of a process of mediation and the three-place pragmatist model of quality or firstness (individual), confrontation or secondness (social) and symbolic unity or thirdness (community). However, it is only beyond this that Honneth sees his real task looming: pinpointing a 'formal concept of the good life' (1992: 275) as a complex of the leading ideas shared by those involved, which, it is important to note, lies behind collectively shared existential challenges, threats or risks and hence goals and values. This concept, embracing the principles of love, rights and solidarity, concerns the final normative horizon which is morally sufficiently open to a diversity of goals and ethically specific enough to allow appeal to material values – but material values the selection and fulfilment of which depend on future social movements and social conflicts. Considering them as elements of the normative infrastructure of social interaction, Honneth regards the forms of recognition as pointing to three basic types of negative experiences of lack of recognition or 'disrespect' (2007b) – abuse, deprivation of rights and degradation (1992: 212) – which play a motivating role in social conflicts. The conclusion he drew from this is of particular significance, for it represents his first step towards the explicit conceptualization of the problem of immanent transcendence from 1994 onwards. Such negative experiences embody at least implicit demands to correct the withholding of recognition. Such recognition is made morally obligatory by normative principles that are available in culture and institutions and thus at least implicitly also present in everyday reality. Although not mentioning the concept, he retrospectively confirmed this when he made clear that his intention with the study of the struggle for recognition was to isolate 'the type of morality which in the social lifeworld . . . is always already effective in the form of claims of recognition . . . [and thus] . . . operates in the form of expectations of recognition' (1999: 252).

In Chapter 4, the concept of immanent transcendence is addressed as the principal theme and is accompanied by a consideration of the remaining problems in the critical theorists' respective conceptions of the status and role of idealization or regulative ideas with reference to the current state of the art. At this stage, however, it is necessary to turn from Critical Theory to a consideration of contemporary pragmatism and its relationship to Critical Theory.

;matism

l accounts, pragmatism as a philosophical movement went into decline in the ..... and was completely eclipsed by mid-century on account of a variety of factors, among which the most important were the Vienna School's neo-positivism; Charles Morris's behaviourism, which paradoxically drew on Peirce and Mead yet represented a reductive two-place semiotics close to neo-positivistic semantics; and eventually the triumph of analytic philosophy's technical stringency, which drowned out these earlier developments. Undifferentiated fragments of the Chicago tradition, especially as represented by Mead, continued to operate subterraneously in the tradition of symbolic interactionism founded by Herbert Blumer as well as in various sociological subdisciplines in an even less recognizable form. It was only in the 1960s and early 1970s that the first signs appeared of the resurfacing of philosophical pragmatism, which reached a high level of visibility in the 1980s and 1990s. This achievement is the basis of the more recent talk of the renaissance of pragmatism. Habermas (2002: 226) reported that when he first visited American universities in 1965, where Carnap's and Wittgenstein's influence had still been in evidence, his mention of the great American pragmatist tradition was met with shrugging shoulders and mutterings of Peirce as odd and Dewey as a fuzzy thinker. The literature (Bernstein 1975; Joas 1993; Delanty and Strydom 2003; Halton 2005) leaves no doubt that Apel's Peirce studies of the 1960s and Habermas's propagation of their central insights played a pivotal role in stimulating the interest of American scholars in recovering their own most typical philosophy and, more generally, its renaissance. On the American side, it was in particular two authors, Richard Bernstein and Richard Rorty, who started the ball rolling, and it was then picked up by Thomas McCarthy and James Bohman.

The older generation

Bernstein: concrete reasonableness

According to Habermas, Richard Bernstein (1932–) was 'the first "real" pragmatist' he had met (Habermas 2002: 226). This was in 1972, shortly after the appearance of Bernstein's book *Praxis and Action* (1971), from which it is apparent that since the late 1960s he had been working towards facilitating interaction between American and Continental philosophy. Well grounded in pragmatism, with a series of publications between 1964 and 1966 on Peirce and Dewey, he seems to have been strongly influenced by Apel's and especially Habermas's writings on Peirce of the 1960s. From here onwards indeed he consistently made an important contribution not only to the revitalization of pragmatism, but also to the exchange between and strengthening of the ties binding pragmatism and Critical Theory. This much is borne out by a series of subsequent book publications, from *The Restructuring of Social and Political Theory* (1976), through *Beyond Objectivism and Relativism* (1983), to *The New Constellation* (1991). Through critical analyses of international debates of the time, all these works seek to cultivate relations between different directions, with the overriding concern to secure and advance what Bernstein called the 'pragmatic legacy'.

Praxis and Action is of particular interest since it sought to clarify relations among four distinct philosophical traditions – Marxism, existentialism, pragmatism and analytic philosophy – from the viewpoint of their shared reservations against the modern contemplative concept of knowledge, or the myth of the given, and their alternative orientation towards human activity, whether conceived as praxis or as action. Of particular interest here is Bernstein's assessment of the relation of pragmatism and Marxism. The core of Marxism, including what he called 'critical Marxism', is represented by 'a radical anthropology' in terms of which social praxis produces and reproduces the complex objective network of historical institutions and practices within which human beings themselves work, give form and are formed, including paradoxically being subjected to alienation, which in turn could become a motivating factor in transformative praxis. Marxism is further clear about the fact that reflection on people and society from the viewpoint of possible emancipation shapes the very image of what human beings are. Its limits become apparent, however, in a tendency towards absolutism and dogmatism due to an inadequate awareness of the norms of critical inquiry, which themselves are not unrelated to the norms of democratic institutions. It is in this respect that pragmatism offers an urgently required corrective to Marxism. Its ideal of an indefinite critical community of investigators has significant consequences for the way in which human activity is seen. Inquiry does not aim at knowledge with an exclusive claim to truth, but serves the development of habits and forms of action contributing to a world characterized by concrete reasonableness – which entails the shouldering of the responsibility of cultivating critical habits and rational forms of conduct, while maintaining openness towards mutual criticism and the future.

The parts of *Praxis and Action* dealing with pragmatism and analytic philosophy were published in German under the title *Praxis und Handlung* in 1975. To this edition Bernstein added an introduction consisting mainly of a thorough critique of Habermas's interpretation of Peirce. Ever since the early 1970s, according to Habermas, Bernstein kept pushing him in the direction of 'a more intense detranscendentalization of Kant' (Habermas 2002: 226). Seeing what precisely this means in the debate between these two authors promises to illuminate not only pragmatism, but also the relationship between pragmatism and Critical Theory. The major problem of Habermas's interpretation of pragmatism, according to Bernstein, was his misunderstanding of Peirce's theory of reality due to a lack of appreciation of the significance of the latter's doctrine of categories for the theory of reality. On the one hand, Habermas undervalued and misconstrued secondness in the sense of the dyadic moment of resistance of reality as something independent of mind and language as a result, on the other, of overemphasizing thirdness in the sense of the triadic symbolic moment of argumentation or justification. It is remarkable, as made clear earlier, that it is only in the 1990s that Habermas conceded and – we may say – detranscendentalized his concept of reality and of truth by fully incorporating the non-epistemic moment of the objective world independent of us. However, there is another side to the debate. Bernstein (1971, 1975) acknowledged that Peirce was a realist in the sense of acknowledging two aspects of reality, namely objective resistance as well as the reality and efficacy of universals or regulative ideas. Yet, despite stressing the latter symbolic moment, he nevertheless insisted on keeping it strictly within the horizon of social practices by considering it exclusively from the viewpoint of the participants and thus denying that it could be approached in the theoretical attitude (Bernstein 1983). Habermas's (1998b: 407) critical response dating from 1985 is, in effect, that this is tantamount to pushing detranscendentalization a step too far. In his view, not only is it possible to theoretically elaborate on this third symbolic moment by, for example, developing a formal pragmatic analysis of the idealizations regulating social practices, but it is necessary to acknowledge also 'the moment of unconditionality built into the universalist validity claims' advanced in such practices. This is the threshold of detranscendentalization over which pragmatists readily step, but Habermas resolutely refuses to cross – in opposition to Bernstein as well as to Rorty.

Rorty: social practice as conversation

The most decisive American impetus towards the renewed development of pragmatism came from Richard Rorty (1931–2007). His turn to pragmatism was motivated by disillusionment with his own philosophical background and was spearheaded by a criticism of academic philosophy, which, indeed, contributed to changes in analytic philosophy, including attempts at a re-appropriation of pragmatist ideas. His elevation of Dewey in *Philosophy and the Mirror of Nature* (1979) to the level of one of the three most significant philosophers of the twentieth century, the others being Wittgenstein and Heidegger, gave rise to the so-called 'neo-pragmatist' movement. From Wittgenstein, Heidegger and Dewey he learned respectively that language is a medium, that there is no subject of knowledge to support truth, and that social practice is primary, but the conclusions he drew from this pointed in a contextualist and relativist direction: signs are purely conventional, humans are solely products of socialization, and social practice is strictly a matter of conversation. Against the background of a criticism of traditional epistemology for the representationalism, foundationalism and essentialism entailed by its emphasis on inquiry geared toward knowledge and truth, he proposed an alternative conception inspired by Heidegger and harking back to the German Romantic poet Hölderlin's idea that we human beings form something like a conversation. As he made clear in *The Consequences of Pragmatism* (1982), the alternative mode of inquiry has to take the form of a conversation that creates the possibility of agreement by allowing only conventional standards emerging from the context itself to constrain the process. Rather than following the pragmatist concept of cognition
and ledge centred on the experience and creative overcoming of problem
he thus tendentially Heideggerianized philosophy and concomitantly
ically dissipated pragmatism into a contextualism which converged
stmodernist perspective. Besides three volumes of philosophical essays,

this position was confirmed by his *Contingency, Irony, and Solidarity* (1989), in which he entertained the utopia of achieving human solidarity, but saw it as possible only in a context where individual freedom to privately pursue aesthetic projects of self-creation is guaranteed. These tendencies have solicited numerous criticisms from both American and European authors – including Apel and Habermas – to the effect that Rorty is skating on rather thin ice in his appeal to Dewey in particular and pragmatism more generally.

The debate about Rorty's position sheds light on some of pragmatism's characteristic features as well as on the relationship between pragmatism and Critical Theory. There are such defining features as the pragmatist concept of cognition and knowledge, Peirce and Mead's interest in Darwin, Dewey's insistence on the critical testing of democratic institutions, pragmatism as a philosophy of purport and so forth, which Rorty ignored. However, particularly significant in the present context is pragmatism as a philosophy of action. Pragmatism, like Critical Theory, sees theory as mediated by practice that serves the interests of the larger community. Peirce provided the normative impetus, whereas Mead pursued social reform and Dewey stressed rational problem solving and the concurrent improvement of democracy. By contrast with both Apel and Habermas, who on this basis regard also pragmatism as a branch of left-Hegelianism, Rorty translates the theory–practice relation into philosophy as an edifying moment in a conventional conversation which he himself admitted is ethnocentric. Not only does he not grasp pragmatism's understanding of itself, which is close to Critical Theory's, as part of a practical philosophy appropriate to the times, but concurrently he also overlooks or explicitly denies the relevance of the tension between institutions and their legitimation, the need for the justification of standards, the necessity of a reference point beyond the conventional, and the importance of social reform and transformation of the existing social order. These are the kind of matters that were at issue in the mutual criticism and debate between Rorty and the second-generation critical theorists. For him, Habermas was caught in a Kantian transcendental trap and needed to completely detranscendentalize to be able to escape at all, whereas, for Habermas, Rorty fell into the bottomless relativist pit of a strict, anti-realist contextualism, thus exhibiting in the extreme the typical weakness plaguing pragmatism: the misunderstanding of 'the anti-Platonic distrust in an ideological misuse of abstract ideas' as the need for 'the denial of the transcending force and unconditional meaning of claims to truth' (Habermas 2002: 228). Most recently, Apel (2003: 172–4) directed his criticism at Rorty's strategy of detranscendentalization, which informs the renaissance of pragmatism and, in his view, represents precisely a reversal of the interpretation he offered in 1967 of Peirce's normative pragmatism.

The younger generation of pragmatists

Two younger American authors with connections to pragmatism as well as Critical Theory are of particular interest in the present context. The first is McCarthy, who relatively early in his career established a relationship with Critical Theory

through Habermas, but in the course of time embarked on an attempt to prag-
matize Critical Theory. The second is Bohman, who studied under McCarthy
and, continuing along the path Dewey opened, seeks to cultivate a closer tie
between pragmatism and Critical Theory. Like McCarthy, who spent some time
in Germany, he sojourned in Frankfurt, the seat of Critical Theory. An account of
the relationship between contemporary Critical Theory and pragmatism would
be incomplete without a consideration of the contributions of these two authors.

McCarthy: critique of impure reason

Having started his academic career as a colleague of Marcuse at the University
of California at San Diego, Thomas McCarthy (1941–) spent the late 1960s and
early 1970s lecturing at the University of Munich, where the relation between
philosophy and politics became still clearer to him and the interests of the students
led him to shift from the philosophy of the physical sciences to the philosophy of
the social sciences, Critical Theory in particular. It is in this context that he took
up contact with Habermas, who henceforth had a decisive impact on his thought.
His first book was *The Critical Theory of Jürgen Habermas* (1978), which, besides
translations of three of Habermas's books, was followed by *Ideals and Illusions*
(1993) and *Critical Theory* (Hoy and McCarthy 1994) – the former critical essays
on such deconstructionists as Heidegger, Foucault, Derrida and Rorty as well as
on Habermas, and in the latter a more detailed account of a pragmatized version
of Critical Theory as against Hoy's Foucauldian deconstructionism. Particularly
interesting in the later book is his recourse to Garfinkel's ethnomethodological
concern with the analysis of social practices.

From McCarthy's book of 1978 runs a line of persistent criticism of some
of Habermas's basic analytical assumptions, such as the labour–interaction and
system–lifeworld distinctions, which opened up a route towards the explicit pragmatization of Critical Theory he would later undertake. Of particular importance
in this respect was his initiation of a wave of immanent or critical theoretical criticism of Habermas's theory of socio-cultural evolution (McCarthy 1978; Strydom
1992). In opposition to Habermas's theory, which on the basis of Piaget's psychology prioritized the developmental logic of formal normative structures, McCarthy
objected that historically specific social life was lost as basic reference point and
thus that the practical meaning guiding interpretation and action was located
beyond situated practical reason in pure practical reason. Parallel to this but at
a different level, he regarded Habermas's discourse ethics as actually a 'discourse
morality' (McCarthy 2001b: 420) which was in need of being rendered ethical by
being made situationally relevant – something Habermas only hesitantly started
doing in *Justification and Application* (1993), containing essays dating from 1990–1.
McCarthy's writings of the first half of the 1990s, especially the exemplary
'Philosophy and Critical Theory: A reprise' (1994a: 5–100), took up the challenge of redressing the balance between pure and situated reason by focusing
on the 'detranscendentalization of reason' and the corresponding articulation of
Critical Theory as a form of 'practically significant, sociohistorical critique of

impure reason' (1994a: 8). Significantly, he regarded this shift in the understanding of reason as having been inaugurated by the left-Hegelians, in which case he
predictably mentioned Marx but at the same time also pointed out that American
pragmatism was originally a variant of this departure. However, even more significantly, he insisted on retaining the import of reason as normative basis for
the regulation and critique of social practices, despite having stepped back from
God's point of view into the concrete socio-historical world.

McCarthy took Horkheimer's programme for Critical Theory as a philosophically oriented, reflexive type of socio-historical inquiry as his starting point since
the German founding figure had appreciated that a materialist critique could
only assume the form of a critique of reason. Rather than a matter of empirical
reduction or sceptical rejection of truth, justice, freedom and responsibility, such
normative ideas needed to be both unmasked, to prevent their distortions from
being used to justify the unjustifiable, and redeemed, to allow them to play their
unique role in the process of bringing into being a better society. Horkheimer was
convinced that the left-Hegelian emphasis on radical, practically oriented reflection
on reason and its realization had to be maintained, yet under twentieth-century
conditions it required that Enlightenment ideas of reason or philosophical utopias
be identified in socio-cultural forms, which are themselves embedded in concrete
social relations and historical processes or tendencies pointing towards improvements in human social life. In McCarthy's judgement, however, Horkheimer
proved unable to find a way of bridging the gap between ungroundable feelings
of compassion for human suffering and rational justification of universal ideals.
Fortunately, a solution to this problem was to be found in Habermas's conception
of communicative rationality in the sense of the possibility of freely constructed
agreements on theoretical and practical issues through consideration and mediation of reasons for and against, regulated by the idea of truth. The trajectory
leading to this solution has its roots in Peirce as far as truth claims in the theoretical domain are concerned and in Mead as regards justice claims in the practical
domain. Having culminated in Habermas, this solution entails that universal ideas
of practical reason and historically specific socio-cultural settings and practices can
be seen as being related and mediated through communicative reason. McCarthy
understood this pragmatic turn towards communicative reason as being central to
the articulation of the relation between Critical Theory and pragmatism.

While stressing left-Hegelianism in both its Marxian and pragmatist versions,
McCarthy acknowledged, like all the critical theorists and their immediate precursors, the importance of incorporating the Kantian moment as a corrective
to Marx and Marxism's overvaluation of materialism. In the preface to *Ideals
and Illusions* (1993), he registered the detranscendentalization of Kant's ideas of
reason, which, in his view, nevertheless did not impair or invalidate the twofold
significance Kant had originally ascribed to them. This same line of argumentation is continued in his contribution to *Critical Theory* (1994a,b). By contrast with
the followers of Nietzsche and Heidegger, who completely deflate these ideas and
reject them as irrelevant, the left-Hegelian tradition always sought to transfer these
ideas to socio-cultural forms and to find socio-practical analogues of them. The

incorporation of ideas of reason in culture and their structuring effect on social practices and relations underline the necessity of taking into account both their positive and negative social functions. McCarthy (1994a: 7) singles out Kant's distinction between the 'assur[ance of] . . . lawful claims' and the 'dismiss[al of] . . . all groundless pretensions' in the *Critique of Pure Reason* that invoke the norm-setting function enabling critique and the obfuscating function calling for critique.

Critical Theory in McCarthy's detranscendentalized or pragmatized version accommodates both these functions of socio-practical ideas of reason: 'their irreplaceable function in cooperative interaction and their potential for misuse' (1993: 4). However, of greater importance still are the consequences for the overall form taken by Critical Theory so conceived. The transformation of transcendental ideas into socio-practical ideas entails that they be brought down from on high and located within the domain of social practices. Teasing out the implications of Habermas's work, McCarthy interpreted this to mean that reason now appears as the pragmatic presuppositions of communication, which, as medium, embraces at one and the same time social orientations and practices as well as the normative ideas giving them direction and guidance. On the basis of this assumption, he is able to submit that 'socio-practical ideas of reason are both "immanent" in and "transcendent" to practices constitutive of forms of life' (1994a: 38). Immanent transcendence is thus given the status of a defining feature of Critical Theory. As in the case of Bernstein, the exact interpretation of this complex of dialectical relations became the object of a domestic dispute between McCarthy and Habermas.

Bohman: plurality and unity

James Bohman (1954–) perceives McCarthy, under whom he studied in the doctoral programme at Boston University in the early 1980s, as someone who persistently sought to reconcile the Critical Theory of the Frankfurt School, as represented by Habermas and Horkheimer, and American pragmatism, as represented by Mead and Dewey. His own work displays a concern with the pursuit of such reconciliation from the viewpoint of the shared vision of these two traditions – what he calls 'critical social science' (Bohman 1991, 1999, 2000, 2001). The common thread leading Critical Theory and pragmatism to this critical vision is their refusal to surrender the normative import of reason and truth even after the detranscendentalization and de-absolutization of these ideas in the wake of left-Hegelianism by the historical school and such figures as Nietzsche and Freud. Despite this common basis and orientation, however, Bohman regards the two programmes for a critical social science as very different – Critical Theory being characterized by a theoretical orientation and pragmatism by a practical orientation. Indeed, they are so different that a reconciliation of the two entails a transformation of Critical Theory, which can be described as a pragmatization of Critical Theory. This 'pragmatic interpretation' or 'pragmatic turn', which displays the strong impact of Dewey, results in what he calls his 'practical approach to critical social science' (2001: 90). Backed up by sympathetic criticisms of McCarthy, this position of his suggests that he is willing to make this move more radical way than McCarthy.

Bohman (1993, 1999) does not speak of left-Hegelianism but sees Criti Theory against the more general background of German idealism, of whi left-Hegelianism was a creatively materialized offshoot. His argument is that the German idealist legacy harbours deficiencies which are compensated for by the introduction of pragmatism, particularly Dewey's continuation of Peirce's thought. Such a step clarifies the political nature, brightens the substantive focus and sharpens the methodological function of critical social inquiry. Critical Theory, in his view, is uniquely characterized by a theory of society that combines explanation and critique in a way which highlights its normative thrust. Its principal weakness, however, lies in the typical concern of its representatives, inaugurated by Marx, with the formulation of the one and only correct comprehensive theory of society that allows not only critical explanation, but also the specification of the goals of the appropriate form of political practice. The undesirable consequence of such a convergence of theory and politics, namely the obliteration or restriction of pluralism, can be undone by the introduction of pragmatism, particularly Dewey's theory of democratic research. Despite the advance it represents, even Habermas's methodologically pluralistic account of Critical Theory requires a still stronger pragmatist input in order to improve its self-understanding of its role in democratic practice and public self-reflection. Critical Theory's weakness also shows up in Marxist ideology critique. In Bohman's judgement, it is a negative form of devaluing or disillusioning critique in so far as it is concerned with the explanation of phenomena by exposing their functions and causes. Only occasionally does it exhibit also the positive pragmatist form of disclosing new actualities, meanings, orientations and possibilities – what he calls a 'pragmatics of disclosure' (1993: 566) – which opens up new ways of seeing, redefines relevance structures and transforms cognitive schemata and cultural models. Critical Theory, therefore, is in need of being corrected and complemented by pragmatism.

Following Dewey, Bohman argues that a pragmatized form of critical social inquiry forms part of the democratic constitution and organization of society as a process of collective problem solving through social cooperation. Critical social science is the institutionalization of societal self-investigation of established practices and the basic norms of cooperation underpinning them, including the practices and norms of social science itself. Embodying both pragmatism's and Critical Theory's political understanding of the relation between theory and practice, critical social inquiry seeks to serve the establishment of equal action capacities through its production of knowledge and stimulation of public reflection on practices and their goals. For this reason, Bohman stresses the 'public testing' or 'practical verification' (1999: 477, 2001: 91) of proposals as pragmatism in particular demands. What has been disclosed by critique in a first reflexive turn has to pass through a 'second reflexive turn' (1993: 569) by being tested, confirmed and appropriated by the audience or, more generally, the public. It is only when critique exerts this 'double pragmatic impact' (1993: 572) that it succeeds in not merely interpreting the world, but actually contributing to changing it.

For Bohman, then, the reconciliation of Critical Theory and pragmatism in critical social science, which itself forms part of democracy, as a mode of inquiry turns on the commitment to 'a normative account of democratic practices of socially organized critical judgment' (1999: 477). Such an articulation of the two traditions allows not just the observance of both the 'plurality' of perspectives immanent in social reality and the possible 'unity' of perspectives pointing beyond a given situation, but also critical inquiry into the 'ongoing tension' as it is being worked through by 'reflective and self-critical practices' (2001: 91).

Conclusion

This chapter was devoted to an exploration of the relation between contemporary Critical Theory and pragmatism with a view to further clarifying the impact of the incorporation of central ideas deriving from the latter on the development of the former. The account started from Apel's seminal Peirce studies, which provided the broad parameters for the pursuit of Critical Theory by Habermas and younger authors such as Wellmer, Eder and Honneth. The focus, however, was on the interaction between Critical Theory and pragmatism, the latter represented by Bernstein, Rorty, McCarthy and Bohman. In so far as this account completed the sketching of the background of the concept of immanent transcendence commenced in the preceding analyses, it forms the basis for the systematic treatment of this key aspect of contemporary Critical Theory.

4   Immanent transcendence as key concept

Introduction

Immanent transcendence is the key concept of contemporary Critical Theory. The previous chapters suggested that the basic insight encapsulated by this concept dates back to the nineteenth century or even the eighteenth and that the explicit formulation and codification of the concept emerged from one of the most important debates in the late twentieth and early twenty-first centuries – namely, the debate between Critical Theory and pragmatism, which itself is at the centre of what has become known as 'the renaissance of pragmatism'. To a certain extent, the 'renaissance of pragmatism' overlaps also with the debate about social criticism and critique. Although McCarthy and Honneth in particular highlighted the concept in the wake of Apel's clarification of the core figure of thought and Habermas's explicit naming of it, its implications for Critical Theory still remain largely opaque. In order to explicate the concept and achieve clarity about its implications, the following paragraphs offer a brief recapitulation of the background of the concept, followed by a more systematic analysis and presentation.

Background of the concept

Emergence and development

Enlightenment, Kant, Hegel and left-Hegelianism

Transcendent ideas are present in all human forms of life, but it is only under certain conditions that they are understood as simultaneously available in, yet transcending, the actual situation as still unrealized ideas which, if realized, could transform the status quo. In medieval Europe, for instance, the religious worldview served to project transcendent ideas into an otherworldly domain beyond history and society. The origin of the modern, more particularly the contemporary concept of immanent transcendence, by contrast, can be traced to that point in history when situation-transcendent ideas for the first time became forces spearheading the transformation of the existing state of society. This was the case with the idea of freedom in the context of the eighteenth-century rights discourse that prepared the way for the French Revolution (Mannheim 1972; Strydom 2000) and then, more generally, with the very concept of 'idea'. Whereas in the seventeenth and early eighteenth centuries the latter merely referred to a formal reference point by comparison with which a concrete phenomenon could be theoretically evaluated, in the course of the eighteenth century the French gave it a practical-rational form which was used to help define and shape the situation in graphic political terms.

As Marx in his critique of post-revolutionary Germany made clear, it is this morally and politically infused, practical concept of idea that philosophers in keeping with circumstances there gave a subjective tone and thus made into the mainstay of German idealism. This genealogy accounts for the central aspect of Kant's founding of idealism: his theoretical 'ideas of pure reason' and 'not completely pure' practical or normative ideas of reason, both of which are not just transcendent ideas but simultaneously also have their own 'immanent use' (1968: 486). Despite his prioritization of practical reason and adoption of a pragmatic point of view, however, the abstractness of his approach precluded the articulation of the relation between immanence and transcendence. In turn, Hegel made 'the Idea' the centrepiece of his thinking, while criticizing Kant from the concrete historical perspective of ethical life. This allowed him to trace in all spheres the role of the rational factor in the process of the idea's historical development with reference to its immanent realization. For him, reason has already been incorporated in the real world and through its effects there renders what exists immanently rational.

However, Hegel's all too ready identification of the rational and the real, transcendent ideas and their immanent realization, and his confinement of the active element to the movement of the idea to the exclusion of the agents or forces actually engaged in realizing its potential, called forth the influential transformative critique of the left-Hegelians. Instead of reconciliation or identification, Marx focused precisely on the discrepancy and contradiction between idea and reality, which had to be seen in the context of the historical processes generated by human activity. Since an idea implied striving towards a goal, this relation needed to be investigated in terms of the actual consequences following from the propagation and pursuit of ideas. As the 'Theses on Feuerbach' projected, this required a multilevel approach that was able to pinpoint and account for both the negative and positive interpretations of an idea and the corresponding consequences which not only deform the existing situation but potentially also point beyond it. While likewise sensitive to the practical consequences of ideas, Peirce was more concerned with the solution of collective problems in a way that simultaneously improves the world in which we live than with associating transcendent ideas with anti-systemic, revolutionary transformation, as did Marx. For Peirce, its imagined effects or consequences provide an indication of the meaning or normative sense of a concept. He insisted, however, that such consequences should be understood not just in terms of action, but with reference to general ideas defining the ends of action. By interpreting our thought, transcendent ideas simultaneously also provide guidance to action. In the process of knowledge production, for instance, concepts such as reality, the interpretation community and concrete reasonableness serve as such situation-transcending ideas. In Peirce's view, this process can be adequately conceived only as taking place in the medium of signs. Against the same Kantian–Hegelian background as his fellow left-Hegelians and hence as centrally concerned with the relation between reason and existence, Kierkegaard in turn redirected the focus from the macro level to the individual. For him, reflexive self-cultivation as a responsible and authentic individual is a necessary condition for the realization of context-transcendent ideas in concrete situations.

Pragmatism

In their respective creative continuations of Kant, Hegel and the left-Hegelians, both the pragmatists and the Critical Theorists in some form or another made central the figure of thought encapsulated by the concept of immanent transcendence. Royce extrapolated Peirce's idea of the indefinite community of investigators in terms of social interaction as the historical human community whose development is directed and guided by the transcendent idea of the ideal communication community. Contrary to Royce's attachment to Hegelian idealism, Mead later elaborated the same basic set of concepts under the naturalistic impact of Darwin. By tracing the process of development of symbolic and linguistic communication from the pre-human to the human level at which situation-transcending ideas come into play, he was able to illuminate the emergence and formation within this medium not only of the self, particularly of moral-ethical consciousness, but also of social relations organized by means of the progressively more generally interpreted idea of the 'generalized other' up to the level of the community of 'universal discourse' (1974: 90, 327). Despite their differences, both Royce and Mead followed more closely the early and late Peirce's insistence on the role of general ideas. James and Dewey, by contrast, limited the perspective in keeping with suggestions of the middle Peirce to everyday problematic situations requiring creative thought and intervention. The emphasis on action meant that they tended to confine the immanent-transcendence configuration within the concrete situational context, with evaluative criteria regarded as being generated strictly immanently with reference to the problems encountered. The lowering of the transcendent horizon nevertheless had beneficial results. This approach led, in Dewey's case, to an emphatic linking of problem solving to democracy and, in James's, to a contribution to the clarification of the problematic of subject formation.

Critical Theory

In their avowed attempt to renew left-Hegelianism and its model of critique, the critical theorists and those immediately preparing the way for them dealt more or less directly with immanent transcendence, albeit without having settled on a name for it. As against vulgar Marxism, Korsch recovered the Kantian ideational moment, but simultaneously went dialectically beyond the transcendental approach. According to his understanding, it was vital to capture the mutual implication of the situational and transcendent moments in the process of societal development. Taking cues from Hegel, Lukács focused on the dynamically interrelated set of relations carried along in the historical process of the formation of society. As a temporal process, it is led by an objective possibility in the guise of the transcendent idea of a fully socialized human form of life which knowl-edge-producing and acting agents seek to realize. Interferences in the process of realization by factors and forces reifying social relations and alienating individuals cause contradictions which, in turn, serve to drive the process forward. Paralleling and forming part of this dynamic movement is a process of knowledge produc-tion and critique which, in Lukács's version, closely approximates the *medium quo* theory of cognition and knowledge shared by Marx and Peirce. Korsch's and par-ticularly Lukács's revitalization of left-Hegelianism provided the core members of the Frankfurt School with an indispensable starting point in their attempts to lay the foundations of Critical Theory.

The problematic of immanent transcendence was central to Horkheimer's tradition-founding contribution. With reference to Kant, he insisted on the crucial role of normative ideas and ideals, but for the purposes of Critical Theory at the same time was adamant that they are less moral than political. Far from being a pure fantasy as it may appear, the idea of 'a rationally organized future society' (Horkheimer 1970: 49), for example, is immanently rooted in every human being and in human activities, forming part of social life and subject to change in the course of attempts to realize their potential. Having in mind here Marx's ontology of labour, Horkheimer did not have at his disposal sufficiently differentiated theo-retical tools to explicate more particularly the precise sense in which such ideas are immanent in historically specific forms of life and yet simultaneously able to transcend such contexts – not to mention seeing the problem clearly enough to name it. In an attempt to consolidate the basic insights deriving from the classics as well as the renewal of left-Hegelianism, Adorno devoted his *Negative Dialectics* directly to an ontological, epistemological and methodological treatment of the problematic of the 'immanent' and the 'transcendent' (1970: 21): how to con-ceptualize and analyse the open historical process of reality in a way that avoids hypostatizing the process through conceptual subsumption and methodologism by capturing its immanent non-conceptual qualitative aspect, on the one hand, and its direction of development guided by a transcendent 'negative sign' (1970: 151), a counterfactual 'cypher' (1970: 277) or an as yet unspecifiable goal, on the other? For Adorno, constellational analysis proceeding from a sign-mediated epistemology and employing analytical models based on language and reading was best suited to the task. Starting from the experience of suspicion engendered by a reified society, this approach could both critically penetrate the hypostatized process and reified society and detect the directional tendencies of the process to which they belong. Appreciating the classical concern with the role of mind in the historical process of society, Marcuse explicitly sought to accommodate ideas of reason in his understanding of the process of reality as well as Critical Theory's approach to it. Rational ideas such as freedom, rights, a liberated humanity and a rational society are contained in the concrete social situation – for instance, preserved in culture and in the human instinctual structure – as unfulfilled yet realizable potentialities which point beyond the existing state of affairs and thus exert a progressive impetus towards their actual realization. Regarding them as both immanent and transcendent, Critical Theory detranscendentalizes such ideas and thus treats them as 'impure . . . transcendent truths' (Marcuse 1972: 141). Together with philosophy, it keeps hold of these ideas through the imagination, but as a constructive endeavour simultaneously seeks to contribute to their realization and thus to the transformation of society by bringing a new world into being. To the extent that he adopted Marxist functionalism, however, Marcuse tended, like his fellow early critical theorists, to subvert this understanding of the relation between immanence and transcendence. Instead of ideas having a foothold in society yet going beyond it in a way that exerts a constitutive and regulative impact on it, they are separated from reality as potentials requiring fulfilment in a one-off revolutionary transformation of society.

Codification

Behind the formulation and naming of the concept of immanent transcendence lies a cooperative relation between Apel and Habermas that goes back to their student days in the mid-twentieth century – the former originally coming more strongly from a Kantian–Heideggerian direction, with the latter closer to the left-Hegelian tradition. Apel's achievement is to have brought these lines of thinking together and, in addition, to have related pragmatism to them in a way that allowed him in the 1960s and early 1970s to clarify the figure of thought at the core of the concept of immanent transcendence. A comparable constellation of philosophical traditions having come to inform Habermas's thinking, it is unsurprising that the same figure of thought took centre stage for him too. By the late 1980s, he was able to name the concept and thus to open a new more precise route for the elaboration not only of his own work, but also of what may be considered the third phase in the development of Critical Theory. It is in this latter context that McCarthy and Honneth in particular grasped the opportunity to highlight the new key concept of contemporary Critical Theory.

Apel

Apel's reconstruction of the figure of thought at the core of the concept of immanent transcendence, what in the late 1960s and early 1970s he conceived of as 'the dialectics of the *a priori* of the communication community' (1980: 281), stretched over a period of some twenty years. It commenced in 1950 with his investigation of the transformation of traditional epistemology by Heidegger's fundamental ontology, which provided the basis for Gadamer's hermeneutics. The crucial step here was the foregrounding of the all-pervasive pre-understanding that allows human existence, which is always already situated in the world, not only to orient towards the future, but also to continually reinterpret it in a self-correcting way relevant to the present. Since this new articulation of the hermeneutic circle neglected the question of justification or validity, however, Apel sought a corrective to it by investigating the problem of the relation between theory and practice as developed in the different left-Hegelian strands represented by Marx, Peirce and Kierkegaard. This underlined the need to inquire into the effective history of dialectics in twentieth-century thinking. Critically pointing up the limitations of both hermeneutics and Marxism, Apel focused on the analysis of the implied set of rather complex relations under the title of 'the dialectics of the situation' (1973, II: 23) and demonstrated the need for a substantive interpretation of the world as a historical situation to mediate between ideal reflection and material praxis. The clarification of this moment of mediation compelled Apel to undertake a series of investigations, beginning with language and passing through pragmatism, especially Peirce's *medium quo* or sign-mediated theory of cognition and knowledge and the role of transcendent ideas or regulative principles, and more generally the pragmatic turn in twentieth-century thinking. This sequence ultimately culminated in Apel's own characteristic 'transcendental pragmatics', which identifies communication as the metadimensional condition and basic principle not only of the social sciences but also of ethics. Here is located what he called 'the dialectics of the *a priori* of the communication community'. According to this core idea of the concept of immanent transcendence, human beings find themselves in a real historical world mediated by communication, while at the same time both presupposing an ideal communication community which endows the real one with meaning and action orientations and counterfactually anticipating the possibility of its realization through active engagement in the real communication community. For Apel, this metadimensional dialectical figure of mediation represents the basic framework of Critical Theory: theoretically, methodologically and normatively.

Habermas

From his re-appropriation of left-Hegelianism in the early 1960s until his explicit introduction of the concept of immanent transcendence, Habermas operated with the same figure of thought as the one Apel so meticulously reconstructed. Initially, it was implicated in his endeavour to establish a type of theory that proceeds from an anticipatory interpretation of society as a whole yet simultaneously cultivates practical intentions, thus keeping the transcendent moment within immanent bounds. By the late 1960s, it was more broadly epistemologically articulated with the assistance of Peirce in terms of an internal relation between forms of knowledge and types of action. Accordingly, he came to see knowledge production as a process that is given form by a framework made up of an experientially generated goal and concurrent practices in the service of social life. Recasting this complex of relations in a communication mould allowed him in the next decade not only to specify the transcendent moment in its role as directing, guiding or regulative instance in terms of claims to validity requiring justification, but also to broaden the perspective to the process of the constitution of society through communicative action and the associated legitimation requirements. This provided the basis for the development of the theory of communicative action in the early 1980s. As he was inspired by Mead's elaboration of Peirce and Kant into a normatively integrated communication-theoretical approach, it does not come as a surprise that the core idea of immanent transcendence, albeit at best only in an implicitly operative form, occupied a central position in Habermas's exposition of the theory. As part of a step in detranscendentalization, he regarded the concept of the lifeworld as bringing the sphere of validity claims down from the transcendent realm of free-floating cultural meanings and incorporating it into empirical, spatio-temporally identifiable contexts of action, so that their normative content was installed as social facts. What Apel earlier referred to as a dialectical contradiction in the communicative framework of social life, Habermas now saw as a tension between the immanent and transcendent moments, which the social actors themselves had to deal with through practices appropriate to the actual situation. This enabled him six years later to conceive of 'situated reason' (1992: 139), in which case pragmatically unavoidable idealizing presuppositions were regarded as pervading everyday orientations and practices and exerting an organizing and unifying effect on them. By 1988–9, he was ready to explicitly name the concept of 'immanent transcendence' and to elaborate on it in its own right in conference contributions which were published later.

On introducing the concept, which he did with reference to Peirce, he submitted that, as communicatively acting humans, we are subject to the movement of linguistic intersubjectivity or the transcendence built into the reproduction conditions of language, without, however, being delivered out to it – transcendence in the sense of the necessity of a situation-transcending pre-understanding or anticipation of an infinite communication community which we are afforded but which is also demanded of us (1991b: 142, 155). Social actors orient themselves towards normative reference points which they can articulate and live up to only in the context of their own languages and forms of life, even though the counterfactual surplus of those orientation complexes far outstrips all actual concrete situations. As the title of *Between Facts and Norms* (1996) alone already unequivocally makes clear, the project of this book was basically structured in terms of the idea of immanent transcendence. The analysis of law and democracy proceeds from the concept of situated reason and focuses on the tension between facticity and validity in the dynamics of the integration of society as a social order which exists through the effective recognition of normative validity requirements. A few years later, Habermas genealogically traced the change in perspective in the wake of the collapse of the universally valid religious worldview, which compelled a shift from 'the transcendent God's eye point of view' to a 'transcendence from within' (1998a: 7), allowing the accommodation of pluralism and the location of the moral point of view within the world itself without losing the possibility of taking distance from the world. The result of Habermas's systematic appropriation of pragmatism in his late work under pressure from Bernstein, Putnam, McCarthy and Rorty as well as Wellmer is what he called his 'Kantian pragmatism'. As a 'detranscendentalization' (2003: 17) or pragmatic deflation of Kant's transcendental philosophy, the concept of immanent transcendence is obviously made central to it. Following an earlier established theoretical strategy, the strict separation between the empirical (the world) and transcendental (beyond the world) is replaced by a relation of tension within the world which compels the actors involved to cope with it themselves and seek to resolve it in keeping with the demands of their world and times. Thus Habermas's late work confirms that the detranscendentalizing step inaugurated by Marx and pursued in the left-Hegelian tradition up to his own work draws a basic distinction and shifts the focus to a set of tension-laden relations which together mark out the basic parameters of the concept of immanent transcendence.

McCarthy

McCarthy was the first to take steps to relate the core of the idea encapsulated by the concept of immanent transcendence emphatically to Critical Theory. This was facilitated by the continuing in-house dispute he carried on with Habermas regarding whether the emphasis should not rather be more pragmatic than transcendental. He took these steps in 1991 and followed them up in 1994 in the context of a debate with the Foucauldian David Hoy. Apparently, he confined himself to Habermas's relevant publications prior to his explicit introduction of the concept, which explains why McCarthy did not employ the expression 'immanent transcendence' despite his acute understanding of the implied figure of thought. It is to his credit, nevertheless, that he in effect signalled the importance of the concept of immanent transcendence for Critical Theory in its contemporary form. This enabled him to characterize Critical Theory as pursuing the programme of a socio-historical critique of impure reason to which the analysis of how ideas of reason work in practice– that is, both positively and negatively – is central. As was the case in Kant, Hegel and the left-Hegelian tradition, reason is retained in a core position, but it is now embedded in concrete situations in the stream of socio-historical processes. Starting from Habermas's proposal to find socio-practical analogues to Kant's ideas of reason, McCarthy goes back to Kant's critical distinction between the double norm-setting and obfuscating potential of ideas of reason to follow the line of development from Hegel and Marx's abortive attempts to reconcile reason and reality, through Horkheimer's unsatisfactory effort to resolve the consequent problems, to Habermas's reconstitution of reason in the medium of communication. To the extent that ideas of reason are sufficiently detranscendentalized or pragmatized, they are transformed into the pragmatic presuppositions of communication, with the consequence that the Kantian distinction between the ideal and the real is relocated within the historically specific socio-cultural world. Socio-practical ideas of reason are pragmatically unavoidable idealizing suppositions which, one the one hand, are actually effective in organizing social practices and social life and simultaneously, on the other, are counterfactual in that they point beyond actual situations. They are thus characterized by a constitutive and regulative duality. It is on this basis that McCarthy was able to state the concept of immanent transcendence unequivocally: 'socio-practical ideas of reason are both "immanent" and "transcendent" to practices constitutive of forms of life' (1994a: 38). He also acknowledged that in everyday practices there is a mismatch at the juncture between the immanent and the transcendent, which attests to the factual force of counterfactual presuppositions. This gap or tension is typically manifested in real problems actually experienced in concrete situations, whether of a psychological, cultural or social-structural kind, which require reflective engagement, critical participation and on-the-spot actions to resolve. Contrary to traditional exaggerated claims regarding ideas of reason and the realization of their potential, however, confronting and dealing with this dialectic of the ideal and the real demands an orientation towards ongoing activity.

Honneth

If McCarthy was responsible for signalling the significance of the concept of immanent transcendence for Critical Theory, Honneth is the author who, explicitly using the term, first highlighted the concept as the key defining feature of contemporary Critical Theory: 'I see the key to updating Critical Theory in the task of categorically disclosing social reality in such a manner that an element of immanent transcendence will again become visible' (2007b: 66). This quotation comes from his professorial inaugural address at the Free University of Berlin in 1993, 'The social dynamics of disrespect: on the location of Critical Theory today'.[1] The lecture contains a significant reference to McCarthy that suggests that his work may have served as a trigger in directing Honneth's attention to the centrality of the concept.[2] In his debate with Nancy Fraser regarding the relation between recognition and redistribution, which was published in 2003, prompted by her reference to 'a dialectic of immanence and transcendence', he once again reinforced the view that immanent transcendence is not just central to contemporary Critical Theory, but indeed its defining concept.

For Honneth, immanent transcendence is the authentic core and identifying feature of Critical Theory as heir to the left-Hegelian tradition. It distinguishes Critical Theory from all other currents and directions of critique by specifying the basic conceptual and methodological requirements Critical Theory has to fulfil and, therefore, also the particular form of normative critique characterizing it. In Critical Theory, transcendence is not simply understood in terms of unfulfilled and in that sense transcending ideals or goals which are still present in actual social situations. To successfully and justifiably adopt a theoretically informed, normative perspective, making a diagnosis, explanation and critique of a social anomaly, disorder or pathology possible, Critical Theory must comply with a stringent condition. It must be able to identify a pre-theoretical foothold for that perspective in reality and thus to root its theoretical and critical endeavour in a moment or movement of immanent transcendence transpiring in social life or the actual situation itself. Such an instance could be marked by any one or a combination of a variety of conceivable manifestations of the emergence or assertion of an emancipatory interest in society – including an element of experience or a practice, unease, malaise, resistance, a new form of subject formation, the making of a public issue, the formation of a collective actor, a social movement, protest action and so forth. In criticism of Fraser's more empiricist approach, however, Honneth insists that in keeping with the left-Hegelian tradition such empirical manifestations by themselves are not sufficient. Rather, they should be seen as pointing to a deeper-seated dimension of social reality which allows what he calls 'a quasi-transcendental justification of critique' (2003: 245; 2009a: 150). It is at this level, strictly speaking, that immanent transcendence is located. Historically, the problem of the emergence of movement in social reality that points beyond its limits has been differently theorized. Marx and Lukács assumed that labour is the vehicle of immanent transcendence, but in the wake of the dissolution of the productivist paradigm critical theorists resorted to other theoretical alternatives. Marcuse came to regard the human drives as the always present and all-pervasive impetus which time and time again presses towards transcending the limits of the social order; Adorno for his part stressed art; and Habermas singled out the movement of linguistic intersubjectivity instead. Honneth's own unique contribution, which is presented against this background, particularly in criticism of Habermas, is an alternative theoretical interpretation of the communication paradigm that seeks to locate the normative presuppositions of social relations in the anthropologically rooted structural conditions of social recognition rather than in linguistic conditions. In his view, Habermas's focus on communicative rationalization or the social process through which the linguistic rules of communicative understanding are developed takes place at such a high level that the moral experience necessary to tie it down immanently in actual social situations is lost sight of. To do justice to immanence, therefore, it is imperative to accommodate the violation of identity claims or claims to social recognition and the feelings of social disrespect and injustice accompanying it over and above the authoritarian, ideological, distorting or obfuscating restriction of intuitively mastered linguistic rules and competences. For Honneth, it is anthropologically based moral experiences such as these, which are given rise to by structural forms of violence and disrespect, that provide the immanent reference point or pre-theoretical anchor for Critical Theory's normatively guided and theoretically informed diagnosis, explanation and critique of social states of affairs.

Systematic presentation of the concept

Against the background provided in the previous section, it is now possible to develop a more systematic analysis and presentation of the key concept of immanent transcendence. This is necessary in order to prepare for the explication of the methodology of Critical Theory put forward in the following chapters.

Basic distinctions

To arrive at the concept of immanent transcendence relevant to the left-Hegelian tradition in general and contemporary Critical Theory in particular, it is necessary to recognize that the transcendent ideas present in all human forms of life are not absolutely transcendent, but point towards a state beyond the present which could be realized, with the result that the actual situation is transformed in some crucial respect. God's point of view or the perspective from eternity must be given up or detranscendentalized, as Habermas submitted, by replacing the distinction between the world and what is beyond the world with the lower-level distinction between the world and practices and processes that are situated and take place within the world. McCarthy reinforced this by advocating the pragmatization of ideas of reason to such a degree that they are transformed into the pragmatic presuppositions of communication and action, which allows that the traditional distinction between the ideal and the real is relocated within the historically specific socio-cultural world.[3]

However, there is also a further, more specific distinction which has been central to left-Hegelianism from the outset and is necessary if room is to be made for a characteristic feature of the world. It is the inherent relation of problematic matching, tension or contradiction pervading the world. The world as such embraces both a real and an idealized dimension, both pragmatically necessary presuppositions such as the pre-understanding of the rules to follow in conduct and the projected idealization of such rules as situation-transcendent ideas to be realized. Accordingly, inner-worldly practices and processes can be regarded as proceeding from the normative bedrock of pragmatic presuppositions, on the one hand, and as being given direction and guidance by transcendent ideas of reason, on the other. Here Apel speaks of a genuine dialectical contradiction between the real and the ideal communication community which has to be resolved through practice, and Habermas of the tension generated by the factual force of counter-factual presuppositions which those involved have to work through themselves, whereas the pragmatists correspondingly focus on problem situations which call for intelligent and creative problem solving. Against this foil, McCarthy identifies a gap between the ideal and the real, which is typically manifested in real problems actually experienced in concrete situations that require reflective engagement, critical participation and action to resolve, whereas Honneth focuses on social pathologies of various kinds which it is the task of Critical Theory to diagnose, explain and critique in a practically relevant manner. The feature of the world at issue here turns on the recognition of the role of reason in human social forms of life rather than its rejection, as in the case of late twentieth-century intellectual tendencies inspired by Nietzsche. The advance in the appreciation of how reason enters social life introduced by Critical Theory and pragmatism since the 1960s takes the form of the embedding of reason in the medium of communication and, more fundamentally, the sign-mediated organization of the latter. On the one hand, it plays a constitutive role in so far as pragmatic presuppositions make communication, action and practices possible and, on the other, as detranscendentalized ideas of reason taking the form of idealized pragmatic orientation complexes, it exercises a regulative function in respect of social life.

The distinctions reviewed above – that is, first, between the world and inner-worldly practices and processes and, second, within the world between pragmatic presuppositions and idealized pragmatic forms standing in a tension-laden relation to one another – lay down the outer parameters of the concept of immanent transcendence. This much can be deduced from Habermas's work. The concept in this sense provides, as Apel's analysis of the metadimensional dialectical figure of mediation earlier already suggested, the basic framework of Critical Theory. It is from this configuration of relations that McCarthy draws the conclusion that Critical Theory is best conceived as the programme for the socio-historical analysis and critique of impure reason which focuses on how ideas of reason work, both positively and negatively in practice. As the diagram (Figure 4.1) illustrates, however, there are many more details which need to be filled in within this parametric framework for a fuller understanding of immanent transcendence and, hence, of Critical Theory.

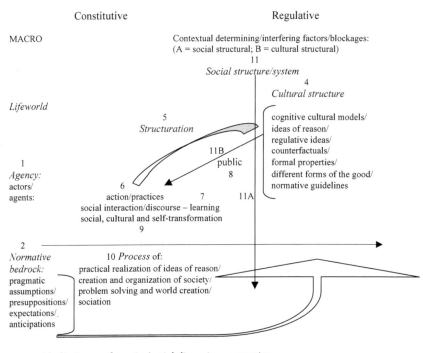

Figure 4.1 Immanent transcendence.

Key: (1) Agency proceeds from (2) a normative bedrock of immanent pragmatic presuppositions that are (3) performatively and/or through social construction idealized into (4) transcendent counterfactual cultural models. These models exert (5) a regulative structuring effect on (6) action and practices taking place through social interaction and/or discourse that carry (7) learning processes in which (8) the observing public plays a significant role. The learning processes make possible (9) social, cultural and self-transformation necessary for (10) the process of the practical realization of counterfactual models at the core of the constitution and organization of society. This process of the interrelation of the immanent and the transcendent is distorted and blocked by (11) determining or interfering forces, factors or mechanisms of (11a) a social-structural and (11b) a cultural-structural kind, which need critical theoretical explanation and critique.

Before considering these details, however, another qualification must be taken into account. It is a crucial one to which Honneth emphatically drew attention. The core idea of the left-Hegelian tradition is indeed that there is a historically accumulated potential which reflection makes or could make apparent so that it could be realized through practice, as Dews submitted (2000), and Critical Theory indeed focuses centrally on the dialectic of immanence and transcendence, as Fraser (2003) put it. Honneth is correct, however, when he insists that in Critical Theory transcendence is not simply understood in terms of unfulfilled and in that sense transcendent ideals or goals which are still present in actual social situations. Over and above empirical manifestations, immanent transcendence is regarded as being located at a deeper dimension of social reality. None of the major representatives of the left-Hegelian tradition and, more specifically, of Critical Theory therefore ever allowed their focus to be exhausted by purely empirical phenomena.[4] Without exception, the left-Hegelians and critical theorists understood empirical phenomena theoretically, even if their theoretical perspectives differed more or less sharply. For instance, Marx and various of his followers emphasized labour, Marcuse the human drives, Habermas language, and Honneth himself the anthropologically rooted moral-psychological need for recognition. Honneth's crucial point is that for Critical Theory immanent transcendence must be understood theoretically in a way that anchors the theoretical perspective in social reality.

Situation-constitutive axes

In Figure 4.1, it is assumed that the most basic distinction between the world and inner-worldly practices and processes provides the outermost parameters of the socio-historical situation representing the object of Critical Theory. The world or socio-historical situation itself is conceptualized in terms of three axes. For Critical Theory, the decisive axis concerns the normative quality of the situation that is captured by the concept of immanent transcendence. This axis rests on the distinction between immanent pragmatic presuppositions underpinning orientations, action and practices, on the one hand, and their idealized, performative, social-discursive construction into counterfactual ideas of reason in the pragmatic form of cultural or socio-cultural models, on the other. The second is the 'agency-structure' (Giddens 1984) or 'lifeworld-system' (Habermas 1984/87) axis constituting the world as a dynamic, structured, action situation which allows scope both for simultaneously enabling and constraining structures and for individual or agential autonomy. The final axis covers the scope and depth levels of the situation, which stretches from the micro via the meso to the macro dimension. The fact that the agency-structure axis is only one among a number of axes and, even more decisively, the fact that priority is given to immanent transcendence indicate that Morrow and Brown's (1994) identification of the defining feature of Critical Theory for the purposes of clarifying its methodology is not entirely plausible. It is not agency-structure that represents Critical Theory's key concept, as he claims, but rather immanent transcendence. As regards the micro–macro relation, it is conceived not along the lines of the well-known figure of 'Coleman's boat' (Coleman 1990) but, as will become clear below, rather in terms of communication theory: certain properties of actors or agents at the micro level which get inserted into the publicly accessible social domain are socially or discursively constructed, through the mediation of communication – that is, interaction and discourse, including the evaluation and judgement of the public – at the meso and especially the macro levels as socially significant social and/or cultural phenomena which, in turn, exert a structuring effect on orientations, actions and practices at the lower levels (Eder 1993; Strydom 2000).

In the case of the decisive immanence–transcendence axis, the assumption is made that the pragmatic presuppositions or expectations carrying orientations, actions and practices become idealized and even institutionalized in the form of cultural or socio-cultural models possessing more or less significant normative import. Such establishment of transcendent pragmatic forms is achieved through social or discursive construction involving fantasy, reflexivity, distantiation and generalization or universalization. The resulting normatively potent ideas of reason allow the anticipation of the generative regulation and continuation or redirection of the process produced by the actions and practices and of the realization to some degree of the normative import guiding it.

Status and authority of regulative ideas

In the context of the renaissance of pragmatism, to which the question of the relation between pragmatism and Critical Theory is central, a dispute about the ontological status of transcendent ideas of reason has arisen, focused on the need for their regulative function. Apel gave pride of place to regulative ideas in his recuperation of Peirce and the development of his concept of the a priori of the communication community. In 1970, for instance, he submitted regarding the most basic regulative principle:

> If one considers that the real communication community that is presupposed . . . in the finite situation never corresponds to the ideal of the unlimited community of interpretation, but rather, is subject to the restrictions of consciousness and interest that are manifested by the human species in its various nations, classes, language-games and life-forms, then from this *contrast between the ideal and the reality of the interpreting community*, there arises the regulative principle of *practical* progress, with which the progress of interpretation could, and ought, to be entwined

– practical progress being 'progress towards realizing that ideal communication community which we must anticipate counterfactually in all attempts at communicative understanding' (1980: 123–4). In his theory of truth of the 1970s, Habermas (1984) initially followed him in this, but this called forth Wellmer's (1986, 1998) repeated criticism of both his and Apel's not entirely justifiable talk of anticipating the realization of the ideal in the real communication community. Under the pressure not only of Wellmer but also of pragmatists such as Bernstein,

Rorty and McCarthy, Habermas (2003) subsequently qualified his position by introducing a degree of 'detranscendentalization' of ideas of reason. Although he recognized that Habermas meant something different by detranscendentalization from Rorty, Apel (2003) nevertheless registered his disagreement with the philosophical implications of this step. From a social scientific perspective, on the other hand, McCarthy (1994a) applauded Habermas's weakening of the transcendental status of Kant's ideas of reason up to the point where they became recast as 'desublimated pragmatic forms' (Habermas 2003: 83). Simultaneously, however, he acknowledged the importance of the regulative role such pragmatic forms or socio-practical ideas play in social life. Bohman likewise gave legitimacy to the regulative function when he underlined the need to consider seriously what reasons – what he called 'reflexive rules' or 'non-local regulative ideas' (1991: 99) – are and the explanatory role they play. Wellmer, who continued his criticism of his fellow critical theorists Apel and Habermas, sharpened his polemic against the former in particular with a piece bearing the revealing subtitle of 'Pragmatism without regulative ideas' (2003) in which he opposes a 'performative' against a transcendental position. In the international discussion of Apel's work around the time of his eightieth birthday in 2002, various authors including for instance Audun Øfsti (2003) and Horst Gronke (2003) came to his defence and showed that the difference between Wellmer and Apel may not be as big as it seems at first sight. Most recently, the American author Eugene Halton (2005)[5] questioned whether Apel's re-introduction of the transcendental is not a regression in the light of what he regards as Peirce's rejection of Kant's transcendental philosophy. On the other hand, Halton also criticized Rorty for developing a Heideggerian–Wittgensteinian position, the leading ideas of which are at odds with pragmatism. For his part, Apel regards any version of the renaissance of pragmatism that jettisons the normative moment represented by regulative ideas as a lack of appreciation for one of Peirce's greatest achievements.

It is apparent that a considered conclusion from the debate regarding the status of ideas of reason as regulative principles in Critical Theory can be reached only by negotiating a relationship between the transcendental and performative extremes. This leads to something like Habermas's desublimated pragmatic forms or McCarthy's socio-practical ideas. Social scientifically, these can be treated as socially significant cultural models (Strydom 2000, 2002) which, in turn, can be analysed in terms of cognitive social theory (Strydom 2006b, 2007).[6] In this respect, it is interesting that Bohman should write: 'Second-order . . . reflexive rules . . . are neither conventional nor interpretive but part of the cognitive ability to judge and assess reasons publicly' (1991: 99). Besides ontological status, the question of the authority of transcendent ideas also arises. Whereas the authority of certain basic regulative principles such as truth and justice is philosophically argued to be unconditioned,[7] social-scientifically it has to be related to moral, ethical, legal and political forces in society in order to do justice to the relation between the immanent and the transcendent. Seyla Benhabib is correct, then, when she leads the authority of transcendent ideas such as cosmopolitan norms back to 'the power of democratic forces within global civil society' (2008: 71).

Tension-laden process of practical realization

Far from a seamless or harmonious one, the relation between immanent pragmatic presuppositions and transcendent counterfactual ideas is a tension-laden
(Habermas 1992) and dialectically contradictory (Apel 1980) one. There is a gap
(McCarthy 1994a) between the two which needs to be overcome or at least mitigated. Transcendent ideas exert a structuring pressure on immanently operative
presuppositions, orientations, actions and practices. Their counterfactual pressure
in the form of a demand for increased reflexivity and a heightened threshold
of justification is experienced as a factual force towards opening up, learning
and transformation in the concrete situation. This tension or contradiction can
be resolved in the actual social situation only through action and practices of
various kinds, depending on circumstances including social interaction, practical discourse, problem solving and transformative collective action, which in the
best-case scenario serve as the vehicle of collective learning. In response to the
'concretization imperative' represented by the relevant idea of reason, such activities are required to follow their own 'transformation imperative' by de-idealizing
the counterfactual demand (Gronke 2003), 'opening' up and broadening out to
receive it, and finally 'closing' again to consolidate immanently the adoption and
realization of the situationally appropriate sense of the idea of reason (Øfsti 2003).

The interrelation of immanent presuppositions and transcendent ideas of
reason and the resolution of the tension or contradiction between them through
action and practices can be conceived as a process of the practical realization
of the potential of ideas of reason. It proceeds by way of both problem solving
and world creation, which are necessary for the constitution and organization of
society. A central thread of this process is occupied by collective learning (Miller
1986, 2002; Strydom 1987, 2008, 2009a; Eder 1999) in the sense of a network of
competing and conflicting immanent and transcendent ideas which, on the one
hand, brings individuals to learn through self-contradiction, to adjust their views
and to develop cooperative relations and, on the other, gives rise to a collectively
achieved outcome in the form of a shared framework. Particularly the former
aspect – self-cultivation, self-transformation or subject formation – requires more
systematic attention in Critical Theory, which has tended to underplay it in favour
of the latter aspect, collective outcomes.

Against the background of historical contributions such as those of
Kierkegaard, James, Mead and Piaget, Habermas's concern with individuation
or reflexive character formation, including in particular the development of
autonomy and moral consciousness, is of vital importance. It secures the normative in the sense of an orientation in terms of rational norms or being affected by
reasons in distinction to the conventional sense of Wittgensteinian rule following
or mainstream sociological socialization-cum-internalization in the sense of an
orientation in terms of practical norms or being obligated by prevailing norms.
Although the transcendent moment is observed, it is at the same time immanently
relevant. It means that the normatively inspired empirical reference point is less
individual strategic action or preference aggregation (liberalism) or group ethos or

ethical self-determination (republicanism) than the process of opinion- and will-formation geared towards problem solving and world creation (deliberationism). As Honneth (1992) has demonstrated, however, the Habermasian perspective has its limits, especially when it comes to subject formation involving the attainment of a sense of self-confidence, self-respect and self-worth. However important, and it doubtless is, the emphasis on ethical autonomy within a framework of the asking for and giving of reasons in public communication effectively excludes the problematic of recognition. Honneth's refocusing of Critical Theory on recognition, therefore, is an important step towards correcting the neglect of subject formation, yet it is by no means sufficient. Today, in a period of drastic societal transformation, one of the most serious problems, as Touraine (2000) for one has suggested, is that of an appropriate subject for the emerging world society. It could safely be ventured that this dire need for an appropriate subject will not be fulfilled by processes of socialization, which Honneth's proposal assumes to be central. More important still will be processes of self-cultivation and self-transformation – something to which Critical Theory pays little attention.

Communicative mediation

However, let us return to the question of immanent transcendence. Rather than a dual relation, therefore, the interrelation of immanent presuppositions and transcendent ideas of reason and the resolution of the tension or contradiction between them implicate something making such mediation possible. Reason is embedded and fluidized in communication, which represents the medium in which the distinction between immanent pragmatic presuppositions and their transcendent counterfactual counterparts are maintained in reality and brought into relation with one another. The process of the practical realization of the potential of ideas of reason and, therefore, the process of collective learning at its core, including both its micro and macro effects, also take place, indeed are possible only in this very medium. It is because of the significance of communication and, moreover, its structure reflected in the system of personal pronouns that the role of the public or anonymous audience in the mediation of the immanent and the transcendent has to be incorporated in a way not reflected in Critical Theory.

Both Critical Theory and pragmatism stress that it is necessary for the critique or knowledge they produce to be publicly tested or verified, yet the implied communicative framework making it possible is never adequately clarified. The focus is largely confined to the first-person/second-person perspectives embodied by the active or directly involved participants in a situation constituted by a social problem or public controversy, while the indispensable role of the third person perspective in the communication process is neglected. This is the case even in Habermas, the leading theorist of the public sphere, and Bohman, a follower of Dewey. The public or anonymous audience embodying the third-person perspective is indispensable to public communication as a process of cognitive-epistemic structure formation. Over and above those actively involved in the actual situation, the public is necessary for the establishment of the epistemic authority of the emerging rules or structures. It represents the party to whom the participants appeal for support in dealing with each other and who, in turn, observes and monitors the participants by evaluating, judging and commenting on their communication and behaviour, thus exerting a significant influence on the definition of reality and the related decision making that emerges from the joint communicative process. As regards the mediation of the immanent and the transcendent, the public represents a level of contingency – 'triple contingency' (Strydom 1999, 2001, 2009a) – over and above the traditionally recognized 'double contingency' holding between alter and ego (Parsons 1977; Luhmann 1995; Habermas 1996) and, as such, is a central factor in rendering immanent the transcendent, making factual the counterfactual or situationally ethicizing the moral.

Theoretical sense of the concept

Having submitted the above regarding the dialectic of immanence and transcendence, it is now necessary to shift to the implied characteristic theoretical concern of Critical Theory. As was clear especially with reference to Honneth, immanent transcendence in the context of Critical Theory does not simply refer to the availability in the actual situation of as yet unfulfilled transcendent ideas which, if realized, would transform the situation more or less drastically. Critical Theory is not able to content itself with discovering an empirical reference point in social reality that is then deemed to provide it with an immanent anchor point and hence justification for its theoretical perspective. It cannot simply appeal to unfulfilled normative claims in the present as concrete evidence for the necessity and justifiability of critique. The relation between immanence and transcendence must be understood in terms of a deeper dimension of social reality. This demand attached to the comprehensive understanding of immanent transcendence, it should be noted in parenthesis, is in line with the differentiated sign-mediated epistemology characteristic of the left-Hegelian tradition – something to which Honneth does not pay attention. The deeper dimension of reality would be an abiding form of human engagement, experience, interests or practices which simultaneously makes social reproduction possible and points beyond all forms of social organization so that it time and time again, not just here and now in the present, gives rise to situation-transcending claims. A related methodologically significant point, stressed by Honneth, is that the very instance which in principle secures the possibility of transcending the actual situation must at the same time also allow the explanation of how normatively meaningful changes and transformations have come about historically in past forms of social organization.

As we have seen, Honneth singles out labour in Marx's case, the human drives in Marcuse's, and language or linguistic communication in Habermas's as the theoretical perspectives from which critical theorists interpreted immanent transcendence and, therefore, identified the required immanent vehicle of possible transcendence. Honneth's own unique theoretical proposal is to make the anthropologically rooted moral-psychological need for recognition central in order to recover the immanent-transcendence problematic required for the revitalization of Critical Theory under contemporary conditions. It is possible, of course, to argue that today the theoretical interpretation of immanent transcendence can be taken yet a step further. In developing his own position, Honneth (2007b; Cooke 2006) acknowledges the continued relevance of the communication paradigm, but against that background sets his own concept of recognition off against Habermas's concept of linguistic communication. However, if the communication paradigm is retained as Honneth proposes, then it is possible to find a new more general theoretical position that goes beyond both Habermas and Honneth by allowing the mediation rather than opposition of language and recognition. This option is made available by the cognitive approach (e.g. Strydom 2000, 2002, 2006b, 2007), which emphasizes mediating dynamic cognitive structures of different levels and scope, including both the micro and macro levels as well as covering both recognition and language. The distinction between the world and inner-worldly practices on which Figure 4.1 is based corresponds in fact to what is regarded as the most basic cognitive phenomenon: that something belonging to the world is nevertheless able to develop a perspective on the world. What is not explicitly depicted in Figure 4.1, further, is the medium in which the process of the mediation of immanence and transcendence takes place, but perhaps the white background of the diagram could be interpreted as such. This medium is represented by communication, which, for Habermas, is manifest as the emancipatory social process of communicative rationalization and, for Honneth, as the moral experiences correlating with it yet overlooked by Habermas. Presupposed by both these conceptions, however, is the process of the formation of cognitive structures, from schemata in the head through organizational models to cultural models or repertoires, and the generative regulative effects these dynamic complexes exert at different levels. Judging from their writings touching on the cognitive, however, this approach is not particularly well dealt with by either Habermas (e.g. 1984/87) or Honneth (e.g. 2007b). In fact, it is possible to demonstrate that, in certain respects, both of them misjudge the nature and relevance of this approach, indeed Honneth more so than Habermas.

Interferences, distortions and blockages

The relation of immanent presuppositions and transcendent ideas becomes palpable and the facing of the tension or contradiction between them is experienced as urgent under particular conditions. Such conditions are given rise to by forces or factors that intervene or interfere in the practical realization of the normative import of cultural models and thus distort or block the process in some way. The challenges, risks and threats which such distortions and blockages present can eventuate in problems or even crises. Despite their overwhelmingly negative character, as both pragmatists and critical theorists have shown, they can also have the positive effect of revealing the structures of reality and thus making possible the development of knowledge about reality. As regards the forces, factors or mechanisms in point, Apel's earlier reference to 'restrictions of consciousness and interest' suggests that they can be of a psychological, social, economic, political or cultural kind. Correspondingly, the distortions or blockages can vary from repressive through ideological and authoritarian to regressive types (Eder 2007; Miller 1986, 2002; McCarthy 1994a; Habermas 1984/87). Repression limits the expression of subjectivity and regression fractures comprehensibility and mutual understanding by distorting communication, whereas ideology limits legality, plurality or publicity by distorting the normative import of cultural models and authoritarianism disallows free information and hence objectivity (Strydom 2009a). In so far as Critical Theory's programme is 'a continuation of the social detranscendentalization of reason' (Honneth 2003: 240) or the 'practically significant, sociohistorical critique of impure reason' (McCarthy 1994a: 8), its task is to explain in terms of real generative mechanisms, typically in the form of social or cultural structures, the interferences in and distortion or blockages of processes of the immanent realization of transcendent ideas of reason and, on that basis, to offer a practically significant critique. Chapter 6 is devoted to a systematic presentation of Critical Theory's methodology, and substantive examples of such critical theoretical explanations and critiques with reference to, for instance, economic, political and cultural mechanisms are presented in detail in the final chapter.

Conclusion

The aim of this chapter was to clarify the status and significance of immanent transcendence as the key concept of contemporary Critical Theory. In the first instance, the concept represents the basic metatheoretical or conceptual requirement with which Critical Theory as a continuation of the left-Hegelian heritage has to comply. It represents the demand that a moment of immanently embodied reason which harbours a surplus of situation-transcendent norms must be identified to serve as the basic anchorage of critical theoretical analysis. This metatheoretical attitude is suggestive of Critical Theory's ontology or orientation to social reality, namely as a process of transformation focalized by the tension-laden interface between the constitution and organization or production and reproduction of society. Closely related to the left-Hegelian constraint, second, the concept encapsulates Critical Theory's defining feature, namely its normative or moral-ethical concern and, hence, its claim to be an essentially critical enterprise. Third, the concept provides the abiding reference point for the theoretical articulation of Critical Theory or, as the succession of basic theoretical concepts from labour through human drives and language to recognition suggests, the theoretical development of different versions of the critical theory of society. In the fourth place, the concept lays down a framework for a multilevel methodology beyond both empiricism and interpretativism which is the principle theme of the subsequent chapters. Finally, the structure of the concept of immanent transcendence corresponds to the three-place sign-mediated epistemology which Peirce and Marx shared in the post-Hegelian period and which Apel and Habermas rehabilitated and vigorously defended. As the key, then, the concept links all the major aspects of Critical Theory – from the ontological and theoretical, through the epistemological and methodological, to the normative dimension.

Part II
Methodology

Critical social scientific knowledge is dependent on a process of development which embraces not only established knowledge, but also morally justifiable practice.

Kari Otto Apel

5   Contemporary critical theorists on methodology

Introduction

The preceding chapters contain the suggestion that the transition from the second to the third generation of critical theorists harbours the possibility of compensating for a weakness from which Critical Theory has been suffering for years. It is the problem of an underspecified and underdeveloped methodological framework, which itself, moreover, is symptomatic of an inadequate connection with social reality. In Part I, it was argued that the establishment of the concept of immanent transcendence, marking as it does the transition in question and thus being characteristic of the new phase in the development of Critical Theory, provides a starting point for corrective action. This key concept represents a rich metatheoretical framework for the elaboration of an adequately specified and transparent methodology that could heighten Critical Theory's relevance and appeal in the substantive social research context, where it is at present under pressure from its competitors and perhaps even outdone in certain respects.

In the light of this promise, the present chapter offers a critical assessment of the methodological positions put forward by contemporary critical theorists from both the Continental Critical Theory and the American pragmatist sides. Of the third generation, Honneth, McCarthy and Bohman are selected since they have submitted the most explicit statements available. Considering that they have Habermas's later methodological writings behind them, the presentation of their positions is preceded by a brief overview of his contribution. A younger author lately associated with the Frankfurt Institute for Social Research, Robin Celikates, is also included on the basis of a recent extensive treatment of the methodology of Critical Theory. He takes important cues from, as well as arguing in certain respects against, another younger author from Frankfurt, Mattias Iser, to whom reference will also be made. For the purposes of assessment, the level of elaboration of methodology is obviously relevant, but of greater importance is the degree to which the methodology is understood as corresponding to the concept of immanent transcendence as well as to the underlying *medium quo* epistemology and its implications.

Habermas: critical-reconstructive social science

By contrast with critical realists who reject all other social scientific approaches but realism in favour of a new version of the old 'essential unity of method between the natural and the social sciences' (Bhaskar 1989: 2, see also 18; see also Danermark et al. 2002), Jürgen Habermas takes the position that: 'Critical social science does not relate to established lines of research as a competitor; . . . it attempts to explain the specific limitations and relative rights of those approaches' (1984/87, II: 375). While recognizing interpretative and nomological approaches, despite their inherent limitations, as having a role in the social sciences, he focuses on his own critical-reconstructive social science (1984/87, II: 397–403; 1990: 21–42), which has both an interpretative-reconstructive and an explanatory component. As against interpretative social science, he stresses the scientific character of Critical Theory, including the desirability of a theoretical approach able to produce objective and explanatory knowledge that can be employed for critical purposes. As against nomological social science, he understands theoretical knowledge to take a realist rather than an empiricist form and thus to make possible reconstructive and socio-historical kinds of explanation which diverge appreciably from the established deductive-nomological, hypothetico-deductive or inductive-probabilistic accounts. This methodological position is ontologically and epistemologically informed respectively by what he in his late work called a 'weak' (2003: 33) or 'soft naturalism' (2005: 215) and a 'pragmatic epistemic realism' (2003: 7). The latter starts from the assumption of human engagement with the world through problems encountered as they arise from the objective context of life and disclose the relevant depth-dimension of reality, about which it is necessary to develop knowledge and a corresponding action plan. Although Habermas put forward the methodological model of his critical-reconstructive social science in the early 1980s, it seems that it had been guided implicitly by Peirce's *medium quo* epistemology, which he discussed in detail for the first time only a number of years later in 1989 in a conference paper published a few years later (1991a, 1992: 88–112). This appropriation was further reinforced ten years later when he outlined his own 'Kantian pragmatism' (2003: 30) in the context of taking up anew epistemology and ontology as problems in theoretical philosophy left in abeyance since the late 1960s. Since the original statement of the model was presented at a conference in 1980 where it was more important to distinguish reconstruction from interpretation, the critical dimension was indeed incorporated yet was not given the desired level of elaboration. The second volume of *The Theory of Communicative Action* made up for this to a certain degree. Until the introduction of Kantian pragmatism, however, his epistemic concept of truth stood in stark contradiction to the explanatory and critical demand for a non-epistemic reference to reality.

According to Habermas's methodological model, the critical theorist does not start by just choosing a theoretical attitude, but depends for an adequate relation to 'the *ratio essendi* of its object' on some movement or occasion arising in the objective context of life that opens up its '*ratio cognoscendi*' (1984/87, II: 401). Such an instance could take the form of a problem, a provocative threat or an objective challenge of some sort in the face of which some aspect of the unproblematically assumed 'background knowledge becomes uncertain' (1984/87, II: 400), creating a 'confusing experience' or a 'communicative disturbance' (1990: 29). In any event, it is a matter of a 'development of society [which] itself gives rise to a problem situation objectively affording contemporaries privileged access to the structures of the social world' (1984/87, II: 403).

In order to make sense of the uncertain, confusing or disturbing phenomenon in question, a 'clarification of the context' (1990: 30) is necessary. A description has to be developed of the shared knowledge and set of relations taken for granted by those involved as well as the public. A description of this kind is not sufficient, however, as it is necessary further to specify the reasons accounting for the phenomenon in question and without which the problematic situation would remain incomprehensible. Such specification requires that the reasons themselves be evaluated and explained. The satisfaction of this requirement demands recourse to a 'presumably universal standard of rationality' (1990: 31) or a situation-transcendent normative reference point. The latter is established through 'reconstruction' (1979: 8–20; 1990: 31) of the competent participant's pre-theoretical knowledge and intuitive mastery of such knowledge at the immanent level, leading to the identification of the relevant 'general and necessary conditions of validity' (1984/87, II: 399; 1990: 31) – whether, social-theoretically, concerning ontogenetically acquired competences or evolutionarily generated innovative structures of consciousness, or, communication-theoretically, the formal features or conditions and rules governing felicitous communication. Such reconstructions are statements that provide descriptions of particular 'rule systems' (1990: 31) or 'cultural forms' (2003: 18) which, as structures of reality, make possible the production and evaluation of orientations, actions, practices and their products. Such statements represent 'theoretical knowledge' (1990: 32, 39) forming part of a philosophical or reconstructive theory of real structures or generative mechanisms, which enables the explanation of a range of phenomena. Explanation requires that the reconstruction in the form of a 'normative theory' (1990: 37) be incorporated in an empirically relevant social theory through which it could be subjected to indirect testing (1984/87, II: 399; 1990: 32, 39). For example, by investigating how situation-transcendent normative structures immanently work in the concrete situation, 'empirical theories' (1990: 32, 39) can explain how certain competences are acquired in the socialization process, how innovative structures of consciousness emerge evolutionarily and become institutionalized or how collectively valid or legitimate communicative outcomes become accepted. Alternatively, they could disprove the applicability of the normative theory, which would then have to be reconsidered and the original reconstruction revised.

The theoretical knowledge established by way of reconstruction, however, can also be employed for another more specific explanatory purpose: critique. Reconstruction facilitates the 'critical function' (1990: 32) by providing a theoretical foil in the form of conditions of validity or a normative reference point against which 'deviant cases' or 'systematic deviations' (1990: 32) such as distorted communication, ideologies, social pathologies and so forth can be shown up and explained. The exercise of critique, however, would require further the specification of a contingently intervening structure or mechanism that brings about or causes the deviance, deformation or deficiency. Here Habermas speaks of 'explain[ing] how this obscurity came about' (1990: 30–1). A substantive example would be a historically informed sociological explanation in terms of 'the systemic imperatives of autonomous subsystems [which] penetrate into the lifeworld . . . through monetarization and bureaucrarization' (1984/87, II: 403). In the light of Habermas's (2003: 30, 38) recent quite drastic revision of his theory of truth from a purely epistemic to an 'epistemic realist' one, or an epistemic one that stresses the necessity of incorporating a non-epistemic moment of something actually existing or of reality, it is clear that critique depends on a type of explanation that targets real spatio-temporally individuated objects, factors, forces, structures, mechanisms or processes – which, of course, does not obviate the need for general concepts or theories and discursive justification. Over and above such a critique, however, a reconstruction could also allow a turn in a 'constructive' (1990: 32) direction by establishing a new standard of understanding, evaluation or orientation and thus opening up a new possibility or perspective. Such a constructive contribution, finally, could advance 'participation in the "universal discourse"' (1990: 36) envisaged by Peirce and Mead in the sense of a better society than the one in which we are living today.

Although not having made a direct link himself, Habermas's late endorsement of Peirce's *medium quo* epistemology (1992: 89–112; 1996: 13–15) can without doubt be taken as being presupposed by his own account of Critical Theory's methodology. Regarding Peirce as among the first to have made the transition from the philosophy of consciousness to the philosophy of language, Habermas not only appreciates that the American philosopher's sign-mediated epistemology is central to his successful rethinking of representation in three-place semiotic instead of two-place mentalistic terms, but also accepts his analysis and ascription of significance to the tripartite nature of the sign and, more generally, of the cognitive process and the development of knowledge. On the one hand, Peirce's third dimension of mediating symbolic forms allows for general or universal concepts making sense only in the ongoing communicative process borne by the larger community of interpretation. On the other hand, the objective property of an actual object – that is, 'something independent of us and thus, in this sense, transcendent' (Habermas 1996: 14) – is maintained by the concrete anchorage of signs in an index linking with a natural sin-sign such as a causal nexus and in an icon relating to a quali-sign capturing a pre-existing quality or similarity. Although such anchorage becomes habitual and hence conventional in social life, Critical Theory not unlike pragmatism by contrast focuses on problem situations or new situations produced by a change of conditions, which call for an intelligent approach and innovative intervention. This is the place of the 'abductive inference' as 'the real knowledge-amplifying element' (1992: 100) which Habermas, like Peirce, sees as forging new linkages among the qualities, objective features and conceptual aspects of the situation on the basis of a lightning insight, a new world-disclosing perspective, an innovative modification of language or a creative hypothesis. The claim advanced on the basis of such a newly forged set of linkages is made sense of, tested for whether it is supported by conventional and natural signs rooted in the object in question, and possibly agreed on in a justificatory discursive process in the community of interpretation guided by the transcendent counterfactual standards of truth and of rightness. Crucially as far as the relation between theory and practice or the translation of critical theoretical knowledge into something practically significant and relevant is concerned, according to Habermas's understanding, this communication community is not confined to science, as Peirce tended to assume, but rather embraces, as Mead made clear, society here and now as well as potentially extending infinitely.

Honneth: critique of social pathologies of capitalist society

Axel Honneth has not stated his methodological position as such in either the same concise and coherent way or the relatively fine technical detail as Habermas did, but his writings are replete with sufficient substantive indications to get a relatively precise overview of it. In broad structural outline, it appears to be comparable to Habermas's, but there are of course marked differences between the two. In an essay devoted to an assessment of social philosophy past and present which was written just after he had consolidated his characteristic position in *The Struggle for Recognition* (1992), Honneth's (2007a) project of returning to and revitalizing social philosophy instead of following in Habermas's footstep by continuing to elaborate political philosophy is unmistakably visible. In another essay published in the same year dealing with the current situation of Critical Theory (2007b), he indicates in precise theoretical terms how his position centred on recognition differs from Habermas's emphasis on language and, by extension, the public sphere and political practical discourse. Whatever the difference between them, however, what is sure is that Honneth explicitly and emphatically places the concept of immanent transcendence at the centre of contemporary Critical Theory's methodology. Indeed, he regards the concept as indicative of the general 'methodological structure' (2003: 239) of Critical Theory as a left-Hegelian legacy which today requires recovery and re-assertion. Critical Theory's methodology has to be thought through and developed in keeping with the demand that a critical analysis of society guided by a reconstruction of normative principles must from beginning to end maintain a connection with 'an innerworldly instance of transcendence' (2003: 238). Having guided his thinking from the early 1990s, this understanding shaped all those methodologically significant statements and indications to be found in his writings since then which together can be regarded as making up his methodological position.[1] Since his assumption of the directorship of the Frankfurt Institute for Social Research, the more detailed aspects of this methodology have started to concern him in particular and, on occasion, he elaborates on methodology in a quite specific research-oriented manner, including reference to particular methods.

In an interview shortly after the turn of the century, for instance, Honneth goes on record as submitting repeatedly regarding Critical Theory that 'there is no need for our own methodological approach' and that all that is required in the pursuit of 'a clear hypothesis of certain social developments, preferably certain social pathologies', is 'a clever way of combing existing methods' (2002a: 268). In his view, the latter could for example include group discussions, structured interviews and qualitative methods such as biographical research and deep interviews incorporating sociological and psychoanalytical assumptions. This focus of his on the triangulation of particular methods can of course not be interpreted as meaning that methodology in the proper sense of the word – that is, the system, logic or theory of methods to which according to his understanding of contemporary Critical Theory the concept of immanent transcendence belongs – can simply be jettisoned. On the contrary, his work is much richer on the topic of methodology than on methods. An attempt at systematizing his various indications and proposals at this upper level yields a relatively clear methodological structure and also puts the more specific level of methods in its proper place. Such a pattern is readily to be found in an important essay of 2004 (Honneth 2004a). In fact, the three principal sections into which the piece is divided provide the key. Against the background of the Critical Theory tradition's concern with the pathological deformation of reason in the historical process of its actualization and realization, which in effect pinpoints the problem of immanent transcendence, the essay follows the more specific tripartite structure of Critical Theory.

The first of the three features responsible for Critical Theory's uniqueness that Honneth (2004a: 338–45) singles out concerns its normative focus. Inspired by Kantian ideas of reason that Hegel ethically transformed, Critical Theory proceeds on the basis of the idea of a concrete rational ethical universal which has become possible historically but is not realized in the present in social relations. Against this normative foil, it searches for social situations that are characterized by negative features constituting a social pathology and indicating a deficiency in social rationality. The motivation for this is the conviction that Critical Theory can provide a diagnostic analysis and critical explanation of what causes the lapse in the social realization of the historically available potential of reason, thus contributing to the alleviation of the situation. Instead of a lack of a guiding ethical universal, a form of common practices would become visible for those involved, according to which they could then orient themselves in the process of cooperative self-realization and the creation of a meaningful common world.

The second characteristic feature of Critical Theory (Honneth 2004a: 345–52) is its unique form of explanatory critique, which depends on a diagnostic analysis of the situation in question. Based on the blurring of the widely accepted positivistic distinction between description and prescription, it seeks to provide a critical explanation of whatever causes the deformation or blockage in the historical process of the realization of reason leading to the social pathology. It should possess such rational force that it enlightens and convinces those involved to transform their thinking and action and to engage in cooperative practices. This type of critique is distinct from a purely normative form of criticism that seeks to expose injustices, whether the liberal form depending on the construction of principles of justice against which violations are identified or the hermeneutic communitarian form depending on the socially accepted values of the given community. Not only does Critical Theory have recourse to the accumulated potential of historically produced values or normative ideas, but it pursues a causally or explanatory critique of a historical and sociological kind of the social str͏ or mechanisms which generate the state of social negativity. Such structure͏s ͏. mechanisms are assumed not only to cause the pathological social circumstances, but at the same time also to induce silence and apathy by disguising the very state of affairs which would otherwise provide urgent grounds for public disquiet, reaction and criticism. Since Marx, Weber and Lukács, critical theorists have always proceeded from the basic premise that capitalism is the root cause in so far as it is a social form of organization which is driven by a social imaginary giving priority to reifying forms of thinking, practices and institutions. However, Critical Theory also assumes that the very process of the realization of reason which has become blocked here is a historical learning process which takes its course mediated by conflicts over the monopolization of knowledge. The future surmounting of the detrimental causal force of the capitalist form of social organization depends on such learning.

The third and final characteristic feature that Honneth (2004a: 352–7) singles out and can be taken as shedding light on his understanding of the methodological structure of Critical Theory concerns the relation of theory and practice – or more precisely, if it is a matter of the primacy of practice over theory, the relation of theory and practice within practice. Wanting to contribute through its explanatory critique to overcoming the social pathology and accompanying suffering, Critical Theory relates reflexively to a potential transformative praxis. This requires reflection on the conditions of the conversion of knowledge into praxis, from the suitability of the explanation and the appropriate perspective for the conversion, through the capacities and readiness of the addressees, audience or public, to what Critical Theory shares with members of society and could serve as a bridge between them. Explanations and perspectives must be well founded and relevant, the real interests of subjects in rational, potentially liberating accounts of social reality must be identified, and beyond common objectives or political projects the only common bond between Critical Theory and its addressees is a space of potentially common reasons, a discursive practice that allows individual subjects to be responsive to better reasons.

That this three-point reconstruction of Critical Theory – or, rather, of its methodological structure, as it can be interpreted – is not just a scholarly exercise on the part of Honneth, but actually reflects how he understands his own methodological position, is apparent from his various descriptions and specifications. For him, Critical Theory's methodological starting point is marked by a suspicion that all is not well in capitalist society and its liberal democratic institutional arrangements: 'the suspicion of a social pathology of capitalist society as a whole' (1999: 249; see also 2007e: 226). This vague feeling that is given rise to by sign-bearers of suffering, such as groups struggling for recognition, directs a sensibility for paradoxical and damaging social developments, deformations, reifications and resulting problems at various levels of society (2002b, 2008, 2009b,c). Any of these could take the form of an actual 'social pathology' (2007a,f) that calls forth a reaction and thus could be identified and eventually be subjected to a thorough 'diagnosis', but to locate them requires a 'clear hypothesis' (2002a: 268). Rather than just a hypothesis in the usual empiricist sense of the term, however, the latter could be interpreted as representing an incisive abduction, a creative moment in the cognitive process, which brings together a theoretical insight and empirical indications with the qualitative feeling of something being wrong. Although not mentioning abduction, Honneth is quite clear about this. The initial feeling engendered by the phenomenon in question allows identification on the part of the critical theorist not simply with an already articulated suffering, but rather with pain that as yet escapes the available public vocabulary and that is imputed from the perspective of the violation of the generalizable interests of everyone informed by a theory of the development of society (2007e: 230). It is such an abductive forging of connections that first allows a pathway toward the identification of an actual social pathology and indicates the direction in which specific explanatory hypotheses could be sought. More concretely, the suspicion of a social pathology is firmed up by taking cues, on the one hand, from socio-cultural conflicts assuming the form of 'struggles for recognition' (1992) involving agents suffering from non-recognition or disrespect and its consequences and, on the other, from the theory of recognition guided by a formal concept of the good life and its reconstructed principles of recognition. This means that both the immanent – that is, the subjects' rational interest in recognition – and the transcendent – that is, the reconstructed normative motif of the good life – as well as the tension between them experienced by people in a concrete situation – that is, the particular struggle against disrespect and for recognition – are given a central position. This set of relations is moreover underpinned by the theory of the process of the formation and deformation as well as the potential winning of recognition.

Once the object of investigation has been constituted by the forging of these various relations, the scene is set, second, for the diagnosis of an actual social pathology. It is at the stage and within such a framework that a combination of a variety of research methods, from group discussions, through structured and in-depth interviews, to biographical research (2002a), is called for in order to describe, makes sense of and begin to fathom the actual situation and its formal structuring features. Depending on the actual case, the diagnosis could employ both psychoanalytical and sociological tools to clarify the different dimensions and features of the pathological phenomenon as well as of the suffering and the motivation to react against it. A diagnosis of this kind establishing the actuality of a social pathology makes available the basis for pursuing the 'explanatory intentions' (2003: 245), which Honneth regards as characteristic of the left-Hegelian tradition in general and Critical Theory in particular. Within the framework of the formal conditions securing adequate identity formation, on the one hand, and the identified social pathology, on the other, the search is now focused on the relevant social development generating the pathology in question. Led by explanatory intentions, it penetrates below the actual social pathology to the depth-structures of reality in search of the 'societal' or 'social-structural causes' (2000b: 101, 103) giving rise to it in the first place. For the relation of the social pathology to the structure of society to be clarified, these causes must be identified. Of particular interest to Honneth are causal mechanisms that systematically deform and damage the conditions of mutual recognition in the family, law and social labour and thus give rise to feelings of violation of legitimate assumptions and expectations of respect, which, through their assertion in social struggles, in turn come to play a role in the moral development of society.

The explanation of the real conditions of a social pathology makes possible the most characteristic, indeed the defining moment in Critical Theory's methodology: the critique of the relevant structural developments of society that systematically have a detrimental effect on intersubjective social relations and processes of identify formation. Honneth indeed insists that Critical Theory distinguishes itself from a purely normative analysis of the present precisely by basing its critique on the explanation of social-structural causes. However, in accordance with the different dimensions specified by the theory of recognition, he regards critique in his own version of Critical Theory as being exercised in three different formats. They are the critique of social pathologies, the critique of injustice and, finally, the critique of reification (2009b: 78–9). The critique of social pathologies manifested in such phenomena as the suffering of members of society from indeterminacy, insecurity, uncertainty, depression and so forth requires the reconstruction of a normative idea of an intact form of social practice for the identification, exposure and denunciation of its cause. Starting from phenomena such as a damaged self-relation preventing members of society from taking an active part in social and political life, the critique of injustice is, second, guided by the normative idea of social relations enabling everyone to appear in public without shame and focused on the identification, exposure and denunciation of conditions preventing people from becoming active participants. The third type, the recently introduced critique of reification, is Honneth's (2008) attempt, partially inspired by Adorno's concept of mimetic rationality, to find a contemporary equivalent for the early Frankfurt School's critique of instrumental reason and Habermas's critique of functionalist reason at the deeper anthropological level of the primordial mode of mutual perception and recognition. It targets the sociality-deforming or -denying 'forgetfulness' of the socially 'constitutive form of recognition of the other' (2009b: 80–1). Thus, it represents a critique of the one-sidedness of reason or of cognition and knowledge and, hence, more substantively of modernity, as involving the repression of the constitutive elements of sociality. Ultimately, however, all three these forms of critique depend on the criticizable phenomena in their focus being led back to global social developments, conditions or social practices – what, in a word, Honneth calls 'societal structures' (2009b: 69), which systematically deform, damage and thus cause social pathologies, injustices and reification.

Although Honneth himself holds that the explanation and critique of the real causal factors or mechanisms operative at this level is defining of Critical Theory, it is the case that his own social theoretical position, as he himself admits (2009d), does not cover this historical and sociological dimension of structures and mechanisms. Although he argues that Critical Theory suffers from a sociological deficit – Adorno and Horkheimer neglecting moral norms and actors' interpretative capacities and Habermas the action-based and conflictual nature of social order, including the economic – and that it could be overcome by making struggles for recognition central (2009a: 83–4), he is yet to demonstrate this latter claim. This lack of a substantive social theory is also the most significant criticism that his work attracted at the symposium on the theme of 'recognition and power' held at the University of Utrecht in 2003 (van den Brink and Owen 2007). The root of the problem is that his strict adherence to action theory and praxis philosophy (1985; see also Basaure 2011) leaves a gap in his social theory which prevents him from accounting for institutional and systemic phenomena and, hence, from engaging in the kind of explanation presupposed by critique.

As regards the practical significance of critique, third, Honneth (2002a: 269) identifies two different avenues. In the course of research, first, a moral vocabulary is used to encourage the recovery from repressed public language of the means to express and articulate moral experiences on the part of research subjects. In a society characterized by a tendency toward one-sided and false self-descriptions, reinforced by positivistic utilitarianism and technocracy, it is necessary to provide alternative critical descriptions that could bring out the submerged and unrecognized moral nuances of conflicts (Boltanski and Honneth 2009: 99). In the case of the trade unions, for instance, the reduction of conflict to wage demands conceals the moral quality of workers' needs. Second, more general audiences are addressed through the presentation of concrete social scientific research findings, for instance uncovering everyday struggles of recognition and their underlying patterns of disrespect. In both these cases, critique opens new possibilities that could be appropriated by research subjects and general audiences as reference points for the creation of new perspectives. In this respect, critique has a disclosing function. In a certain sense, it relates to the kind of 'disclosing critique' (2000a) he ascribes to Horkheimer and Adorno's *Dialectic of Enlightenment* (1969), a book designed to provide new positions or content which could enter and stimulate public discussion and debate. Critique involves an insistence on and a visionary articulation of the surplus of meaning and untapped normative potential of the principles of recognition, which are always incorporated in a deficient form in the institutional order (Boltanski and Honneth 2009: 99–100). Although Honneth decouples Critical Theory's critical role from direct political activism in the light of potential dangers such as instrumentalization and manipulation, he is adamant that critique, through its different formats, does seek to have practical significance in the form of 'consciousness-raising effects' or 'reflexive emancipation' (2002a: 269), which could be a factor in alleviating operative forms of disrespect in social life. In relation to his or her audience, the critical theorist adopts not the position of the classical party or movement intellectual exhibited by Lukács, for example, but instead the position of the social scientist addressing the scientific community and of the 'critical intellectual' (2009b: 64) addressing the democratic public as a whole in the knowledge that the measure of the validity of the proposals made is their acceptance by the discursively oriented public. The critical intellectual should be distinguished, however, from the 'normalized intellectual' (2007e) typical of our time. Rather than taking intellectual positions within the bounds of the political consensus on the political issues of the day and with an eye on the *Zeitgeist* in order to deliver quick persuasive arguments with a direct effect on opinions in the public sphere, the critical intellectual proceeds from a well-founded theory to problematize widely accepted models of practice, needs schemata and attitudinal syndromes with a view to contributing indirectly to a medium-term re-orientation and a learning process with long-term consequences.

Honneth's methodological position embracing three levels – a social pathology as object, diagnostic analysis involving reconstruction and eventuating in explanatory critique, and finally linking with addressees to convert knowledge into praxis – could be illuminated further by a brief consideration of the development of his view of Critical Theory's model of critique. The debate about critique and social criticism, or strong and weak critique, provided the stimulus for his expanding understanding of it. In 2000, stimulated by contributions of such authors as Rorty, Bohman and van den Brink, he considered the relevance of disclosing critique for Critical Theory. Judging from various statements (2002a, 2007e, 2009b) stretching over a number of years, there can be no doubt that he came to regard disclosure as an indispensable aspect of critique. In the same year, he presented a more comprehensive model. Reacting to Rorty and Walzer's characterization of strong, external, context-transcending critique from the viewpoint of weak, hermeneutic, contextual criticism as at best paternalistic and at worse despotic, Honneth (2007c) first showed that the left-Hegelian tradition has always sought to recover the criteria for critique from social life itself. Marx's demand that a well-founded ideology critique of capitalism must appeal to the normative ideals incarnated in social reality itself finds its equivalent in contemporary Critical Theory in the procedure of reconstruction. However, besides reconstruction, the Critical Theory model also has two more dimensions, namely constructivist and genealogical critique. The constructivist form, which predominates in liberalism, involves the construction of normative principles for the criticism of injustices in the institutional order on the basis of a generally agreed-on procedure. The genealogical form, which was lately highlighted by Foucault, had actually been made part of the Critical Theory model by Adorno and Horkheimer already in the early 1940s in the face of the National Socialist corruption of normative principles for their instrumental purposes. The three-dimensional Critical Theory model embracing reconstruction, construction and genealogy, presumably also incorporating disclosure, which Honneth presented here, obviously lacked the historical-sociological form of explanatory critique. It is in particular after the Utrecht conference of 2003, where it came to light that the principal weakness of his recognition-theoretical position could be addressed only by the development of an adequate social theory and theory of power, that he took corrective action. A major aim of the important article on the intellectual legacy of Critical Theory under the title of 'Eine soziale Pathologie der Vernunft' (2007d) was to characterize explanatory critique as the unique feature of Critical Theory. This argument was reinforced with the publication of the collection *Pathologien der Vernunft* in 2007, as the preface makes clear. The Critical Theory model of critique now started to assume its proper proportions. Recently he also insisted that he proceeds from the assumption of 'the structural priority of the capitalist commodification imperative' (2009a: 84). The assertion of this priority and therefore the centrality of explanatory critique, of course, does not yet fill the theoretical gap.

Finally, that Honneth's understanding of Critical Theory's methodology, over and above the concept of immanent transcendence and the multidimensional model of critique, may well be implicitly structured by the three-place sign-mediated theory of knowledge presupposed by left-Hegelianism since at least Marx and Peirce, is suggested by his robust response to Fraser's allegation that he is epistemologically caught in the trap of the 'myth of the given'. Not only does Honneth (2003: 245) emphatically reject the implication that he represents an 'unmediated' mentalist position, but he also continues to offer an account that unmistakably exhibits the assumption of a mediated or *medium quo* epistemology. On the one hand, he objects to the allegation that he remains in empiricist or positivist fashion fixated on 'the given' and hankers after an absolute starting point. On the other, he sets in dynamic relation three moments corresponding to Peirce's firstness, secondness and thirdness. First, diffuse feelings about the normative legitimacy of social orders are, second, semantically shaped by established principles of recognition operating under historically specific social conditions and, third, the social claims to which such feelings give rise as well as even the historically prevailing versions of principles under which this occurs are subject to moral justification in a publicly relevant debate with potential practical significance for the organization of social life that provides the framework for the emergence of the feelings in the first place. Although this *medium quo* epistemology is visible only obliquely at the presuppositional level, Honneth can hardly be clearer regarding the assumptions about knowledge underpinning Critical Theory's methodology as he understands it.

McCarthy: reconstructive pragmatic critique of impure reason

In his understanding of Critical Theory and its methodology, Thomas McCarthy (1994a) is throughout guided by the left-Hegelian concern of how socio-practical ideas of reason actually work in practice. This concern was historically preserved by both Critical Theory and pragmatism, and recent developments have allowed these two directions to be brought closer together and their relation to be articulated in a manner that renders this common concern more precise. McCarthy regards the twentieth-century pragmatic turn towards communicative reason, particularly as consolidated by Habermas, as being of central importance in this respect. The foregrounding of communicative reason has not only resolved problems left standing by the early Frankfurt School, but also provided the means to employ insights from both the Critical Theory and pragmatist traditions to develop a more sharply focused conception of Critical Theory's research programme and corresponding methodological structure.

Although using only circumlocutions rather than the term itself, McCarthy clearly operates with an acute understanding of the concept of immanent transcendence as the central defining feature of the overall structure of Critical Theory's methodology. His characterization of Critical Theory as a programme for the 'practically significant, sociohistorical critique of impure reason' (1994a: 8) is comprehensible only in terms of this concept. Critical Theory proceeds from the distinction between universal ideas of practical reason and historically specific socio-cultural settings and practices, and treats the two poles as being related and mediated through communicative reason. The latter is itself detranscendentalized, pragmatized or deflated to the level of pragmatic presuppositions of communication in the guise of socio-practical ideas of reason such as truth, justice, freedom and responsibility. Reason taking this socio-cultural form is the medium that embraces at one and the same time social orientations and practices as well as the normative ideas giving them direction and guidance. In approaching its object in the course of seeking to fulfil its task, therefore, Critical Theory is focused on 'socio-practical ideas of reason [which] are both "immanent" in and "transcendent" to practices constitutive of forms of life' (1994a: 38). Accordingly, McCarthy regards Critical Theory as a 'non-foundationalist critique of impure reason' (1994b: 223) which continues 'the philosophical critique of reason' yet doing so 'in the medium of social, cultural and historical studies' (1994a: 31). It is centrally concerned with 'critical analyses of rationalization processes' in the sense of processes of the practical activation and realization of ideas of reason or socio-practical ideas that have a structuring – that is, constitutive and both regulative and critical – and a potentially transformative impact on social relations under historically specific socio-cultural conditions.

In comparison with Honneth, who gave a recognition-theoretical twist to the communication paradigm that Habermas originally introduced, McCarthy (1994a: 64–74) put forward a very different yet equally interesting proposal. To enhance the communication approach theoretically from a pragmatist viewpoint, he took recourse to ethnomethodology and conversational analysis as represented by Garfinkel and Pollner respectively. His reason for this step is to strengthen Critical Theory's version of the practical realization of reason by both ethnomethodology's and conversational analysis's meticulous attention to the ongoing process of maintaining social order through the accountable construction of the contextually relevant, rational properties of practical activities. That this proposal possesses not only theoretical but at the same time also methodological promise is suggested by the fact that both process thinking and the analytical focus on the structuration of the process could benefit from this addition.[2] McCarthy singles out the schemes of interpretation and expectation identified by ethnomethodology, such as the supposition of rational agency and of an independent reality, which are shared in so far as the participants reciprocally impute them to one another and hold each responsible for justifying their actions by providing good reasons. The aim is to conceptualize more clearly the practical ways in which the real and the ideal or the immanent and transcendent are articulated and mediated in everyday interaction and practices and, thus, to pinpoint the practically rational 'meaning-in-practice' through which 'abstract formal structures and procedures' become 'locally particularized' so as to constitute or transform specific social settings (1994a: 81). McCarthy advises that analyses of such mediation should seek agreement with available evidence and other relevant social scientific theories, all with a view to making a contribution to the practical realization of reason, even if only an indirect one.

Methodologically, the marriage of the two left-Hegelian variants on the other hand shifts the weight in favour of Critical Theory. It entails that the conventionalism of pragmatism, particularly ethnomethodology's notorious theoretical and methodological 'indifference' (1994a: 96) in the sense of its limiting descriptive orientation and abstention from all judgements, is overcome through Critical Theory's commitment to context-transcendent standards. By insisting on maintaining this transcendent normative basis, McCarthy is emphatic about the need to secure methodological space for critique. Critique, for its part, is 'a polymorphic, multilayered and multidimensional enterprise' which need not and cannot be carried out 'in the same way or at the same level of specificity' (1994a: 18). Considering that socio-practical ideas of reason have both a norm-setting or regulative significance and an obfuscating potential, as Kant already stressed, McCarthy (1994a: 82, 1994b: 224) accordingly regards critique as having not only a negative exposing or ideology-critical function, but simultaneously also a positive, affirmative, justificatory function. Over and above justification, however, critique could also be directed at improving, correcting or overhauling accepted normative standards. In such cases, it draws on the normative surplus of meaning inherent in socio-practical ideas, which points beyond their mere regulative function to their critical corrective, subversive and deconstructive potential (1994a: 21, 39, 75). In dependence on Habermas, McCarthy regards critique, both in the sense of the exposure of the obfuscating potential and as the deconstruction, subversion or critical correction of socio-practical ideas of reason, as complementary to and hence presupposing the 'reconstruction' (1994a: 21, 82, 1994b: 225) of their implicit and explicit validity. It is thus obvious that reconstruction is a crucial methodological moment in a critical theoretical description, interpretation and analysis of a situation embracing both immanent social orientations and practices and the transcendent normative ideas giving them direction and guidance.

Besides guarding its ability to engage in critique by keeping a reconstructive hold on context-transcendent standards, however, Critical Theory cannot start research in theoretical and methodological indifference either. Rather than arbitrarily selecting just any object or conducting ad hoc ethnomethodological experiments, it focuses on problems which arise in everyday practices at the tension-laden or misaligned juncture – 'the gap' (1994a: 77) – between the immanent and the transcendent where the factual force of counterfactual presuppositions impacts on the concrete situation. Critical Theory's cognitive interest guides it towards problems that are actually lived, felt and experienced under particular circumstances, especially problems with a moral, ethical and political significance calling for reflective engagement, critical participation and appropriate action to resolve. Such problems often stem from 'unconscious determinations of our thought and action' (ibid.) – whether of a psychological, cultural or social-structural kind or, more typically, an interdependent complex of all these – and, therefore, Critical Theory's object of inquiry is less the problems as such from which it starts than the conditions or factors giving rise to them. These could be institutional, social-structural or cultural-structural settings or factors which either 'encourage' or 'discourage' certain orientations, practices and normative standards or 'place unreasonable risks and burdens' on them (1994a: 57). These are the real, independent, objective roots to which Critical Theory points in order to 'explain' (1994a: 73) the aporetic tensions and discrepancies signalled by lived, felt and experienced problems, while its critique of the conditions giving rise to these problems in turn depends on such explanation.

McCarthy identifies a variety of what he calls 'methodologies of critical social theory' that could contribute to 'socio-cultural studies of reason in practice' (1994a: 81–5). Among the ones he considers relevant are thick descriptions, interpretative approaches of various kinds, historical studies of reason in context and the reconstruction of rule systems. However, he neither presents them with a systematic or comprehensive intent nor really enters into an exposition that links those approaches with Critical Theory as a 'critique of impure reason with practical import' (1994a: 8). The social, cultural, historical and reconstructive studies he lists all exhibit in some form or another what he regards as the key methodological attitude, namely the adoption of the perspective of a 'critical-reflexive participant' (1994a: 81, 43), which avoids the partiality of both the insider participant's and the outsider observer's point of view. This posture is compatible with different modes of reflective inquiry which retain contact with social practices, while taking distance from them in order to critically examine their validity claims, both implicit and explicit. Such critical scrutiny could lead to either the ideology critique of groundless pretensions or the reflective affirmation of justifiable claims, or both. The ultimate common element he discovers in these modes of inquiry, however, is their 'reconstruction' (1994a: 82) of social practices. It is doubtful, however, whether all of the approaches mentioned are capable of reconstruction, considering Habermas's careful distinction between reconstruction and interpretation. Given this difference, the approaches listed do not necessarily reach the depth of Critical Theory's explanation-based critique of causal conditions or factors, but can be regarded as making descriptive, interpretative, critical historical and reconstructive contributions to the diagnostic analysis of actual situations that precedes explanation-based critique. As regards explanation, considering his rejection of systems theory, McCarthy's (1991) position leaves him with the same problem as Honneth of not being able to deal theoretically with precisely those institutional and systemic phenomena that need to be explained to render critique ultimately cogent.

Like Honneth, McCarthy does not systematically reflect on his epistemological assumptions and hence forgoes articulating his methodology, which in any case is not systematically presented either, in conjunction with corresponding epistemological considerations. There can be no doubt about the fact, however, that he operates with the three-place *medium quo* theory of cognition, knowledge and action presupposed by the left-Hegelian tradition. Not only does he explicitly reject 'the Cartesian–Hobbesian paradigm of the solitary subject' (1994a: 27), but he consistently defends a pragmatic position and on a number of occasions refers to Peirce himself. More specifically, the basic dimensions of the threefold sign-relation that inform the overall methodological structure of Critical Theory are all unmistakably, albeit somewhat dispersed, present in his account – and, indeed, with some suggestive references to methodology. First, the qualitative moment of felt problems (1994a: 77) is depicted as opening the route, second, towards actual situations and their real, independent, objective determinants (1994a: 77), facilitating and limiting conditions (1994a: 57) and factors (1994a: 73) that are deictically and indexically referenced (1994a: 67) and play an indispensable role in explanation (1994a: 73), while, third, the significance of general concepts (1994a: 67–8) for the achievement of intersubjective understanding and agreement is underlined. This third moment is further understood in the extended sense given to it by Peirce, Mead, Apel and Habermas of the consideration of reasons pro and con in a communication community leading to rationality in both theory and practice (1994a: 27–8) – with the proviso, however, that it is fallible since the process is directed towards a universal audience (1994a: 76, 77), which renders it in principle open ended. McCarthy importantly conceives of the mode of operation of this communication community in terms of an incessant shifting to and fro among first-, second- and third-person perspectives in the dynamics of which socio-cultural representations, including presumably critical theoretical knowledge and critical contributions, are constructed, modified and accepted under the pressure of the active presence of others as well as of observing spectators (1994a: 73, 89, 92). This pragmatic conception of communicative rationality is the key to the way ideas of reason work in practice and, therefore, to understanding the relation between theory and practice.

Bohman: democratically organized critical social inquiry

According to James Bohman, Critical Theory provides little or no clarity about its unique methodology, whether the social organization of critical inquiry, its own unique form of explanation or its form of verification (2000: 299, 309). To compensate for this failure, he establishes a relation between pragmatism and Critical Theory in order to arrive at a pragmatic critical social science. Although not stressing left-Hegelianism as such, he is fully aware of the common heritage of pragmatism and Critical Theory, which they emphasize and exploit differently. The core element of their shared background that allows their reconciliation is their steadfast refusal to jettison the normative import of reason even after its nineteenth-century and, once again, twentieth-century deflation. In this respect, Bohman stresses the indispensability and unavoidability of 'non-local . . . [or] . . . transcending . . . second-order . . . [or] . . . reflexive rules' emerging from social practices, which function as 'regulative ideals in the Kantian sense' and are 'neither conventional nor interpretative but part of the cognitive ability to judge and assess reasons publicly' (1991: 99, 100). Although he does not use the concept of immanent transcendence explicitly, the retention of reason and recognition of its regulative significance for social life is more than enough to indicate that a thorough understanding of the problematic underpins his position. Accordingly, the sweep of his vision embraces both the 'plurality' of perspectives immanent in social reality and the possible 'unity' of perspectives transcending and thus pointing beyond a given situation as well as the 'ongoing tension' between the two that requires critical inquiry; such inquiry could facilitate its being worked through by the 'reflective and self-critical practices' of those involved themselves (2001: 91).

From the pragmatist perspective, Bohman (1999, 2000) sees more clearly and is therefore able to outline more explicitly than the Continental critical theorists of all generations the social organization of critical social inquiry. The latter forms part of the cooperative process of the democratic constitution and organization of society and, as such, it is responsible for any associated research. In that context, it is charged with the investigation of the institutional and related practices involved as well as the basic norms of cooperation on which they depend, including its own practices and norms. In executing this task, it seeks to develop socially useful and meaningful knowledge, collectively valued goals and critically justifiable norms of cooperation. The task itself requires the characteristic methodological feature of critical social science, namely critique.

In Bohman's view, Critical Theory is uniquely characterized by a combination of explanation and critique in a way that highlights its normative thrust. The logic of its 'critical explanation' is both explanatory and normative (1991: 211). The way in which Critical Theory's inherited Marxist ideology critique is typically exercised, however, given a negative form of devaluing or disillusioning critique by being confined to the explanation of phenomena through exposure of their functions or causes, is inadequate. In so far as it neglects the opening up of new actualities, meanings, ways of seeing, orientations and so forth, it needs the complementary support of a 'pragmatics of disclosure' (1993: 566): a positive pragmatist form of disclosing of possibilities. Rather than an ad hoc procedure, such a disclosure is informed by the critical theory of society as a theory which provides a 'general interpretative framework' (2000: 316–17). An example of a critical-normative theory of society that Bohman discusses in a number of his writings is Habermas's theory of communicative action. The task of critique is to break up, dissolve and transform reified modes of seeing and asking questions, values, cultural schemes and ideologies and thus to open up new possibilities of self-understanding and action. This it does by creating new cognitive and cultural contexts, which could lead to the transformation of orientations and relations with the world, whether social relations or cultural meanings.

Both the negative devaluing and the positive disclosing moments of critique depend furthermore on an explanatory moment to complete the logic of critical explanation. Generally speaking, explanation takes the form of a causal account with reference to power and domination impacting on social relations or to obstacles standing in the way of certain processes or developments (1991: 211, 226). In the wake of the post-empiricist recognition of the inapplicability of general laws, however, such explanation requires to be conducted in terms of appropriate 'causal mechanisms', which could be any of a wide range, depending on the field of operation or level of specificity. Bohman mentions general intentional, non-intentional and macro-sociological mechanisms and, more specifically, unconscious repression or displacement, restriction of communication or discourse, privatism and depoliticization (1991: 48–9, 200, 213). Although writing on occasion that 'the identification of various mechanisms would always be an *ad hoc* affair' (1991: 200), he could certainly not have intended this statement to mean a denial that causal mechanisms fall within the purview of theoretical knowledge.

Once again mobilizing the strength of pragmatism, as in the case of the social organization of critical social inquiry, Bohman offers a clearer account than any of the critical theorists of how the knowledge, goal clarification and justifications developed by critical social science could become practically effective. In this case, he insists on the necessity of the 'public testing' or 'practical verification' (1999: 464, 466; 2000: 306, 309) of the findings, particularly critical explanation, offered by critical social science. This can be accomplished by taking practically relevant inquiry a reflective step further, a 'second order sort of testing' (1999: 464), that can be carried out only by a public. The second-order reflection allows the members of society affected or, more generally, the public to evaluate, judge and accept or reject what is proposed (1999: 465; 2000: 307–9). Testing or verification of this kind could lead either to the instrumental or strategic fulfilment of behavioural expectations in accord with legitimate social norms, or to a questioning and more or less drastic transformation of the enabling framework of social cooperation itself – that is, either to problem solving or to world creation. Critical social research most typically, then, opens the way for collective self-reflection through public democratic discussion and thus for potential cooperation, ultimately leaving it to the participants and those affected themselves to solve the problem at issue or to change their world (2000: 308, 320). Rather than an epistemological or theoretical one, the relation between theory and practice is above all a practical and, indeed, a political problem.

Celikates and Iser: reconstructive critique

Robin Celikates, as Honneth (2009e) points out in his foreword to the former's book, takes up anew a question that was central to the first-generation critical theorists but largely neglected by the second generation on account of their almost single-minded concentration on the question of the normative foundations of critique. Instead of focusing on how the normative standards adhered to by Critical Theory could be theoretically justified, he is once again concerned with the epistemological question of how the critical theorists' knowledge relates to the pre-scientific competences and judgements of ordinary members of society. What is interesting about his treatment of this problem, however, is that he does not only seek to draw out the methodological implications of the relation between observer and participant or theorist and addressee, but provides an account of Critical Theory's methodology which in effect places the concept of immanent transcendence at its very core. Unlike Mattias Iser, on whom he draws and who links 'reconstructive societal critique' (2008: 12) explicitly to it, Celikates does not mention the concept as such in the course of the discussion. This is apparently because he pits a methodological model inspired by psychoanalysis against

Honneth's left-Hegelian version, but that his understanding is nevertheless shaped by the concept is confirmed by the following statement: 'To insist on the decision: either immanence or transcendence, is tantamount to regressing to traditional logic' (Celikates 2009: 187, quoting Adorno). His focal concern is clearly the relation of continuity and discontinuity as well as of mediation between societal self-understanding and the ability and necessity of Critical Theory to go beyond it.

Formally not unlike Iser, who locates reconstructive critique between 'internal or immanent critique' and 'external or transcendent critique' (2008: 9), Celikates develops his 'post-pragmatic' account of the methodology of Critical Theory by contrast and comparison with two contrary conceptions of critique: one an older well-established position and the other a more recent innovation which is becoming increasingly consolidated and internationally influential. While Bourdieu's scientistic model of external critique (Celikates 2009: 52–97) and Boltanski's interpretative pragmatic model of internal critique (2009: 136–57) represent the parameters, Celikates locates Critical Theory's critical reconstructive methodology between these two methodological hierarchical and methodological egalitarian extremes. Proceeding from a Durkheimian epistemological break, Bourdieu establishes an asymmetrical relation between the critic and ordinary members of society and conceives of the critic as an omnipotent scientist observing from a distance the participants, who are locked into the naturalized perspectives associated with their particular positions. This hierarchical structure, however, has two complementary negative consequences. The critic gives up, on the one hand, every possibility of explicating and drawing on the intuitive everyday knowledge of the participants and, on the other, loses the ability to connect with the participants and to expect their receptivity to critical insights and cooperation in the process of practically realizing them. Proceeding from the ethnomethodology inspired centrality of the reflexive structure of social practice and hence an assumption of symmetry, Boltanski by contrast regards social action and critical reflection as being on exactly the same plane and sharing a common structure. Since ordinary everyday routines of coordination and cooperation involve reflection and questioning of commonly presupposed representations of order, every social practice harbours corresponding forms of justification and critique. This egalitarian structure means that critique takes the form of a descriptive account of the way in which the participants themselves evaluate and judge their own circumstances. Critical sociology becomes transformed into the sociology of critique. Yet this methodological egalitarianism has its own one-sidedness and associated problems. The basic assumption of a commonly shared critical capacity overlooks not only inequalities in reflexive and critical abilities but, more importantly still, the societal conditions which determine, impact on, distort or block either or both the acquisition and exercise of such reflexive and critical abilities. Although it is apparent that the weakness of Boltanski's methodological egalitarianism requires compensation by a theoretical turn making possible a critique of societal conditions, Celikates is emphatic that it will take more and, indeed, something else than a re-importation of Bourdieu's hierarchical methodology. His proposal is a form of 'reconstructive critique' (2009: 159), which he recovers from the psychoanalytical methodological model Habermas presented in the late 1960s. This compares and contrasts with Iser's conception of reconstructive critique based on the left-Hegelian idea of immanent transcendence, which he finds articulated in Habermas in terms of relations of understanding and in Honneth in terms of relations of recognition, and beyond which he wants to go by means of the synthetic idea of 'communicative recognition' (Iser 2008: 12–13).

Celikates conceives of Critical Theory as social praxis and makes central the reflexive capacities of ordinary members of society, which both are immanently practised and make transcendent critique possible. In relation to the original reflexivity of everyday life, Critical Theory's characteristic reconstructive critique represents a second level of reflexivity, which is able to diagnose 'second order pathologies' (2009: 166) as well as to adopt a related form of 'metacritique' that delivers a 'critique of societal conditions' (2009: 174). A second-order pathology is a state in which the actors suffer from a reflexive deficit and are consequently unable to recognize, understand or criticize a problem situation of, say, injustice or alienation. Any of a range of societal conditions at the second level could be the cause of such 'blockages' (2009: 174) or 'structural reflexive deficits' (2009: 168) at the first level by impairing, impeding or preventing either or both the acquisition and exercise of reflexive capacities – for instance, inadequate socialization practices or a hegemonic or ideological justification regime that naturalizes social relations or individualizes collective problems. The 'diagnosis' (2009: 169) of such pathological reflexive deficits is in the first instance achieved formally rather than substantively by reconstructing the necessary conditions required by the actors under their concrete circumstances to be able themselves to raise and answer the question of the negative quality and criticizability of their situation. An adequate theory of society has to capture this dimension of structural possibilities opened up by the conceptual structure of language at the categorical level. Like Iser (2008: 10), who stresses the importance of explanatory social theory as against the moralistic narrowing of Critical Theory by the second generation's obsession with normative foundations, Celikates regards this reflexive task of Critical Theory as being complemented by its critical task of 'explaining' and 'criticizing' (2009: 171, 173) the debilitating effects of social relations, self-understandings and symbolic orders. Causal factors must be 'empirically identified and explained . . . by means of a case-specific, testable hypothesis . . . in the usual way . . . employing the generally accepted test procedures' (2009: 183, 235). The empirically substantiated, theoretically formulated, hypothetical construction or reconstruction obtains its character as critique from the fact that it stands in a relation of tension to the prevailing self-understanding of the actors, who are caught in a state requiring not only a transformation of the situation, but also self-transformation in the sense of eliminating or diminishing the structural reflexive deficits plaguing them.

A central and innovative part of Celikates' contribution, which effectively places Iser's conception well in context, is his distinction among three types of reconstruction: the early Habermas's psychoanalytical conception, the later Habermas's formal-pragmatic conception and Honneth's left-Hegelian conception of reconstruction (2009: 188–94). His own preference is for the first one, which he critically plays out against the remaining two. The significance of this account becomes clear when one considers that reconstruction is not only central to the methodological self-understanding of contemporary Critical Theory, but at least by implication also the means of articulation of the overall concept of immanent transcendence. Reconstruction specifies the general methodological structure laid down by immanent transcendence.

According to Celikates' understanding, the three reconstructive approaches differ in terms of both what they reconstruct and how they reconstruct. The psychoanalytical model selects concrete pathologies and their genesis, the formal-pragmatic model universal rules and competences, and the left-Hegelian one the rational and normative content of a particular practice or form of life. This means that, as far as their respective objects are concerned, the first is historically specific, the second abstract and unhistorical and the third in between these poles. As regards procedure, the psychoanalytical model integrates theoretical reflection and dialogue with the addressees, whereas the formal-pragmatic model privileges the ideal-typical reconstruction of rules systems and developmental logics, and the left-Hegelian one follows stages in the process of the historical realization of reason driven by struggles of recognition. In Celikates' view, both the formal-prag-matic and the left-Hegelian models have a range of problematic methodological consequences. On the one hand, both favour constitutive structures rather than contingent socio-historical structures – that is, structures respectively of communi-cative relations and of recognition relations rather than normatively directing and guiding ideas and ideals won from concrete, historically specific social practices, institutions and interpretative systems marking the possible self-understanding of the actors. On the other hand, both privilege a macro process that transpires above the heads and behind the backs of the participants – that is, the concep-tion of reconstruction making sense, in the formal-pragmatic case, only in the context of a self-interpretation of reason and, in the left-Hegelian case, only in the framework of the history of struggles of recognition being the history of the progressive realization of reason. Considering these tendencies, not only do the formal-pragmatic and left-Hegelian methodological models nurture a basic philo-sophical concern that separates reconstruction and critique and places them in an awkward relation to empirical social research, but their undervaluation and inability to actualize the relation between theoretical reflection and its addressees expose both as dialogically deficient or monological approaches. Both the later Habermas's and Honneth's conceptions of reconstruction are therefore marred by an untenable '*monological* identification of *constitutive* structures' (2009: 191). On the basis of these arguments, Celikates opts for psychoanalysis as the paradigmatic example for the interpretation of the overall methodological structure of Critical Theory characterized by reconstructive critique.

Considering his central concern with the epistemological question of how the critical theorists' knowledge relates to the pre-scientific competences and judgements of ordinary members of society, strengthened as he thinks by the psy-choanalytical model, it comes as no surprise that Celikates regards a communicative or what he calls a 'dialogical' (2009: 188) relation between Critical Theory and its addressees as a fundamental aspect of its methodological structure. Accordingly, Critical Theory's characteristic social-theoretically based moment of explanation and critique must be exercised in such a manner that hypothetical constructions or reconstructions aimed at affording the actors new insights into their situation and empowering them to act are dialogically linked with their still-operative reflexive capacities and stimulate them to 'reflexive self-understanding . . . acceptance . . . [and] . . . self-transformation' (2009: 173, 227, 234). Here dialogue obtains a meta-status since, despite the weighing of reasons and empirical testing for or against a reconstructive hypothesis belonging to the very core of Critical Theory, only dialogue between critical theorists and their addressees makes possible such weighing and testing. It is on the basis of this dialogical relation, which locates Critical Theory immanently in social life yet allows a reconstructive critical turn beyond to feed practical insights and stimulation back into social life, that Celikates is able to regard critique as social praxis. Considering his methodological understanding of Critical Theory in terms of a concern with pathologies, their diagnosis and explanatory reconstructive critique, all within a dialogical framework extending to the members of society, it is moreover possible to conclude that Celikates operates with assumptions that are consistent with the *medium quo* epistemology of the left-Hegelian tradition.

A number of questions can be raised about Celikates' presentation of the methodology of Critical Theory, however. The first is whether his interpretation of the left-Hegelian conception of reconstruction in terms of Honneth's Hegelian attachment does not unduly narrow down that more general position. Peculiarly enough, despite his adoption of the psychoanalytic model, Celikates closes his analysis with a positive quotation from the young Marx which confirms the relevance of left-Hegelianism over and above Honneth's version. In addition, it should be remembered that Honneth, as became apparent in an earlier chapter, fails to recognize Peirce as a representative of left-Hegelianism and thus, despite his recourse to Mead, does not incorporate pragmatism adequately into his understanding of Critical Theory. This means that the left-Hegelian understanding of immanent transcendence and of reconstruction cannot be reduced to Honneth's and, on that basis, be replaced summarily by the psychoanalytical model.

A related question is whether there is not a tension between Celikates' emphasis on the importance of the formal dimension of an adequate theory of society which is linked to the conceptual structure of language, on the one hand, and his outright rejection of the reconstruction of abstract and unhistorical structures, on the other. There can be no doubt about the fact that the categorical dimension of structural possibilities requiring conceptual analysis is of the utmost importance to Critical Theory, which of course does not imply that it should become an independent philosophical concern in its own right. In earlier chapters it became clear just how central this issue was in the course of the early twentieth-century combating of vulgar Marxism and the recovery and revitalization of the left-Hegelian tradition. It is interesting to note that Iser, who explicitly adopts the concept of immanent transcendence, regards the matter in terms of mediation rather than separation as Celikates does. Reconstruction brings together and interrelates the immanent interpretative moment and the transcendent constructivist moment (Iser 2008: 82).

Third, the question arises of what Celikates achieves with his not infrequent references to empirical social research and hypotheses regarding social-structural blockages which need to be empirically verified and explained. He indeed argues for embedding this step in a dialogical process involving the addressees, but the fact that he is content to settle for 'generally accepted testing procedures' and 'the usual ways of confirming empirical hypotheses' (2009: 235) suggests that this is the weakest link in his methodological account. No thought whatsoever is given to this crucial aspect of Critical Theory's methodology, not to mention consideration given to developments in this area since the debates of the 1960s (e.g. Bhaskar 1989; Bohman 1991). Iser is emphatic about the necessity of a 'causally explanatory theory of society' to allow critique 'to refer to *something*' and to account for factors such as societal structures and mechanisms (2008: 67, 76–7, 82), yet he also persists in speaking in an undifferentiated way of 'empirical' (2008: 65, 76) questions and research and of explanation.

Finally, Celikates takes an emphatic position on dialogue as a meta-institution providing the necessary communicative relation between Critical Theory and its addressees, but he also acknowledges the persistent absence of the necessary forums and procedures that could accommodate such dialogical exchange. Since in his view this communicative problem cannot be resolved by calling on the public sphere as informal context of discourse, he refers it strictly to the concrete research context where the critical theorist must relate to a relevant category of members of society as both research subjects and addressees of critique. Far from being without merit, this description captures an important dimension of critical social research, yet it could be asked whether Celikates is not misled by his choice of the psychoanalytical model. Does he not propose to simplify matters to direct relations between critical theorist and addressees, thus ignoring the situation that has to be faced under the complex contemporary conditions of the communication, discourse or media society in which public opinion and hence the public play a crucial role? By contrast, Iser considers the relation between Critical Theory and its addressees in terms of what he calls the 'bridging function' of critique, but, rather than confining it to a direct relation between critical theorists and a particular section of the population, he mentions the role of 'public opinion' and the necessity therefore of considering the influence of discourses transpiring in civil society (2008: 67–8, 79–80). Elaboration of what precisely is involved, however, is still required.

Conclusion

To conclude the assessment of the positions of a number of contemporary critical theorists, this chapter draws attention to four points in particular regarding the methodological understanding of contemporary Critical Theory that bear brief restatement.

First, there can be no doubt about the fact that contemporary critical theorists more or less explicitly comprehend the concept of immanent transcendence as laying down the general structure of the methodological approach appropriate to the new version of Critical Theory, which distinguishes them quite sharply from the earlier generations. Having a foothold in actual reality and generating a dialectical tension immanently, the transcendent normative moment that both demands and guides reconstruction cannot be projected outside existing society as though nothing good, not even a single good reason, could be found in it. Nor should it be treated exclusively as a question of quasi-transcendental conditions providing abstract and unhistorical normative foundations for critique.

Second, it is apparent that contemporary critical theorists operate with a grasp of the *medium quo* epistemology originally assumed by the young Marx and spelled out by Peirce. However, a more explicit consideration and closer observance of the sign-mediated nature of cognition, knowledge production, problem solving, meaning creation and their application in the real world would undoubtedly lead to a more differentiated and specific articulation of the methodology of Critical Theory than they offer. All the necessary elements are present in the reviewed presentations, but a coherent and fuller statement remains a desideratum.

This is in particular apparent, third, in respect of the not altogether satis-factory accounts available in contemporary Critical Theory of its supposedly defining methodological feature of critical explanation or explanatory critique. Contemporary critical theorists such as Honneth, McCarthy and Bohman as well as Celikates and Iser of course concern themselves with Critical Theory's critical explanatory orientation toward societal transformation processes and structures, conditions or causal mechanisms generating social pathologies, actu-ally lived problems and ideologies, yet two weaknesses are clearly visible. First, the implied objective or reality moment is not given the treatment it requires – a problem exacerbated by the fact that the theorists discussed neither consider the epistemological demand involved nor clarify the ontological implications of interchangeably talking of the empirical dimension, actuality and reality, nor do they command or even recognize the necessary social-theoretical resources to deal with societal processes and structures. Second, the type of explanation appropri-ate to this dimension remains to be explicated. The undifferentiated reference by Honneth and others to hypothesis formation fits very uneasily in the context of an epistemological and methodological approach that claims to be unique and, in any case, is very different from the scientistic approach. Even after Bohman (1991), who has made an important contribution to assessing the new philoso-phy of social science in the post-empiricist era and drew attention to the logic of explanation, a gap persists. Considering the account offered by these theorists, it would seem as though Critical Theory has learned nothing or has nothing to learn from the structural and realist types of explanation, which can be reckoned to be among the best achievements of the transformative methodological debates of the 1960s and 1970s. It appears as though Habermas's life-long wavering and the resulting ambivalent statements, especially as indicated by his infamous theory of truth, may well have contributed to the uncertainty, lack of clarity and vagueness that have plagued and continue to plague Critical Theory at this most decisive juncture. Another contributory factor is the focus of the second and largely also the third generation of critical theorists on the problematic of the normative foundations of critique, while the latest shift is towards renewing the epistemological question of the relation between critical theorists and audience, leaving by the wayside an important methodological aspect of Critical Theory.

Finally, the communicative framework within which Critical Theory develops its knowledge and within which it could attain practical effect receives much more attention than ever before, due in particular to the conception of communicative rationality shared by contemporary critical theorists and its pragmatist embedding in democracy, but also to the critical testing of these assumptions. Bohman's Deweyan grasp of critical social inquiry as forming part of the self-investigative process of a democratic society is important, yet a stronger sense of the possibility of world creation and transformation will have to be brought in to counter pragmatism's complacency about cooperative problem solving. Celikates' granting of meta-status to dialogue and his specific focus on critique as part of social practices borne by ordinary members of society oriented toward transformation, as well as Iser's reference to public opinion, both complement Bohman's approach formally and practically. The general understanding of the presupposed communicative framework allows contemporary critical theorists to include in their reflections on the potential practical efficacy of Critical Theory the relation between the knowledge it produces and its addressees or, generally, 'the public'. What is not sufficiently taken into account, however, is the dramaturgical nature of the process of the communication and communicative monitoring of knowledge, that is, the active participation of actors on a virtual stage and the observing, evaluating, judging, commenting and opinion-forming public, which plays a significant, situation-specific, structuring role in the process of construction by embodying ethically incarnated, transcendent regulative and critical principles. Celikates turns away from the public in order to focus on the direct relation of Critical Theory to its audience in the concrete research context; Honneth speaks vaguely of publicly relevant debates, general audiences and a discursively oriented public; Bohman recognizes the importance of the public yet tends to identify it with one of the actors on the virtual stage; McCarthy very importantly appreciates the vital significance of the relations among the first-, second- and third-person perspectives in the dynamic process of communicative construction, including the communicatively mediated impact of the active presence of others and observing spectators, but does not analyse it – not to mention explicating it with special reference to the public's crucial role in an indispensable moment of Critical Theory's methodology; and Iser recognizes the importance of taking into account public opinion and hence public discourse, but then leaves it at that.

Against this background, it is possible in the next chapter to focus in a concentrated way on the methodology of contemporary Critical Theory in its own right.

6   The methodological framework of critical theory

Introduction

From the previous chapter it is clear that, although the concept of immanent transcendence is generally understood as being indicative of the methodological structure of contemporary Critical Theory and actually determines the way contemporary critical theorists pursue it, there are certain aspects of this methodology that need explicit and even urgent attention. These aspects will have to be covered in the present chapter at least up to the point at which Critical Theory's methodology can be presented in a reasonably comprehensive and coherent matter.

First, an aspect that is currently largely implicitly operative but in a conscious and explicit form would undoubtedly benefit the differentiation and articulation of Critical Theory's methodology is the *medium quo* or sign-mediated epistemology presupposed by the concept of immanent transcendence. Although the second generation, Apel in particular but also Habermas, stressed its importance, contemporary critical theorists are at best only intuitively aware of the nature of this epistemology and, therefore, not in a position to exploit it for the purposes of explication, developing and justifying their shared methodology. Second, a weakness of Critical Theory calling for improvement concerns an aspect that is brought to light precisely by a conscious reflection on its epistemological underpinnings – namely, the objective or reality moment to which correspond the generative or causal societal structures or real mechanisms with reference to which the phenomena on which Critical Theory brings its critique to bear are explained. Since Habermas's endeavour to compensate for the weaknesses of first-generation Critical Theory, the concern with normative foundations has taken on a life of its own to such an extent that it tended to marginalize the question of reality and explanation. This asymmetrical focus was further reinforced by the defensive position into which Critical Theory was forced by the unrelenting attacks launched against it from the interpretative side in the context of the international debate about critique. Then there are examples of critical theorists such as Honneth and McCarthy, as we have seen, who represent a position based exclusively on action theory and praxis philosophy, which is theoretically too weak to support the kind of explanation required by Critical Theory. As a consequence, contemporary critical theorists do not make sufficiently clear what precisely Critical Theory's distinguishing type of explanation-based critique consists of. It is this open flank that invites the attacks of genealogical critics (Foucault 1986a), critical realists (Bhaskar 1989) and critical sociologists (Bourdieu 2001). A third aspect needing clarification of its methodological significance is the pragmatics of Critical Theory, particularly the communicative framework within which the moment of pragmatic reception of its findings takes place. Along with this, it is vital to explicate the self-referential implications for Critical Theory itself of its knowledge production and involvement in such a communicative context.

This chapter is divided into three sections. Considering that the concept of immanent transcendence represents the core of the methodological structure of Critical Theory, attention is first given to the methodological implications of this concept. The second section is devoted to the sign-mediated epistemology that Peirce originally spelled out but which is presupposed by the left-Hegelian tradition more generally. The detailed presentation is warranted by the advantage it has for developing a clear and transparent understanding of Critical Theory's methodology. In the final section, these benefits are reaped in the form of an analytical presentation of the three principal moments of this methodology.

Methodological implications of immanent transcendence

Contemporary critical theorists understand the concept of immanent transcendence (see Figure 4.1) as the master concept of the left-Hegelian tradition, which, as such, lays down the general methodological structure of Critical Theory. Immanent transcendence, as was made clear in preceding chapters, refers to accumulated historical potential in the form of socio-practical ideas of reason or cultural models that reflection in the form of critical disclosure makes or could make apparent so that the potential is or could be realized to some degree through appropriate social practices. Such historically accumulated socio-practical reason does not exhaust itself in a mere ought, normative obligation or idea projected outside of existing society, however, but is emphatically regarded as always already operative in structuring social life by directing and guiding or potentially critically regulating social practices to some degree and in some way. In general methodological terms, the concept of immanent transcendence thus directs Critical Theory to focus on the dialectical tension that serves as the dynamic impetus of the ongoing process of the constitution, reproduction, organization and transformation of society, including the self-transformation of the agents. This is the tension generated at the interface between social orientations and practices, on the one hand, and their reflexive rules, formal properties or counterfactual presuppositions in the form of cultural models characterized by a penumbra of surplus meaning, on the other.

For the more particular purposes of the production of practically relevant theoretical knowledge, however, contemporary critical theorists operate with another related concept, which has become central to the methodological self-understanding of Critical Theory – namely reconstruction. Specifying the general methodological structure laid down by immanent transcendence by providing the means for the articulation of the overall concept, reconstruction indicates the general methodological direction of Critical Theory. This direction can be characterized, for short, as reconstructive explanatory critique that is backed by social theory. The methodological implications of immanent transcendence are thus best spelled out while keeping in mind the concept of reconstruction.

There are three important methodological implications of the concept of immanent transcendence that are of direct relevance for the clarification of Critical Theory's methodology aimed at in this chapter. The first is the mediation of the internal and external references embedded in the tension-laden dialectical relation between the immanent and the transcendent at the core of Critical Theory's object. The concept of reconstruction is central in this case. Closely related to reconstruction is the flexible modulation of the relation between the participant's and the observer's perspectives. The second implication concerns the methodologically relevant theoretical significance of immanent transcendence, which brings a number of different nuances into view. Finally, a methodologically important implication following from the preceding relates to the nature of the context within which the concept of immanent transcendence applies and, hence, the dimensions that need to be taken into account in approaching any social situation.

Mediation through reconstruction

The function of reconstruction in Critical Theory's methodology, first, is to identify, recover and make explicit the structuring force of both pragmatic presuppositions and possibilities of the concrete situation and the formal or universal structures refracted as ideas of socio-practical reason and expressed in ethically relevant cultural models which are necessarily implied or presupposed by the social practices or form of life in question. The essence of the mediation problem to which reconstruction is the solution consists of having to bring the reconstructed immanent and transcendent structures in relation to one another without underplaying or even cancelling out the other (see Figure 6.1). In the end, of course, this has to be adequate to the actual way in which those involved themselves cope with and resolve or fail to resolve the tension under the particular conditions characteristic of their situation.

The problem of reconstructive mediation between the immanent and the transcendent becomes graphically clear from a consideration of the key methodological

I		T
• pragmatic presuppositions of actors, orientations, actions, institutions etc. in the concrete situation • possibilities contained in the actual situation	 Reconstruction	• formal or universal structures of practices or forms of life (e.g. communicative, recognition) • socio-practical ideas of reason • cultural models

Figure 6.1 Reconstruction.

attitude adopted by contemporary critical theorists, namely the perspective of the 'critical-reflective participant' (McCarthy 1994a: 81; Bohman 2001) or 'an internal perspective transferred to the outside' (Honneth 2007e: 226).[1] This posture avoids the one-sidedness not only of the insider participant's viewpoint, but also of the outsider observer's viewpoint. It makes possible simultaneously maintaining contact with the concrete situation and taking the distance necessary for establishing its presuppositions and critically examining their explicit and implicit validity claims or normative import. Whereas the participant's viewpoint is carried out in the first instance through a moment of internal or immanent interpretation of the actors, their orientations, social practices and institutions in the actual situation, the viewpoint of the observer is given effect through a constructive moment identifying the structures necessarily presupposed by what transpires in the concrete situation. Reconstruction thus brings together, transforms and interrelates the immanent interpretative moment and the transcendent constructive moment in such a way that the reconstructive-interpretative and the reconstructive-constructive moments support the taking of a critical view both of the concrete situation and of its categorical – not only but especially its normative – framework. Reconstruction in this sense is not accomplished once and for all, which distinguishes it from Rawls's Kantian constructivism, but requires regular iteration in the form of moral self-reflection revising the move from the immanent to the transcendent (Menke 2000; Cooke 2006, 2009; Benhabib 2008).

Two important aspects of reconstruction warrant mention here. First, reconstruction in the above sense makes possible a genetic- or neo-structuralist type of explanation (Habermas and Luhmann 1971: 280–1; Habermas 1979: 8–25, 1984: 18–9) which, by contrast with the empiricist focus on observable surface correlations indicating regularities or laws as well as the interpretative focus of intersubjectively understandable meanings, has benefited from the cognitive and structuralist revolutions and, accordingly, identifies the deep-seated, formal, generative and regulative set of elements and relations that lay down the parameters of what transpires in the actual concrete situation. It can more properly be called reconstructive explanation. Although the formal set of structures established by reconstruction is obviously associated most strongly with the transcendent moment, the centrality of mediation to reconstruction entails that it is not confined to it. On the immanent side, the reconstructive task is to draw out the relevant possibilities inherent in the actual situation on the basis of pre-theoretical knowledge in the form of real generative mechanisms (Habermas 1979: 16, 1984: 19; Outhwaite 1987: 86, 2000: 232–3). Second, reconstructive critique, which is possible only on the basis of such a depth structure, takes both a negative exposing and a positive disclosing form – two forms of critique that are intimately connected. Immanent reconstructive critique takes a negative form in targeting what is amiss with the self-understanding of actors, their orientations, practices, relations and institutions, and a positive form in disclosing new possibilities, interpretations, orientations, modes of organization or protest or transformative potentials available in the situation. Transcendent reconstructive critique takes a negative form in exposing distorted, ideological, naturalized or reified and such features of socio-practical ideas of reason or cultural models, and a positive form in disclosing surpluses of meaning contained in ideas of reason or cultural models that are ignored, only partially or selectively used in practice or not recognized at all. This still leaves, of course, the explanatory moment, which accounts for whatever contingent material, structural or real forces, factors or mechanisms cause what is amiss and goes unnoticed in the actual situation and/or why semantic potentials of cultural models are deformed and treated inadequately. This dimension of explanation, the moment of critical explanation or explanatory critique which is central to Critical Theory, is dealt with below in a more appropriate place.

Multilevel theoretical significance

The second major methodological implication of immanent transcendence attaches to the theoretical significance of the concept. As was evident earlier, immanent transcendence is theoretically a very rich concept. It is the key concept of Critical Theory as a social theory or theory of society and, as such, it possesses a multidimensional significance. To begin with, the above paragraphs touched on the formal dimension of the theory of society, which is linked to the conceptual structure of language, allowing the reconstruction of the categorical structures presupposed and semantic potentials or structural possibilities inherent in concrete practices and forms of life. The methodological sense of this was explicated in terms of reconstruction, reconstructive explanation and reconstructive critique.

The second theoretical sense of immanent transcendence is one requiring emphasis here – namely, the fundamental substantive theoretical perspective it implies in so far as, from the viewpoint of Critical Theory, it concerns not just a concrete situation and its formal features, but some instance of a force deeply rooted in concrete social life that persistently, time and time again, exerts pressure towards transgressing, transforming and overcoming the status quo (Honneth 2003, 2007b). Methodologically, this sense of the concept theoretically specifies what is to be reconstructed – whether the structures of a self-creative and self-transformative practice (such as labour), linguistic communication or relations of recognition.[2] This theoretical concern is a characteristic feature of Critical Theory and has to be observed as an essential aspect of its methodological framework. Without it, reconstruction and its explanatory and critical implications are certain to lose their focus.

Immanent transcendence has yet another important methodologically relevant theoretical sense. It relates to the centrality of the concept of the dialectical tension and contradiction at the interface between the facticity or concretely settled and inertial quality of the actual situation and the critical regulative force exerted on it by socio-practical ideas of reason or the semantic import of cultural models. Of particular importance here, theoretically, are those contingently intervening, interfering, impeding, retarding, deforming or blocking forces, factors, structures, mechanisms or related processes which only a historical-sociological materialist or realist theory of society is able to specify and identify and thus make available as *explanans* in a causal explanation that can contribute to a critique of an undesirable, unjustifiable, pathological state of affairs. This is the moment of explanatory critique, which, dependent as it is on a substantive theory of society normatively contextualized by reconstruction, is the uniquely characterizing or defining feature of Critical Theory. Despite being of defining significance, however, it is probably the weakest moment in the available accounts of contemporary Critical Theory's methodology, as argued in the previous chapter, and therefore requires more attention here. Whereas second-generation critical theorists learned something about reconstructive explanation from the cognitive and structuralist revolutions, the third and fourth generations still need to come fully to grips with this moment of explanatory critique and its particular object. Contemporary accounts of explanation by critical theorists exhibit an awareness of the gains represented by the reconstructive approach, but little or no clarity is to be had regarding the nature of the objective or reality dimension, the disclosure of this dimension, the moment of explanatory critique and its relation to the reconstructive explanatory model. Lately, Habermas (2006) approached the distinction between reconstructive and explanatory critique with his contrast of 'normative theory' and 'empirical research'. In addition Honneth has re-asserted the importance for Critical Theory of 'the sociological explanation . . . of the pathological deformation of reason' (2007f: 40), but on all accounts his own theoretical resources for accomplishing this are in rather short supply (van den Brink and Owen 2007; Basaure 2011). In the case of explanatory critique, the reference is to an independent objective feature of reality exerting a causal structuring or generating force that represents not a causal regularity, as in Humean-inspired empiricism, but rather a real societal structure, system imperative or mechanism. The talk of the empirical identification and explanation of causal factors, testing in the usual way by means of generally accepted procedures and so forth shows that contemporary critical theorists still tend to be caught in the dominant mode of empiricist thinking. However, this is patently incompatible with Critical Theory's explanatory critique as well as post-empiricism. Perhaps, there is something to be learned at this particular level from the procedure of 'retroduction' analogically and metaphorically employed in critical realist social science (e.g. Bhaskar 1989).[3]

To begin with, explanation, generally speaking, is an account that offers directions for how to deal with reality, for instance in order to transform it. Its strategic sense, therefore, is to point towards a crucial juncture where appropriate intervention could potentially lead to such transformation and self-transformation of reality. A reconstructive explanatory model and a moment of explanatory critique of a contingently interfering structure, mechanisms or related process play complementary roles here (Figure 6.2). On the one hand, immanent transcendence together with reconstruction lay down the situational parameters within which the *explanans* – that is, the real mechanism representing the contingent obstacle blocking the process of the practical realization of structural possibilities or potential socio-practical rationality – accounting for the *explanandum* – that is, the problem or pathology to be explained – must be located and identified. The reconstructive type of explanation offers an account of the possibility and constraints of the actual situation by specifying the formal set of elements and relations generating and regulating it. By contrast with the surface-level empiricist model of explanation, correlating observable variables with a view to establishing regularities,

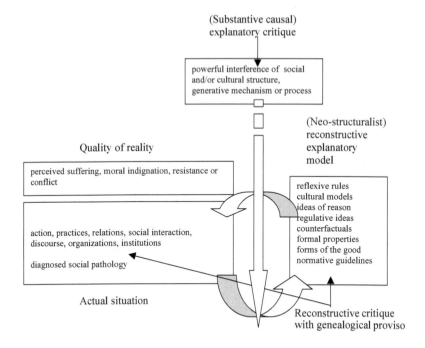

(Substantive causal)
explanatory critique

powerful interference of social
and/or cultural structure,
generative mechanism or process

(Neo-structuralist)
reconstructive
explanatory
model

Quality of reality

perceived suffering, moral indignation, resistance or
conflict

reflexive rules
cultural models
ideas of reason
regulative ideas
counterfactuals
formal properties
forms of the good
normative guidelines

action, practices, relations, social interaction,
discourse, organizations, institutions

diagnosed social pathology

Actual situation

Reconstructive critique
with genealogical proviso

Figure 6.2 Explanation: reconstructive explanatory model and explanatory critique.

reconstruction burrows down to the deep level of structural rules or causal mechanisms which are unobservable yet can be ferreted out. The in-depth reconstructive
explanatory model of formal features of the actual situation directs the attention
towards the crucial juncture where intervention could possibly stimulate transformation and self-transformation of reality. Explanatory critique, on the other hand,
in dependence on the depth revealed by the reconstructive explanatory model
and led by the substantive theory of society, zones in on an instance of powerful
interference of a societal structure or causal mechanism which could prove to be
decisive for a successful and meaningful transformative critique. The moment of
explanatory critique takes the form of the actual location and identification of the
contingently interfering societal structure, mechanism or related process and an
explication of its distorting or blocking causal impact giving rise to the problem
felt and vaguely perceived in the first instance. The methodological priority that
Critical Theory assigns to problem situations, provocative threats, challenges and
social pathologies underlines the vital role of phenomena which disclose the real
structure or mechanism in pinpointing exactly what needs to be explained.

Forming part of the procedure of reconstructive explanatory critique is
a moment of critically reflecting on the reconstructed formal structures in the
awareness that their normative force could have been instrumentalized, corrupted
or subverted for the purposes of creating precisely the opposite effect. This is an

aspect of genealogical critique of which Foucault reminded contemporary critical theorists such as McCarthy and Honneth, but the precedent for this 'genealogical proviso' (Honneth 2007c) in the left-Hegelian tradition is to be found in Marx's (1963; Brunkhorst 2004) moderate thesis of the relapse of enlightenment into superstition or autonomy into heteronomy central to his analysis of Louis Bonaparte's victory in 1851 – that is, before Nietzsche and later Horkheimer and Adorno (1969) generalized it into a negativistic claim applying to society as a whole. Rather than in this generalized form, it enters Critical Theory as a state of affairs that is possible only under certain determinable circumstances.

The Critical Theory literature contains a disparate range of suggestions about the theoretically significant mechanisms operating in social situations, some of which are relevant to reconstruction and others to explanatory critique. Their more precise identification has become increasingly urgent since the emergence of the post-empiricist understanding of social science, which demands explanation with reference to mechanisms rather than in terms of regularities or laws. Table 6.1 makes explicit and systematizes various disparate assumptions and proposals regarding possible mechanisms contained in the literature.[4] The generative, relational and transformative mechanisms are the ones that play a role in the generation and social integration of society by making an input into the constitution, reproduction, organization and transformation of the latter. The contextual mechanisms at one and the same time provide both more or less positive enabling and more or less negative constraining conditions for the operation of the aforementioned mechanisms. Since Marx and particularly again since Lukács, the left-Hegelian tradition has of course focused principally on capitalism as the source of negative constraint. To it Habermas has added the bureaucratic state, which intervenes in social life through the medium of administrative power.

Table 6.1 Generative mechanisms

	Sphere		
Mechanism	*Intellectual-instrumental*	*Moral-practical*	*Aesthetic-practical*
Macro-cognitive and structural: contextual	Science and technology Economy	State Civil society	Ethicized cultural structure
Meso-cognitive transformative: collective learning	Intellectual purposive	Moral-practical democratic	Endetic (transposing feelings into needs)
Meso-cognitive relational: association	Theoretical-technical opportunity-creating networks	Movements enhancing means for solidarity building	Networks exploring and consolidating subject identities
Micro-cognitive generative: competences	New ideas	Normative innovation	Claims making of new kind of subject

Science and technology have become closely associated with capitalism and the state, and culture itself could also be a source of mechanisms. Be that as it may, it is in their highly varied constraining impacts that the contextual mechanisms are causally efficacious in generating the kind of problems or pathologies in social life in which Critical Theory is interested. From this more differentiated perspective, the institutional complexes associated with each of the intellectual, moral and aesthetic spheres can be regarded as relatively autonomous, but also as allowing for interpenetration or mediation with the neighbouring complexes. Accordingly, some practices may belong predominantly in one of the spheres, yet stretch across others for stabilization or motivation. Mediation also occurs on the vertical plane in the interplay of micro, meso and macro mechanisms.

A monocausal explanation and critique of a given social phenomenon or state of affairs in these terms, given the interplay between mechanisms, is rarely possible. This is obvious from a consideration, for example, of such familiar negative modern phenomena as commodification (e.g. capitalism), authoritarianism (e.g. fascism), instrumentalism (e.g. Holocaust or exploitation of nature) and ideologization (e.g. nationalism or racism). Often forming part of such pathological manifestations, moreover, is repression or the silencing of need articulation and participation, as well as obfuscation in the sense of distorting communication, manufacturing public opinion or manipulating the relation between active agents and the monitoring public.[5]

Nature of the socio-historical situation

The third and final methodological implication of the concept of immanent transcendence concerns the nature of the socio-historical situation of which the dimension indicated by immanent transcendence itself forms an essential part. The concept thus draws attention to the different contextual dimensions that need to be taken into account methodologically in approaching a social situation representing the object of Critical Theory. These dimensions can be portrayed as the basic axes structuring any situation relevant from the perspective of Critical Theory (see Figure 6.3). Immanent transcendence designates the normative axis of the situation to which Critical Theory in characteristic manner gives priority. The second lifeworld–system or, somewhat differently, agency–structure axis represents the dynamic temporal dimension of the situation, and the micro–meso–macro axis as the spatial dimension captures the scope and depth of the situation. In addition, it should be noted that the situation as structured by these three axes is manifested in the concrete on three cross-cutting analytically distinct and, therefore, methodologically important ontological dimensions. In a vocabulary owing something to the structuralist legacy but that would be more properly conceived processually in terms of semiotic mediation, as will become clear in the next section, they are the superficial empirical level, whose quality is signified by an icon, the deeper level of actuality (*Wirklichkeit*) which is signified by indices of various kinds, and finally the deepest level of reality (*Realität*), where the objective structures or real mechanisms generating the actual features and quality of the situation are confirmed as existing and operating.

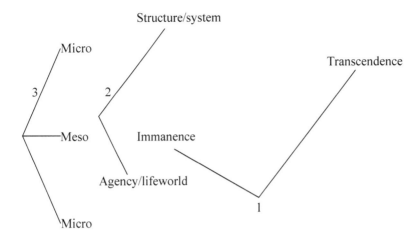

Figure 6.3 Dimensions of the objective situation: three axes.

Having clarified the major methodological implications of the concept of immanent transcendence, it is now necessary to consider Critical Theory's *medium quo* or sign-mediated epistemology for the purposes of offering as clear a statement of its methodology as possible. As established in the previous chapter, this is a dimension of which contemporary critical theorists are at best only intuitively aware and, therefore, which they do not make use of for the purposes of explicating, developing or justifying their shared methodological approach.

Three-place sign-mediated epistemology

A principal argument of this book is that a considerable advantage will accrue to any attempt to clarify and state as transparently as possible the methodology of Critical Theory if it is done with an explicit awareness of the epistemology presupposed by the left-Hegelian tradition. This is the *medium quo* or three-place sign-mediated epistemology with which, according to Apel, the young Marx operated in his seminal 'Theses on Feuerbach', for instance, and which Peirce later independently developed in fine detail. Subsequently, as was argued in previous chapters, both critical theorists and pragmatists, for example Horkheimer and Dewey, operated at least implicitly with this epistemology, which made their work distinct from the output of their competitors in the scientific, interpretative and orthodox Marxist traditions. Apel's and Habermas's bringing together of Critical Theory and pragmatism once again drew attention to this epistemology but, despite having restated it in some detail, Apel (1974, 1980, 1995) much more so than Habermas (1991a, 1996), they neglected the more specific task of linking it emphatically to Critical Theory and explicating its methodology in those terms. This is in all probability why the third generation as well as the emerging fourth generation have fallen back into just operating implicitly or intuitively with its basic principles. The claim advanced here, by contrast, is that a clear and sharply profiled understanding of Critical Theory's methodology is possible if it is developed in conjunction with an explicit reflection on its characteristic epistemological underpinnings.

Taking cues from Peirce and his principal interpreter in Critical Theory, Apel, it should be noted at the outset that to speak simply of epistemology here is not quite adequate. Peirce's thinking concerns not just knowledge or, better, a process of knowledge production, but a broad semiotic or meaning production process, which, moreover, also has an ontological counterpart. Knowledge production, including the practice of Critical Theory, is but a part of a much more encompassing process which includes the constitution of society and the development of the universe. Far from being isolated activities, cognition and knowledge production are contributions to problem solving and world creation necessary for the production and reproduction of society and for the maintenance of a sustainable relation to nature. This means that the production and validation of knowledge can by no means be confined to the scientific context, but of necessity has both a social and public significance and consequences for nature. To this should be added, finally, the important observation that self-referential implications – especially, the taking of responsibility – follow for Critical Theory itself from its involvement in such a set of constitutive, knowledge production and regulative relations.

The threefold sign relation

To begin with, the most basic relation in terms of which we understand the process of constitution and, therefore, also knowledge production is represented by the triadic sign-relation or function, itself a process of mediation, according to which a sign signifies or refers to something for an interpreter:

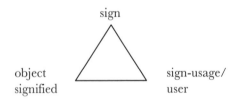

First, the sign has a material aspect and as such forms part of the constitution of the world in which sign-users or interpreters participate and, therefore, cannot be regarded as just a figment of the imagination. Second, the object to which the sign refers is real, which means that it is not just sense data, as in empiricism, nor merely an intentional object or phenomenon, as in phenomenology and interpretativism, nor is it simply a fiction or simulated virtual or hyper-reality, as in post-structuralism and post-modernism. It certainly figures in any discourse, but then it must be acknowledged that discourse necessarily involves the pragmatic presupposition of a common objective world. The sign-user or interpreter, finally, is not just an individual; but a community, in fact, a real communication community stretching beyond the scientific community as well as a temporally infinite, unlimited or ideal communication community representing a regulative and hence also a potentially critical principle.

The three moments of the semiotic process – the sign, the object referred to and the sign-user – are mutually interdependent. Presupposing each other, the exclusion of any one would methodologically amount to a reductive or abstractive fallacy of some kind which entails an inadequate mediation, short-circuiting or reification of the process of cognition, knowledge production, communication and practical realization. The contemporary tendency to give priority to interpretation, one could even say the current interpretative obsession, harbours this danger. It should be pointed out, by contrast, that the fact that the objective moment is part of a semiotic process of which the synthetic moment is an interpretation does not imply that the objective reference becomes redundant. As a materialist or realist theory of society, in any event, Critical Theory has a sharp focus which demands that in the pursuit of its explanatory and critical tasks it refer to something in the commonly presupposed objective world. In the case of its characteristic reconstructive explanatory critique, it must be stated clearly to what reference is made. The generative and causal mechanisms outlined in the above provide suggestions of what such objects of reference could possibly amount to (see Chapter 8 for illustrations).

Types of signs and universal categories

The process through which a sign-user or communication community comes to interpret and understand the object signified by a sign as something specific is made possible and mediated by a number of different types of signs – namely icons, indices and symbols:

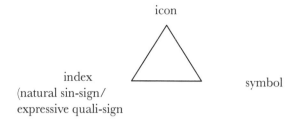

These three classes of signs respectively bring distinct ontological dimensions into play in the process of mediation. The ontological aspects are represented by the three universal categories Peirce called 'firstness', 'secondness' and 'thirdness'. Considered in relation to the three classes, these aspects shed light on the specificity of the different types of signs. Correspondingly, icons capture the singular quality of reality felt and perceived, indices the dyadically confronted, experienced and identified object, and symbols finally the triadic representative interpretation which interrelates and brings these various moments into a consistent unity:

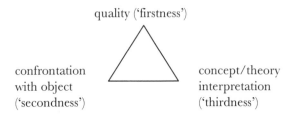

quality ('firstness')

confrontation with object ('secondness')

concept/theory interpretation ('thirdness')

   The quality of reality is of great important to Critical Theory, as is indicated by the central role assigned to suffering, moral indignation, resistance or conflict as qualitatively felt and perceived manifestations of the state of a society. It points towards the methodological priority critical theorists give to problems, challenges, threats, crises or pathologies. Such iconic significations provide Critical Theory with a starting point and a lead for a systematic investigation of its object domain by opening up the structure of reality. Given the processual interrelation of these three moments, the perception of the quality of reality and the confrontation with the object are simultaneously informed, but in a flexibly mediating sense, by relevant conceptual, theoretical and interpretative insights deriving from Critical Theory's own tradition as well as the other social sciences.

Dimensions of reality

The universal categories cover more specific dimensions of social reality, which are methodologically of the greatest importance. These dimensions stretch from the surface empirical level, through the objective level of the actual concrete situation and its real structuring or generative mechanisms, to the level of reality as validated and collectively accepted as such:

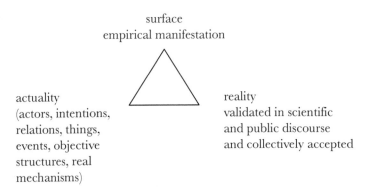

surface
empirical manifestation

actuality
(actors, intentions,
relations, things,
events, objective
structures, real
mechanisms)

reality
validated in scientific
and public discourse
and collectively accepted

The universal categories and the three dimensions corresponding to them indicate that the ontological implications of the epistemology under discussion diverge from empiricism's one-dimensional ontology. The distinction among the empirical, actual and real dimensions is of the greatest importance for an adequate understanding of Critical Theory's methodology. In this respect, there is a certain similarity between Critical Theory and critical realism. The talk of levels or 'stratification' (Bhaskar 1978: 170) here is somewhat misleading, however, considering that the empirical, actual and real dimensions are mediated moments in a semiotic process, yet the structuralist vocabulary of surface and deep structures is nevertheless meaningful. For a materialist or realist theory of society concerned with societal structures and their transformation, adequate observance of the objective dimension is not only vital, but also characteristic of Critical Theory. This orientation is strengthened by its incorporation of pragmatism, which is focused on the resolution of real problems. In the first instance, as discussed earlier in terms of immanent transcendence, the task is to reconstruct the actual situation up to the point that a formal set of elements and relations is reflectively abstracted that accounts for or explains the situation by specifying its parameters, constraints and generative regulation. Critical Theory as a substantive theory of society comes into its own, however, in its search for objective structures or real mechanisms that operate in and shape the actual situation and its surface qualities, especially structures or mechanisms interfering in them, distorting them or blocking potentially positive developments and thus giving rise to unjustifiable or pathological qualities calling for critical diagnosis and explanatory critique. In respect of its concern with the objective dimension, Critical Theory differs from various other epistemological positions. The difference from empiricism was mentioned earlier. It diverges particularly sharply from interpretativism in so far as the latter eschews a theory of society and insists on intertextuality and the never-ending concatenation of interpretations, not to mention declaring the concern with reality a metaphysical aberration. Critical Theory's option for a weak naturalistic ontology and pragmatic epistemic realist epistemology distinguishes it also from critical realism which, while avowedly focusing on generative mechanisms, nevertheless tends in the direction of an ontological realism. As we have learned from Peirce through Apel, Habermas and Bernstein, reality is a tension-laden concept – a tension given with the fact that reality is in process. As something on which the objectivity of knowledge depends, 'reality' on the one hand refers to an objective actuality and the structures or generative mechanisms underlying it. On the other, it cannot be secured by reference to the objective world alone since its establishment requires also a cooperative process of the search for truth through the public exchange of arguments. In the end, however, reality nevertheless must again surpass such discursive agreement in so far as it is something independent and transcendent, not reducible to agreement among the interlocutors. It is this tension between the reference to a structure or mechanism and the agreement about it within the horizon of the future possibility of a different judgement and agreement that constitutes the fallibility and conditionality in principle of scientific knowledge, including that of Critical Theory.

Modes of inference

In the course of the process through which an understanding of a signified reality is acquired, the community-based interpreter or investigator obtains a grasp and develops knowledge of reality through distinct yet interrelated modes of inference – namely abduction, induction and deduction:

Deduction and induction are two traditionally well-established inferential modes that are strongly identified with the empiricist tradition. Deduction is a logically correct or necessary inference, such as an axiomatic theoretical statement, that establishes a generality which could play a guiding role in the development of knowledge, yet under particular conditions could turn out to be false. Induction, by contrast, has the role of making available particulars that, in turn, could assert their authority as against purported generalities under specific spatial and temporal conditions, the end result being either the confirmation or falsification of such deductions. For Critical Theory, however, abduction is methodologically of vital importance. It is one of the aspects that distinguish Critical Theory from its competitors as well as from other methodological directions criticized by Horkheimer already in the 1930s and again by Habermas in the 1960s. In particular, the place of the positivistically reductive mode of inference called 'hypothesis' in empiricism is taken by abduction in Critical Theory. Adorno, for instance, criticized hypotheses since they are designed to establish regularities or what can be regularly expected, and: 'What can merely be expected is itself a piece of societal activity, and is incommensurable with the goal of critique' (Adorno et al. 1976: 69). The characteristic abductive inferential mode has always been central to the epistemological and methodological understanding of the critical theorists, although they did not necessarily call it by its technical name. Its origin, in any case, lies in the left-Hegelian tradition, Peirce having formalized a mode of thinking that at the time was clearly exhibited also by Marx. It is what Horkheimer and Adorno had in mind when they criticized the scientistic conceptual pair of induction and deduction and insisted on 'a thought process' (Horkheimer 1970: 43) or a dialectical procedure or constellational mode of thinking (Adorno 1970; Adorno et al. 1976) which draws specific elements together and forges clarifying relations. It is what Marcuse (1972) had in mind when he emphasized the importance of 'fantasy' or 'imagination' in Critical Theory, and it was the intent of C. Wright Mills, with a pragmatist-critical theoretical education in his wings, when he famously coined the phrase 'the sociological imagination' (1970). In Mills's phraseology, abduction amounts to making a creative, insightful, potentially fruitful and practically effective connection in a historically specific context among 'personal troubles of milieu' at the micro level, 'public issues of social structure' at the macro level and, crucially, 'master symbols of legitimation' such as freedom or reason at the normative level. These three moments obviously correspond to Peirce's categories of firstness, secondness and thirdness respectively, whereas the identification of socio-practical ideas such as freedom and reason is an indisputable reference to the transcendent reconstructive moment.

Modes of engagement with reality

The inferential modes brought to bear on the empirical, actual and real dimensions identified above presuppose particular modes of engagement with social reality on the part of the knowledge producer as an embodied being and member of a communication community. A particular quality of reality, for example suffering or a social conflict, provides a cue or affects the knowledge producer who undergoes sensations and has feelings accompanied by a vague perception of the situation. Such a qualitative impression opens up an access route to the object, which is experienced and existentially engaged with as something independent in the form of a detailed investigation and analysis of the actual situation and its structuring or generation. Finally, the resulting concept and theory formation, explanation and critique are tested and validated in the scientific and broader societal communication community and, in positive cases, given practical effect.

being cued and/or affected/
feeling/vague perception

experience-based   concept and theory formation
collection of information   testing and validation in
interpretation   scientific community and public
analysis   practical application
reconstruction   transformation and self-
explanation   transformation
critique

Having been cued or affected, the engagement with the object domain is guided by experience of various kinds. Far from being limited to the traditionally emphasized observational or sensory experience, 'communicative experience' (Apel 1980: 110; Habermas 1988: 92) necessary for interpretation and immanent reconstruction is called upon as well as historically specific socio-political or 'living experience' (Adorno et al. 1976: 69), which is prioritized by Critical Theory. The engagement with the object domain, the actual situation, as we saw previously, takes place within the parameters laid down by immanent transcendence and is carried out in particular by reconstruction. Reconstruction specifies the formal set of elements and relations generating and regulating the actual situation and thus provides an explanatory model accounting for its possibility and constraints. The depth level opened by reconstruction in turn provides the background against which explanatory critique, which is so important for Critical Theory as a substantive theory of society, becomes possible. In a positive case, the outcome of reconstructive explanatory critique adds to the conceptual and theoretical development of Critical Theory and, having passed through the discursive crucible of argumentation in both the theoretical and practical contexts, exerts a practical effect evidenced by a transformation and self-transformation of reality for the better.

The pragmatics of Critical Theory

The epistemology selectively presented here from the perspective of Critical Theory's methodology has had an impact in its broader form on the development of philosophy in the twentieth century, particularly the philosophy of language, which passed through the linguistic and the pragmatic turns, progressively shifting from an emphasis on syntax through semantics to pragmatics. Accordingly, the figure below seeks to capture the structures of language mediation in terms of the triadic semiotic scheme:

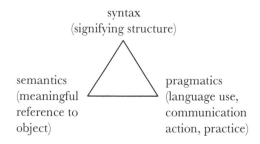

syntax
(signifying structure)

semantics
(meaningful
reference to
object)

pragmatics
(language use,
communication
action, practice)

It is interesting to note that pragmatics and the more general so-called 'pragmatic turn', which for their part have contributed to the so-called 'renaissance of pragmatism', represent in a certain sense a recovery and recuperation of previously forgotten aspects of the process theorized by the semiotic theory of signs. Of particular importance is that language use and communication, but also action and practice, were once again brought to the fore. It is the case, nevertheless, that much of what passes under the title of pragmatics, the pragmatic turn or neo-pragmatism is actually a deficient form of the full process of mediation. Irrespective of whether it is a matter of neo-Wittgensteinian, neo-hermeneutic, neo-Aristotelian, neo-Hegelian, neo-pragmatist or pragmatic social science, all of these versions of the interpretative turn suffer from a reductive or abstractive fallacy of some sort.

Typically, the objective dimension or the reality moment is excluded, and a more or less impoverished form of pragmatics or practice is presupposed. For Critical Theory, explanation, critique and the potential practical relevance of the explanations and critiques it develops are of defining significance, and critical theorists are aware of the fact that the practical efficacy of its findings and proposals is decided in the medium of communication and exchange between Critical Theory, its addressees and the general public. It is the case, of course, that contemporary critical theorists could gain greater clarity about what is involved in such pragmatic reception processes by analysing more closely the communicative context and the structure and dynamics of the process of communication transpiring within its bounds. The threefold structure of communication, basically indicated by the system of personal pronouns and reproduced both in the organization of the public sphere into a virtual stage with actors monitored by the public and in the reflexivity of this whole arrangement, needs to be properly thought through and taken into account in Critical Theory's methodology. The equally neglected related question of media – understood as material sign-mediated or semiotic communicative means complementing communicative action (Rusch 1999; Schmidt 1999; Baecker 1999) – also calls for more attention in Critical Theory. Nevertheless there is no doubt about the fact that Critical Theory's addressees and the members of the public are not regarded as oversocialized like the traditional *Homo sociologicus* or 'cultural dope', but instead are treated as cognitive agents who themselves are in a position to grasp the insights of Critical Theory's explanatory critiques, to engage in self-transformative and social-transformative practices and to understand the resulting processes reflexively as learning processes. Closely related is Critical Theory's concern, following Kierkegaard, Nietzsche, Freud and Mead, with subjectivity as a centre of vulnerability, the embodiment of a rational capacity, a source of resistance and innovation, and a receptive resonance surface. What these considerations suggest is that we are here concerned not simply with an epistemology or a theory of cognition and knowledge, but at one and the same time more broadly with a theory of communicative practical testing and reception and of the practical relevance and application of knowledge – indeed, a theory of social practice that relates to both the creation and organization of society and the development of nature.

Principal methodological moments

In the previous sections, Critical Theory's theoretical, normative, epistemological and ontological dimensions were clarified with a view to offering as clear and transparent a statement as possible of its methodological framework. All the necessary elements were touched on and can now be systematically related and elaborated where required. Although the following account of this framework unavoidably takes the apparent form of the presentation of each of its principal methodological aspects in isolation, it should be stressed that the overall perspective is a semiotic processual one in accordance with the threefold logic outlined earlier. Rather than simply isolated aspects or separate dimensions which occur or are followed in a linear sequence of stages, therefore, the methodological rules singled out – that is, problem disclosure and constitution, diagnostic reconstructive explanatory critique, and scientific-public validation (see Figure 6.4) – represent interrelated moments in a broad multidimensional process in the context of which they stand in a relation of mediation and interpenetration to one another. Critical Theory's methodology thus mirrors the process of knowledge and meaning production, which forms part of the social practices whereby society is created, reproduced and organized and its relation to nature is maintained. As part of these social practices, Critical Theory is able to contribute to problem solving and world creation only to the extent that it is communicatively connected with its addressees and, more generally, the public.

Problem disclosure and constitution

The first moment attests to the methodological priority that critical theorists assign to problems, challenges, threats, crises, pathologies – but of course not just any problem. Critical Theory characteristically differs from the standard approach shared by various other methodological directions of simply starting from a given scientific problem or arbitrarily choosing a methodological or theoretical attitude. Critical Theory depends on some occurrence, development or change in the objective context of life or society itself to give rise to a phenomenon of some kind that offers those involved a glimpse of a relevant structural or generative aspect of social reality and thus a privileged access route to acquire an understanding of it. Some instance – whether of suffering, the expression of moral indignation, resistance, struggle, conflict or the like – opens up the possibility of gaining knowledge of the structures or mechanisms generating social reality by rendering uncertain, questioning or problematizing the taken-for-granted background assumptions underpinning everyday social life and thus allows an appropriate cognitive or knowledge-producing relation to be established with reality. Besides opening up reality, giving methodological priority to problems, challenges, threats and so forth at the outset also establishes a connection between the knowledge production process and practice. Critical Theory shares this general orientation with its left-Hegelian cousin, pragmatism, which regards genuine problems as objectively produced and as emerging from existential problems or practical troubles which are confusing, conflicting and disorienting and thus call for inquiry, clarification, transformation into a definite problem and the development of a practically meaningful solution. The difference between the two, however, is that Critical Theory is particularly selective in what it regards as an appropriate problem. In keeping with the centrality of the concept of immanent transcendence, preference is given to problems arising in the wake of the deformation or prevention of the historical process of the actual social realization of reason – what are called 'social pathologies of reason' (e.g. Honneth 2007f).

This initial moment of problem disclosure in Critical Theory's methodology is captured by Peirce's category of 'firstness', which coincides with a material

I
PROBLEM DISCLOSURE AND CONSTITUTION

(1) through a sign-bearer (e.g. suffering people) vaguely
feeling and perceiving an iconically presented quality of an
objectively disclosed problem situation
(2) initial logical-imaginative abductive linking of problem
situation, its possible diagnosis, and its theoretization

('firstness'/icon)

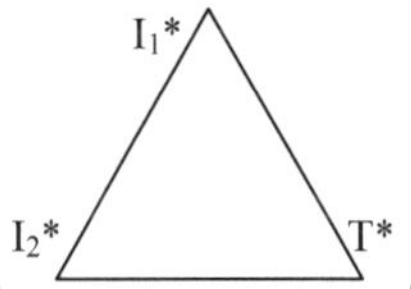

I_1*

semiotic process of
sign mediation

I_2*   T*

('secondness'/index)   ('thirdness'/symbol)

II   III
DIAGNOSTIC RECONSTRUCTIVE   SCIENTIFIC-PUBLIC VALIDATION
EXPLANATORY CRITIQUE   AND PRACTICAL APPLICATION

(1) diagnosis: (1) theoretical discourse:
• identification of problem (e.g.   • concept and theory formation
pathology, crisis) in concrete   • scientific validation of reconstruction,
context using descriptive analysis,   identification of problem, explanation of
quantification and interpretation   its cause(s) and critique, i.e. reality
• reconstruction under genealogical   intersubjectively confirmed
proviso specifying formal set of   (2) practical discourse:
elements and relations constituting   • practical testing through relating to
and generatively regulating the   addressees and the public
actual situation   • pragmatic reception
• reconstructive explanation   • problem solving and world creation
accounting for possibilities and
constraints of the situation
• reconstructive critique targeting
both negative features and positive
potentials at immanent and
transcendent levels
(2) substantive theoretical
explanatory critique in terms of
structure(s) or real mechanism(s) as
causal factor(s) generating the
problem

Figure 6.4 Methodology of Critical Theory.

*Firstness and secondness are immanent, whereas thirdness is transcendent (in the mediated sense
applying throughout).

sign-bearer expressing the singular quality of such an instance of objective movement. An iconic embodiment of the unusual, strange or disturbing quality of
something – a change, event, new actor, identity, word, semantics, symbol,
breakdown of mutual understanding, protest, conflict and so forth – attracts the
attention, arouses the emotions, unease, moral indignation, curiosity or concern
and gives rise to a mood or feeling that something is amiss and a vague perception
of the world as being out of joint. For Adorno, suffering is such a qualitative
expression of 'living experience' that demands the attention of the critical theorist; for Habermas, it is the feeling of 'becom[ing] uncertain' in the wake of the
breakdown of background assumptions. For Honneth, as in the aforementioned
case, Critical Theory's methodological starting point is made possible by a suspicion that all is not well in capitalist society and its liberal democratic institutional
arrangements: 'the suspicion of a social pathology of capitalist society as a whole'
(1999: 249). More generally, a variety of examples of shifts in the objective order
of society can be cited that played a central role in iconically signalling the quality
of reality and thereby not only disclosing problems, threats and challenges, but
also opening up new perspectives on the possible structuration or generation of
reality, which proved significant for the understanding of reality by both the members of society themselves and the theory of society. Historically, violence and
conflict have played an important role in making problem situations visible and
disclosing the world in ways that shaped the formation of new kinds of experience
and action as well as corresponding knowledge production processes (Strydom
2000). The processes leading to the emergence of the modern state and the rise
of capitalism, for instance, opened an entirely new range of problems which were
to become the basis not only of modern social movements and the normative and
political imagination of modernity in which new values were generated, but also
of the social sciences, including the left-Hegelian tradition and Critical Theory
itself. The same is the case, since the dropping of the nuclear bomb, with the opening of new risk and global perspectives, which not only allowed the experience
of equally global ecological and intercivilizational or cosmopolitan problems, but
also directed the attention to the presupposed ideas of reason or ethical universals
and the forces distorting and blocking their appropriate actualization (Strydom
2002).

At the opening stage of Critical Theory's production of knowledge, the participant's perspective predominates. The opening up of reality by a shift or alteration
in the objective order of society and the rendering visible of the structures or
generative mechanisms of reality is by no means the preserve of the critical theorist. He or she shares with the members of society involved or affected the very
feelings, emotions and mood such an eventuality generates. Indeed, in many a
case the critical theorist is in the first place dependent on the responses of the
members of society to become aware of what is happening. A particular quality
of reality, for example the suffering of a specific group or the resistance of another
against oppression, affects the critical theorist in a way which connects him or
her emotionally and perceptually with reality. The mood of the time, the feeling

of unease, lack of well-being or malaise that serves as material sign-bearer, if not widely shared, is manifest in particular sections of the population or specific groups whose reactions, responses, resistance, actions, struggles, identity forma-tion, claims, slogans or the like attract the attention of Critical Theory and spur it on in its pursuit of knowledge that could make a difference to the constitution of society.

Since the initial perception of the quality of reality is but a moment in a process that interrelates with the remaining moments, the iconic pointing towards a possible confrontation with something particular in the object domain is simultaneously, albeit only tentatively, informed in a flexibly mediating sense by potentially relevant conceptual and theoretical assumptions or anticipations. They are obviously influenced by Critical Theory's own tradition, but could also be shaped by broader intellectual resources. It is in this mediation among the three moments that the abductive inference or, rather, imagination or fantasy has its place. Through it the disclosed problem is constituted as the object of investigation. Being a more than merely logical and a less than purely speculative thought process, abduction is the only source of new knowledge. It is the vehicle of the creative forging of innovative linkages among the qualities, objective features and conceptual aspects of the situation in question. This it is able to do, however, only because, on the one hand, it captures the lightning insight, new world-disclosing perspective or innovative modification of language brought about by the change in the objective context of life and, on the other, it latches emotively and perceptually onto the qualitative singularity of reality. C. Wright Mills's explication of 'the sociological imagination' as establishing a creative, insightful, potentially fruitful and practically effective relation in a historically specific context among personal troubles of milieu, public issues of social struc-ture and master symbols of legitimation still stands as the paradigmatic concrete exemplification of the operation of abduction. Abduction is thus a variety of relational thinking that is able to imaginatively establish connections among the agentic and structural, the spatial and temporal, the micro and macro and the immanent and transcendent – vitally the normative – dimensions of social situations in the object domain.

The iconically encapsulated feature of reality representing the qualitatively felt and perceived manifestations of the state of a society is of great methodological importance to Critical Theory since it provides not only a starting point, but also a lead into the object domain. Opening up reality and revealing its structures and generative mechanisms, a qualitative impression clears an access route to an object which, in a second step, is experienced and existentially confronted and engaged with through a detailed investigation and diagnostic analysis of the actual situa-tion and its structuring or generation. The emotionally and perceptually evocative iconic representation directs the attention towards problems, deformations, reifi-cations and paradoxical and damaging social developments or social pathologies and, moreover, makes possible the eventual pinpointing of exactly what needs to be explained and be subjected to practically relevant critique.

Diagnostic reconstructive explanatory critique

The second moment in Critical Theory's methodology involves engagement with its object domain. From initially focusing on some quality of reality directed by its methodological prioritization of symptoms of phenomena in need of explanation and critique, Critical Theory next shifts to the identification of the problem in question in the context of the problem situation and its conditions. This is a basic diagnostic task which is both analytical and normative, including reconstruction, and is presupposed by the subsequent explanation and, particularly, the kind of critique that is characteristic of Critical Theory. This means that Critical Theory's engagement with its object traverses a number of methodologically distinct yet closely interrelated dimensions.

The diagnosis is opened with a comprehensive descriptive analysis of the actual situation. The situation is covered in all its aspects, from the spatial micro–macro depth axis, through the dynamic temporal agency–structure or lifeworld–system axis, to the normative immanence–transcendence axis. The description is achieved through the mobilization of relevant methodological resources, including quantification and interpretation where helpful. Interpretation is of particular importance for the development of a diagnosis which avoids an overly objectivistic or paternalistic treatment of the social actors involved in the situation or affected by it. However, in so far as Critical Theory is interested not only in an adequate grasp of the actual concrete situation but also in the real structures or mechanisms generating it, more than these familiar social scientific tools is required. This is where Critical Theory's characteristic methodological means of reconstruction enters. It takes Critical Theory far beyond both empiricist and interpretative approaches by allowing a penetration of the various layers of the actual concrete situation to the deep level of structural rules or generative mechanisms which, although neither empirically observable nor interpretatively discernable, can be unearthed with the appropriate methodological means.

Reconstruction fulfils a multidimensional task. First, it has to identify, recover and make explicit the structuring or generating force not only of the pragmatic presuppositions and possibilities of the concrete situation, but also of the formal or categorical structures refracted as socio-practical ideas of reason and expressed in ethically relevant cultural models which are unavoidably at work and thus presupposed by the social practices and relations in question. In doing so, it is in principle subject to a genealogical proviso in that the normative content of any of its results could turn out already to have been corrupted or reversed into its opposite. Instead of directing and guiding, a leading normative idea may have turned into a means of subjection to power and domination. On the one hand, the immanent pragmatic presuppositions and possibilities of the concrete situation are constitutive of the concrete situation, while on the other the formal set of transcendent structures are responsible for its regulative generation. What precisely is reconstructed in respect of these various immanent and transcendent features of the situation is theoretically determined in terms of what is accepted as the immanent force deeply rooted in concrete social life, which persistently, time and time again, exerts pressure towards transgressing, transforming and overcoming the status quo – for instance, labour, communication or recognition. Second, reconstruction has to put the reconstructed immanent and transcendent structures of the situation in relation to one another in a manner that shows how they mutually contribute to the constitution and regulative generation of the social practices, relations and form of life. The critical reconstructive demonstration of such mediation provides a framework of the formal features of the unobservable yet methodologically accessible depth-level structural rules or generative mechanisms of the actual concrete situation. This framework represents the set of elements and relations that lay down the parameters of what takes place in the actual concrete situation. As such, it plays the role of an explanatory model that makes possible a reconstructive explanation of the situation, social practices, relations and their possibilities and constraints in terms of their constitutive presuppositions and guiding socio-practical ideas. At this point, the reconstructive explanatory model must be subjected to a genealogical test to determine whether the regulative generation captured by its framework is actually intact and free from instrumentalization or misuse for contrary purposes. The reconstructive explanatory model is methodologically vital in two respects. First, it forms a basis for a reconstructive critique of the situation and, second, it opens the way for the culmination point of the second moment of Critical Theory's methodology, namely explanatory critique.

Arising from the basis of the depth-structure revealed by the reconstructive explanatory model, reconstructive critique takes a multidimensional form. Not only does it embrace an immanent or internal and a transcendent or external form, but each of these forms of critique goes in two directions. Immanent reconstructive critique negatively targets deficient forms of social self-understanding, orientations, practices, relations and institutions, and positively discloses new possibilities, interpretations, orientations, modes of organization and protest or transformative potentials contained in the situation. Transcendent reconstructive critique negatively exposes unjustifiable features of socio-practical ideas of reason or cultural models, and positively discloses surpluses of meaning harboured by socio-practical reason or cultural models that go unnoticed, are brushed aside or are only selectively employed in practice. In its course, a genealogical-critical test may be required. Once the methodological process progresses to this level, an adequate diagnosis of the nature of the situation is reached and an identification of the particular problem or social pathology is accomplished. At this point, therefore, an explanation-based critique of the phenomenon in question is in sight.

Explanatory critique, the defining aspect of Critical Theory's methodology, has the task of accounting for whatever causes the problem or social pathology characterizing the situation. Its concern is with the contingent yet powerful interfering, distorting, deforming or reifying structure, mechanisms or related processes that give rise to the unexpected, strange or disturbing quality of social reality that drew the attention in the first instance, but more concretely in particular also to the deformation and lack of exploitation of possibilities in the actual situation and the distortion of the semantic potentials of cultural models and their inadequate practical employment. In tracking the *explanans* represented by some causal force, explanatory critique is specifically led by the substantive theory of society's specification of possible structures or mechanisms, while more generally operating within the framework outlined by the reconstructive explanatory model and the deep structural level opened up by it. This model directs the attention towards the crucial juncture where intervention in the form of explanatory critique could possibly stimulate transformation and self-transformation of reality. Explanatory critique focuses in on what exactly would explain the problem or pathology, namely the real causal structure or mechanism representing the contingent deforming factor, obstacle or blockage that, if identified, could be transformed to allow a more adequate and justifiable practical realization of structural possibilities or socio-practical rationality. In the context of Critical Theory's second methodological moment, explanatory critique reaches its goal with the actual location and identification of the contingently interfering societal structure, mechanism or related process and a critical explication of its distorting or blocking causal impact that gives rise to the problem originally vaguely felt and perceived.

Critical Theory's engagement with its object domain, then, passes through diagnostic analysis, reconstruction involving both reconstructive explanation and critique and, finally, the defining culmination point of explanatory critique. The outcome of these steps becomes the central concern of its third methodological moment.

Scientific-public validation and practical application

The third and final moment of Critical Theory's methodology is circumscribed by the parameters of the communication and interpretation community within which the process of knowledge production, meaning creation and practical utilization in the form of problem solving and world creation takes place. It is a communicatively mediated and, therefore, an audience- and public-oriented moment in which discourses of different types and scope provide crucibles through which Critical Theory's reconstructive explanatory critique has to pass if it is to advance scientific development and prove practically efficacious. On the one hand, there is the more specific, scientifically relevant theoretical discourse and, on the other, the more general practical discourse in which Critical Theory relates to its audience and the public. Only in this public, open and inclusive medium of argumentation can critique link up with and be part of the process of social praxis in a way that avoids both theoretical or epistemological and practical authoritarianism (Cooke 2006, 2009).

Implied by its communicative and discursive nature, this third methodological moment is simultaneously a reflexive one in a number of different senses. Reflexivity involves the ascertaining of the conditions of the epistemic function and the socio-genetic relevance of the knowledge production and practical application process. Not only is the critical theorist included in his or her own theory but, like the theory, the theorist is part of the process of the constitution and transformation of the object of the theory. Critical Theory thus forms part of the social practices of the constitution and transformation of the object. Both its conditions of genesis and its conditions of validation and application are rooted in these practices and the related process and are therefore affected by the social context. On the one hand, the critical theorist objectifying the object does so from a particular position in the scientific field and, on the other, the knowledge produced makes sense only in the social world. Beyond Critical Theory's scientific relation to its object and its social relation to the knowledge it produces, however, there is, third, the properly epistemic relation between the object and knowledge of the object. Irrespective of the critical theorist's position or the social interest in knowledge, the object itself makes certain demands on the knowledge produced about it, and the existing knowledge has significance for the validity of the knowledge claims made about the object (compare Maton 2003). This last dimension needs to be stressed since none of the interdisciplinary organization of Critical Theory originally envisaged by Horkheimer, the democratic organization of critical social inquiry as advocated by Bohman following Dewey, or the organization of critical social science so as to exercise collective critique as demanded by Bourdieu adequately covers epistemic reflexivity in the proper sense of the word. In its third methodological moment, accordingly, Critical Theory has to engage in multilevel reflexivity in order to clarify its own conditions and to justify itself on a number of dimensions: its conceptual, theoretical and methodological elaboration relative to its own tradition and more broadly the social sciences and philosophy; the genesis of its knowledge production relative to the social practices of the constitution of its object; the practical relevance and application of its knowledge relative to the transformation of its object; and self-referentially its knowledge as an instance of responsible participation in the process of elaborating and developing reality. The importance of self-referentiality as a condition of the production and practical efficacy of knowledge for Critical Theory's effective contribution to the advancement of social science and to the appropriate development of society as well as society's relation to nature cannot be over-emphasized.

As a social scientific enterprise, Critical Theory is at all levels of its practice subject to scientific validation. Scientific validation is pursued though a communicative or, more specifically, a discursive practice which takes the form of argumentation in the context of 'theoretical discourse' (Habermas 1984/87, I: 19). Such discourse is a medium for the activation of various forms of reflexivity. Through the argumentative provision of reasons, plausible alternatives are considered and proposals developed and strengthened, and contested claims are tested, criticized, rejected or accepted. This discursive practice is brought to bear on the knowledge production process as a whole. From the start and throughout, concept and theory formation and related methodological judgements, which as part of the third methodological moment stand in a relation of mediation to the other moments, are discursively tested, as are all the phases in the process of knowledge production, from the abductive inference, through the diagnostic analysis and reconstruction, to the explanatory critique and the validation and communication of the findings. Far from adopting a dogmatic position, therefore,

Critical Theory willingly exposes itself to testing and criticism and, where necessary, participates in argumentation, both inside its own ranks and in the wider social scientific community.[6]

Apart from its epistemic function secured by theoretical discourse, Critical Theory also possesses socio-genetic significance in the sense that it forms part of a much more encompassing process. Since it contributes to the problem solving and world creation necessary for the production and reproduction of society and for the maintenance of a sustainable relation to nature, the production and validation of its cognition and knowledge can by no means be confined to the scientific context, but of necessity has social and public significance. It is only once pragmatic reception and acceptance occur that Critical Theory's practically relevant epistemic contribution is socially or publicly validated. This is where 'practical discourse' (Habermas 1984/87, I: 19) over and above theoretical discourse enters. The assurance of Critical Theory's socio-genetic relevance and practical efficacy depends on a second-order or reflexive type of testing, 'public testing' or 'practical verification' (Bohman 1999: 464, 466), which is possible only through the establishment of a relation with addressees and the public. In such a context, Critical Theory engages in communication as a form of action, communicative action as a form of orienting action. In practical discourse, a norm of action is subjected to testing in order to determine whether the concurrent claim that it is right or legitimate that it should be followed is collectively valid and thus acceptable to those concerned and affected. In these terms, Critical Theory's communication of the result of its diagnostic reconstructive explanatory critique serves the activation not just of reflexive competences, but in particular of modes of action. It communicates an ethical orientation for action, a context-transcendent reference point, a norm to follow in order to attain a problem-solving or world-creating goal which in some sense entails self-transformation and the transformation of reality. The communication of such an orientation is supported by a critical explanatory reference to a causal social structure or mechanism. The understanding it seeks in such a context has less to do, therefore, with interpretativism's concern with empathy, circular hermeneutic exchange or the fusion of horizons than with 'pragmatic understanding' (Rusch 1999: 173) – that is, providing an ethical orientation that stimulates the development of a new understanding which relates to action. To achieve such a pragmatic result, Critical Theory thus proposes a norm by suggesting or, rather, imputing an orientation as a means of understanding that stimulates reflection and action. The basic assumption of such an imputation is that the addressees are ethically autonomous (Cooke 2006, 2009) – that is, vulnerable human beings and sensitive cognitive agents who themselves are able to grasp the point of Critical Theory's explanatory critique, to engage in self-transformative and social-transformative practices and to understand the resulting processes reflexively as learning processes (Honneth 2004a: 352–7).

Establishing a relation with an addressee or audience and more generally the public and, hence, participating in a practical discourse demands an appropriate communicative infrastructure. To begin with, the disciplinary language of the social sciences and of Critical Theory in particular represents a system of com-munication offering a whole repertoire of communication means and strategies. For the purposes of pragmatic reception, however, this system of communication needs to be 'conventionalized' (Rusch 1999: 182). Rather than simply a matter of making the language more readily accessible, however, this requires that it be made understandable as a part of the social practices whereby society is consti-tuted and transformed and self-transformative self-cultivation is engaged in. Here Critical Theory, particularly critique, comes into its own as part of 'social praxis' (Celikates 2009). Conventionalization could thus include even unconventional or idiosyncratic linguistic and rhetorical devices such as exaggeration, metaphor and chiasmus or the surprising joining of words such as, for example, 'culture-industry' (Horkheimer and Adorno 1969: 128), 'repressive tolerance' (Marcuse 1969b), 'distorted communication' (Habermas 1970: 115) or 'colonization of the lifeworld' (Habermas 1984/87, II: 331) and so forth (Honneth 2000a: 59–60, 2007e: 231–2).

In so far as Critical Theory's interest lies in ethically orienting or reorienting action, however, this is of course also where the well-known difficulties of the practical efficacy of communication appear. It has the advantage granted by its methodological prioritization of problem situations or social pathologies, yet the difficulties are by no means negligible. Since there are no conventionally estab-lished routines, coordination arrangements, institutions or communication forums to bridge the cognitive gap in society between Critical Theory and its addressees and the public, it is vulnerable to the same limitations as any attempt to inten-tionally pursue communicative effects. They include the dispersed nature of the temporal staggering of communicative effects and dependence on the diversity of personal presuppositions as well as of both situational and general parameters and conditions (Rusch 1999). Besides the standard intrascientific media of journals, workshops and conferences, more specific thought could profitably be given in each case, beginning with the neglected textual form of social scientific knowl-edge (McCarthy 1994a: 90; Honneth 2007e: 231), to appropriate media capable of generating the scarce resource of the attention of the addressees or public. However, also the status, role and goal of the critical theorist should be reflected on. The critical theorist is no longer a general intellectual as had been assumed by the Enlightenment *philosophe*, nor a party or organic intellectual as represented by Lukács and Gramsci respectively, but instead a 'critical intellectual' who in turn has to be distinguished from today's 'normalized intellectuals' (Honneth 2007e). Whereas these last appear in their numbers in the media to inform and shape public opinion regarding relevant day-to-day political issues, the critical theorist is more concerned with going back behind the assumptions of publicly accepted definitions of problems and exposing through critical explanations the constructed nature of such definitions. Rather than unquestioningly accepting the political consensus of the day, the critical theorist probes, questions and problema-tizes the background assumptions of such a consensus and accounts critically for it by means of a historical-sociological explanation which unearths the complex of social and cultural conditions making it possible. It is only in this way, after all, that prevailing deformed modes of classification, perception, desiring, understanding and acting can be denaturalized and prepared for transformation.

In any case, just as Critical Theory does not presume to be the epistemic authority to which all and sundry has to submit, as though critical theorists know beforehand and throughout what ought to be the case, in the same way it is far from laying claim to a direct relation between theory and practice, as though the application of social scientific knowledge will immediately lead to the desired state of affairs. As but one among a number of participants – indeed one with a particular orientation – in a much wider collective learning, problem-solving and world-creation process, which is itself characterized by a non-linear mode of unfolding, it is more generally dependent on a medium- and longer-term process of a growing familiarity among members of society with its critical diagnoses. An important step in this process is, for instance, the sudden and increasing recognition since the 1960s among social scientists of all persuasions of the existence and, indeed, indispensable contribution of the critical approach. Related to this is that strain of the expressive revolution of the late twentieth century which attests to the enhancement of the reflexive and critical capacities of many ordinary members of society (Boltanski and Honneth 2009). Whatever the difficulties, communicative acts are always consequential in some sense, even when they apparently fail (Rusch 1999). On the one hand, it could establish awareness of a problem and/ or of the communicator, which is the starting point of pragmatic reception, and thus trigger conscious or unconscious cognitive constructions on the part of the addressees or members of society. On the other, disillusionment and frustration could trigger learning effects and thus improvements in Critical Theory itself. In cases where Critical Theory does succeed and pragmatic reception results in the reorientation of action, self-transformation and social transformation, a concurrent social or collective learning process occurs which contributes to problem solving and world creation.

Since the process of practical verification or public testing and pragmatic reception forms such an important part of Critical Theory's third methodological moment, it is worth dwelling on the methodological significance of the largely neglected communicative framework within which the fate of its findings and proposals is decided as well as the structure and dynamics of the communicative process whereby it happens. Some critical theorists (Habermas 1996, 2006; McCarthy 1994a) touch on the matter yet without developing it, whereas others (Bohman 1999; Honneth 2004a; Iser 2008; Celikates 2009) tend to focus on the Critical Theory–addressee relation without taking the larger set of communicative relations into account. As a starting point serves the threefold structure of communication represented by the system of personal pronouns designating the first person or ego, the second person or alter and the third person or Other. This structure is writ large and reproduced in the organization of the public sphere in the form of a 'virtual stage' (Habermas 2006: 419) with actors, ego and alter, who are monitored by the observing, evaluating, judging, commenting and opinion forming public (Strydom 1999, 2009a; Eder et al. 2002; Eder 2007). Representing the third point of view, the public ethically embodies and thus renders concrete and specific, albeit with a certain ambivalence itself requiring critical vigilance and evaluation, the situation that defines normative principles. Critical Theory's relation to its addressees is never purely a relation of double contingency between ego and alter, but in principle a threefold one that is epistemically and socially shaped by the 'triple contingency' (Strydom 1999, 2009a) attaching to the third point of view – that is, the temporally manifested, collectively acceptable, possible closure beyond both necessity and impossibility, implied by the public's ethical incarnation of the moral point of view. This element of immanently embodied transcendence or situationally actualized formality or counterfactuality is an inherent dynamic and structuring factor in the process of communication and exchange between the actors on the virtual stage, that is, between Critical Theory and its addressees. It makes present other voices embodying the pressure of potential questioning, disagreement and contestation (McCarthy 1994a: 89, 92). As such it is essential not only for 'the peculiar reflexivity of the public sphere that allows *all* the participants to reconsider what they perceive as public opinion' (Habermas 2006: 419), but by the same token also for their mutual cognitive construction of a collectively valid, acceptable and hence practically effective interpretation of Critical Theory's proposed ethical action orientation. An important aspect of Critical Theory's third methodological moment, particularly the practical discourse phase in which it is tested whether Critical Theory is in fact part of a continuing process of social praxis, therefore, is the observance of the shaping impact of the third point of view on pragmatic reception as it mediates between the actual situation and its transcendent reflexive rules. It makes possible a collective learning mechanism at least potentially allowing 'triple contingency learning' (Trenz and Eder 2004; Strydom 2008b, 2009a) in the sense of socially engaged actors on the virtual stage learning with reference to the monitoring public whose ethical incarnation of normative principles in turn depends on being informed by the situationally relevant concerns of the actors on the stage. This mechanism is at work not just in the public communicative context of day-to-day political issues where normalized intellectuals prioritize persuasive techniques to gain quick results in the democratic exchange of opinions. It is even more important in the case of critical theorists seeking through reconstructive explanatory critique to problematize the conditions and presuppositions of a whole form of life with a view to stimulating and reinforcing a process of long-term ethical re-orientation of a population trusting in the prevailing modes of classification, perception, desiring, understanding, acting and engaging in practices.

Several self-referential implications that follow for Critical Theory itself from its involvement in the kind of communicative context sketched above were mentioned a few paragraphs earlier. One such implication, however, warrants special emphasis at the close of an account of Critical Theory's methodology. It concerns responsibility. In this case, it is well to recall that this communicative context implies not just knowledge production, but at the same time also constitutive and regulative relations. Critical Theory has not only an epistemic function, but also a socio-genetic and socio-cognitive relevance and significance. Both its function and

relevance should be seen, furthermore, within the context of the larger set of relations of which it forms a part – namely, a persistently reconstituted socio-cultural
world which, although relatively autonomous, is continuous with a natural historical process stretching many millions of years back into the past and pointing to the
future. In this context, both the production and employment of knowledge form
part of a process in which signs mediate between reality and those who engage
with reality through the interpretation of signs. All three moments are at all times
involved in the temporal semiotic process. Far from being simply an imaginary
concatenation of figments of the mind, signs are an essential material element in
the process of the constitution of reality. It is incumbent on us, the sign interpreters, therefore, to use signs correctly and appropriately, and to learn to do so is to
acquire the ability to participate responsibly in the process of historical elaboration
and evolution, both natural and socio-cultural. Every act of cognition, knowledge
production and generation of pragmatic understanding in which Critical Theory
engages is an act of taking responsibility. It places the self-reflective, learning, self-
critical and sign-interpreting subject, which is not simply the individual, within the
broader framework of an unfolding natural and socio-cultural process in which it
is required and presumed to participate responsibly.

Conclusion

Aiming at as clear a statement as possible of contemporary Critical Theory's methodology, this chapter was opened by an illumination of its parameters by spelling
out the methodological implications of the key concept of immanent transcendence. The methodological centrality of reconstruction and explanation-based
critique was stressed in particular. To render the process of knowledge production as part of the constitution of reality comprehensible, in its relation both to
reality and to social practice, the presupposed sign-mediated epistemology was
presented next. On this basis, it was then possible in the third and final part of the
chapter to offer an outline of Critical Theory's methodology in terms of its three
semiotically mediated methodological moments. The first is problem disclosure
and constitution, in which case Critical Theory, proceeding by abductive reasoning, prioritizes problems or social pathologies of reason brought to attention by a
shift in the objective order of society itself. The second is the more differentiated
engagement with the object domain by way of a diagnostic analysis aimed at identifying the problem or social pathology together with its conditions in the actual
concrete situation as well as the interfering societal structures or real mechanisms
with reference to which it could be explained and critiqued. Reconstruction in the
form of the establishment of a reconstructive theoretical or explanatory model
and the development of a reconstructive critique plays an indispensable role in
the diagnosis. It provides the presupposition for the culminating explanation and
critique of the phenomenon in question, which is possible only in terms of a
substantive theory of society. The third methodological moment, which is above
all characterized by multilevel reflexivity, concerns the scientific as well as public
discursive testing of Critical Theory's mode of procedure, findings and proposed

critical-ethical action orientation, which eventuates, in felicitous cases, in its pragmatic reception and practical application.

Against this background, the next chapter compares and contrasts Critical Theory's concept of critique with a number of currently prevalent competing conceptions.

7 Varieties of critique
Critical Theory compared

Introduction

The purpose of this chapter is to sharpen the profile of contemporary Critical Theory by comparing it with other currently accepted approaches that claim to represent a form of critique or social criticism. Against the background of the debate about critique from the 1960s to the present, it offers a perspective on what may be considered the contemporary international field of critique. At first sight, the latter may appear as a reproduction of the antinomic field of hermeneutics and critique, but it is only when one appreciates that it is actually more diverse that Critical Theory's profile becomes visible. Although the unrelenting attack against both explanatory conceptions of critique based on social theory and the hegemony of the scientific viewpoint gave rise to the widely accepted distinction between 'internal' and 'external' critique, the parameters of the debate allow for the mediation of immanent and transcendent critiques in a way that, in certain cases, calls for the inclusion of the viewpoint not merely of the observer but also of the marginalized and excluded.

In the opening section of the chapter, the necessary framework for the comparative exercise is established, guided by Critical Theory's key concept of immanent transcendence. In the main section, the different approaches are then comparatively assessed with the aim of highlighting what is distinct about contemporary Critical Theory's concept of critique. Of importance are close rivals such as Bourdieu's critical sociology, Foucault's genealogical critique and Bhaskar's critical realism, but of great relevance lately is also Boltanski and Thévenot's pragmatic sociology with its central notion of critical practice. To be able to map the field in a way that permits Critical Theory's profile to be comparatively accentuated, however, reference is also made to the positions of Walzer, Rorty and Rawls, which have helped to shape the context during the past two decades. From this overview, it is evident that, although Critical Theory did and could further benefit from a dialogue with other critical approaches, its overall configuration, which emanates from the notion of immanent transcendence, is quite distinct.

The comparative framework

To identify different positions on critique or criticism that are relevant to highlighting Critical Theory's profile, a potentially fruitful strategy is to take cues from the protracted debate about critique. Having started with Critical Theory's rise to prominence in the 1960s against the background of the linguistic-pragmatic turn and the cognitive and structural revolutions and in the context of the positivist dispute and Habermas–Gadamer debate, over the following decades it was periodically revitalized by new developments and new participants with competing views. Among them are in rough chronological order Bourdieu, Foucault, Rawls, Bhaskar, Walzer, Rorty, Boltanski and Thévenot, McCarthy and Honneth. With the recent publications of the emerging fourth generation of critical theorists in Frankfurt, such as Iser and Celikates, the debate is once again intensifying. Considering the most important positions and associated forms of critique in this debate, it is possible to proceed to a graphic classification of different types of critique (see Figure 7.1). The classification itself is arrived at by means of the model of immanent transcendence put forward in Chapter 4 and employed in the presentation of Critical Theory's methodology in Chapters 5 and 6. In the following section, this classification serves as a map of the territory to guide the comparative profiling of Critical Theory's characteristic form of critique.

Since Walzer's and Rorty's interventions, reinforced by arguments of commentators (e.g. Bohman 1991; Kemp 2003), the distinction between 'internal' and

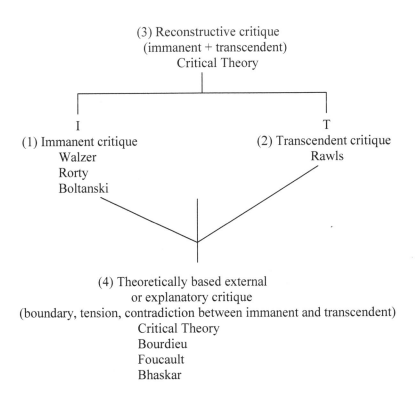

Figure 7.1 Types of critique.

'external' critique has become established as standard in the literature up to the very recent publications of younger critical theorists such as Iser and Celikates. Although this distinction is useful up to a certain point, it is not adequate to the task of laying out the whole field. Instead, the distinction between the immanent and the transcendent is used here in order to allow, with reference to the boundary, tension, contradiction or conflict between these two moments, the further dimension of explanation from a viewpoint supported by a sociological, materialist or realist theory of society. Crucial here are both the instance in social reality harbouring the potential to transcend the actual situation, which instance provides the critical perspective with an immanent foothold, and the causal mechanism giving rise to the problem features of the situation calling for critique. This more complex set of parameters is required if justice is to be done to Critical Theory's concept of critique.

Whereas some theorists can be classified under one particular form of critique, others represent more complex positions involving some combination or other of different forms. Walzer as well as Rorty put forward an immanent interpretative form of social criticism, with the latter differing from the former in so far as he adds a world-disclosing dimension. Rawls's suggested constructivist criticism could be regarded as a transcendent form of critique. On the basis of a consensual procedure of justification, it involves the construction of normative principles beyond society which allow a criticism of social institutions. Several authors, each in a particular way, combine immanent and transcendent forms of critique. This is an innovation that Habermas spearheaded and, therefore, following his use of reconstruction, it could be called reconstructive critique, although not all the theorists adopt this title. Both Honneth's critique of recognition relations and McCarthy's critique of impure reason fall in this category. Although Boltanski and Thévenot's pragmatic sociology of critique is an immanent form of critique, its uniqueness depends on the methodological decision to immanently assimilate the transcendent level in the form of 'orders of worth'. Like Habermas's, Honneth's and McCarthy's positions entail acknowledgement of the concept of immanent transcendence according to which theoretically specifiable presuppositions underpinning social reality already contain the normative import necessary for a critique of the existing social order. Considered in its full breadth and depth, however, this dimension is lacking in Boltanski and his associates' work. Habermas himself of course represents a still more complex position which, over and above reconstructive critique, also brings in a form of critique with reference to causal mechanisms – a dimension poorly, if at all, supported by Honneth and McCarthy's theories. Since it involves an objectifying historical-sociological explanation, it could be regarded as an external form of critique – but then only in the sense of 'internal exile' (Honneth 2007d: 225–6). Both the younger critical theorists Iser and Celikates defend at least verbally a position with the same complexity as Habermas's, both somewhat misleadingly calling it simply reconstructive critique. Bourdieu and Foucault as well as Bhaskar, again each in his own particular way, represent a form of external critique. Although there is therefore a certain comparison as regards external critique between contemporary Critical Theory, on the one hand, and critical sociology, genealogical history and critical realism, on the other, the contrast in other respects is rather marked.

In order to obtain a sharply defined comparative view of Critical Theory, the types of criticism or critique represented by Walzer, Rorty, Boltanski and his associates, Bourdieu, Foucault and Bhaskar are selected for more detailed discussion in the following section.

Comparison of types of critique

In the opening event of the debate concerning critique in the 1960s, Habermas's emancipatory ideology critique called forth strong opposition from Gadamer because Habermas on the one hand acknowledged that such critique remains embedded in language as the context of tradition but, on the other, insisted on the possibility and necessity of having recourse to infra-linguistic conditions such as labour and domination through which the constraints of reality make themselves felt. This confrontation cleared the way for the continuing contestation between the idea of a critical social science and the interpretative tradition. Against this background, the type of critique that Habermas (1990: 21–42) subsequently associated with his critical-reconstructive social science in the early 1980s in the context of playing reconstruction out against interpretation, once again met with opposition – this time articulated in different registers. This type of critique has different roots, which account for the divergent objections levelled against it and, hence, the alternative forms of critique or criticism proposed instead. On the one hand, formulated in terms of reconstruction with its constructivist element of reflexively abstracting the formal features of the real normative intuitions or expectations of competent social actors, critique takes the form of exposing deviant cases or unjustifiable violations of the principles in question. Rather than just normative considerations, on the other hand, Habermas envisages here explanatory reference also to social structures, mechanisms and processes, which are the topic of social theory (1984/87, II: 397–403; 2006).

Interpretative social criticism: Walzer

Having the contextualism and communitarianism of the cultural or interpretative turn in general and the opposition between interpretation and external critique prefigured by the Habermas–Gadamer debate in his wings, Michael Walzer (1987, 1988) defends an interpretative form of criticism from a standpoint within moral philosophy. Since his central intuition coincides with Gadamer's formula of the fusion of horizons, he gives priority to the tradition and practices of the form of life to which the critic belongs. Social criticism must take its cues from the constitutive self-understanding or self-interpretation of the community or, more broadly, society. The assumption is that the socially established values of the community make possible the identification of problems calling for criticism. According to his well-known figure of thought of three paths of social criticism (1987), both critique with reference to the 'discovery' of some real factor or structure – that is, reconstruction and explanation – and critique in terms of the 'invention' of criteria – that is, construction – are not only impossible but also practically ineffective. According to him, critique can take only one form, namely interpretation – a thick form which depends on the interpretations available in the community or society. Critics who either discover some external reference point or invent new criteria in terms of which they seek to develop a criticism distance themselves, by the very nature of their respective approaches, so far from the practices or form of life in question that they are incomprehensible to the social actors involved and thus render themselves incapable of convincing them and instigating the changes they deem necessary. Any remotely successful attempt at criticism must start from and retain a connection with the values inherent in the practices and form of life and entertained in some form by the social actors. Walzer takes the necessity and unavoidability of interpretation as rendering both forms of critique based on reconstruction and explanation redundant.

Walzer undoubtedly makes an important point. It concerns the need for any critic to establish and somehow maintain an immanent connection with the social practices and form of life in point. The thrust of the argument can be taken to be the compelling one that critique must take the form of social praxis. The question, however, is what exactly his demand entails, particularly considering the fact that any tradition, value or social practice is subject to a variety of possible interpretations. To assert the appropriateness of a kind of thick interpretation, as Walzer does, only highlights the central problem of his proposal – namely, the plurality of possible carriers of the constitutive self-interpretation of the community or society and, therefore, the proliferation of possible reference points serving as cues for the critic. What can one expect from a thick interpretation in a contemporary pluralist society, that is, if it is at all possible in such a context? What is the self-interpretation of the community or society, and where is it to be found? Walzer (1988) himself appeals to a confusing series of vehicles of social self-understanding, from national history and the critic's culture, through the hopes of the people and the ideals of the political leaders, to some group or other. Although he is against every form of external critique, he even admits that '[s]ometimes, of course, the critic must stand alone' (1988: 234). This incoherence indicates that Walzer has no clarity about how the reference point and therefore justifiable standards for social criticism are to be identified (Rosa 2004). He fails to clarify not only what precisely is to be interpreted, but also how this is to be done. His position is thus characterized by both a theoretical and a methodological deficit. These deficits are intensified by the inherent limits of the interpretative approach in so far as it is confined to a particular form of life, tradition or society. In the context of the currently emerging world or global society, for instance, the problem of methodological nationalism has come to attention owing to the urgent need for a more appropriate methodological cosmopolitan perspective (Beck 2006; McCarthy 1994a: 86–93). In light of this development, Walzer's proposal seems to be wavering between methodological nationalism, on the one extreme, and the much more imprisoning stance of what by analogy may be called methodological communitarianism or traditionalism, on the other, without any possibility of contributing to any of the currently pressing global problems calling for critique.

Interpretative world-disclosing critique: Rorty

Richard Rorty (1989) in the first instance endorses a comparable yet more contextualist conception of immanent interpretative social criticism by supporting an anti-Kantian or pro-neo-Hegelian idea of a relation to the practices of a particular community. Not only does he reject Habermas's appeal to the transcendent moment of universal validity, but he also questions the more concrete left-Hegelian idea of alienation with its implication of a base – that is, a concrete or ethical universal – for a critical perspective beyond the actual state of society. Rather than a critique of arbitrary and inhuman social restrictions thrown at society in the name of humanity, therefore, he recommends instead 'protesting in the name of the society itself against those aspects of society which are unfaithful to its own self-image' (1989: 60). Here Rorty questions both the assumption of the superiority and authoritative position of the critic and the concept of ideology together with its implication that people unconsciously maintain systematic false beliefs and thus are in need of consciousness raising. The desire to obliterate the distance between the critic and the community brought about by the critic's adoption of the observer's or outsider's perspective motivates Rorty's often repeated turn against theory. This turn is directed against reconstructive theory, which appeals to real essences such as intuitive action competences, but he also takes it in the direction of denying the possibility of making reference to causal structures or mechanisms, which are the central concern of a sociological or materialist social theory. This is the epistemological dimension of his argument, which goes back to his well-known book, *Philosophy and the Mirror of Nature* (1979).

The position Rorty argues for most consistently, however, is not a straightforward interpretative form of criticism, whether based on moral, contextual or epistemological presuppositions, but rather a world-disclosing one. Instead of references to Gadamer, his work teems with appeals to Heidegger's idea of world disclosure. The presuppositions in this case are obviously of an aesthetic kind. Rather than wanting either to clear some obstacle away or to burrow down to hidden depths based on inquiry, the best way to approach a questionable practice of a community, according to Rorty, is the imaginative, creative and poetic articulation of a new alternative practice. Not exposure, demystification or explanation is required, but linguistic innovation, a new metaphor, a new vocabulary that opens up potentials, possibilities, options or alternatives and thus serves the setting of a goal to be achieved. In so far as an achievable goal is linked to world disclosure, the Heideggerian perspective is obviously enriched by a pragmatist complement. Of the normative interest shared by pragmatism and Critical Theory, however, little or nothing is in sight. At the same time, the concern with the relation between theory and practice, or disclosure and reception, and the question of the conditions of such a transfer is subjectivistically reduced (Honneth 2007d: 49).

Like Walzer, Rorty reinforces important points that accompanied Critical Theory from its emergence in a new form. To the requirement of an abiding immanent connection with social reality and the clarification of the status of the critic he adds also the need to rethink the problematic indicated by the concept of ideology. Again like Walzer, he does not provide any positive indications of how any of these desiderata could be addressed. One is often left with the impression that his largely dismissive gestures lead to a recasting and postponement of these very problems. On the other hand, it is not the case that Critical Theory has all along been completely oblivious of these issues. The central problem of Rorty's position, however, is the glaring contradiction between his '*ideally* liberal society' (1989: 60) in which everyone has already accepted the norms that potentially could invalidate their own practices, and the present state of society, including numerous forms of persistent injustice, even after the touted definitive triumph of liberalism. The latter obviously requires explanation and critique over and above normative criticism and devising a new vocabulary. This discrepancy raises a series of questions about his methodologically important proposal of world disclosure (Kelly 2000; Iser 2008). Rorty proposes that the imaginative, creative and poetic articulation of alternatives would reveal current practices to be unnecessary evils and thus would prepare their displacement, yet he does not indicate any practices or even classes of practices to which such alternatives could or should be developed. His all too quick discarding of one particular form of ideology, the semantic form, instead of rethinking it in the pragmatic terms in which he himself deals, seems to be part of what prevents him from doing so. Observance of the inner-worldly learning processes that Habermas stresses but Rorty rejects in favour of world disclosure could also be helpful in identifying relevant practices. A further question is whether the imagining and articulation of an alternative would alone be sufficient to show up and contribute to the transformation of an unjust practice. Does this proposal not underestimate the problem of there being something that needs to be overcome or eliminated? Why is it that alternative practices are so easily imagined and articulated, yet remain elusive while the unnecessarily evil ones endure? This cannot simply be regarded as a matter of a Kuhnian anomaly, as he suggests. As in the case of Walzer's strictly internal or immanent criticism, these problems in Rorty's proposal of immanent world disclosure highlight the absence of a theory of society, and its outright dismissal of social scientific inquiry unmistakably signals his lack of interest in methodological matters.

Sociology of critique: Boltanski and associates

What Walzer and Rorty fail to demonstrate methodologically, Luc Boltanski and associates such as Laurent Thévenot and Eve Chiapello work out in detail in their pragmatic sociology of critique. As the shift from Bourdieu's critical sociology suggests, Boltanski's new departure is based on a basic methodological principle that is the direct opposite of Bourdieu's. Orthodox critical sociology proceeded from the assumption of an epistemological break between science and common sense which not only separates the two, but simultaneously lends superior authority to the former. In the sociology of critique, by contrast, its place is taken by the principle of 'symmetry' (Boltanski and Thévenot 1991: 24) inspired by the interpretative turn. This principle fixes the assumption that the descriptive language and explanatory principles of the social sciences are on a par with the modes of justification and critique employed by ordinary social actors. Ignoring this dimension, critical sociology puts too much emphasis on the external point of view and lacks the necessary normative resources required to be able to denounce social injustices. The relation between social science and social actors is activated by problem situations of questioning and critique, dispute, conflict or crisis in which those involved are compelled to engage in practices of justification and critique in order to test whether the attribution of qualifications or the evaluation of persons are legitimate. Situations of this kind are ubiquitous in everyday life under modern conditions and represent the privileged site of investigation for the sociology of critique. The question is, however, whether Boltanski and Thévenot have the full range of theoretical resources necessary to identify the critically relevant situations.

Rather than a purely interpretative situational analysis, Boltanski and Thévenot have recourse to the formal normative dimension of the situation. Their version of reconstruction, as it could be regarded, takes the form of identifying with reference to different models of extant political philosophy the different semantically articulated sets of rules or repertoires of grammars having a bearing on the regulation of the situation. Rather than just one, as stressed in moral philosophy, however, they identify a number of formalized orders of worth or the good in terms of the kind of arguments appropriate to each. As parametric conditions, these rules or grammars both enable and constrain the cognitive capacities or competences of actors, allowing them to engage in reflexive practices of justification of action and of critique. These normative orders are able to have a regulative impact on a situation, however, only to the extent that, below their formalized form, they are simultaneously inscribed in the arrangement of objects characteristic of distinct worlds in everyday life – what Boltanski and Thévenot somewhat arbitrarily call the world of inspiration, the domestic world, the world of public opinion or fame, the civic world, the market world and the industrial world. Although the authors stress ordinary actors' justification and critical competences, they admit that the actors for the most part unconsciously follow the given rules, whether in their formal or inscribed manifestation. Considering Critical Theory's key concept of immanent transcendence, it is interesting to note that the central importance ascribed to these two dimensions – the reflexive competences of actors expressed in everyday practices of world-related self-understanding and the complex of justificatory normative orders regulating the practices and making possible their coordination and, hence, agreement or compromise among the disputants – indicates that Boltanski and Thévenot's position is one that in effect operates with the distinction between the immanent and the transcendent dimensions and focuses on their mediation in everyday problematic situations. In fact, justification and critique involve testing the cogency of the relation between the particular and the general. This relation, however, is kept strictly within immanent bounds.

Starting from a problem situation, concrete analysis traverses three dynamically interrelated dimensions: action or practices, rules regulating the practices and at the symbolic level the semantic repertoires or narratives giving coherence to the rules, depending on the field of action or world to which they apply. Boltanski and Thévenot regard such integrated normative and pragmatic analysis, involving the observance of a plurality of formalized rules and object-based worlds having a bearing on a social situation, as making possible a relational position that neutralizes the substantialist assumptions built into standard social scientific concepts such as culture and group and, therefore, as cutting across and mediating the dualistic conceptions of culture and society, representations and structure, and communication and system. A single problem situation could thus generate a whole matrix of mutual or criss-cross critiques due to the different normative orders and worlds that could be brought into play at the same time. The pragmatic sociologists nevertheless single out two forms of unveiling or critique in particular. The first is a 'purifying' or corrective critique and the second a 'radical' critique (Boltanski and Thévenot 1991: 270–8). The former arises in the context of a disagreement and takes the form of an internal critique which challenges the application of a normative principle, for instance the violation of the achievement principle by a promotion due to nepotism, rather than questioning the principle itself. By exposing the deviation from the principle, it aims at reinforcing the validity of the principle by purifying the conditions of its application and thus making the situation more just. The latter arises in the more extreme case of a clash or conflict and takes the form of a radical questioning of the applied normative principle or its appropriateness to the situation in question. By appealing to a transcendent criterion, it aims at overturning the situation by introducing to it a different principle relevant to another world altogether. Although transcendent, such a critique nevertheless remains tied to the logic of the justification and critical practice in train since, according to Boltanksi and Thévenot (1991: 285), there is no external vantage point above the worlds and the plurality of justificatory regimes.

Pragmatic sociology's major contribution from the perspective of Critical Theory is readily apparent. Boltanski and his associates' basic assumption is that there is a structural similarity between everyday practices of justification and the mode of procedure of critical sociology. Examples abound in everyday life of the 'critical exposure of motives' and the 'revealing of interests behind arguments aiming at disinterestedness or the common good' which correspond to sociology's attempt at 'unmasking shams and ideologies' (Boltanski and Thévenot 1991: 24). This means that, although it is intentionally conceived as a shift from critical sociology, the sociology of critique does not amount to an outright rejection of critical sociology, or even of ideology critique, but rather establishes the important point that critique is a form of social practice. Yet there are a number of problems associated with this proposal, as hinted at above, which are important for understanding just how Critical Theory differs from it.

To begin with, a basic methodological decision leads to a not entirely unfamiliar contradiction. Despite the fact that Boltanski and Thévenot grant that social actors employ rules of which they do not have knowledge, that is, rules the authors themselves as well as other experts are able to command, they take Bruno Latour's methodological advice to follow the actors and, consequently, cast sociology in the mould of an action-oriented reflexive exercise which always comes too late and, therefore, is unable to identify any structures or mechanisms operating above the heads or behind the backs of the actors. The fact that different degrees of distantiation is quite possible, even if one accepts that critique is a social practice, and one has to, suggests that the pragmatic sociologists overlook an available contact point for a critical sociology. The problem resulting from their methodological decision is clearly visible in Boltanski and Chiapello's (2005, 2007) treatment of the 'spirit of capitalism'. In neo-Marxist fashion, the historically variable economic system is regarded as being impelled by an insatiable profit-maximizing drive which is supported by a normative elaboration serving to secure sufficient loyalty and acceptance of the principle of efficiency. The normative logic of development of capitalism, which has an impact on its material form, is marked by a periodically repeated sequence of the critical dissolution of the legitimacy of the social order it generates and the subsequent regaining of legitimacy. This means, paradoxically, that critique has the function, indispensable to the longevity of the system, of both transforming and stabilizing capitalism.[1] The authors investigate the relation between critique and social order only at the action level and, furthermore, never ask after the driving force impelling the system in the first place.

This failure points up a serious theoretical deficit. First, the pragmatic sociologists lack the necessary theoretical means, which is an absolute requirement of the left-Hegelian concept of immanent transcendence, of discriminating the significant from the less significant problem situations in contemporary society and, further, of specifying what force or tendency in social reality it is that harbours the possibility of meaningful normative transformation. Second, the assumption that all social actors are in command of the same level of competence to justify, criticize, pragmatically employ the range of normative grammars and mobilize the inscribed object worlds excludes the possibility that social conditions could lead to the unequal distribution of competences and the structural limitation and obstruction of the ability to use them. This glaring absence of a theory of society indicates that the orthodox critical sociology against which Boltanski and his associates set themselves off, granted that it overstates the possibility of assuming an external point of view as well as the monolithic nature of social reality, is by no means completely mistaken in focusing on the unequal distribution of economic and cultural resources and, hence, the unequal development of competences and opportunity structures for the exercise of competences. Social practices and their normative logics, be they justificatory and critical practices, without exception take place within the context of social conditions of some kind or another, some of which are limiting rather than enabling.

Critical sociology: Bourdieu

Although Pierre Bourdieu focused precisely on the inequalities and generative social conditions that Boltanski and his associates neglect, thus exhibiting certain similarities with Critical Theory, his critical sociology is closer to orthodox versions of critical social science, including mid-twentieth-century Critical Theory, than to contemporary Critical Theory. In fact, there are very sharp differences between critical sociology and Critical Theory. Two crucial features in respect of which Boltanski and Thévenot depart from Bourdieu are also among those on which Critical Theory differs from him. They are his basic epistemological-methodological and social ontological assumptions.

Epistemologico-methodologically, the most prominent feature of Bourdieu's position is what he calls 'the break' (e.g. Bourdieu, Chamboredon and Passeron 1991: 13; Bourdieu 1977: 1) between everyday opinion and scientific discourse. He frequently refers to authors such as Durkheim and Bachelard, which indicates that he proudly stands in the French tradition of the *coupure épistémologique*. Following Bachelard and Canguilhem, who stressed that immediate knowledge is fruitful as a starting point but only to the extent that it is left behind, Bourdieu (1977, 1990) from the days of his anthropological research in North Africa understood this break with reference to the phenomenon of gift exchange on two distinct yet interrelated levels (1977: 4–6): what he called 'the twofold truth of the gift' (Bourdieu 2000: 191). On the one hand, the reciprocal gift givers engage in a social practice that they sincerely regard as honouring their opposite number with an act of gratuitous, unrequited generosity. On the other, the carefully considered lapse of time between the gift and countergift indicates to the observer the temporal nature of the social practice – a feature that is the hidden condition of the pre-reflexive 'practical sense' as well as of unconscious 'strategic' orientations on the part of the participants. Whereas in his view Mauss remained captivated by the self-understanding of the actors and Levi-Strauss reduced it to a timeless structure, Bourdieu insisted on focusing on the mediation of the two dimensions by social practice as it temporally unfolds according to the pre-reflexive grasp that the participants have of the game. In his judgement, this change in perspective shifts the emphasis to the essentially strategic or economic and hence non-normative nature of the exchange practice and thus fulfils the requirement of the break in accordance with Bachelard's principle, according to which 'the *immediate* must give way to the *constructed*' (Bourdieu, Chamboredon and Passeron 1991: 82). On this foundation Bourdieu erects his theory of practice with its threefold theoretical architectonic of field or structure, habitus and practice (1977, 1990).

In an interview, Bourdieu submitted that he introduced the idea of practical knowledge possessing its own particular logic, in one respect, to acknowledge that, 'in a sense, agents know the social world better than the theoreticians' and, in another, to indicate that 'they do not really know it', so that 'the scientist's work consists in making this practical knowledge explicit' (Bourdieu, Chamboredon and Passeron 1991: 252). When the interviewer pressed him to clarify how the practical knowledge is made explicit, suggesting 'reconstruction', he insisted on the importance of 'construction' instead and went on to evade the question. What he did not recognize is that the relation between structure, habitus and practice, besides a strategic economic component, also has a normative dimension that is reconstructable for the purposes of explanation and critique, as is done by contemporary critical theorists in terms of the concept of immanent transcendence and the mediation of the participant and observer perspectives. Throughout his work right up to his late publications (e.g. Bourdieu et al. 1999: 607–26), it is apparent that the first part of the above equation – the knowledge of the agents – possessed little if any methodological significance for him. Despite claims that his genetic-structuralist approach allows the overcoming of dualisms such as the actors' self-understanding and sociology as a science, subjectivism and objectivism, action and structure and so forth, the required mediation was never accomplished. The principal features of his critical sociology are the model of the break and the related maintenance of an asymmetrical relation between everyday opinion or *doxa* and the privileged position of the critical sociologist, the latter of which is moreover underpinned by an objectivistic and more generally a decidedly scientific, if not scientistic in the sense of sociologistic, epistemology. There is, however, a persistent attempt on his part to mitigate these features through what he calls 'a second break' (1977: 2), namely the development of critical sociology as a reflexive enterprise which objectifies its own objectivism. The extent to which this form of reflexivity is successful becomes evident by contrast with Critical Theory.

Ontologically, Bourdieu's basic assumptions about the nature of social reality correspond to his epistemologico-methodological option for an objectivistic conception of critical sociology. Theoretically (Bourdieu 1977, 1990), society is constituted by social practices that are generatively structured from below by the habitus in the sense of enduring dispositions acquired through socialization, on the one hand, and structured from above by the social structures making up the social field within which the practice takes place, on the other. The classification systems of the social field are internalized and embodied to form the habitus, which provides the agent with a theoretical and practical relation to self and world, enabling participation in social practices. A social practice is borne by a number of agents, each with its own habitus and variable amounts of economic, social and cultural capital and hence power, and takes place in a social field, whether economic, political, artistic, scientific or other, which brings to bear on the agents the objective relations between their different positions, endowments and power, with the result that the agents are caught up in a permanent struggle to improve their capabilities and positioning in the field. Practices, according to Bourdieu's conceptions of the 'dialectic of strategies' (1977: 3) and the 'logic of practice' (1990: 80, 145–6), are led by strategies serving the improvement of position and capital. On this basis, he rejected both finalist and mechanistic approaches. The former, typically employing the concept of rules, which is far too ambivalent for Bourdieu, regards practices as being directed and guided by consciously set goals, whereas the latter treats practices as though they are mechanical reactions determined by antecedent conditions. Instead, practices should be theorized, on the one hand, as objective adaptations to structurally set goals and, on the other, as strategic moves objectively organized by the habitus as a generative and structuring source. Despite rejecting what he saw as a false dilemma, however, it is remarkable that Bourdieu's own analyses tend strongly towards the mechanistic pole of structural determination and the reproduction of structural conditions.

This tendency is moreover strengthened by structuralist assumptions regarding a 'homology' between structure and habitus (1977: 86, 143–58; 1990: 60). To the extent that the practical sense is an anticipation of the exigencies defined by the objective structures of the field, it guides agents by means of a belief or *illusio* (1990: 66–7) that not only underpins their participation by linking it to the collective belief in the meaningfulness and objectivity of the practice, but also excludes the possibility of reflecting on and breaking through the pre-reflexive nature of the generative accomplishment of the habitus and the structural conditions behind the belief. This objective illusion, which is central to the reproduction of any and every society, accounts for the superficial 'spontaneous sociology' of ordinary everyday members of society and the misleading euphemizing language or *doxa* in which it finds expression (Bourdieu, Chamboredon and Passeron 1991: 20–4). It is this all-pervasive collective illusion, spontaneous folk theorizing and *doxa* that make it absolutely imperative for sociology at all cost to break decisively with immediate knowledge and opinion.

On the basis of the break, critical sociology's task is twofold, in keeping with its combination of a Kantian concept of 'epistemological critique' and a Marxian concept of 'social critique' (Wacquant 2004). First, it requires the dissolution of *doxa* and, closely related to it, also of sociologies that just reproduce *doxa*, supported by an intellectual critique of the historically developed conceptual and theoretical instruments of sociology. This step is complemented by a social or institutional critique requiring the development of objective theoretical knowledge by means of which unconsciously operating, unobservable structures and mechanisms can be exposed. This 'unveiling task' (Bourdieu 2000: 5–8) is aimed at 'breaking the unanimity which is the greater part of the symbolic force of the dominant discourse' (1998: viii) and compelling the discovery of 'the truth of the collective unconscious' (1990: 146). On the one hand, Bourdieu acknowledged the difficulty of achieving such a practical effect of enlightenment and emancipation, noting in particular the inertia of social structures and typical reactions of resistance, rejection and denial of sociological explanation and critique. On the other, his firmly held view that the 'innumerable acts of recognition' required for participation in social practices and thus, more generally, for the functioning of the field render reflexivity, questioning and critique impossible (1990: 68), paradoxically undercut his claim that critical sociology has an enlightening and emancipatory purpose.

It must be stressed that the problems plaguing Bourdieu's critical sociology by no means simply invalidate his contribution. His substantive work and its practical effects go far beyond his particular stipulations. Neither the relevance of an epistemological break and of objectification as necessary moments in social scientific practice for the identification of social inequalities, structures and mechanism, nor that of the social ontological importance of structures and mechanisms can be denied. What is impossible to justify, however, is Bourdieu's tendency to generalize and absolutize the essential epistemologico-methodological features of social science and, furthermore, in complementary fashion to reduce the plurality of practices, including ones allowing reflexivity and critique, to routine practices serving the reproduction of the social structure, thus rendering impossible a practical link between critical sociology and its addressees. By contrast, contemporary critical theorists have been at pains to avoid these errors associated with orthodox critical social science.

Although Bourdieu never succeeded in giving a systematic presentation of the methodology of his critical sociology, as the incomplete publication project announced in *The Craft of Sociology* (Bourdieu, Chamboredon and Passeron 1991) shows, his work does reveal three mutually implicated principles (Grenfell 2008: 219–27) which bear a certain resemblance to Critical Theory: construction of the object, three-dimensional analysis of the object domain, and reflexive self-objectivation. However, the differences stand out. Motivated by a 'personal interest in unveiling . . . breaking the enchanted circle of collective denial' (2000: 3, 50), Bourdieu's critical analyses typically start from certain problem social consequences of symbolic power. The first methodological step takes the form of the construction of the object (Bourdieu, Chamboredon and Passeron 1991: 33–55, 147–99; Bourdieu and Wacquant 1992: 220–1, 227–33) involving a relational mode of thought which approaches Critical Theory's abductive mode of inference. Yet it is rather difficult to see how his denunciation of 'lived experience' as deplorable subjectivism and naïve humanism (1977: 4) and insistence on the Durkheimian positivistic procedure of definition could be reconciled with his constructivism and its abductive overtones. Already at this stage, the limits of Bourdieu's objectivism become apparent. The second methodological step consists of the systematic analysis of the object domain in terms of the levels specified by his theory of practice. At the upper level, the field is analysed both on its own terms and with reference to its relation to other fields impinging upon it, particularly the governance field of power. At the lowest level, the habitus of each of the participating agents is analysed. Field and habitus are connected through the relational analysis of the objective structure and laws of the relations among the distinct positions in the field as they become profiled in the course of the competitive struggle of the agents. By concentrating on the differential capital endowment and power of the agents in order to develop an unveiling critical analysis, it is obvious that Bourdieu operates with normative considerations, yet in characteristic crypto-normativist manner he denies this and insists on a non-normative economic-strategic focus and the mechanistic laws of the field. In comparison with Critical Theory, therefore, the occasionally employed concept of 'reconstruction' clearly possesses no methodological meaning in his work. This also explains why he reductively conceived of his research subjects as 'informants' (e.g. Bourdieu and Wacquant 1992: 228) rather than as social actors capable of reflection, judgement, critique, learning, self-transformation and world creation.

The most interesting difference with Critical Theory lies at the third methodological moment, where Bourdieu locates the defining feature of his critical approach: its reflexive character. Through 'the sociology of sociology', 'participant objectivation' or 'epistemic reflexivity' (e.g. Bourdieu 1993: 49–53, 2000: 118–22, 2001; Bourdieu, Chamboredon and Passeron 1991: 69–77; Bourdieu and Wacquant 1992: 36–46, 253–60), critical sociology is required to objectify its very own objectivism. This is required because of sociology's peculiar epistemological status, which rests on a blurred boundary between common sense knowledge and science. Since the very social conditions making it possible are simultaneously also the source of the typical errors to which sociologists are exposed, sociology's participation in social life, its being part of social knowledge, its objectification of its object of study and its production of knowledge about the social world must all be subjected to relentless objectivation. This enables sociology to attain freedom from constraints or limits, which benefits its analyses as well as its status as an epistemologically justified and practically efficacious social science. The initial break made with immediate social knowledge must be reflexively repeated at this second level to overcome unconsciously operating presuppositions or biases. Bourdieu frequently gave to understand that he drew his model of this form of reflexivity from the sociology of sociological knowledge, but this is somewhat misleading since his leading idea in this respect actually derives from Bachelard's vision of the 'scientific city' in which the organization of science allows a fully developed set of critical relations of social control. Whereas the sociological concept of reflexivity concerns the relation between subject and knowledge, Bachelard's concept focuses on the relation between subject – that is, science or the scientific community – and object. It is this latter dimension that Bourdieu had in mind when he characteristically insisted on objectifying sociology's objectification of its object. For this reason, he rejected (Bourdieu and Wacquant 1992: 71–2) not only Alvin Gouldner's idea of reflexivity tied to the sociology of sociology, but also the subjectivist or narcissistic social form of reflexivity which has become so widely accepted in the wake of phenomenology, ethnomethodology, the strong programme and postmodernism. An additional reason is that his Bachelardian concept stresses collective rather than individual reflexivity, which explains why he spoke of 'the collective work of critical reflexivity' (2000: 121; 2001). Accordingly, the individual sociologist can indeed be expected to shoulder the burden of reflexivity, but it is the collective organization of sociology and the sociological community at large upholding proper scientific standards as well as a generalized exchange of critiques that alone could ensure reflexivity and control over the knowledge produced. On this basis, Bourdieu committed himself to contributing towards the establishment of the necessary social conditions for justifiable and practically adequate social scientific knowledge. What is needed is the collective reflexive analysis of the collective objectification of the social world which would critically unveil not just the sociologist's biases, but above all 'the truth of the collective unconscious' (Bourdieu 1990: 146) structurally shaping practices in the social scientific field.

Although Bourdieu's position resonates with Critical Theory's ideas regarding the discursive and democratic organization of social science, there is a marked difference between their respective conceptions of the conditions of critical social scientific knowledge. At the outset, it is interesting to note the difference in epistemological assumptions. Bourdieu's (e.g. 1990: 4) adherence to the structuralist theory of signs presupposing the twofold distinction between signifier and signified contrasts sharply with Critical Theory's threefold semiotic theory of signs. In Bourdieu's understanding, which centres on the genetic structuralist relationalism captured by the field–habitus–practice formula, collective reflexivity would unveil the fact that knowledge is produced from particular positions in the social scientific field in the course of a competitive struggle in which all of the participants seek to realize their social interest in maximizing their own capital and power. By so doing, it would critically cleanse the field and thus contribute to a more secure social science and practically efficacious knowledge. From Critical Theory's perspective, however, this is a rather partial understanding of collective reflexivity – indeed, one that further reveals Bourdieu's tendency towards objectivism and scientism. The problem is that, for him, collective reflexivity is principally a matter of objective reflexivity in terms of relationalism, which is supplemented by social reflexivity through the organization of science and the scientific community (Maton 2003). Against the background of Critical Theory's sign-mediated epistemology as well as its third methodological moment, it is obvious that something of the greatest importance is missing here. Possibly on account of his over-exaggerated campaign against academic disinterestedness and misrecognition, Bourdieu does not command a dimension of epistemic reflexivity which, besides a social interest in enhancing their own positions, gives its due to a cognitive interest of critical social scientists in improving knowledge of the social world and rendering such knowledge sufficiently practically relevant to contribute to the improvement or alleviation of pathological social states of affairs. This gap has a number of implications – implications, important to note, that all have a bearing on a moment of transcendence beyond the struggle between competing social positions in the field of knowledge production, a moment that is not to be found in Bourdieu. First, the gap can be filled only by incorporating the relation between the object and knowledge of the object, as for instance in Critical Theory's adoption of a pragmatic epistemic realist epistemology which grants reality an independent status and regards knowledge of it as discursively established and therefore in principle fallible and corrigible. Since this dimension is not covered by Bourdieu, his talk of 'epistemic reflexivity' is without a foundation. Second, knowledge of the social world must be developed in such a way that it is at least potentially practically relevant. As this implies intersubjectivity, the requirement is twofold: that knowledge is, on the one hand, produced according to a collectively justifiable methodology and, on the other, rendered potentially practically relevant by starting from the knowledge of social actors and eventually subjecting it to practical testing or public verification involving the addressees and, more generally, the public.

Despite that fact that both share an interest in a theoretically based type of external or explanatory critique, the methodological difference between Bourdieu's objectivistic and scientistic critical sociology and Critical Theory, deriving from their respective understandings of epistemic reflexivity and the conditions of social scientific knowledge, could hardly be greater.

Genealogical critique: Foucault

A number of prominent authors belonging to or associated with the second generation of critical theorists (e.g. Habermas 1987; Taylor 1986; Fraser 1989) have not only doubted Michel Foucault's ability to offer a critical social science, but also raised serious objections to his project. Since his death, however, material by Foucault has been published that compels a revision of this assessment. In one publication, Foucault emphatically claims that his 'critical history of thought' philosophically stands in 'the critical tradition of Kant' (1998a: 459). In another (1998b: 440), he even admits not only the similarity between the French tradition of the history of science and the German tradition of the history of reason, but also that, had he been familiar with the work of the Frankfurt School and the avenues it had opened up, he would have been saved many an error, fumbling and detour. In the well-known late essay 'What is Enlightenment?' (1986a; also 1982), he confirmed his appreciation of Kant as well as the centrality of the concept of critique, but simultaneously also made clear the characteristic twist he gave this tradition by introducing the genealogical approach. By contrast with the older critics, consequently, contemporary critical theorists are inclined to a more chari-table interpretation of Foucault. They acknowledge not only his distinct form of genealogical critique, but considering the challenge it represents also stress the need for Critical Theory to learn from Foucault's innovation (McCarthy 1993, 1994a; Honneth 2007c; Saar 2007, 2009; Iser 2008).[2]

Although Foucault's career opened with doctoral work on Kant (1961), he dedicated his research over the next decade and a half to his project of Nietzschean-inspired critical history, which he codified in 1971 in 'Nietzsche, Genealogy, History' (1986b). It was not until approximately 1978 that he returned to Kant and a reconsideration of the heritage of the Enlightenment (Hanssen 2004: 295; McCarthy 1993: 60). Since this was intended to provide a broader basis for his position, a brief consideration of this late phase in his development could contribute to a better understanding of his characteristic form of genealogi-cal critique.

Starting from Kant's interpretation of the Enlightenment, Foucault regarded critique as a 'limit attitude' (1986a: 45) which avoids fixing on either the immanent or the transcendent by hovering over the boundary between the two. It coincides with the attitude of modernity, which is a mode of relation both to contemporary reality and to the self. Being focused on the inherent quality of modernity while simultaneously imagining it differently and transforming it, it takes the form of a confrontation of what is real – wanting to be free but not being free – with the practice of liberty. Critique is therefore a continuous reactivation of the attitude or ethos of a permanent questioning of our historical era by means of a type of interrogation whereby our relation to the present and to ourselves is prob-lematized. Under current conditions, however, it can no longer be confined to an epistemological critique investigating the limits of knowledge, as did Kant, but must be transformed into a practical critique which could transgress the existing reality. Foucault's reference to 'practical critique' and, reinforcing it, to critique as 'recapturing something eternal that is not beyond the present instant, nor behind it, but within it' (1986a: 39), brings to mind the left-Hegelian transformation of the Kantian critique and its core idea of immanent transcendence. Although this points to a certain affinity between Critical Theory and Foucault, it is of course his choice of the much later Nietzschean mutation of this line of development that provided the substance of his conception of critique and accounts for the big difference and challenge that genealogical critique represents for Critical Theory. Genealogical critique is carried out in the medium of historical analyses of the contingent conditions that, on the one hand, have shaped the existence, self-understanding and practices of the subjects involved in a complex and even paradoxical way and, on the other, harbour the possibility of a transgression of the limits of the situation particularly through self-transformation. Its focal point, marked by the border between what subjects have become and what they could be, is represented by those practices through which different sets of conditions become interrelated and interfere with one another to give rise to paradoxical and ambiguous outcomes.

The nature of Foucault's genealogical form of critique gains a sharper profile when it is located in the framework of his social ontological assumptions. Under the impact of structuralism and serial historiography, Foucault (1998b,c) approached social reality as a transformable system which called for the study of the conditions making transformation possible. Rather than adopting the biological metaphor of evolution, social reality must be conceived as embracing different time spans such as short cycles, twenty-five-year cycles, secular trends and long *inerties*, each of which carries its own type of events or processes. Being responsible for both discontinuity and continuity, this variety of events or processes is essential to the transformation of societies. Given the complexity and determining effect of the hidden layering of diffuse, atmospheric, polycephalic events, a structural explanatory approach rather than a conventional causal approach is required, not to mention an interpretative one. The former would be ineffective because of the complex and circular relations among the different dimensions. The latter would be particularly inappropriate since the events or processes in question are for the most part invisible and therefore unknown to the contemporaries. The aim of the structural approach is to identify the transformations of which society is actually capable.

Inspired by Nietzsche's genealogical approach to history, Foucault (1986b, 1998a) pared down this broad programme to the analysis of the conditions under which particular relations between subject and object are formed and transformed in a way that brought knowledge into play. In the wake of structuralism's rejection of phenomenology and the concurrent problematization of the concept of the subject, his interest was, as against structuralism, in retaining the concept of subject yet, as against phenomenology, finding a new way of posing the question of the subject. Taking it as the general theme of his research, he concentrated on the mode of subjectification or subject formation taking place in the context of a larger set of relations. The central problem was 'to determine what the subject must be, to what conditions he [sic] is subject, what status he must have, what position he must occupy in reality and in imagination, in order to become a legitimate subject of this or that type of knowledge' (1998a: 459). Since Foucault adopted a historical and processual mode of thinking, the conditions in question could be conceived neither from a purely formal nor from a merely empirical point of view, but needed to be approached as historically variable and situated within a particular practical context. Only on this basis could the concept of social reality integrate the two distinct dimensions of the subject – being subject to someone else's control, and having an identity based on self-knowledge, conscience and the ability to resist – in a way that would allow the implicated knowledge and power at work in the situation to be brought out and analysed.

Foucault's social ontology thus embraces three major dimensions. On the one extreme are the events or processes with their associated technologies and kind of knowledge that define the historical context within which subjectification occurs. On the other extreme is the subject or subjectivity, which is conceived from the viewpoint of practices as being constituted in a historically specific practical context and, therefore, as being historically variable. In the third place, practices establish a mediating context of application and allow the interrelation of knowledge and subject as well as the bringing into play of power, indeed different kinds of power, as a constitutive force in the whole set of relations. This framework was designed to serve Foucault's overall purpose of writing a critical history of basic modes through which human beings in Western culture and society are made into appropriate subjects. Accordingly, his major works are historically detailed, remarkably systematically interrelated studies of distinct modes of subjectification in which all three principal dimensions are involved, but with a different emphasis in each case. The early studies focused on knowledge as represented by scientific practices such as linguistics, economics and biology, which constituted human beings as speaking, labouring or living subjects; the studies of his middle period took as its central theme power as represented by dividing practices such as the asylum, clinic and prison, which transformed human beings into the insane, the sick and the criminal; and, finally, the late studies of sexuality concentrated on the self and the various practices and technologies whereby individuals relate to themselves in making themselves into sexual subjects.

Although this systematic comparison and contrast of historical modes of subjectification suggests that Foucault rooted his problematizing genealogical critique in an external position that opened a perspective also on the contemporary form of subjectivity, he often adamantly denied that he was a theorist of power and that he as historian contributed anything relevant to a critique of his own time. Yet his generalizations regarding power and his related appeal to Kant's refocusing of philosophy on the question of what and who we are in the historically specific world in which we live, dating from his last years, tell a different story. They make unequivocally clear that his 'critical analysis' is concerned with 'the problem of the present time' (1982: 216), which, for him, is 'the form of power which subjugates and makes subject to' in distinction to the feudal form of 'domination' and the nineteenth-century form of 'exploitation' (1982: 212). Accordingly, his 'starting point' was the contemporary form of 'resistance', namely the 'anti-authoritarian . . . struggles against the "government of individualization"' (1982: 211, 212). These struggles in the first instance drew attention to and gave voice to the widespread contemporary sense of being 'trapped in our own history' (1982: 210), which, in turn, can be led back principally to the new kind of 'power of the pastoral type', which arose with 'the modern state' and 'spread out into the whole social body' through 'the family, medicine, psychiatry, education and employers' (1982: 214, 215). In his late essays, Foucault is entirely explicit about the aim of his critical analyses. On the one hand, it is 'to imagine and build up what we could be' and thus 'to promote new forms of subjectivity'. This is necessary, on the other hand, to be able 'to get rid of this kind of political "double bind", which is the simultaneous individualization and totalization of modern power structures . . . to liberate us both from the state and from the type of individualization which is linked to the state' (1982: 216).

The model of genealogical critique (Saar 2007, 2009) as paradigmatically exhibited, for instance, by Nietzsche's *On the Genealogy of Morality* (1994) and Foucault's *Discipline and Punish* (1979) is characterized by the procedure of exposing the paradoxical reversal or collapse of socially accepted and operative normative ideals into practices of disciplining and normalization which stabilize power structures, domination and repression – what Honneth calls 'the procedure of genealogical exposure' (2000a: 63). This figure of thought owes something to Hegel as well as Marx, who both noticed 'the relapse of autonomy into heteronomy' (Brunkhorst 2004: 260; Habermas 1987), but it was Nietzsche who, as late outrider of post-Hegelian historicism, first radically analysed this paradoxical trap by using genealogical historicization to presenting moral codes as equivalent to coercive force or violence.

Adopting Nietzsche's approach, Foucault followed the same basic procedure of a historicizing description with a critical exposing intent, which, in his case, is supported by more systematically elaborated theoretical assumptions: first, the genealogical conception of the subject as being constituted in a historically specific social process in which it is subjugated yet retains some independence and the ability to resist; and, complementing it, what later emerged as a theory of power as a productive force mediated through historically specific practices which also bring knowledge into play in the process of constitution. Traversing these different dimensions, the historicizing description is at one and the same time a history of subjectification, a history of practices and a history of power, which, together, provide an analysis of phenomena whose interrelation and complexity can be made intelligible only by a multidimensional and processual approach. The central object is the formation of the subject or self and the emergence of particular subjectivities in the practical context representing the field of power. However, rather than a history relating to the past, as is obvious from the fact that Foucault starts from the 'problem' of our today being 'trapped in our own history', the genealogical account is oriented towards the present. It is essentially a description of our own prehistory which is intended to give the contemporaries an insight into the contingency of what they accept as necessary and thus to open the possibility of jettisoning the compulsion and instead being, thinking and doing things in a different way. Its historically specific focus on a particular process of power-drenched self-formation means that genealogical critique is situation-oriented and thus shorn of all universal significance. Accordingly, Foucault regards the critic neither as a universal intellectual addressing humankind, nor as an organic intellectual addressing a social class, but instead as a 'practical . . . situated . . . intellectual' who develops a 'diagnosis . . . by following lines of fragility in the present' (1998b: 450) with a view to addressing those caught up in that situation.

As in the case of Critical Theory, the genealogical approach can also be characterized in terms of three distinct methodological moments which are nevertheless mutually implicated. First, Foucault starts from the general problem of the present's being paradoxically caught up in its own history and specifies it with reference to some form of resistance which expresses itself against the form of power operative in the situation. Although it is a problem produced by society itself and not simply an arbitrarily chosen one, the actual selection is nevertheless led by systematic considerations. In Foucault's case, these considerations are clearly reflected in the progressive shift of the focal point of his project from an emphasis on knowledge first to power and then to the self. The second methodological moment is a diagnosis of the situation, which is identified in terms of a historically specific practical context interpreted as a field of power and antagonistic strategies in and through which the process of subjectification takes place. Although general theoretical assumptions about subject formation and the exercise of power are of the utmost analytical importance at this stage, a characteristic feature of the genealogical approach comes strongly to the fore here. It consists of the radical constructivist nature of genealogical critique, which, notwithstanding the critic's location within a particular local situation, depends for its problematizing effect on a step back or distantiation and the adoption of an external standpoint. It is a constructivism, however, that differs sharply from the normatively oriented Kantian constructivism of Rawls and, partially, of Habermas. On the basis of an assumption of a level of complexity entrapping those involved in society, a range of relevant historical evidence is mustered only to be integrated in an unconventional way into a quite speculatively constructed genealogical narrative of the power-drenched emergence and formation of the subject. It is constructed in this manner in order to maximize the calculated problematizing effect on the prevailing assumptions, practices and processes which are taken as self-evidently positive.

> [The] diagnosis . . . does not consist in a simple characterization of what we are but, instead – by following lines of fragility in the present – in managing to grasp why and how that which is might no longer be that which is.
>
> (Foucault 1998b: 450)

Where Critical Theory proceeds reconstructively, Foucault employs a radical constructivist form of critique, and, where Critical Theory has explanatory recourse to real social structures, mechanisms and processes, Foucault draws in a nominalist manner on historical evidence of practices, processes and human responses in order to sketch a speculative scenario or formulate an exposing genealogical narrative about how a particular rationality became subverted and, as a consequence, how a subject emerged partially deformed by being penetrated by power not only from the outside but even from the inside itself. During his strictly Nietzschean period before his return to Kant, the Enlightenment and the connection with the

Frankfurt School, Foucault renounced every concern with the normative dimension of social reality and regarded every demand for a normative justification of genealogical critique as part of the blackmail strategy of those wedded to Kantian transcendental and Enlightenment ideas. It is in view of this refusal to acknowledge the normative assumptions unavoidably made by his depiction of disciplining, normalization and repression as morally evil that Honneth brands genealogy a 'parasitic procedure of critique' (2007c: 63). In his late essays and interviews, however, Foucault is more explicit about the normative implications of genealogical critique. It is 'work carried out by ourselves upon ourselves as free beings' (1986a: 47), undertaken in the name of 'autonomy', 'liberty' or 'freedom' (1986a: 41, 44, 46, 50), with a view to opening up 'the space of concrete freedom' in the sense of 'possible transformation' (1998b: 450) or 'transgression' (1986a: 45). Yet these normative implications are not given effect in genealogical critique, which remains negative in that neither the reason for the necessity of the transgression nor what could or should be done after the transgression is described, indicated or even suggested. The normatively reticent Foucault is adamant that the diagnosis 'never has a prescriptive value' (1998b: 450).

The debate about critique of the past two decades has created a context in which a particular feature of genealogical critique has become highlighted. It came to light in the wake of the introduction of the concept of world-disclosing critique and its application to certain writings of Nietzsche, Horkheimer and Adorno as well as Foucault in view of the peculiar rhetorical form and quality of the texts in question – all works exemplifying the genealogical narrative genre (e.g. Bohman 1993; Van den Brink 1997; Honneth 2000a; Saar 2007, 2009). This feature, clarified best by Saar in relation to Foucault, defines the third methodological moment of genealogical critique. It concerns the form of presentation of the critical-historical, problematizing diagnosis which, far from being an appendix or gratuitous embellishment, is an essential part of the genealogical method. Although more moderate than its Nietzschean model, Foucault's version also exhibits the general qualities of a genealogical narrative that proceeds by abstraction, condensation, chiasmus and metaphorical illustration, which is presented with an existential urgency in the medium of affective-rhetorical exaggeration, dramatization and hyperbole. It does not appeal as directly as did Nietzsche's texts, but his genealogical historicizations of the present likewise both implicate and address an audience, particularly the reader of the text. The audience orientation built into the dramatic presentation is specifically calculated to evoke or induce a new way of seeing and experiencing the social world and thus to change the accepted value beliefs. By giving an alienating description of the social world, by revealing or stating something unexpected or even shocking, it seeks to provide insight into contingency, for instance, that the familiar social world rests on 'a precarious and fragile . . . base of human practice and history . . . [which] . . . can be unmade' (Foucault 1998b: 450). While trying to produce a destabilizing doubt or even an artificial crisis in self-understanding, it appeals to the addressees to embark on reflexive self-interrogation and self-transformation. The overall aim of genealogical critique presented in its dramatic textual form is the opening up of a space for the enlargement of freedom by shifting the boundaries of the unduly limited consciousness through the creation of a sense of possible transformation or transgression. As a limit attitude, however, Foucault's genealogical critique remains negative. It resolutely sticks to the boundary, refusing to cross over from the immanent to the transcendent, and in typical normatively reticent if not abstinent manner declines to offer any normative suggestions, let alone prescriptions.

From the viewpoint of contemporary Critical Theory, genealogical critique has to be acknowledged as a unique, meaningful and potentially practically effective form of critique which, unavoidably of course, faces the familiar difficulties of all attempts to intentionally create communicative effects. Unlike other versions of critical social science, however, it is also notable that Foucault's emphasis on the subject allows the development of a subject theory (e.g. Butler 1997), in some sense comparable to the role of psychoanalysis on Critical Theory (Honneth 2007d), which could account for the motivational structure and possibility of being addressed by critique in the interest of a rational transformation. As the lasting contribution of the Nietzschean line of development to the elaboration of the notion of critique, it has to be taken into account by any critical approach. Despite the irritating normative poverty of the genealogical approach, critical theorists are paying increasingly charitable attention to its unique denaturalization thrust, which differs from yet complements the same drive of their own more classical conception of critique. Saar (2007, 2009) has been promoting the relevance of the particular form of the genealogical narrative genre, but the danger here is its overuse and exhaustion, as has been the case with Foucault's critical histories, which have tended to lose their critical edge. Honneth, for his part, has given genealogical critique a more restricted interpretation with a view to incorporating it explicitly into Critical Theory's left-Hegelian model. Horkheimer and Adorno (1969) had already *de facto* achieved this on the basis of their experience of National Socialism when they added a metacritical perspective to Critical Theory, which has the task of checking whether the meaning of the normative ideas to which it appeals has changed, become instrumentalized or been lost. For Honneth, the normative ideas that Critical Theory reconstructs and constructively deploys in its critique of society stand in this sense permanently under 'a genealogical proviso' (2007c).

Critical realism: Bhaskar

Critical realism, which is associated with Roy Bhaskar (1978, 1989) and a number of associates (e.g. Sayer 1992, 2000; Archer et al. 1998), who have gained a following in Britain and also in Scandinavia (e.g. Danermark et al. 2002), is claimed to have become an international movement presenting a challenge to every other philosophy of social science. Despite Outhwaite's (1987, 2000) longstanding attempt to stimulate debate between Critical Theory and critical realism, however, critical theorists understandably continue to ignore the work of authors who unmistakably draw on the achievements of Critical Theory yet continue to trade on what seems like a wilfully inadequate characterization of it, while hardly being able to conceal their hostility toward it. This situation of antagonism and indifference allows neither the similarities nor the differences and even less the actual and potential mutual learning between the two critical approaches to be identified and acknowledged.

Like the contemporary version of Critical Theory, critical realism arose in and helped to shape the post-empiricist situation. Against the background of Scriven, Hesse and Harré's problematization of positivism's deductivist theory of the structure of science, Bhaskar insisted that the Humean criteria of causality and law are not merely insufficient but in fact lack necessity and, therefore, require the restitution of the ontological realism under-emphasized and even marginalized since the modern epistemological turn. Its central intuition is an ontology that acknowledges the existence of reality independent of consciousness and statements ('intransitivity'), a universal nomic dimension securing the necessary continuity of facts ('transfactuality'), and a differentiated power-imbued quality allowing emergence ('stratification') (Bhaskar 1998: xii–xiii). Together, these features provide the basis for the characteristic threefold critical realist distinction of the empirical, the actual and the real, which corrects the positivist or empirical realist tendency to collapse experience, events and the generative mechanisms giving rise to events and the experience of them. This distinction is of cardinal importance for the critical realist concept of science and its methodological structure. Science has an independent object, produces knowledge as an epistemologically relative social product, and follows a dialectical process of moving from manifest phenomena to the deep structure by first describing something, then constructing and testing a possible explanation and, finally, fulfilling its aim of discovering the mechanism generating it. In turn, the discovered mechanism then provides the starting point for the next cycle of progressing from descriptive to theoretical or explanatory knowledge (Bhaskar 1978: 248; 1989: 12, 19; 1998: xvii). Although there are a number of similarities between critical realism and Critical Theory here, barring the over-emphasis on ontology in Bhaskar as well as his followers (e.g. Sayer 2000), this conception transferred to social science is rather one-sided. Critical Theory understands both the starting problem and the aim of critical social science quite differently since it regards critical social scientific knowledge as being dependent upon a process of development which embraces not only established knowledge but also morally justifiable practice, for which the vehicle is communication. Critical realism's problematic tendency towards ontologization and scientism becomes apparent here. The social conditions of the constitution of the problem investigated scientifically as well as of the resolution of the problem receive little or no attention.

Initially, Bhaskar called his philosophy of science 'transcendental realism' (1978) to indicate that, although standing in the Kantian tradition, it simultaneously differed from Kant in that a transcendental argument for the possibility of science was presented from an ontological rather than an epistemological standpoint. Already at this early stage, he envisaged extending this philosophy from the natural to the social sciences and, once he had embarked on this new phase, the designation changed to 'critical naturalism' (Bhaskar 1989) instead.

Correspondingly, the meaning of critique also underwent a change. He indeed retained the transcendental refutation or critique of empirical realism for application to both positivist social science and hermeneutics. However, the new critical naturalism was presented as salvaging not only the positivist emphasis on generality or causal laws and the hermeneutic concern with a pre-interpreted reality, but also as being capable of explaining social phenomena in terms of real structures or generative mechanism and, owing to its being part of the very processes it explains, by the same token exercising 'critique' (Bhaskar 1989: 22). In the 1980s, the implied concept of 'explanatory critique' (Bhaskar and Collier 1998) became the theme of the third phase in the development of critical realism. The name 'critical realism' emerged only in the course of time through the merging of the two previously adopted expressions, transcendental realism and critical naturalism.

What strikes the reader familiar with the history of Critical Theory and its place in the philosophy of social science is Bhaskar's strategy of, on the one hand, giving Critical Theory an unjustifiably one-sided treatment and, on the other, falling back on Marx's notion of ideology critique, which had been extrapolated and made clear in the first place by representatives of the critical tradition. At first sight, this strategy seems to be motivated by the desire to advance his position as a unique synthesis at the expense of the earlier achievements of the critical theorists, but on closer inspection it becomes apparent that there are two systematic grounds accounting for it. The first concerns his interpretation of the history of the philosophy of social science and the second the priority he ascribes to natural over social science. Neither of these is defensible and each in its own way misleads him in his dealings with Critical Theory.

In Bhaskar's view, the history of the philosophy of social science is a 'historical see-saw, an oscillation to-and-fro between [two] basic positions', namely, positivism and hermeneutics (1989: 18). First, according to his interpretation, Comte and Mill's positivism called forth a reaction from idealism represented by Dilthey, Simmel, Rickert and Weber. Second, the early Wittgenstein, Russell and Moore countered idealism by developing logical atomism, which, in turn, gave rise to the countermove of the later Wittgenstein and Oxford ordinary language philosophy. Third, the 'sophisticated hermeneutics' that this latter reaction spawned in the work of Anscombe, Dray, Taylor and Winch then stimulated a parallel development on the continent. It took the form of the 'critical and dialectical hermeneutics of Gadamer, Apel and Habermas', which, for its part, immediately drew an attack upon itself by Popper and his followers. Much could be said about this rather selective and misleading interpretation, which excludes a series of crucial Continental developments and confuses others, but one argument in particular needs to be made. It concerns Bhaskar's two-dimensional oscillation model. If one adopts a more systematic and long-term perspective, it becomes apparent that the social sciences and philosophical reflection upon them have not two, but in fact three basic sources: the emergence of hermeneutics in the sixteenth century; the institutionalization of modern science in the 1660s; and, finally, the seventeenth- and eighteenth-century Enlightenment idea of critique. From the Reformation, the 'Great Instauration' and the struggle against absolutism run three major intertwined developments which are integral to the social sciences to this very day. Characteristic of Bhaskar's interpretation of the history of the philosophy of social science, then, is his lack of recognition of the third critical line of development and, more broadly, his concomitant neglect of the complex relations of mediation among the three lines. His history-of-ideas interpretation excludes not only the encompassing early modern societal discourse historically contextualizing the development of knowledge on the basis of major social movements (Strydom 2000), but also a series of nineteenth- and twentieth-century methodological disputes which remain incomprehensible without taking account of the contribution of the critical tradition (Strydom 2008a). It is obvious that Bhaskar's two-dimensional model not only severely curtails his ability to appreciate Critical Theory but, ironically, cannot account for his own attempt at synthesis, which actually seeks to bring together basic insights deriving from precisely the three basic social science directions. Having started from natural science and wanting to pull all other developments back into the science tradition, he fails to see this.

Bhaskar indeed allows for certain differences between the natural and social sciences, but the monistic overtones of his demand for 'an essential unity of method between the natural and the social sciences' (1989: 2, see also 18) translates into hostility towards established lines of research and even a call for their elimination: 'Humean theories of causality and law, deductive-nomological and statistical models of explanation and criteria of confirmation, Popperian theories of scientific rationality and criteria of falsification, together with the hermeneutical contrasts parasitic upon them, must all be totally discarded' (1989: 45). Despite the meaningfulness of established lines of research, for instance a convincing defence of statistics notwithstanding its inherent limitations (Pratschke 2003), this monistic demand is nevertheless still echoed by Scandinavian critical realists: 'the nomological (law-seeking) method must be rejected . . . Nor is the answer any method inspired by phenomenology or hermeneutics' (Danermark et al. 2002: 163).

Second, Bhaskar's prioritization of natural over social science entailed by this new version of the unified science doctrine represents a problem. Inspired by, for example, Keat and Urry's (1975) observation that, in his argument in the 1960s for a tripartite methodological framework for the social sciences, Habermas perpetuated a positivist misunderstanding of the naturalistic tradition, Bhaskar insists on classifying Habermas and Apel as belonging to the hermeneutic tradition. His reason for this is that they remained inextricably enmeshed in the 'antinomic problem-field' (1989:123) of positivism and hermeneutics, with the result that their position is just an 'inversion of characteristically positivist themes' (1989: 19). This rather forced interpretation is shaped by Bhaskar's conviction that a proper understanding of the social sciences and an adequate solution to their methodological problems 'depend upon a more adequate conception of natural science' (1978: 245) – by which, needless to add, he has in mind his own realism. Besides not having given due consideration to Habermas and Apel's relation to the critical tradition, their more pragmatist rather than positivist approach to science, their understanding of Critical Theory as social science and the realist moment of the latter, Bhaskar overlooked the fact that the emergence of post-empiricism was made possible not by natural science but by a series of social scientific interventions, from Kuhn's sociological history of science, through the cognitive and structuralist revolutions, to Critical Theory, which his own position presupposes. Rather than turn to natural science to make sense of critical social science, as he demands, we therefore need to revitalize the critical tradition.

Bhaskar introduces critique on the basis of his not entirely unfamiliar-sounding social-ontological assumptions and casts it in a strictly scientific mould. Social reality is a process of transformation in which emergent social phenomena are reproduced and transformed by relationally connected positions and practices. Considering that all social phenomena are dependent on positional practices and practices in turn on beliefs that themselves relate to preceding beliefs, not all of which can be explained or rationally changed by the agents, evaluation and, where necessary, judgement of falsity is a transcendental necessity. From this it follows that social scientific 'ideological explanation' (1989: 64) is a condition of rational practices and thus indispensable and unavoidable. The provision of such an explanation brings about a shift from facts to values and therefore entails a critique of the belief in question, the practice sustaining it and the social structure or social relations generating it. It is this figure of thought, by the way, that Bhaskar developed in the 1980s under the title of 'explanatory critique' (Bhaskar and Collier 1998) in a focused attack against the positivistically accepted Humean fact–value distinction, rejecting the naturalistic fallacy with the argument that facts logically entail values. It should be noted that, in the left-Hegelian tradition, the distinction between description and prescription has been blurred since Hegel in order to gain a normative reference point for a critical explanation of the distortion or prevention of the realization of reason under historically specific conditions (Honneth 2007d: 39–40). Be that as it may, since such explanation and critique are possible only on the basis of a justifiable theory that is able to explain false beliefs, Bhaskar (1989: 70) assigns this task to science and science alone. There is no need for a uniquely critical social science since science, particularly explanatory social science, to which explanatory critique is unique, is by definition critical and, hence, emancipatory. For this purpose he returns to the mature Marx, while attacking what he regards as the anti-naturalist and anti-scientific followers of Marx – the target unmistakably being Critical Theory. Marx 'the scientist' demonstrated not only how critique is achievable through the central methodological procedure of 'retroduction' (Bhaskar 1989: 70), but also how science is definitively demarcated from ideology. Here all the well-known problems associated with an external form of critique forcefully emerge, and that despite Bhaskar's frequent appeals to a pre-interpreted reality, the need for hermeneutic adequacy, social science being part of social reality as a transformative process rendering it critical, and social science as being about a subject matter for an audience. Among these problems are scientism, objectivism, the 'anterior disruption' or epistemological break between science and common sense, the hegemonic, imperial paternalism or epistemic authoritarianism of the scientist critic, the underestimation of the communicative, reflexive and critical capacities of the social actors, and the relation of critical realism to its audience as regards both the initial constitution of the problem and its eventual resolution. Then there is also the crucial problem of the instance immanent in social reality indicating the potential transcendence of the actual situation that is to be theoretically identified and is the vehicle of potential progress both in knowledge and in morally justifiable practice. These epistemological problems, as we have seen earlier, are faced by all external forms of critique, including those of Bourdieu and Foucault as well as Critical Theory itself. The decisive question is how critical realism methodologically deals with these problems. To the extent that critical realism approximates an orthodox position, a comparison in this respect would place it closest to the scientistically inclined Bourdieu, but then the latter's critical sociology has a reflexive dimension it lacks.

In its fourth stage, Bhaskar (1998: xix–xxiv) proposed to enhance critical realism by taking it through a dialectical phase. This step provides reference points for seeing more clearly certain similarities between critical realism and Critical Theory. They concern not only ontological levels – Bhaskar's empirics, actuality and reality corresponding to Critical Theory's Peircean–left-Hegelian notions of firstness, secondness and thirdness – but also the process of the development of knowledge and of reality – Bhaskar's dialectical process of 'the *absenting of constraints* (which could be viewed as absences) on *absenting absences or ills*' (1998: xix) corresponding to Critical Theory's Peircean–left-Hegelian pragmatic semiosis. Against the background of Critical Theory's methodological structure sketched in previous chapters, but with due caution regarding unwarranted dialectical overconfidence, these similarities stands out sharply. Conceived dialectically, according to Bhaskar, the scientific process opens its 'first moment of non-identity' with the concept of 'absence'. This unlocks to the 'second' moment or 'dialectical edge', which pivots on the concept of absence or negativity and immediately leads to 'referential detachment, existential transitivity and thence ontology' with all its categories 'from constraint to dialectical contradiction to rhythmic spatio-temporal efficacy'. The 'third level', centring on the concepts of 'totality' and 'concrete universal', is implied by the emergent phenomena generated by the 'contradictions within and between entities'. As regards its nature as a process that rests on the activity-dependence of social structure, this set of relations can be considered as having a 'fourth dimension' of 'transformative praxis, the unity of theory and praxis within praxis'. This process is driven by 'the logic of dialectical universalization', which seeks to 'absent all dialectical constraints' and is guided by the regulative idea of 'the eudaemonistic or good society which [is] already implicit in the most elemental desire' (Bhaskar 1998: xix, xxiii–xxiv). The purely formal parallel between critical realism and Critical Theory regarding the three-level methodology and progress guided by an idea of reason should be obvious.

At the core of this complex as it is manifested in critical realism as social science is what Bhaskar, following Hanson, Harré and Hesse, calls 'retroduction' (1989: 12, 19). The development of science follows a three-phase scheme according to which a phenomenon is identified, an explanation is then constructed by means of retroductive reasoning, and finally a generative mechanism explaining the phenomenon is identified. Retroduction occupies the central place in this dialectical process of the development of knowledge. Now, when one notes that reconstruction is to Critical Theory what retroduction is to critical realism, then the sharp and decisive difference between the two positions becomes graphically clear. The most remarkable thing about critical realism is that, despite Bhaskar's appeals to a pre-interpreted social reality, transformative social praxis, emancipatory explanatory critique, truth as a condition of science, and lately the eudaemonistic or good society, there is no proper provision in his outline of the transcendental structure of science for the normative dimension without which critical social science is impossible. In this respect, it is noteworthy in addition that Bhaskar conceives of human activity essentially in a non-normative manner: 'Now human activity is in fact a more or less continuous stream in time of more or less deliberate, more or less routine causal intervening in the world, subject to the continuing possibility of reflexive self-awareness' (1989: 82).

Over and above induction and deduction, retroduction in critical realism is a mode of inference that proceeds by means of theory, analogy and metaphor with the aim of explaining a phenomenon by discovering and identifying the causal mechanism generating it. It is apparently called retroduction because of the counterfactual nature of the mode of argumentation involved: constructing an idea or 'building a model . . . of a mechanism, which *if* it were to exist and act in the postulated way would account for the phenomenon in question' (1998: 12). This orientation, however, could not be more different from the explicitly asserted type of counterfactuality characteristic of reconstruction in Critical Theory. For the latter, reconstruction supported by abductive reasoning is essentially normative in that it is concerned with the reflexive abstraction of the pragmatic presuppositions informing social actors, action and practices. Critical realism, by contrast, orients retroduction directly toward the task of discovering a causal mechanism without the support of such normative analysis, and then it banks on the resulting explanation triggering an automatic, potentially critical shift from facts to values. The concept of retroduction, which has been adopted from the philosophy of natural science, is obviously not sufficiently differentiated and sensitive for use on its own in critical social science. The methodological framework of Critical Theory encapsulated by the concept of immanent transcendence and within which reconstruction finds its place, as made clear in previous chapters, allows an analytical distinction between the reflexive abstraction from real presuppositional structures of normatively significant regulative ideas of reason and the search for and discovery of real structures or mechanisms that could explain powerful interferences causing social pathologies. Critical Theory indeed has a definite realist dimension, as Outhwaite (1987, 2000) has argued, and in this sense it compares closely with critical realism – particularly regarding the causes of powerful interferences in social relations. Here Critical Theory could learn from critical realism to be more aware and attentive to the realist nature of these concerns and to be more explicit about the mode of inference or reasoning – that is, retroduction – involved in dealing with it. Yet it differs sharply from critical realism in terms not only of the normative dimension and its implications for the concept of critique, but also of the mode of procedure for arriving at a certain normatively relevant aspect of reality. It concerns the pragmatic presuppositions of social actors, action and practices. In critical realism, the normative dimension is allowed in at the tail end as a mere effect of scientific explanation bringing about a shift from facts to values, and there it is left hanging in the air with no support by, for instance, recognition of the nature and problems of the relation between critical realism and its audience. Critical realism admits reality on the side of the agents or the members of society only in the form of reasons as causes, and it has no means available to come to grips with normatively important pragmatic presuppositions. Retroduction is differently oriented and insensitive to such real structures possessing normative significance. Failing the wherewithal for the iterative reflexive abstraction of such reality-based normative import, critical realism has no basis for appealing to totality, a concrete universal, the good society and so forth – that is, apart from the vacuous and teleologically problematic 'logic of dialectical universalizability' (Bhaskar 1998: xix). By contrast, contemporary Critical Theory gives central place to reconstruction within the framework of the left-Hegelian idea of immanent transcendence, which demands the theoretical ability to specify an instance immanent in social reality itself that possesses and demonstrates the potential to transcend the actual situation by bringing about transformation, including self-transformation.

Conclusion

The march through the contemporary international field of critique provided the opportunity, by way of the comparison and contrast of a number of currently relevant conceptions of critique or criticism, to highlight the profile of contemporary Critical Theory.

The moral-philosophical and contextualist demand voiced by Walzer and Rorty that the critic must maintain a substantive interpretative relation with the social form of life criticized, albeit fraught with problems, has a certain force that Critical Theory seeks to satisfy by means of the reconstruction of normatively significant presuppositions immanent in social life. By contrast with construction, such reconstruction is not accomplished once and for all, but has to be appropriate to the historically specific context and, therefore, the need for iteration is associated with it. The world-disclosing critique Rorty proposed on the basis of his epistemological rejection of realism is first of all taken into account by Critical Theory at the very outset of abductive problem constitution with reference to a development in social reality that reveals an object calling for diagnostic analysis. Drawing on available indications, especially indications of absences, it also elaborates in a positive critical manner on possibilities or alternatives at the immanent level of actors' self-understandings and social practices as well as at the transcendent level of ideas of reason or cultural models. As against both Walzer and Rorty, Critical Theory insists on the indispensability of theory in accomplishing these various tasks and, further, maintains an awareness of the level of reference so as to avoid falling in the trap of methodological nationalism, not to mention methodological traditionalism. With Boltanski and associates Critical Theory shares not only respect for the reflexive and critical capacities of social actors, as is indicated by, for instance, the concepts of communicative competence and communicative power, but also the prioritization of problem situations inducing justificatory practices in social life as reference points for social scientific analysis. By contrast with the sociology of critique, however, it is on a theoretical basis more selective in ascribing social significance to problem situations and insists on the need to take into account inequalities in the distribution of reflexive and critical capacities and opportunities to exercise them and, by extension, the social conditions responsible for such structural distortion.

In so far as Bourdieu is interested in precisely such inequalities and social conditions, there is no disagreement between critical sociology and Critical Theory, but on closer inspection the differences quickly mount. Chief among these are Bourdieu's scientistic and objectivistic epistemology, rigid structuralist ontology, underestimation of the capacities of agents, normatively stripped strategy-oriented theory of practice and, above all, philosophically impoverished sociologistic conception of reflexivity, which is incapable of accommodating social scientifically important considerations concerning the relation between the object and knowledge of the object. In both the left-Hegelianism of the 1840s and the Frankfurt School of the 1940s, the awareness of the problem of the relapse of autonomy into heteronomy had been alive in the critical tradition, but it took Foucault's revival of Nietzschean genealogical critical history to alert Critical Theory in the late twentieth century to the need to look more closely at the intertwined power relations and resulting paradoxical reversal of expectations, norms and ideals lurking beneath normative foundations, positive potentials, structural possibilities and opportunity structures. At the same time, Foucault's focus on subjectification also underlined the importance of considering anew the problem of subject-formation – a problem that becomes increasingly urgent as the emergence of world society accelerates. On the negative side, the fact that Foucault's critical genealogical rhetoric proceeds on the basis of a Nietzschean perspectival epistemology and an underlying nominalist positivistic ontology rules out his form of critique as a comprehensive alternative to Critical Theory.

Critical realism, in turn, differs from Critical Theory not only in its natural science-inspired scientism and objectivism as well as the consequent imperialism of its methodological monism, but above all in its tendency to over-emphasize ontology and, quite predictably, even to pursue it *ad absurdum*, as illustrated by the later works of Bhaskar and some of his followers. What the two approaches do share is the post-empiricist concern with explanation with reference to real causal mechanisms. Here Critical Theory could learn from critical realism to be more explicit and emphatic about its own differentiated left-Hegelian ontological assumptions for the purposes of explicating its multilevel methodology. Not just the distinction among firstness or empirics, secondness or actuality (*Wirklichkeit*) and thirdness or reality (*Realität*) is relevant, but in particular also the last: the real generative or causal mechanisms and the corresponding retroductive mode of inference appropriate to their explanation. Yet this is at the same time the very juncture where Critical Theory decisively parts way with critical realism. Instead of ontological realism, it adopts a pragmatic epistemic realism. Whereas retroduction may be helpful in the explanation of causal mechanisms, the characteristic feature of Critical Theory is reconstruction, which is specifically designed to fully incorporate the normative dimension, which critical realism admits only in an extremely anaemic form. Critical Theory's characteristic emphasis on the normative dimension distinguishes it sharply from critical realism. Unlike the latter, this emphasis leads it to recognize that science is part of society through communicatively mediated structures and processes which need to be taken into account in the very practice of science. The immanent orientation of reconstruction secures this at an early stage of the scientific process and, by making audience-oriented practical discourse part of Critical Theory, knowledge production is re-linked to social practice at the final stage. It is the status each assigns to normativity, therefore, that accounts for why critique as social praxis is the defining feature of Critical Theory but only of adjectival significance in the case of critical realism.

8 Methodology in action

Introduction

Having clarified Critical Theory's methodology in the foregoing, this final chapter is aimed at illustrating its application by presenting a series of concrete examples drawn from the research of established critical theorists. Each case is presented in sufficiently transparent terms to provide a model for the organization of research. That it is not a matter of mechanical application, however, is apparent from the fact that the selected authors, besides dealing with very different topics, emphasize different aspects of the methodology and employ different methods in their research.

The first example of Critical Theory's methodology in action is Jürgen Habermas's recent outline of the potential of normative theory for empirical research with reference to mechanisms intervening in, distorting and blocking the epistemic import of democracy. It is followed, second, by Axel Honneth's analysis of the transposition of the late twentieth-century cultural ideal of self-realization into a means of institutional manipulation and exploitation that leaves a series of currently typical pathologies of individualism in its trail. In the third example, Thomas McCarthy focuses on the traces of its racist legacy still to be found in contemporary liberal political philosophy and theory. The fourth and final exemplary case is Klaus Eder's analysis of the use of sustainability in European environmental policy to mobilize the population and the role it plays in the emergence of a European society.[1] Each of the examples is presented in terms of the three methodological moments of Critical Theory: first, problem disclosure and constitution of the object, second, diagnostic reconstruction and explanatory critique and, finally, scientific-practical validation.

Habermas: distortions of the epistemic import of democracy

In the opening example, Jürgen Habermas (2006) is concerned with the question of whether democracy still has an epistemic dimension in the context of the kind of political communication that has become associated with the media society. It is indeed not a piece of substantive research, but rather the development of a framework for the analysis of political communication in contemporary society which is intended to clarify how the normative theoretical focus characteristic of Critical Theory can be applied in the course of substantive research. Although the text is largely theoretically oriented, it is nevertheless eminently suited to illustrate Critical Theory's methodology in action.

A close consideration confirms that the overall theoretical-methodological idea informing the text is immanent transcendence. Although not explicitly used, it is suggested by the distinction between the normative and the empirical in the subtitle and, more importantly, captured by the central statement, 'Ideas enter into social reality via the idealizing presuppositions innate in everyday practices and inconspicuously acquire the quality of stubborn social facts', with the result that, 'In the course of everyday practices, actors are always already exposed to a space of reasons' (2006: 413). Then, in a footnote, Habermas quite explicitly characterizes this as a 'conception of a detranscendentalized reason, the normative content of which is incorporated into social practices' (2006: 423). Rather than simply a direct confrontation of the immanent with the transcendent or the real with the ideal, however, the relation between social practices and normative ideas is methodologically treated in terms of a 'critical' approach which focuses on the 'contingent constraints' conditioning the process of realization or concretization and seeks to identify and explain the 'specific causes' of such constraints. The detection and explanation of such causes is made possible theoretically by normative ideas which, however, must first be won through the reconstruction of presuppositions underpinning everyday social practices.

Problem disclosure and constitution of the object

Habermas's starting point is the sense of a negative quality appertaining to contemporary Western democracies. On the face of it, certain things seem to work reasonably well, but in 'real-life politics' (2006: 414) communication is not proceeding in the way it is expected to. His suspicion is that democratic political communication is plagued by 'communication pathologies' (2006: 416). This problem has become apparent in the wake of recent developments and changes affecting public communication. To make sense of what this negative quality implies requires abductively or logically yet imaginatively establishing relations among micro and macro phenomena as well as a related normative point of view. On the one hand, Habermas notes that there is prima facie evidence of concerns about the relevance of issues, the availability of information, the quality of contributions and, related to these, a lack of legitimacy. On the other, he sees that these concerns must be linked to the higher-level conditions of public communication, which he suspects are subject to intervening contingent constraints. Normatively, this relational set is completed by means of the principle of democracy. The key to it, however, is the brilliant abductive insight encapsulated by the chiasmus, or apparently internally contradictory construction, 'systematically distorted communication' (Habermas 1970: 115) which is here investigated in the form of 'pathologies of political communication' (2006: 420). This is the leading concept for the diagnostic analysis to be conducted in order to properly identify the nature of the communicative pathologies in question and, on that basis, to explain and criticize it in terms of a causal mechanism or conjunction of mechanisms.

Diagnostic reconstruction and explanatory critique

Central to the diagnosis of the pathologies of political communication is the reconstruction of the normative pragmatic import of everyday social practices relevant to public communication and democracy. In certain respects, such reconstruction depends on both description and interpretation in order to achieve the reflexive abstraction and statement of the normative principles or ideas of reason having a foothold in, yet simultaneously generatively regulating, those social practices. Once these principles as necessary conditions for the generation of democratic public communication and democracy have been reconstructed, Habermas takes it that we have 'nonarbitrary standards for the identification of the causes of communication pathologies' (2006: 416). The first step in this descriptively and interpretatively supported reconstruction aimed at establishing a reconstructive explanatory model requires the critical clarification of the concept of democracy. Habermas's basic theoretical assumption that linguistic communication is a force immanent in society which harbours the potential for the recurrent problematization and transcendence of the status quo directs this step. What must be reconstructed, according to this theoretical perspective, are those real generative mechanisms of democracy as a communicative process whereby collective problems are resolved and a common world is constructed. For this purpose, Habermas considers the 'institutional design of modern democracies' and the 'normative bedrock' it presupposes (2006: 412). The design brings together three elements by allowing the private autonomy of individuals and public democratic citizenship to be mediated in the public sphere in a way that links society and the state. This institutional arrangement arises from three basic normative presuppositions which it is designed to actualize in the concrete and to protect. They are equality, political participation and public opinion, which, respectively, are protected and guaranteed by civil liberties, communication rights and an independent public sphere.

The first outline of the reconstructive explanatory model of democracy emerging here allows Habermas then to engage in a reconstructive critique of the political philosophies that currently play a structuring role in actual democracies. They all incorporate the basic normative and institutional elements of democracy mentioned above, but they do so with widely varying emphases. The liberal tradition stresses above all the liberties of private individuals or freedom, republicanism the participation of active citizens or equality, and finally deliberativism the formation of considered public opinion or solidarity. If one systematizes the different models of democracy implied in Habermas's discussion (see Table 8.1), then the basis and direction of what we may regard as his reconstructive critique become graphically clear. This critique is at bottom informed by his basic theoretical position and thus employs the reconstructed normative import of democratic linguistic communication as the measuring rod to evaluate the different political philosophies. On the one hand, a negative critique of the one-sidedness and limitations of contemporary thinking and therefore widely held beliefs about democracy is directed at both the economically based, goods-oriented liberal and

Table 8.1 Models of democracy

Component	Model		
	Liberalism	*Republicanism*	*Deliberativism*
Principle	Rights and liberties	Inclusion and equality	Deliberation
Domain	Economic	Communitarian	Epistemic
Medium	Rational choice	Political ethos	Public opinion
Mode of constitution	Individual preference aggregation	Collective ethical self-determination	Cooperative value- and will-formation, problem solving and world creation
Substance	Goods	Feelings	Reasons

the communitarian-based, affectively oriented republican philosophy. On the other, a positive critique seeks to disclose a neglected dimension of democracy and thus to bring out a different emphasis. It gives weight to deliberation, particularly the epistemic quality of deliberation reflected in public opinion, which is built up in a cooperative process of value- and will-formation in which good reasons are considered, tested and accepted.

The reconstructive critique leads Habermas to adopt the 'deliberative paradigm' (2006: 413), on the basis of which he then proceeds to fill out and refine the reconstructive explanatory model in the form of what he calls the 'communication model of democratic legitimacy' (2006: 416). Through a much closer analysis of the democratic process, the aim here is to construct a model that is not only normatively rich, but at the same time substantively applicable. It must both make possible the diagnosis of the communication pathologies from which democracy in contemporary Western societies is suffering and guide the search for, and the formulation of fruitful hypotheses for the identification of, the causal social structures or mechanisms giving rise to those pathologies. Without such a substantively oriented reconstructive model neither the explanation of the pathologies nor the critique of the conditions reproducing them is possible. In this case, substantive theoretical considerations of a historical and sociological kind are presupposed.

In deepening the reconstructive analysis, Habermas takes as the principal empirical reference point of the deliberative paradigm the 'democratic process' (2006: 413) with which the expectation of the generation of legitimate collective decisions is associated. This contrasts sharply with the liberal emphasis on the process of the aggregation of private interests and the republican emphasis on collective self-determination. The presumption of a reasonable, generally acceptable outcome of democracy is justified in so far as the process of communicative-discursive deliberation follows a procedure of cooperative value- and will-formation that is public, inclusive and transparent. This is possible only on condition that public discourse actually plays a central role in the democratic process. Discourse is generated by the routine asking for and giving of reasons and concurrent modes of justification which form part of ordinary everyday social interaction. In turn, it stimulates communicative action beyond routine behaviour. By mobilizing relevant topics and claims, promoting the critical evaluation of contributions and soliciting rationally motivated yes or no stances, discourse activates normative ideas and standards such as truth (a shared objective world, information), rightness (respect for the Other, mutual recognition, legality, plurality, publicity, transparency) and sincerity (truthfulness, need articulation), which provide a 'space of reasons' (2006: 413) or a justificatory framework. It is through the discursive medium, with one foot in ordinary everyday interaction and the other in a space of reasons, that normative ideas which are intuitively present in social interaction explicitly enter social reality and have a structuring effect on it. It is in this reflexive discursive way that democratic deliberation acquires an 'epistemic dimension' (2006: 413) or 'cognitive potential' (2006: 414). This element refers to the quality of deliberation that permits those involved to cognize the collective problem at issue in a reasonable way, to develop defensible knowledge about it and to justify its interpretation as well as making decisions about it in terms of good reasons. This is the decisive quality of deliberation in the sense of truly democratic political communication. Its presence transforms political communication into a mechanism that enhances cooperative learning and collective problem solving – and, we may add, world creation. There is not a conceptually necessary relation between democratic deliberation and epistemic or cognitive quality, however, but it is an empirical question whether the democratic process possesses this quality. It is a question of contingent conditions which have to be established by the social scientific investigation of a particular case. Where this quality is lacking, Habermas's diagnostic concept of a pathology of political communication applies. His suspicion is of course that it is at least in part the case in contemporary Western democracies.

Turning to the available research findings against the background of this reconstruction of the normatively significant reflexive rules emerging from and generatively guiding communicative practices, Habermas discovers support for his view regarding the epistemic or cognitive potential of political communication. Varied studies of small groups, focus groups and mediation groups confirm that deliberation improves cooperative learning, value- and will-formation, and the acceptance of outcomes of such processes as legitimate. Yet he is not satisfied that these findings can be generalized to what he calls 'real-life politics' (2006: 414) in contemporary democratic societies. Frequently recurring phenomena such as irrelevant topics and claims, the dearth or paucity of information on the issues at stake, the selective nature and poor quality of contributions, and a lack of legitimacy suggest that the democratic process is often neither properly public nor inclusive, and even less transparent. Particular factors, forces or processes, certain structures or mechanisms, must be at work which distort the discursive dynamics of political communication and interfere with the normative requirements of the process. Here Habermas suspects 'powerful interventions' (2006: 415) in the democratic process and, more generally, in the 'power structure of the public sphere' (2006: 418) to be the distorting factors. On the one hand, the reconstruction that culminated in the idea of a public, inclusive and transparent democratic process that is generatively regulated by normative principles in such a way that it produces legitimate outcomes possessing epistemic import allows a reconstructive critique of social practices or communication processes which deviate from this normative standard. Such practices and processes could be criticized both negatively, exposing their failings, and positively, disclosing available opportunities that are excluded or neglected. On the other hand, an explanation and hence a critique of such deficits in democratic deliberation and its legitimacy which could lead to a transformation for the better requires more than an appeal to normative principles. Although normative reconstruction and critique is central to and even characteristic of Critical Theory, the explanation and critique of social pathologies is its still more defining feature. It demands the location and identification of real causally efficacious social structures or mechanisms. In terms of the proposal made in Chapter 6 (see Figure 6.3), the latter may be conceived as contextual mechanisms which should be analytically distinguished from the generative, relational and learning mechanisms responsible for the production of the process of democratic political communication, but with which they could enter into a relation in the concrete case. Habermas in effect calls on contextual mechanisms when he tentatively mentions 'the power of the media' as well as 'the strategic use of political and social power' (2006: 415) as general indications of potential locations of the intervening mechanisms giving rise to 'pathologies of political communication' (2006: 420). The challenge at this stage is to draw on the normative perspective opened by the reconstruction for the purposes of delimiting an area within which potentially fruitful hypotheses regarding causal mechanisms can be formulated.

Despite his intense concern with the normative dimension, Habermas entertains illusions neither about the nature of mass communication as the basis of public opinion nor about the power structure of the public sphere. On the one hand, mass communication is dominated by a type of abstract mediated communication that disallows face-to-face relations and reciprocity between speaker and addressees and thus prevents egalitarian exchanges and shared practices of collective decision making. On the other, the public sphere is an intermediate system of communication in which different kinds of power borne by actors with unequally distributed resources or 'capital' meet and compete – from political power, through social and economic power, to communicative power in the sense of public influence on decision making. However, not the abstractness of communication, the asymmetry of speaker–addressee relations, or even the power structure of the public sphere necessarily renders impossible or disqualifies fruitful political communication. The highly mediated communication enables a plurality of different actors wielding distinct kinds of power, which are not illegitimate per se as long as they adhere to the rules of the game, to engage with one another in a consequential way. Indeed, the relation of the actors both to each other and to the anonymous public guarantees the 'peculiar reflexivity of the public sphere that allows *all* participants to reconsider what they perceive as public opinion' (2006: 419). Across the system as a whole, the various communicative contributions are discursively filtered up to the point that the core institutions of the political system are able to make largely legitimate, formally binding decisions. Where legitimacy is lacking and pathologies of political communication become apparent as a consequence, a closer investigation of the mechanisms intervening in the power structure of the public sphere is called for. This is where Habermas stresses the 'critical thrust' (2006: 420) that the deliberative model possesses for substantive analysis.

The closer, more detailed and concrete analysis of mass communication and the public sphere by means of the normatively sensitive deliberative model brought Habermas a step closer to the mechanisms causing communication pathologies. The abstract communication, asymmetrical relations and power structure of the public sphere are compatible with intact discursive dynamics and normative requirements and thus legitimate outcomes only if two conditions are fulfilled. The first is a 'self-regulating media system' which is sufficiently 'independent' of its social environment to exclude powerful interventions and the consequent distortion of communication (2006: 411, 420). The second is a sufficient response from 'anonymous audiences' or the public to maintain a 'feedback' loop between the media system in which politicians, journalists and commentators appear, on the one hand, and civil society, on the other, so as to secure a virtuous inter-relation between formal and informal communication processes of value- and will-formation (2006: 411, 421). If the media system's independence is fractured or the feedback between the discourse of those who appear in the media and civil society is interrupted or, even worse, if both occur, then any of a number of possible pathologies of political communication is virtually inevitable. The final step, then, is the identification of whatever causes these debilitating effects – that is, tendencies pointing in the direction of social pathologies and contradictions, particularly contingently operating causal mechanisms. It should be noted that, for Habermas, pathologies are not mere reflexes, as Marxist functionalism holds, as though they are purely manifestations of a repressive integration orchestrated by an oligopolistic economy and authoritarian state. Beyond the general tendency of capitalist modernization, the contradictory relations among the various components of society, particularly between the economic and political system, on the one hand, and civil society and the lifeworld, on the other, must be investigated in a careful and unbiased way to unearth the causal mechanism operating there.

The conditions Habermas identified serve him as detectors for the discovery of specific 'powerful interventions' causing the communication pathologies that at the very outset he regarded as the scandal in need of explanation and critique. Accordingly, he proposes to search for causal variables in the form of distorting mechanisms in two areas: first, the independent self-regulating media system and, second, the feedback loop between the formal and informal processes of political communications. On inspection, it is obvious that the contingent variables he pinpoints in these two areas presuppose his substantive theory of society put forward in *The Theory of Communicative Action*, namely 'a theory of capitalist modernization developed by means of a theory of communicative action' to which is central the well-known thesis of the 'colonization of the lifeworld by the system' (1984/87,

II: 375, 355). According to that account, historical-evolutionary processes have led to the differentiation of the capitalist economy and the administrative state from the everyday communicative practice characteristic of the lifeworld, and in the modern period have gained such a degree of autonomy that their respective media, money and bureaucratic power, were able to begin to colonize the life-world by displacing its proper medium, communication. The major 'contingent constraints' (2006: 420) he isolates within the context of the general tendency of capitalist modernization, such as the state, the market, private interests, social class and the reduced ability of citizens and representatives of civil society to use their cognitive, reflexive, critical and communicative competences in a meaningful and constructive way in political communication processes, all align perfectly with this theoretical framework of his.

As regards the distortion of the independent self-regulating media system, Habermas focuses on causal mechanisms of a statist, private interest and civil soci-etal kind (2006: 420–1). The incomplete differentiation of the media system from the political system is manifest in the state monopolization of broadcasting, such as in Italy, which could involve belief-forming processes varying from paternalism through authoritarianism to ideologization. Powerful intervention in the inde-pendence of the media also takes the form of temporary dedifferentiation, such as for example the manipulation of the public by various governments in the run up to the Iraq war in the name of nationalism, patriotism and security. Although Habermas does not mention in this context that such appeals could equally well serve larger militarization, geo-political or global governance goals, his critique elsewhere of the tendency towards a 'Hobbesian security state' (2005: 324–65) is relevant here. The interventions of private interests can be ordered according to the same range from incomplete differentiation to temporary dedifferentiation. The phenomenon of corporate ownership of the media as well as powerful corpo-rate interests, supported by particular academic communities such as the Chicago School of economics, which fracture the independence of the media system in the service of political influence and pressure on political decision making, has increased at a disturbing rate during recent decades. The reverse of such statist and private economic distortions of the independent self-regulating media system appears, for instance, in the form of a lack of a responsible press. The damaged independence of media systems shows up in the inability of journalists as repre-sentatives of civil society to devise and communicate effective counterframings of significant issues in the news – the US press in the run up to the Iraq war being the paradigmatic example.

The second area that Habermas delineates as containing contingently operat-ing distorting mechanisms is the feedback loop between the formal and informal processes of political communications (2006: 421–3). The feedback he has in mind here concerns the ability of the citizens to respond to issues on the public and political agenda and thus to make a meaningful input into the process of political communication. It is an indispensable contribution to the common con-struction of public opinion on any particular issue, but even more important is that it is a constitutive element of the reflexivity of the public sphere as such.

Without this feedback, the various participants or 'players on the virtual stage of the public sphere' (2006: 419), as Habermas calls it, are not able to reconsider and revise what they perceive as the collective understanding of the situation. In parenthesis, it should be pointed out that Habermas neglects to analyse fully the communicative structure and set of relations involved here: he presents it as a twofold relation of actors on a stage opposite an audience which he equates with civil society, whereas after the late twentieth-century communication revolution and enlargement of the system of intermediation the relation is actually of a threefold nature, in which case the 'anonymous audiences' (2006: 411) he refers to but leaves unanalysed cannot simply be identified with civil society as such (see Strydom 1999, 2001, 2006a). However that may be, he singles out two important categories of mechanisms causing interruption in the feedback loop, thus distorting political communication in a manner that diminishes the epistemic or cognitive quality and potential of democracy. First, the class structure as evidenced by social deprivation and cultural exclusion shapes the political public sphere in a manner that both restricts access and limits participation. Diffuse phenomena in civil society and the lifeworld, such as alienation, feelings of powerlessness, apathy, indifference, lost of trust in politics and cynicism, are partially generated by the class character of the public sphere and reinforced by the content and formats of a degenerating mode of political communication. Second, the nature of political communication is itself negatively affected by 'the colonization of the public sphere by market imperatives' (2006: 422). It takes the form of the redefinition of politics in market categories. Encouraging civic privatism and an anti-political mood, it stretches from the commodification of media content and modes of reception, via the personalization of politics, dramatization and simplification of issues and polarization of differences in opinion, to the privatization of public broadcasting and the emasculation of political journalism, which is vital to adequate political communication. Both these categories of distorting mechanisms relate to historically formed, contradictory social structures which must be investigated in their contemporary manifestation and interrelation.

Scientific-practical validation

Considering Habermas's analysis of powerful interventions that damage the independence of the media system and interrupt the communicative feedback loop of the public sphere against the background of Critical Theory methodology presented earlier, it is obvious that all three of its moments are present, at least in some form. Both the first – problem disclosure and constitution of the object – and the second – diagnostic reconstruction explanatory critique – are well covered by Habermas's text. In particular, reconstruction and the manner in which its normative dimension allows a diagnosis of a social pathology and thus opens the way for a theoretically based explanatory critique of the causal mechanism proved exemplary. As regards Critical Theory's third methodological moment, namely scientific-practical validation, Habermas dealt only formally with explanatory critique. This is because he addressed an audience of social scientists with a view to demonstrating the relevance of his critical-reconstructive version of Critical Theory, rather than developing and presenting a full-blown critique. The fact that the analysis was verbally presented at a conference and published in a scientific journal means that his proposal has entered the stage of scientific validation. In fact, the present discussion of the analysis from the viewpoint of its methodological structure is part of that stage.

Practical testing or verification will be possible only if particular proposals are followed up, properly researched and presented to a differently composed audience, at least a more general one, than the conference participants and the social scientific readers he has addressed so far. However, even if the third methodological moment is truncated, there can be no doubt about the ethical orientation of Habermas's proposals for explanation and critique. Already in their current form they are oriented towards being pragmatically received as relevant not only to problem solving but also to world creation: solving the problem of democracy's unfulfilled epistemic promise and thus creating a more legitimate political organization of society. To take up and pursue the proposals for an explanatory critique of the mechanisms distorting and blocking the epistemic import of democratic political communication is the task of the current and emerging generation of critical theorists.

Honneth: contemporary pathologies of individualization

In the second example of Critical Theory's methodology in action, Axel Honneth (2004b) starts from the disturbing increase in the incidence of feelings of inner emptiness and depression in contemporary society and pursues the intuition that an elective affinity between cultural and social processes lies behind it. This emphasis indicates that he activates Critical Theory's methodology from a different, in a sense even an opposing, theoretical angle from Habermas. Whereas Habermas focuses on language communication or understanding, Honneth adopts instead the theory of recognition; whereas Habermas takes the idea of autonomy in the sense of collective democratic self-constitution and self-organization as his normative guideline for the evaluation and critique of the actual degree of communicative understanding achieved, Honneth shifts from the moral-practical political sphere to the ethical-practical one in order to prioritize the normative idea of the good life. This normative reference allows him to evaluate and criticize the actual degree of self-realization or attainment of the good life achieved. His analysis draws on a wide range of studies on different aspects of contemporary capitalist society.

Problem disclosure and constitution of the object

The abductive inference that informs Honneth's critical analysis brings together social suffering, the organization of contemporary capitalist society and the theory of recognition focused on the good life. The problem situation that provides him with a starting point is indicated by currently typical individual modes of activity, comportment and experience. These phenomena are evidently associated with significant societal developments of the recent past. At the most banal level, the widespread propensity to make idols out of any fleeting value, or to 'have fun', and to pursue hectic and enervating activities such as jogging, gym exercise, high-risk sport, or to 'work hard and play hard', is the first tentative indication that a structural transformation has occurred which may have more thoroughgoing social consequences. Honneth also considers the plight of people due to what Bourdieu and associates called 'the weight of the world', namely the constraining conditions generated by deregulation, flexibilization, unemployment, unprotected labour, exploitation of immigrant labour and, more generally, the transformation of society into a market. However, on closer inspection of these forms of suffering which are obviously manifesting the return of the nineteenth-century 'social problem', he insists on pushing on in order to find forms of social suffering that are typical of contemporary society. The mounting clinical evidence of an increase in the incidence of depression and feelings of inner emptiness since the 1980s, which he judges to be an unprecedented form and level of social suffering in the history of capitalist societies, convinces him of the prevalence of what he calls contemporary 'pathologies of individualism' (2004b: 474). This negative social state is what calls for a diagnosis of both an analytical and normative kind, and the leading inductive insight for its accomplishment is that the process of self-realization which is supposed to lead to adequate individual development needs to be investigated.

Diagnostic reconstruction and explanatory critique

For the purposes of the diagnostic analysis of contemporary pathologies of individualism, Honneth falls back on the tradition of the 'sociological diagnosis of modernity' (2004b: 464), from which he borrows two master theoretical concepts. The first is the Weberian concept of 'rationalization', which captures the objective socio-structural process of the opening of possibilities and options for societal differentiation, and the second is the Durkheimian concept of 'individualization'. These two concepts are essential to his analysis of contemporary capitalist society, but to give them a proper analytical and critical edge a normative dimension is required. Rather than taking the two classical concepts over uncritically, however, he is aware of having to avoid the one-sidedness of Weber's emphasis on the criterion of purposive-rationality as much as the ambivalence of Durkheim's concept. Individualization can on the one hand be taken to refer to the life-history of the individual as an objective process observable from the outside and, on the other, as pertaining to the increase in personal autonomy as an inner fact manifest from the participant's perspective. Given Honneth's theoretical stance and the need to extrapolate a normative sense of individualization that would make possible a critical evaluation of the contemporary situation, it is this latter aspect that becomes the focus of reconstruction. His approach to this task is first to follow Georg Simmel's analysis of different historical interpretations of individualism and then to pull it through to contemporary interpretations. The large variety of available interpretations threatens to render the concept opaque, including ancient moral-ethical individualism of equality; Romantic and contemporary aesthetic individualism of authenticity; modern institutional individualism between responsibility and conformism; self-interested or egocentric individualism from the nineteenth-century possessive to the contemporary unencumbered variety; and contemporary autonomous individualism from the self-interested to the moral-ethical type. Nevertheless it is possible to see the different relevant strands in the 1960 and 1970s under new socio-structural conditions contributing to the emergence of a new kind of individualism: 'a new, late-modern stage of conscious individualism' (2004b: 468) which has its counterpart in a new 'cultural ideal [of] self-realization' (2004b: 470–1).

Having established the conceptual pair of rationalization and individualization as the basic theoretical means for diagnosing the social pathologies of contemporary capitalist society and having given them a normative-critical edge through a reconstructive exercise, Honneth continues the analysis by tracing the processes that, involving a confluence of diverse dynamics, gave rise to the new form of individualization during the 1960s and 1970s and provided it with a context from the 1980s onwards. First, post-war socio-structural processes laid the material foundation for the appearance of this new conscious, claims-making individualism by opening up a multiplicity of objective possibilities and options. Among them were the expansion of the service sector, upward social mobility, educational opportunities and vocational choice, career advancement, growth of income and leisure time, reduction of the formative influence of social milieux, and the diversification of ways of life and lifestyles (2004b: 468–9). In parallel with these processes, second, a series of socio-cultural developments and transformations took place which simultaneously implicated orientations and attitudes and gave rise to new cultural ideals. Increasing consumption of luxury items, in the service of intensifying the feeling of being alive, called forth and was strengthened by massive investment in the production of intensity-enhancing consumer goods. Concurrently, the culture industry stressed this need as an authentic feature of the time that everyone should be seeking to fulfil. Existing rigid expectations concerning individual conduct were eroded and fell away, while cultural traditions previously reserved for the few, such as artists, entertainers and celebrities, became increasingly available to a growing number of people. Consequently, modes of interpretation deriving from Romanticism, bohemianism and avant-garde art regarding life as experimental realization and the human being as a desiring subject received broad acceptance (2004b: 469–70). In this context, claims to individual self-realization became a normal feature by the late 1960s and 1970s. At the level of personality, these processes found their correlate in the new late twentieth-century form of individualism. It is characterized by the surrender of a fixed map of personal identity and, instead, an emphasis on grasping the possibilities for personal identity as something to probe and reveal through experimental self-discovery. Individual biography was thus transformed into the conscious pursuit of a tentative process of self-actualization and self-realization, underpinned by a commitment to crafting one's personality as the unique, distinguishing feature of the individual (2004b: 470).

Whereas socio-cultural and personality developments of this kind are on the one hand stimulated by socio-structural processes and institutional developments, on the other their survival and continued development depends on supportive socio-structural and institutional responses. During the 1980s not only such supportive responses became observable, but at the same time also institutional developments taking advantage of and capitalizing on the new individualism, its claims to self-actualization and self-realization and the corresponding new cultural ideal. This is where Honneth locates what he calls a 'paradoxical reversal' (2004b: 467). This idea reflects Honneth's position as being in line with the left-Hegelian tradition of Critical Theory, which is characteristically concerned with the deformation or blocking of the realization of reason or the rational potential of ideas of reason such as self-realization under specific historical conditions. These paradoxical developments are clearly displayed by the restructuring of the industrial and service sector at the time and its subsequent extension across the institutional order. The claims raised by individuals were taken up in institutional developments and incorporated in institutional expectations as external demands on individuals, so that the ideal of self-realization they pursued became inverted into a compulsion. Key institutions adapted to the new ideal of self-realization and transformed it into an efficacy-enhancing model of what life ought to be like. The goals at which the claims to self-realization aimed were transposed into support for the system by being made into a reason legitimizing far-reaching institutional restructuring, deregulation and de-institutionalization. Although in the 1970s the American sociologist Daniel Bell predicted that a contradiction had developed between the newly emerged hedonistic-narcissistic everyday morality and capitalism which would have serious consequences for the capitalist work ethic and productivity, Honneth notes that this sociological prognosis was not borne out. Since the 1980s, there is no conflict between the new individualism and the functional requirements of the capitalist economy. Individualism, the pursuit of an aesthetic identity, self-realization and the experimental attitude have not only been used to legitimize and restructure the economy and to deregulate industry and the service sector, but have also been transformed into a productive force (2004b: 471). To be sure, however, this accommodation is by no means without a cost. It is paid for by a widespread new form of social suffering which is unprecedented in capitalist societies, in terms of both type and scope. It is indicated by such symptoms as feelings of inner emptiness, being superfluous, lacking a purpose and, in the extreme, depression. These symptoms and this new form of social suffering describe the characteristic 'pathologies of individualism' of our time which Honneth in the first instance set out to diagnose.

By way of the reconstruction that Honneth undertook in the course of developing his diagnosis of contemporary pathologies of individualism, he established that a new form of individualism had emerged which found its cultural counterpart in the ideal of self-realization. The reconstruction culminated in his finding that the normative import of these new practices of individualism guided by the ideal of self-realization is to be found in the promise of increased qualitative freedom which would allow the attainment of well-being or the good life. We may regard this complex as Honneth's reconstructive explanatory model. It not only explains the situation by making clear the real mechanisms such as the immanent orientations, expectation and practices generating the transcendent ideal of self-realization, which in turn regulates those practices. At the same time, the model allows a reconstructive critique. Measured against the normative standard of self-realization, the actual symptoms of inner emptiness, superfluity, purposelessness and depression are all negative phenomena which need to be critically exposed as being in contradiction with the widely accepted and institutionalized normative ideal. In a critical disclosing sense, on the other hand, there may also be positive potentials hidden in the orientations, expectation and practices, which could be made explicit and given effect – a critical dimension Honneth does not pursue. Now, it is this reconstructive explanation and critique, which is central to the diagnostic analysis, that opens the space for a critical explanation or explanatory critique of the pathologies of individualism with reference to their causes – that is, the causal structures or mechanisms giving rise to the negative social situation of which they are the symptomatic manifestation.

Honneth is adamant that a monocausal explanation cannot account for the pathological state of contemporary society, nor would a moralistic explanation that seeks to pin it to an intentional or deliberate strategy on the part of some agent or another, such as a sly managerial class. What precisely needs to be explained is 'why the claim to self-realization was increasingly made into an institutional demand' (2004b: 472). Why is it that in the course of the last third of the twentieth century individuals were slowly but surely and eventually massively confronted with the expectation and even demand that they be flexible, take the initiative, develop themselves, engage in life-long learning and take responsibility for themselves? An appropriate explanation must pinpoint the causal mechanisms at work that gave rise to this outcome as an unintended end result. In order to do so, a range or chain of distinct processes, each with its own history and internal logic and dynamics, has to be taken into account in such a way that their interrelation and confluence or the 'elective affinity' (2004b: 472) drawing them together are acknowledged. While keeping in mind the increase in diffuse everyday expectations of self-realization and the emergence of a corresponding cultural ideal, Honneth points to three processes of structural transformation that can be regarded as the major causal mechanisms. Reference to the electronic media, the advertising and fashion industry and finally the business enterprise satisfies the explanatory requirement (2004b: 472–4). The electronic media prepared the way by projecting the ideal of a creative and original style of life. As increasing numbers came to experience this ideal as a demand on identity formation and started to follow it, even if subliminally or unconsciously, a tendency towards the pursuit of a standardized pattern of searching for an identity arose. The advertising industry instrumentalized the individual demand for self-realization for the purposes of a faster turnover of consumer goods by subliminally promising the provision of means for the attainment of an original lifestyle. It was joined by the fashion industry and together their finely differentiated and nuanced offering of images of an authentic life as well as the necessary aesthetic resources to achieve a distinctive self-presentation gave rise to a self-propelling spiral of stylistic innovation and individual uptake. The restructuring of the industrial and service sector replaced Fordism with the flexible post-Fordist mode of production, which provided the context for a new interpretation of workers, no longer as employees or personnel, but instead as human resources, creative entrepreneurs or self-employed who was called upon to be creativity, flexible and take responsibility for themselves. A new form of interviewing of applicants made employment dependent on the convincing self-presentation of employees and the indication of a will to realize themselves in their work. This was reinforced by making a periodic self-presentation of goals and demonstration of their having been reached part of reflexive governance. These and other measures appealing to individual self-realization served the legitimizing of the restructuring of the business enterprise, including deregulation and de-institutionalization, a flexible labour market, dissolution of trade unions, individual responsibility, scrapping of fixed job descriptions and life-long learning – all of which contributed to the marketization of society. Besides restructuring, the claims to self-realization together with individual inclination and drive were instrumentalized as a productive force in the capitalist economy. In time, the new institutional paradigm spreads from the economy to other institutions, with the result that individuals, employees, members of society and citizens of the state were all transformed into objects of institutional demands.

These various mechanisms account for the emergence and nature of what Honneth calls contemporary 'pathologies of individualism' (2004b: 474–5) but, rather than merely explaining, their exposure simultaneously also issues in a critique of the pathological state of contemporary society and the forces causing it. In a matter of two decades, the developments serving as vehicle for the paradoxically deforming and blocking mechanisms both transformed the normative ideal of self-realization pursued through the course of life into an ideology and instrumentalized it into a direct productive factor for the deregulated economic system. Honneth's qualification of this productive factor as 'a peculiarly misused one in capitalism's modernization' (2004b: 471) communicates a strong critical force. It points to the orchestrating instance of the various transformational processes that he earlier referred to by way of the Weberian concept of 'elective affinity' as being capitalism. It is the 'institutional transformations [of] Western capitalism' (2004b: 474) that allowed the paradoxical reversal of the ideal of self-realization and the engendering of the new forms of social suffering which make up the typical pathologies of contemporary society. What precise mechanism may be involved in these capitalist processes – for example, time relations, the forced acceleration of all activities (e.g. Pels 2003; Strydom 2004; Rosa 2009) – Honneth leaves unconsidered. However that may be, by ideologizing and misusing the individual search for self-realization as an instrument of economic development and spreading a standardized form of fictional biographies and lives as a productive factor, these institutional processes hollowed out and deformed the normative ideal of

self-realization into 'an emotionally fossilized set of demands under whose consequences individuals today seem more likely to suffer than to prosper' (2004b: 474).
Not only are individuals psychically overburdened by a diffuse external compulsion, but these processes at the same time actively contribute to the encouragement
and diffusion of typically contemporary frivolous, hectic and enervating activities
which conceal the very feelings of emptiness, superfluousness, purposelessness and
depression from which an ever-increasing number of individuals are suffering.
The negative exposing aspect of the explanatory critique targets both the social
conditions that operate as causal mechanisms in generating the pathologies and,
characteristically of Critical Theory, also the disguising of those conditions by
convictions and practices that are produced by those very same mechanisms. The
earlier normative reconstructive critique, which focused on the deviation of actual
self-realization practices from the ideal of self-realization, is thus complemented
by a causal explanatory critique, which traces a socio-historical process of the
deformation and blocking of the realization of a rational universal and locates
the deforming and blocking mechanisms operative in it. The positive aspect of
the explanatory critique, on the other hand, consists of the disclosure of reflexive
and critical competences that could be recovered beyond their currently deformed
and blocked deficient form and could be activated in the service of undoing the
undermining and paradoxical corruption by processes of production and institutional organization of society's avowed commitment to creating adequate living
conditions for its members.

Scientific-practical validation

Considering his work more generally and going by assumptions and indications
apparent in the text under discussion, there can be no doubt about the fact that
Honneth gave serious thought to the final methodological dimension of his
research on pathologies of individualism in contemporary capitalist society. As
regards scientific validation, the research was published both in German (2002b)
and in the English version (2004b) referred to here with a social philosophical
and social scientific audience in mind. Honneth's work, including this piece of
research, has already been for some time the subject of wide-ranging international
analysis and discussion in philosophical and social scientific circles, which form
part of the theoretical discourse representing the medium of its scientific validation. His contributions and suggestions are also taken up and built into related
research and thus subjected to ongoing conceptual and social scientific testing.

As regards practical testing or verification, the first thing that strikes one about
the piece is the title 'Organized self-realization'. It is a carefully thought-through
combination of two opposing words which results in a chiasmus, which signals
precisely the paradoxical process of reversal or inversion it seeks to diagnose,
explain and criticize. Not only does it capture the attention and imagination, but
it also slows things down and stimulates reflection on the current state of society.
It is underpinned by the assumption that the potential addressees, on the one
hand, have experience of the reality being analysed and possibly suffer to some

degree from the diagnosed pathologies of individualism and, on the other, possess the cognitive, reflexive and critical competences necessary to grasp the basic negative and positive insights communicated by the explanatory critique and to begin to engage in self-transformation, if not yet practical transformation. The presentation of the research, both title and substance, is geared towards linking up with these competences of ordinary everyday members of society and the social practices in which they actually and potentially engage. The further assumption is made, which is borne out by cases from the history of the reception of Critical Theory, that the critic should neither try to bring about nor expect an immediate effect and transformation, but rather has to patiently shape contributions toward a medium- and longer-term process of the reflexive incorporation of critical insights into ordinary everyday social practices. It is Honneth's view that the task of the critical theorist is to work towards a well-founded, radical re-orientation by problematizing the background assumptions of the prevailing consensus and thus to convince those concerned of the questionable status of the conventionally accepted mode of practice.

McCarthy: the racist legacy of liberal political philosophy

In the third example of the application of Critical Theory's methodology, Thomas McCarthy (2001a; see also 2004) critically examines why liberal political philosophy continues to maintain a theoretical position that ignores the highly relevant phenomenon of racism despite acknowledging that it is a persistent problem. Although some of the early modern liberal authors such as Locke did benefit by being shareholders in the slave trade, this dissonance is less plausibly explained directly by economic or power factors than by a deforming mechanism operative in a more subterranean way in everyday practices, namely widely accepted cultural interpretation and evaluative schemata. Rather than just classical early modern liberalism, however, this explanatory mechanism and hence the critique it makes possible can be extended also to contemporary political philosophy, particularly liberalism as for instance represented by John Rawls. The text makes use of documentary or textual analysis and draws on a range of studies of racism. Although it does not claim to be a full-blown report on completed research but rather issues in a theoretical-methodological outline that calls for more specific substantive research to be undertaken, it is nevertheless exemplary of Critical Theory's methodology.

Problem disclosure and constitution of the object

McCarthy's starting point is a sense of a problem gained on considering the dominant contemporary Anglo-American liberal political philosophy, particularly as represented by its doyen, John Rawls, in such influential works as *A Theory of Justice* (1985) and the later *Political Liberalism* (1993). At the core of this philosophy, there is a mismatch between the universalistic claims to liberty, equality and justice for all proclaimed in its normative theory and the particular circumstances or present state of society with its visible fault lines and cleavages. What McCarthy finds astonishing and in his view undoubtedly stands for a serious problem representing an eminent object for Critical Theory, is the 'obvious lack of cognitive dissonance' (2001a: 630) in political philosophy, as he calls it. Political philosophy is apparently able to live undisturbed with a basic contradiction at its very core. A suggestion as to what the nature of this problem may be comes from mid-twentieth-century developments in American society and the global order. Among them are the American Civil Rights movement and the global decolonization struggles which highlighted the fact that, throughout the entire modern period, race served not only as a central marker of the distinction between inclusion and exclusion, free-dom and domination, equality and inequality, but also as a means for institution building and the organization of society.

From this perspective, the contradiction in political philosophy emerges as that between its own normative theoretical position, which studiously ignores the prob-lem of racism, and the implicit support for and even advantage obtained from the racist social structure. This abductive insight to the effect that the phenomenon of race is the key to understanding the problem nature of liberal political phi-losophy thus presupposes the making of a logical-imaginative, potentially fruitful and practically effective connection in a historically specific context among the micro, macro and normative levels. The lack of cognitive dissonance in con-temporary liberal political philosophy has to be imagined in the socio-historical context from which liberalism originally arose and which still shapes it today, and then linked to universalistic claims to liberty, equality and justice and the socio-historical deformation and blockage of their normative import. What needs to be done research-wise is, first, to develop a diagnosis of the problem involving an analysis of the socio-historical context of liberalism that allows the identification of a structure or mechanism generating the problem – race being the guiding idea – and then, second, to provide an explanation and critique of liberalism in a way that could change the assumptions and self-understanding of liberal political philosophy.

Diagnostic reconstruction and explanatory critique

The first step towards the diagnosis of the problem of cognitive dissonance is to analyse the relevant aspect of Rawls's liberal political philosophy. The focus is on the normative dimension, which, for McCarthy coming at it from the angle of Critical Theory, requires a reconstructive approach involving the critical-reflective participant. The analysis must reciprocally relate or mediate the intuitive knowledge from the perspective of the insider with the counterintui-tive knowledge from the perspective of the outsider (2001a: 640). McCarthy's basic supporting theoretical perspective, comparable to Habermas's emphasis on language and Honneth's on recognition, is praxis, or historically situated and hermeneutically interpreted practice whereby social reality is constituted and transformed. Investigating Rawls's writings with this methodological requirement in mind, it is striking that he indeed acknowledges the problem of racism as one of the most important with which contemporary society is confronted yet does not include it as an object of analysis in his philosophy. McCarthy's (2001a: 634–6) search for a reason for this apparent discrepancy leads to Rawls's basic distinction between ideal theory and nonideal theory. Following the strict Kantian tradition, Rawls adopts a constructivist approach (2001a: 635), which by abstraction from social life articulates the basic principles of justice according to which a well-ordered liberal society in which all enjoy liberty, equality and justice can be constructed. The political philosopher's argument for this ideal procedure is that he is pursuing a realistic utopia, a utopia that is attainable considering the available knowledge about the laws and tendencies of society. All chance factors of a natural, historical and social kind must be excluded, just like all contingent consequences and effects. This means that the problem of racism is in effect relegated to nonideal theory.

By contrast with Rawls, who excludes it, McCarthy reconstructively incorporates racism. The reconstruction shows that, in this case, it is not a matter of the actual realization falling short of the ideal, but exactly the reverse – namely, that Rawls's ideal construction of the principles of justice in the exclusive terms of general facts about society loses touch with the actual circumstances and the present state of society. McCarthy (2001a: 637) traces this tendency back to the Humean distinction between fact and value, which has become a standard feature of Anglo-American political philosophy and political theory, especially under the impact of twentieth-century positivism. It is the division of labour established by this distinction that leads to the disabling of an evaluative or comprehensive normative approach in Rawls and, more generally, in liberal political philosophy. Employing his reconstructive model, which acknowledges the transcendent socio-practical principles of liberty, equality and justice but simultaneously insists on recognizing the deforming phenomenon of racism, McCarthy is able to present a multilevel reconstructive critique of Rawls. Not only is the latter's constructivist approach one-sided, giving priority as it does to the transcendent observer's perspective to the exclusion of the participant's point of view, but by the same token his political philosophy is uncritical and indeed becomes 'ideological' (2001a: 639). Rather than a value-neutral position based on general information about society which every reasonable person would have to accept, Rawls's constructivist ideal theory presents 'a value-laden picture of the social world which enjoys broad acceptance in the community of liberal theorists' yet is highly contested (2001a: 638). This reconstructive critique calls for the adoption of an objectifying outsider's perspective to identify 'the elements of the situation' (2001a: 640) that enter into and render political values contested. What needs to be investigated more closely to complete the diagnosis of the cognitive dissonance of liberal political philosophy, therefore, is both the context of origin and the context of application of ideal theory, which the latter in unreflexive manner ignores. The suspicion or abductive insight leading McCarthy here is that the nature of the political-theoretical problem has undergone a subtle change. Whereas classical political philosophy theoretically accommodated to racial subordination or provided a justification for it, contemporary political philosophy brushes the problem under the carpet – that is, by relegating it to nonideal theory.

At the centre of political philosophy's socio-historical context of origin McCarthy locates the so-called 'European miracle' (2001a: 627), which, as closer inspection reveals, depended on control of intercontinental exchange and trade, especially the Atlantic trade and European markets. In turn, this control presupposed the conquest and settlement of America, the subjugation and extermination of indigenous populations, and the transfer of forced labour to European-controlled areas involving some 12 million African slaves. Considering that Atlantic trade was the dominant component of global exchange from the seventeenth to the nineteenth century, it would not be too far fetched to conclude that, if racial slavery did not became the pacemaker of European economic expansion, it was at least one of its essential ingredients. These developments were supported by an imperialist ideology which metamorphosed from 'Christians versus heathens', through 'civilised Europeans versus uncivilised savages', to a fully developed theory of racial hierarchy by the late eighteenth and early nineteenth century. The thrust of this theory, the doctrine of 'white supremacy' (2001a: 628), would later during the nineteenth-century European expansion provide ideological cover for colonial domination in a wide variety of particular situations in Africa, Asia and the Pacific. The means for making distinctions between inclusion and exclusion, freedom and unfreedom, equality and inequality and for structuring and organizing colonial life was race. The far-reaching consequences of this departure made themselves felt throughout the modern period in the guise of a 'global racial formation' (2001a: 630). Reflection on this context of origin makes evident the sense of 'race'. Rather than referring to a fixed biological property, it is a complex of social meanings, a social construction, which links up with social, political, legal, economic and psychological realities so as to take the form of a device by means of which identities, institutions and whole institutional orders are shaped and organized.

It is remarkable that, despite its central significance, race was systematically marginalized in the principal political philosophies, from liberalism, which chose to emphasize the ideal in a way that left no room for race and the racial hierarchy, to Marxism, which chose to focus on social class and thus at best regarded the racial hierarchy as derivative of economic relations. Beyond marginalization, however, McCarthy quotes evidence that the majority of classical liberal theorists were not only aware of the racial system of white supremacy, but actually complicit in its emergence. John Locke and Immanuel Kant are cases in point (2001a: 628–9, 631–3). Locke was an original shareholder in the Royal African Company, chartered in 1672 to monopolize the English slave trade, and regularly increased his investment. Although he considered slavery so vile and miserable that an English gentleman would not plead for it, his philosophical and legislative contributions single him out as a spiritual father of both liberalism and racial slavery. Kant, for his part, explicitly rejected slavery as well as colonialism and developed the most refined philosophical statement of the moral point of view, but on the other presented the most highly philosophical restatement of the popular racism of the period of conquest and enslavement prior to the nineteenth century. His colour-coded division of the human species based on detailed knowledge of the biological accounts of racial difference of the day, anticipated the racial 'science', so-called, of the nineteenth century. Furthermore, by propounding the view that non-Europeans required European tutelage to realize their moral capacity and humanity, he in effect made available a justification for global white supremacy. Whereas the lack of cognitive dissonance in the classical liberal authors speaks rather loudly through their self-serving accommodation to racial subordination or justification of it, in McCarthy's view the same deficiency is still in evidence in contemporary liberal political philosophy, albeit in a different form due to the transformation of the political-theoretical problem. Having lost their legitimacy, slavery and *de jure* racism no longer require justification, but now there is accommodation to persistent *de facto* racism. This occurs through the unreflective absorption of certain prejudices and stereotypes of the time which lead contemporary liberal theorists to cordon the problem off in nonideal theory outside the purview of political philosophy. A glance at its context of application confirms that the lack of cognitive dissonance is as acute as ever in liberal political philosophy.

Both analytically and normatively, it should be obvious, the diagnosis of the problem from which McCarthy started out has reached its goal. What is required at this stage is the adoption of an objectifying outsider's perspective, both the observer's and the excluded's, in order to explain the dissonance with reference to a causal mechanism and on that basis to present a critique of it. For this purpose, McCarthy (2001a: 630, 639, 641–2) takes his cues from Habermas, but not without a side-glance at the feminists' explanation of the sex–gender system and Foucault's genealogy of modern metanarratives of universal principles. From a feminist point of view, theorists under-theorize problems because they share the assumptions and understandings of their society, with the result that basic differences are frequently taken as natural and unchangeable rather than as historically variable social constructions. Foucault's genealogical histories reveal that claims about universal principles are accompanied by unacknowledged impure power-drenched demands made in the name of reason. Habermas, for his part, comparably insists that external conditions cannot go unacknowledged if a philosophical or social scientific account is to avoid becoming ideological. Accordingly, McCarthy assigns a central role to implicit socio-cultural background assumptions as the mechanism causally most directly responsible for the pathological lack of cognitive dissonance plaguing political philosophy. These background assumptions are what Habermas regards as images or models of society which are drawn from the pre-understanding of society's structures, dynamics, problems, challenges, dangers and potentials. They enter normative theoretical constructions tacitly and not only play a covert role in disagreements and conflicts among theorists and social and political actors, but also operate in unconscious and unacknowledged ways in the constitution and organization of society. Race, understood as a socially constructed complex of social meanings which relates various dimension of social reality to one another, forms part of precisely such an image or model of society. It functions as a device whereby identities, institutions and whole institutional orders are shaped and organized and, as such, it substructures liberal political philosophy in an unacknowledged way, rendering it cognitively deficient and ideological.

McCarthy's explanation of the lack of cognitive dissonance with reference to a real causal mechanism – that is, race as a socio-cultural device operating in an unacknowledged way in the generation of identities and institutions as well as theories – is at one and the same time a critique of liberal political theory. Although he is not explicit about it, it is clear that the critique has two distinct yet interrelated dimensions. It is a negative exposing critique and a positive disclosing critique. As a negative critique, first, it exposes the fact that liberal political philosophy imports prejudices and stereotypes into its theory of society. This is possible since it unreflectively shares a widespread pre-understanding of society. This unreflective attitude is strengthened by that fact that liberal political theory gives no attention to external conditions such as the present circumstances and the current state of society and, in addition, ignores how the current state of society historically came to be what it is. Given all this, liberal political philosophy becomes ideological and thus effectively legitimizes persistent but deeply unjustifiable features of the status quo. The disclosing critique, second, brings out certain possibilities or potentials and proposes corresponding options. Liberal political philosophers must make the image or model of society underpinning their theorizing into an explicit theme. In doing so, they must simultaneously develop an appreciation for the dialectical relation between the ideal and the real which would enable them to allow mediation or reciprocal interplay between the two moments, rather than continuing to harp just on the ideal and consequently to develop a one-sided, abstract, constructivist normative theory. To achieve such a more rounded and balanced position, it is necessary to combine intuitive knowledge from the insider's perspective with counterintuitive knowledge from the outsider's perspective – with the outsider being understood not just as the liberal constructivist observer, but at the same time also as the external observer concerned with the identification of real causal mechanisms, who, in turn, is supported by the perspective of the excluded, which is rooted in their actual experience of racism. McCarthy (2001a: 642) thus stresses that the limitations of liberal political philosophy can be overcome only by combining constructive and reconstructive analysis to recover the normative dimension of social reality and, further, by relating such analysis to the interpretative, analytical and explanatory aims of a historically sensitive social science as well as to the practical transformative aim of critique. It is in this sense, which is effectively a reproduction of the methodological structure of Critical Theory, that he recommends a shift 'from normative to critical theory' (2004: subtitle).

Scientific-practical validation

In the early 1990s, McCarthy presented his programme for the pursuit of Critical Theory in the form of a 'practically significant, sociohistorical critique of impure reason' (1994a: 8). His work presented here from a methodological viewpoint falls within the framework of this research programme and forms part of a more specific project on racial injustice on which he has published in 2001 and 2004. Although both this programme and project have already entered the scientific discourse, the medium of scientific validation, he is acutely aware of the relatively tentative nature of different aspects of the work so far. He is very careful in pointing out, for instance, that the alternative theoretical strategy for an adequate theory of racial injustice which he is in the process of elaborating is still in an underdeveloped state. Similarly, he stresses that in many instances his research on race and racism still needs to go beyond the laying down of abstract methodological requirements. Although it is thus evident that a good deal of work is yet to be done, there can be no doubt about the fact that, as far as scientific validation is concerned, McCarthy's contribution possesses a high degree of plausibility. Indeed, besides anti-Semitism, which was of much importance to the early Frankfurt School, it is understood to be an important contribution to an aspect of the modern world and of contemporary society that has not received the required attention in Critical Theory.

As regards practical validation, McCarthy intentionally presents his work on racism as having a practical orientation. It is for this reason that he targets a specific audience, his addressees being liberal political philosophers and theorists, of whom Rawls is the leading figure. Although Rawls died a number of years ago, his theories of justice and liberalism possess paradigmatic significance. Addressing his audience, McCarthy reconstructs liberal political philosophy in such a way that he appeals to them by highlighting both its positive and negative features. On the one hand, he shows critical appreciation for liberal political philosophy's constructivist approach as well as its significant concern with a theory of justice. On the other, his focuses his diagnosis, explanation and critique, both normative and causal, on its glaring lack of cognitive dissonance and both identifies and explicates the nature and mode of operation of the mechanism of race. To this he adds recommendations for the correction of the deficit as well as the enhancement of liberal political philosophy. Central to these is the methodological recommendation to complement construction with reconstruction. All of these positive and negative evaluations and recommendations are intentionally addressed to liberal political philosophers and theorists in a way that could contribute to a change in their unreflective assumptions, pre-understandings and images or models of society and, by extension, their approach. No one expects an immediate massive transformation, but in the medium and longer term McCarthy's reasoned explanation and critique may well help initiate transformation in liberal political philosophy, leading to a better theory and understanding of society and, more generally, moving the problem of racial injustice to the centre of social and political attention so as to become an explicit topic of public debate and discussion.

Eder: sustainability as an ideological mobilization device

The fourth example of Critical Theory's methodology in action is Klaus Eder's (2001) analysis of the practical actualization of reason in terms of the distinct uses that different official and civil society actors make of the idea of sustainability in the context of European environmental policy making. The resulting relations of tension, competition and conflict reveal the process of the making of a distinctly European society and render possible an explanation of environmental policy-making in terms of the changing European class structure which questions both the official interpretation in terms of a North–South divide and the Brussels elite's widely entertained harmonious image of a democratic and inclusive European society. The piece forms part of a research network's study of environmental movements, discourses and policies in Southern Europe and, in various respects, Eder draws additionally on the findings of a range of collaborative European research projects of the past decade or two of which he was the coordinator.

Problem disclosure and constitution of the object

The problem serving as Eder's starting point is not an arbitrarily chosen one, but has been given rise to by a shift in the objective order of society itself – namely, the change induced by European environmental policy making and its consequences. The high level of activity of the Brussels bureaucracy, on the one hand, and public mobilization resonating with a significant number of citizens, for instance widespread protest by farmers, workers and the unemployed, on the other, give the impression of a potential crisis. Eder recognizes this shift as creating an opportunity to see social reality more clearly and to gain unprecedented access to it for producing knowledge about what structures or generates it. At the centre of European policy making is a new concept, the recently established and by now widely accepted idea of 'sustainability'. Together, this concept and the diverse protests against the affects of environmental policies are an iconic signification of the problem quality of the situation in Europe regarding environmental policy. This quality invites critical sociological investigation.

The first step in methodological engagement on Eder's part following this objective disclosure of a potential problem, the constitution of the object of study, takes the form of an abductive forging of logical and imaginative relations among three distinct dimensions in the historically specific context of late twentieth- and early twenty-first-century Europe. The protests on the ground by farmers, workers and the unemployed who are negatively affected by European environmental policy (micro level) are related to the action of the bureaucratic elites in Brussels who force through aspects of environmental policy that prove to be detrimental to several sections of the population (macro level) and, finally, the profusely yet quite differently used concept of sustainability central to environmental policy (normative level) is regarded as the connecting link between the previous two levels. On the basis of this relational thinking, Eder's leading abductive insight is that, rather than focusing on the implementation of environmental directives as is usual, the concept of sustainability is the key to understanding the problem situation that arose in the wake of European environmental policy making.

What needs to be done, therefore, is to analyse the practical rationality inspired by the master legitimizing symbol or, differently, the process of the practical realization of the idea of sustainability, particularly the diverse and even conflict-ing practical uses made of the concept by different actors. This requires that policy making and the process it sets in train be embedded in the social context, which itself is caught in a process of transformation. The rationale for environmental policy making may be that it is good for the environment, but it in fact has a much wider social impact. It affects different sections of the population in unique ways and, correspondingly, calls forth a variety of different responses and action pat-terns which, in turn, transform society by sending the process of its constitution in a different direction. Such an analysis of contextualized, normatively oriented, practical rationality promises to provide a diagnosis of the latent crisis situation surrounding European environmental policy making and to pinpoint the genera-tive mechanisms involved.

Diagnostic reconstruction and explanatory critique

For the purposes of a diagnosis of the latent crisis situation surrounding European environmental policy making, Eder (2001: 25–32) adopts a theoretical position that prioritizes process and has three interrelated moments. It is a theory of soci-etal transformation or a theory of the construction or making of society, with an action, a structural and a normative dimension. As regards the action-theoretical dimension, first, European environmental policy making opens up a field of opportunities. Thus stimulating and soliciting increasing mobilization, a growing number of actors enter the environmental field, some doing so to improve the environment, and others taking advantage of opportunities from the perspective of their own interests. The entry of increasing numbers with different, competing and even conflicting orientations gives rise to a social field of environmental strug-gle in which the likelihood of conflict grows. As regards the structural-theoretical dimension, second, the social field of environmental struggle increasingly tends to transgresses national boundaries within Europe. The actions of interrelated actors generate an emergent social reality. They give rise to the formation of new European structures and a process of Europeanization, with the result that a European society is beginning to emerge. The outcome of the unleashing of this structuration process is uncertain, but it is possible that either a 'self-organizing European society' or a 'European society made in Brussels' (2001: 26), either one driven by the people or one driven by the elites, will become established. The nature and character of the future European society is the stake of the struggle in the environmental field. The normative dimension of the theory, third, recon-structively specifies the normative reference, legitimizing symbol, socio-practical idea of reason or 'regulative idea', as Eder (2001: 50) calls it, which emerges from the practical engagement of the different actors and comes to direct and guide them in their actions. In his reconstruction of the social field of environmental struggle, Eder starts from the communication taking place in the European public sphere, more particularly the 'discourse on sustainability' (2001: 30) in which are institutionalized the rules of how to relate to environmental matters but which is differently appropriated by the actors in the field. The reconstruction of the field in terms of its normative dimension reveals, on the one hand, the context-transcendent 'notion of sustainability' (2001: 30) functioning as regulative idea and, on the other, a number of different practical uses of the idea by competing and conflicting actors immanent in the field – three to be precise. The Brussels elites took up the idea of sustainability and shaped it into a 'device' (2001: 31) which is useful for policy making and enforcement; national media and governments made it into a 'master frame' (2001: 31) for communicating, promoting and defending national interests; and, finally, different sections of the population – farmers, workers, the unemployed – appropriated the idea in reaction to the elite device and national master frame by forming 'practical frames' (2001: 31) in terms of their own lifeworlds and using it to mobilize and orient their collective action. Accordingly, legislation, monitoring and mobilization are three distinct practical uses that not only reproduce the notion of sustainability, but recursively are also generatively regulated by this regulative idea. The reconstructive model – as we may regard it – at which Eder thus arrives permits an explanation of the social field of environmental struggle which at the same time makes possible a critical evaluation of the different practical uses of the notion of sustainability. It entails further the critique of the stereotype of the North–South divide resting on the assumption of good and bad environmental directive implementers and, by contrast, the recommendation to consider instead the variety of different practices whereby society is being constituted.

The analytical framework with its normative thrust having been established, Eder is able to embark on a substantive diagnostic analysis of the latent crisis situation engendered by European policy making. In his view, this policy making itself can be regarded as a social field that, on the one hand, opens opportunity structures for the formation of collective actors and collective action and, on the other, brings new constraints into being. Among the latter are new structural arrangements and new cleavages or class structures. As such, environmental policy making activates a public space in which the participating actors appear and engage in increasing communication, both everyday social interaction and discourse. In the discursive context, actors are defined not by what they have in mind, but by what they communicate. For example, they may think that they are in some way doing something for the environment or relating to environmental matters, but they are simultaneously competing, conflicting or cooperating with others and thus contributing to a larger process of social constitution and transformation in which, significantly, the direction of development and structuration of Europe is at stake. Far from being simply a matter of policy making and of dealing with the environment, therefore, policy is in fact a mechanism in the making of European society. It is in this context that the sense as well as urgency of the normative evaluation of both the different uses of sustainability and the resulting structures becomes evident.

The actual analysis, including the identification of social actors (2001: 32–44) and the decomposition and recomposition of the process of interrelation of the actors (2001: 44–50), is accomplished by such methods as media analysis of the discourse of sustainability, comprising both frame analysis and discourse analysis, documentary analysis of official materials and self-presentations produced by actors, interviews and qualitative analysis.[2] In order to penetrate the process of interrelation of actors and thus the resulting structure formation, Eder starts from the actors in the field – that is, the transnational Brussels elite, the nation-state actors and the people as collective actors – to construct what he calls 'three worlds of sustainability' (2001: 44–6) and locates them within the structural context fostering opportunities as well as constraining relations and cleavages. In keeping with the theoretical framework, the aim of this analysis is multilevel: to identify the use of the notion of sustainability by different actors, to reveal relations of cooperation, tension, competition and conflict between actors and, finally, to bring to light the structures formed through the actions, interactions, discourses, cooperation, competition and conflict which, in effect, represent the structuration of the emerging European society. Table 8.2 presents a summary overview extrapolated from Eder's verbal account which contrasts the three worlds of sustainability – namely, the Brussels 'transnational elite world', the 'nation-state world' and the 'popular world', each with its own constitution, institutional substructure, orientations to the good life, appropriation of the notion of sustainability, typical mode of action, the centre of gravity of its position, the kind of relation it maintains with the issues concerned and, finally, the kind or interest at stake for each.

Two important points reflected in the table need to be made explicit. The first relates to Eder's diagnosis of the problem European situation from which he originally started out. The appearance of an at least latent crisis following in the wake of European environmental policy making, according to his analysis, arises from the fact that the situation is wrongly analysed and evaluated by the Brussels elite.

Table 8.2 Worlds of sustainability in the constitution of European society

| | Actor | | |
World dimension	Brussels elite	Nation-states	People
World	'Transnational elite'	'Nation-state'	'Popular'
Base	EU	National institutional system	Local needs and experiences
Institutional core	Transnational deliberative bodies	Corporatist arrangements	Lifeworlds
Shared interests	Public issues	National interests and identity	Ordinary everyday concerns
Metaphors of the good life	Translations of economic interests	Minimization of economic transaction costs	Moral economies with class-specific notions of nature
Use of sustainability	Policy device/strategy	Master frame	Practical frame
Modus operandi	Legislation	Monitoring	Collective mobilization
Stance	Coercion: imposing a regime on EU society	Loyalty	Voice (or loyalty?)

The crisis is traced back to failing national compliance with environmental directives, which then gives rise to the wrong-headed 'stereotype of a North–South divide' in Europe (2001: 49) which is widely repeated throughout the different national media institutions. Following the stereotype, the Southern European countries are the 'environmental bad guys' (2001: 35) because they consistently fail in some way or another to implement European environmental directives. Considering the different worlds of sustainability and the vastly different corresponding practical uses made of the idea of sustainability, however, it becomes evident that it is by no means a matter of national compliance and hence of a divide between nation-states or countries. Rather, European environmental policy making has intervened in the process of the constitution and transformation of society and, as a result, has engendered a change in the relations between different sections of the European population, who themselves, in turn, are compelled to respond to the consequences of the policy making. Not national compliance with or implementation of environmental directives should be the analytical reference point, but the 'diversity of reactions' (2001: 49) instead. Once this is appreciated, the cherished stereotype dissipates in thin air. This is the punchline of Eder's reconstructive critique, which is negatively directed against the erroneous perception of the European situation and positively points to a potentially constructive and meaningful role for the regulative idea of sustainability.

The second point concerns Eder's basic theoretical position. In so far as he treats the three worlds as being coordinated by the European discourse of sustainability and thus as being interrelated and regulated by the rules of discourse, in particular the regulative idea of sustainability, his position approximates Habermas's communication theory. In so far as he treats the context-transcendent principle of sustainability as being ethically incarnated in different and even competing ways in terms of divergent ideas of the good life, however, he mitigates Habermas's over-emphasis on the Kantian moral point of view by shifting to a position approximating Honneth's Hegelian concern with concrete ethicized universals. This sociologically informed combination is central to his methodological approach. It reflects his basic, albeit at best only suggested, assumption of the immanent-transcendence complex and makes possible the reconstructive explanation of the relation between the regulative idea of sustainability and its different uses as well as the reconstructive critique of the limitations of the different practical uses. Significantly, the combination also has the advantage of allowing him to go beyond both Habermas and Honneth. Whereas Habermas focuses on the potential end result of the discursive process rather than the process itself, and whereas Honneth commands no theory that could get to grips with structure formation, Eder makes precisely the process of structure formation at the core of the emergence of society his focal point.

It is this process of the constitution of a European society and the implicated structure formation that forms the centre of gravity of Eder's socio-historical explanation of the problem European situation in terms of the real mechanisms involved. As is characteristic of Critical Theory's critical explanation or explanatory critique, this explanation would also be the vehicle of Eder's ultimate goal

– both an exposing and a disclosing critique of European environmental policy making. To begin with, Eder isolates three distinct mechanisms that play an indispensable role in the process of the making of European society. The first is what we may call the generative mechanism of a plurality of actors with different cultural-institutional characteristics and goals who possess the necessary competences to make a difference in social reality. The second, what we may call the relational mechanism, consists of the interrelation or association of the actors in such a way that networks of relations are formed. The third and final, what we may call the contextual mechanism, refers to facilitating and constraining structures that are given rise to by the generative and relational mechanisms and, in turn, provide a context for them and recursively work back on them in a structuring manner. An investigation of the structuring that the operation of these various mechanisms has produced in Europe shows, according Eder's account, that from both a temporal and a spatial point of view national determination has declined and that the national perspective consequently runs up against its limits. At the end of the Cold War, the world shrank and, spatially, the emergence of organized blocks of societies such as the Americas, Europe, Asia and now also Africa increasingly eliminate divisions. Under these contextual conditions, it comes as no surprise that European environmental politics has grown into a unified field of action in which a common discourse and related actions compel different social groups to interrelate in ways that transgress borders. This is where Eder locates the process of 'the emergence of European social structures, the making of a distinctly European society . . . not as the ideal project of policy makers, but as the reality generated through collective action with all its cleavages, conflicts and coalitions' (2001: 49). Of necessity, this requires a step back from nations to classes.

The process of structure formation gives evidence of a changing class structure rather than the disappearance of class. The most remarkable feature of the class structure is the deterritorialization and transnationalization it has been undergoing under the new contextual conditions. The different classes cut across national boundaries, while the 'complex system of elite action' intensifies this by having the effect of fostering a 'system of class relations in Europe' (2001: 45). The change in the class structure implies that new cleavages are appearing and closer investigation of the actions and interests involved bears out that these cleavages turn on the position actors occupy in the 'system of economic dependence in European society' (2001: 44). The key conflict in this new context is between popular collective action, on the one hand, and transnational elite action and loyal national proxies, on the other. On this basis, Eder regards the different practical uses of sustainability as indicating that environmental policy making is embedded in the 'system of European class structuration' (2001: 45) and 'shaped by an economically divided Europe' (2001: 44). The basic causal mechanism he identifies and refers to for the purposes of explaining the problematic European situation, therefore, is one that can be understood only in terms of the operation and mutual implication of the generative, relational and contextual mechanisms responsible for the process of the formation of the structures of European society – namely, class and the emerging system of class relations in Europe.

A critique of European environmental policy making follows immediately from this explanation in that the account sheds new light on it. Environmental policy making becomes properly intelligible only in terms of the changing system of European class relations in which it is embedded and the associated conflict which it is partly responsible for initiating and fuelling. Eder's critique is two-dimensional, as is typical for Critical Theory, having both a negative exposing and a positive disclosing dimension. Negatively, the critique first targets the stereotype of the North–South divide in Europe. It is exposed as a legitimizing device for national actors in the loyalty game in which they seek to publicly portray their relation to Brussels and the environment in a positive light. The use of this device is not without a range of negative consequences for relations between nation-states and the inclusion of certain section of the population. Second, the critique exposes sustainability in its official interpretation as a legitimizing device which is used by the transnational Brussels elite or dominant classes in a power game to homogenize the European population into a loyal following. However, the homogenization efforts simultaneously produce their opposite, namely quite severe exclusionary effects. It is these unintended and unacknowledged consequences that account for the mobilization of farmers, workers and the unemployed and, more generally, the concomitant process of societal self-organization. On this basis, Eder very pointedly exposes the widely entertained harmonious image put forward by the European elite of a democratic and inclusive European society as a 'delusion' (2001: 50). Rather than simply a negative devaluation or rejection of Europe and European policy making, however, the critique also has a positive disclosing side. It is emphatically presented as having been designed 'to identify the options (or non-options) available' (Kousis and Eder 2001: 19) to those involved. Eder's central point in this respect is that the conflict between the people and the political elites, which the latter mistakenly interpret as an indication of a crisis situation, is in fact an entirely normal phenomenon. The dynamics driving the process of structure formation will come to a standstill without it, ending in a crisis of stagnation which leaves the structural possibilities or potentials inherent in the process fallow. This disclosure is aimed at allowing all actors involved to develop a better understanding of their role in the constitution of European society and thus to reconsider, revise and strengthen their participation in and contributions to this vital process.

If one of the characteristic tasks of Critical Theory is to problematize the prevailing consensus by showing the questionable nature of the background assumptions underpinning it and thus to open the way for a realizable radical re-orientation, then Eder has provided the necessary intellectual material for this in the area of European environmental policy making with his diagnostic explanatory critique. One step remains, however, and that is whether those concerned, both social scientists and the various actors in the field, can be convinced of the questionable status of the conventionally accepted understanding and mode of practice.

Scientific-practical validation

As regards scientific validation, Eder's piece under discussion here forms part of a large project of an extensive research network in the context of which every aspect of it passed through the crucible of theoretical discourse. The piece was also built on the achievements of a range of earlier large research projects, all of which were thoroughly discussed during the research process and after completion. Its publication in a prominent social scientific book series means, furthermore, that since 2001 it has been subject to scientific consideration. The process of theoretical discourse and scientific validation continues.

This brings us to the question of practical validation. Eder's basic assumption about the addressees of social scientific research and, in particular, of messages containing explanations and critiques that are relevant to the practical concerns of social life, is evident from what he writes about the object of social scientific study. In his view, qualitative data are much more significant than quantitative data which quickly run up against the limits of the extensive methodological approach since 'the object of study changes constantly, not only by virtue of it being studied and observed, but also because of it being the object of reflexive action by the actors' (2001: 37). This suggests that he appreciates that not only the subjects under study but also the audience possess action and communicative competences which can be activated by their reflexive capacity and sent in a critical direction for the purposes of acting on and transforming social reality. Without an assumption of this kind, neither the possibility nor the meaning of practical verification or public testing can be understood.

Eder is acutely aware of his addressees. As is borne out in particular by his exposing critique, they are first of all the political elites, both the Brussels elite and the national actors. The negative critique of their ideological uses of regulative ideas and stereotypes as legitimizing devices with unacknowledged negative consequences is directly addressed at them. For this reason, a particular publisher and a particular book series, one on 'Environment & Policy' which is noted by the European and national policy experts, have been deliberately chosen. Very careful thought has clearly gone into the identification of the appropriate addressees and both the preparation and presentation of the research finding so as to engender a practical effect. However, the political elites are not the only addressees. As the positive disclosing critique shows, Eder had in mind, over and above the political elites, especially the ordinary civil collective actors in the environmental field. It is well known that for the purposes of their collective mobilization and action these actors do take account of relevant social scientific information. Eder understands that they are not only the most vital component in the process of the constitution and structure formation of society, but absolutely indispensable if a 'self-organizing European society' rather than a 'European society made in Brussels' (2001: 26) is to become established, and therefore he seeks to bring this responsibility to their attention. The book series mentioned above is equally relevant from the perspective of having a practical effect in the case of these civil collective actors. To determine whether and what practical effect this work has had up until now would require independent research.

Conclusion

In this chapter, four examples from the research literature – Habermas, Honneth, McCarthy and Eder – were presented in order to illustrate the application of Critical Theory's methodology as it passes through its three principal moments as framed by the concept of immanent transcendence.

In the case of the first – problem disclosure and constitution of the object – the employment of the abductive inference and hence relational thinking regarding an objectively generated problem was stressed. The more complex second moment of diagnostic reconstruction and explanatory critique allowed the investigation of the different examples in terms of how they, on the one hand, established a normative reference point for diagnostic purposes and, on the other, went about offering an explanatory critique of the problem situation in question. Of importance were, first, the procedure of reconstruction and the real generative mechanisms from which it reflexively abstracted normative import and, second, in particular the specific nature of the causal mechanisms referred to for the purposes of explanatory critique. Rather than a monocausal account, the authors typically appealed to a complex conjunction of different mechanisms (see Figure 6.3) which became visible from a normatively led abductive viewpoint. Habermas referred to political and economic power mechanisms rooted in the social structure; Honneth to an array of economic mechanisms linked to a cultural mechanism; McCarthy to a cultural mechanism rooted in economic and political mechanisms; and Eder to a political power mechanism rooted in the class structure. Finally, an assessment was made in each case of both the scientific and practical validation process to which it is subject.

It is hoped that the transparency of the analyses of these outstanding pieces of research will contribute to a better understanding of Critical Theory and its methodology and, by the same token, advance research within the framework of this unique, acute and indispensable left-Hegelian theoretical and research tradition.

Notes

Introduction

1   The dimension of subject formation is also touched on throughout, but deserves more systematic treatment than can be offered here owing to lack of space.

2   It could also be argued that, given more general advances following in the wake of the cognitive revolution, it is quite possible today to develop a new, more abstract theoretical viewpoint for Critical Theory which is able to incorporate and make sense of currently available perspectives, while simultaneously going beyond them to a more general level. Although indications are offered along the way, a systematic development of this alternative theoretical approach is not possible in the present context.

3   See Strydom (1999, 2001, 2006a) on 'triple contingency'.

1 Classical foundations

1   Here reference is made to the theses and not to page numbers.

2   In Peirce's case, reference is conventionally made to the paragraphs of his *Collected Papers* – here 5.2 referring to volume 5, paragraph 2.

2 Appropriation of the classical foundations

1   Here Korsch quotes from Marx's posthumous papers.

3 Contemporary Critical Theory and pragmatism

1   The importance of this question and the intensity with which it is being discussed are documented by the proceedings of a conference held in honour of Apel at the time of his eightieth birthday in 2002 (Böhler et al. 2003), which continued a line of argument also heard at a similar event when he turned seventy-five.

2   Recognizing Apel's seminal contribution to laying the groundwork for the contemporary phase in Critical Theory's development does not necessarily commit one to every aspect of his position – particularly his rather controversial claim to final foundational grounding (*Letztbegründung*).

3   The reference here is to 'Between philosophy and science: Marxism as critique', which dates back to 1960 and was originally published in 1963.

4   On Wellmer generally, see Honneth (2007a: 201–15).

5   Professionally a sociologist, Eder does not present himself as a critical theorist, but his work leaves no doubt about the critical dimension of this former collabo-

rator of Habermas.

4 Immanent transcendence as key concept

1　This lecture was subsequently published in 1994, and in 2000 it was included in a volume of collected essays (Honneth 2000b) – the latter being available in English as Honneth (2007b).
2　It is likely that Fink-Eitel's review essay on Habermas titled 'Innerweltlichen Transzendenz' (1993), to which Honneth refers elsewhere, also played a role.
3　In the current international intellectual context, the distinction at issue here in effect opposes not only the widespread kind of idealism deriving from Heidegger, which stresses an all-engulfing movement of meaning, but also the contrary equally influential naturalism appealing to Quine, which subjects everything to an all-conditioning natural process. A dimension of action and practice must be accommodated.
4　An important part of the motivation of the early Frankfurt School's polemic against the sociology of knowledge, for example, was precisely Mannheim's lack of a theoretical basis in his treatment of transcendent ideas in *Ideology and Utopia* (1972).
5　Rockmore (2002) takes a comparable position on both Apel and Rorty.
6　This means that such forms are not purely culturalist phenomena. They have roots in the biologically formed cognitive endowment of human beings, yet must be presupposed and can serve as secure normative foundations only on the basis of a practical commitment.
7　This is a highly controversial issue, not only between pragmatists and critical theorists but even among the latter themselves, which cannot be addressed here. See for example Aboulafia et al. (2002) and Böhler et al. (2003).

5 Contemporary critical theorists on methodology

1　Together with Honneth's two essays referred to earlier, 'Pathologies of the social' (2007a) and 'The social dynamics of disrespect' (2007b), a series of his publications from the first years of the new millennium are most helpful. Among them are 'The possibility of disclosing critique' (2000a), 'Rekonstruktive Gesellschafskritik unter genealogischem Vorbehalt' (2007c), 'The point of recognition' (2003) and 'A social pathology of reason' (2004a). This last essay together with the one on reconstructive critique with a genealogical proviso (2007c) provide perhaps his clearest, most coherent and comprehensive statement of the overall structure of Critical Theory's methodology. His book on *Reification* (2008) and several recently published discussions (2009a,b,c; Boltanski and Honneth 2009) shed further valuable light on his methodological understanding.
2　Theoretically, this move harbours a significant implication in that the recourse to insights from ethnomethodology potentially opens the route for the systematic development of the communication paradigm from a cognitive theoretical viewpoint (e.g. Eder 1996; Strydom 2000, 2002, 2006b, 2007), which would provide a more secure and detailed grasp of the structuration of the process of the practical realization of socio-cultural ideas of reason without forfeiting the vital normative dimension.

6 The methodological framework of critical theory

1　This perspective turns on the crucial distinction between interaction and discourse (Strydom 2006a).
2　My own proposal beyond these familiar theoretical interpretations of Critical

Theory is what may be called cognitive structuration or, rather, sociation (Strydom 2000, 2002, 2006b, 2007, 2011).

3   In turn, analogy and metaphor depend on sign mediation, which is neglected by Bhaskar.

4   Suggestions of a disparate range of mechanisms are to be found in Habermas (1984/87), Miller (1986, 2002), Bohman (1991), McCarthy (1994a, 2001a, 2004), Eder (1999, 2007), Brunkhorst (2005), Honneth (2007f) and Benhabib (2008). For a more elaborate presentation, see Strydom (2011). As late as 2006, Honneth (2009a: 156) stressed the need for a theory of mechanisms but admitted that it represents a deficit in his theory.

5   It should be obvious that the systematization of mechanisms presented here is more general and therefore goes beyond the theoretical positions of both Habermas and Honneth. The systematization is basically conceived from the viewpoint of cognitive social theory with allowance for structure formations that recursively exert significant contextual impact. It mediates between Habermas's and Honneth's respective language-theoretical and the recognition-theoretical positions and thus acknowledges the relative right of both, while nevertheless shifting to a more encompassing theoretical position. The presentation of this position, however, is beyond the scope of this book (Strydom 2000, 2002, 2006b, 2007, 2009b,c, 2011).

6   As we know from the history of the social sciences, in the case of controversies transcending Critical Theory's boundaries, discourse can take the form of a methodological dispute. Examples abound (Strydom 2008a), from the Haym–Twesten debate, the *Methodenstreit* and the *Werturteilstreit*, through the sociology of knowledge dispute, the functionalist debate, the positivist dispute and the explanation–understanding controversy, to the current pragmatist debate and the increasingly intense debate about the concept of critique. Where argumentation among social scientists comes up against insufficient knowledge and uncertainty, with the result that rational disagreement or the agreement to disagree prevails, we speak of an 'epistemic discourse' (von Schomberg 1992: 262). It is also possible that such lack of knowledge and uncertainty could open social science to public debate, in which case a public scientific controversy is the result.

7 Varieties of critique

1   This entails a 'Hegelianized theodicy' (Schnädelbach 1987: 26) of capitalism according to which the negative is there solely for the benefit of the positive.

2   The development of Critical Theory's relation to this form of critique was reinforced by the conference on Foucault held in Frankfurt in 2001 (Honneth and Saar 2003).

8 Methodology in action

1   Lack of space prevents the inclusion of the originally intended parallel discussions of the research of Brunkhorst (2005), Beck (2006; Beck and Grande 2007), Benhabib (2008) and Claudia von Werlhof (Projektgruppe Zivilisationspolitik 2009).

2   Eder insists that 'Qualitative data, treated with care and according to the logic of scientific inference, produce much more valid information than any quantitative study. Quantitative data . . . are more of an additional device' (2001: 37).

Bibliography

Aboulafia, M., Bookman, M. and Kemp, C. (eds) (2002) *Habermas and Pragmatism*. London: Routledge.

Adorno, T. (1970) *Negative Dialektik*. Frankfurt: Suhrkamp.

Adorno, T. W., Albert, H., Dahrendorf, R., Habermas, J., Pilot, H. and Popper, K. R. (1976) *The Positivist Dispute in German Sociology*. London: Heinemann.

Apel, K.-O. (1962) *Die Idee der Sprache*. Bonn: Bouvier.

Apel, K.-O. (1967) 'Einführung: Der philosophische Hintergrund der Entstehung des Pragmatismus bei Charles Sanders Peirce', in K.-O. Apel (ed.) *Charles S. Piece: Schriften I*. Frankfurt: Suhrkamp, pp. 13–153.

Apel, K.-O. (1970) 'Einführung: Peirces Denkweg vom Pragmatismus zum Pragmatizismus', in K.-O. Apel (ed.) *Charles S. Piece: Schriften II*. Frankfurt: Suhrkamp, pp. 11–211.

Apel, K.-O. (1973) *Transformation der Philosophie*, Vols I–II. Frankfurt: Suhrkamp.

Apel, K.-O. (1974) 'Zur Idee einer transzendentalen Sprachpragmatik', in J. Simon (ed.) *Aspekte und Probleme der Sprachphilosophie*. Freiburg: Alber, pp. 283–326.

Apel, K.-O. (1977) 'Types of social science in the light of human interests of knowledge', *Social Research* 44(3): 425–70.

Apel, K.-O. (1980) *Towards a Transformation of Philosophy*. London: Routledge & Kegan Paul.

Apel, K.-O. (1981) *Charles S. Peirce*. Amherst, MA: University of Massachusetts Press.

Apel, K.-O. (1984 [1979]) *Understanding and Explanation: A Transcendental-Pragmatic Perspective*. Cambridge, MA: MIT Press.

Apel, K.-O. (1995) *Charles S. Peirce*. Atlantic Highlands, NJ: Humanities Press.

Apel, K.-O. (1998) *Auseinandersetzungen in Erprobung des transzendental-pragmatischen Aufsatzes*. Frankfurt: Suhrkamp.

Apel, K.-O. (2003) 'Wahrheit als regulative Idee', in D. Böhler, M. Kettner and G. Skirbekk (eds) *Reflexion und Verantwortung: Auseinandersetzungen mit Karl-Otto Apel*. Frankfurt: Suhrkamp, pp. 171–96.

Apel, K.-O., von Bormann, C., Bubner, R., Gadamer, H.-G., Giegel, H. J. and Habermas, J. (1971) *Hermeneutik und Ideologiekritik*. Frankfurt: Suhrkamp.

Archer, M., Bhaskar, R., Collier, A., Lawson, T. and Norrie, A. (eds) (1998) *Critical Realism*. London: Routledge.

Baecker, D. (1999) 'Kommunikation im Medium der Information', in R. Maresch and N. Werber (eds) *Kommunikation, Medien, Macht*. Frankfurt: Suhrkamp, pp. 174–91.

Basaure, M. (2009) 'Foucault and the "Anti-Oedipus Movement"', *History of Psychiatry* 20(3): 340–59.

Basaure, M. (2011) 'Continuity through rupture with the Frankfurt School: Axel Honneth's theory of recognition', in G. Delanty and S. Turner (eds) *Handbook of Social and Political Theory*. London: Routledge.

Beck, U. (2006) *The Cosmopolitan Vision*. Cambridge: Polity.

Beck, U. and Grande, E. (2007) 'Cosmopolitanism: Europe's way out of crisis', *European Journal of Social Theory* 10(1): 67–85.

Benhabib, S. (1986) *Critique, Norm and Utopia*. New York: Columbia University Press.

Benhabib, S. (2008) *Another Cosmopolitanism*. New York: Oxford.

Bernstein, R. (1971) *Praxis and Action*. Philadelphia: University of Pennsylvania Press.

Bernstein, R. (1975) *Praxis und Handlung*. Frankfurt: Suhrkamp.

Bernstein, R. (1976) *The Restructuring of Social and Political Theory*. Oxford: Blackwell.

Bernstein, R. (1983) *Beyond Objectivism and Relativism*. Oxford: Blackwell.

Bernstein, R. (1991) *The New Constellation*. Cambridge: Polity.

Bhaskar, R. (1978) *A Realist Theory of Science*. London: Harvester.

Bhaskar, R. (1989 [1979]) *The Possibility of Naturalism*. London: Harvester.

Bhaskar, R. (1998) 'General introduction', in M. Archer, R. Bhaskar, A. Collier, T. Lawson and A. Norrie (eds) *Critical Realism*. London: Routledge, pp. ix–xxiv.

Bhaskar, R. and Collier, A. (1998) 'Explanatory critiques', in M. Archer, R. Bhaskar, A. Collier, T. Lawson and A. Norrie (eds) *Critical Realism*. London: Routledge, pp. 385–94.

Bleicher, J. (1980) *Contemporary Hermeneutics*. London: Routledge & Kegan Paul.

Böhler, D., Kettner, M. and Skirbekk, G. (eds) (2003) *Reflexion und Verantwortung: Auseinandersetzungen mit Karl-Otto Apel*. Frankfurt: Suhrkamp.

Bohman, J. (1991) *New Philosophy of Social Science*. Cambridge: Polity.

Bohman, J. (1993) 'Welterschließung und radikale Kritik', *Deutsche Zeitschrift für Philosophie* 41(3): 563–74.

Bohman, J. (1999) 'Theories, practices, and pluralism: A pragmatic interpretation of critical social science', *Philosophy of the Social Sciences* 29(4): 459–80.

Bohman, J. (2000) 'Demokratischer und methodologischer Pluralismus: Eine pragmatische Interpretation der kritische Forschung', in S. Müller-Doohm (ed.) *Das Interesse der Vernunft*. Frankfurt: Suhrkamp, pp. 299–327.

Bohman, J. (2001) 'Participants, observers, and critics', in W. Rehg and J. Bohman (eds) *Pluralism and the Pragmatic Turn: The Transformation of Critical Theory – Essays in Honor of Thomas McCarthy*. Cambridge, MA: MIT Press, pp. 87–113.

Boltanski, L. (2008) 'Die pragmatische Soziologie der Kritik heute: Gespräch mit Mauro Basaure', *Berlin Journal für Soziologie* 18(4): 1–24.

Boltanski, L. and Chiapello, E. (2005) 'The role of criticism in the dynamics of capitalism', in M. Miller (ed.) *Worlds of Capitalism*. London: Routledge, pp. 237–67.

Boltanski, L. and Chiapello, E. (2007) *The New Spirit of Capitalism*. New York: Verso.

Boltanski, L. and Honneth, A. (2009) 'Soziologie der Kritik oder Kritische Theorie? Ein Gespräch mit Robin Celikates', in R. Jaeggi and T. Wesche (eds) *Was ist Kritik?* Frankfurt: Suhrkamp, pp. 81–114.

Boltanski, L. and Thévenot, L. (1991) *De la Justification*. Paris: Gallimard.

Bourdieu, P. (1977 [1972]) *Outline of a Theory of Practice*. Cambridge: Cambridge University Press.

Bourdieu, P. (1986 [1979]) *Distinction*. London: Routledge & Kegan Paul.

Bourdieu, P. (1990 [1980]) *The Logic of Practice*. Cambridge: Polity.

Bourdieu, P. (1993 [1984]) *Sociology in Question*. London: Sage.

Bourdieu, P. (1998) *Acts of Resistance*. Cambridge: Polity.

Bourdieu, P. (2000 [1997]) *Pascalian Meditations*. Cambridge: Polity.

Bourdieu, P. (2001) *Science de la science et reflexivité*. Paris: Raisons d'Agir.

Bourdieu, P. et al. (1999) *The Weight of the World*. Cambridge: Polity.

Bourdieu, P., Chamboredon, J.-C. and Passeron, J.-C. (1991 [1968]) *The Craft of Sociology*. Berlin: de Gruyter.

Bourdieu, P. and Wacquant, L. (1992) *An Invitation to Reflexive Sociology*. Cambridge: Polity.

van den Brink, B. (1997) 'Gesellschaftstheorie und Übertreibungskunst', *Neue Rundschau* 1: 37–59.

van den Brink, B. and Owen, D. (2007) *Recognition and Power*. Cambridge: Cambridge University Press.

Brunkhorst, H. (2004) 'Critical Theory and the analysis of contemporary mass society', in F. Rush (ed.) *The Cambridge Companion to Critical Theory*. Cambridge: Cambridge University Press, pp. 248–79.

Brunkhorst, H. (2005) *Solidarity*. Cambridge, MA: MIT.

Bubner, R., Cramer, K. and Wiehl, R. (eds) (1970) *Hermeneutik und Dialektik*, Vols I–II. Tubingen: Mohr.

Butler, J. (1997) *The Psychic Life of Power*. Stanford, CA: Stanford University Press.

Celikates, R. (2009) *Kritik als soziale Praxis*. Frankfurt: Campus.

Coleman, J. (1990) *Foundations of Social Theory*. Cambridge, MA: Harvard University Press.

Cooke, M. (2006) *Re-presenting the Good Society*. Cambridge, MA: MIT Press.

Cooke, M. (2009) 'Zur Rationalität der Gesellschaftskritik', in R. Jaeggi and T. Wesche (eds) *Was ist Kritik?* Frankfurt: Suhrkamp, pp. 117–33.

Danermark, B., Jakobsen, L. and Karlsson, J. C. (2002) *Explaining Society: Critical Realism in the Social Sciences*. London: Routledge.

Delanty, G. and Strydom, P. (2003) *Philosophies of Social Science*. Maidenhead: Open University Press.

Dewey, J. (1927). *The Public and Its Problems*. New York: Holt.

Dewey, J. (1938) *Logic, the Theory of Inquiry*. New York: Holt.

Dews, P. (2000) 'Die Entsublimierung der Vernunft als Habermas' Leitgedanke', in S. Müller-Doohm (ed.) *Das Interesse der Vernunft*. Frankfurt: Suhrkamp, pp. 144–74.

Dubiel, H. (1988) *Kritische Theorie der Gesellschaft*. Weinheim: Juventa.

Eder, K. (1988) *Die Vergesellschaftung der Natur*. Frankfurt: Suhrkamp.

Eder, K. (1993) *The New Politics of Class*. London: Sage.

Eder, K. (1996) *The Social Construction of Nature*. London: Sage.

Eder, K. (1999) 'Societies learn and yet the world is hard to change', *European Journal of Social Theory* 2(2): 195–215.

Eder, K. (2000) *Kulturelle Identität zwischen Tradition und Utopie*. Frankfurt: Campus.

Eder, K. (2001) 'Sustainability as a discursive device for mobilizing European publics', in K. Eder and M. Kousis (eds) *Environmental Politics in Southern Europe*. Dordrecht: Kluwer, pp. 25–52.

Eder, K. (2006) 'Making sense of the public sphere', in G. Delanty (ed.) *Handbook of Contemporary European Social Theory*. London: Routledge, pp. 333–46.

Eder, K. (2007) 'The public sphere and European democracy', in J. E. Fossum and P. Schlesinger (eds) *The European Union and the Public Sphere*. London: Routledge.

Eder, K. (2009) 'Rational action, communicative action, and the narrative structure of social life', in S. O'Tuama (ed.) *Critical Turns in Critical Theory*. London: Tauris, pp. 63–79.

Eder, K., Giesen, B., Schmidtke, O. and Tambini, D. (2002) *Collective Identities in Action*. Aldershot: Ashgate.

Eder, K. and Schmidtke, O. (1998) 'Ethnische Mobilisierung und die Logik von Identitätskämpfen', *Zeitschrift für Soziologie* 27: 418–37.

Fink-Eitel, H. (1993) 'Innerweltlichen Transzendenz', *Merkur* 47(3): 237–45.

Foucault, M. (1961) 'Introduction to Kant's "Anthropology from a Pragmatic Perspective"', translated by Adrianna Bove, <www.generation-online.org/p/foucault1.htm> accessed 12 May 2010.

Foucault, M. (1979 [1975]) *Discipline and Punish*. Harmondsworth: Penguin.

Foucault, M. (1982) 'The subject and power', in H. L. Dreyfus and P. Rabinow, *Michel Foucault*. London: Harvester, pp. 208–26.

Foucault, M. (1986a) 'What is Enlightenment?', in P. Rabinow (ed.) *The Foucault Reader*. Harmondsworth: Penguin, pp. 32–50.

Foucault, M. (1986b) 'Nietzsche, genealogy, history', in P. Rabinow (ed.) *The Foucault Reader*. Harmondsworth: Penguin, pp. 76–100.

Foucault, M. (as Maurice Florence) (1998a) 'Foucault', in J. D. Faubion (ed.) *Aesthetics, Method, and Epistemology*. New York: New Press, pp. 459–63.

Foucault, M. (1998b) 'Structuralism and post-structuralism', in J. D. Faubion (ed.) *Aesthetics, Method, and Epistemology*. New York: New Press, pp. 433–58.

Foucault, M. (1998c) 'Return to history', in J. D. Faubion (ed.) *Aesthetics, Method, and Epistemology*. New York: New Press, pp. 419–32.

Fraser, N. (1989) *Unruly Practices*. Cambridge: Polity.

Fraser, N. (1997) *Justice Interruptus*. London: Routledge.

Fraser, N. (2003) 'Distorted beyond all recognition: A rejoinder to Axel Honneth', in N. Fraser and A. Honneth, *Redistribution or Recognition?* London: Verso, pp. 198–236.

Fraser, N. and Honneth, A. (2003) *Redistribution or Recognition?* London: Verso.

Gadamer, H.-G. (1975 [1960]) *Truth and Method*. London: Sheed & Ward.

Giddens, A. (1984) *The Constitution of Society*. Cambridge: Polity.

Grenfell, M. (ed.) (2008) *Pierre Bourdieu*. London: Acumen.

Gronke, H. (2003) 'Die Relevanz von regulativen Ideen zur Orientierung Mit-Verantwortung', in D. Böhler, M. Kettner and G. Skirbekk (eds) *Reflexion und Verantwortung*. Frankfurt: Suhrkamp, pp. 260–82.

Habermas, J. (1954) *Die Absolute und die Geschichte*. Neuwied: Luchterhand.

Habermas, J. (1970) 'Toward a theory of communicative competence', in H. P. Dreitzel (ed.) *Recent Sociology No. 2*. London: Macmillan, pp. 115–48.

Habermas, J. (1972 [1968]) *Knowledge and Human Interests*. London: Heinemann.

Habermas, J. (1974) *Theory and Practice*. London: Heinemann.

Habermas, J. (1979) *Communication and the Evolution of Society*. London: Heinemann.

Habermas, J. (1984) *Vorstudien und Ergänzungen zur Theorie des kommunikativen Handelns*. Frankfurt: Suhrkamp.

Habermas, J. (1987 [1985]) *The Philosophical Discourse of Modernity*. Cambridge: Polity.

Habermas, J. (1984/87) *The Theory of Communicative Action*, Vols I–II. London: Heinemann.

Habermas, J. (1988 [1967]) *On the Logic of the Social Sciences*. Cambridge: Polity.

Habermas, J. (1990) *Moral Consciousness and Communicative Action*. Cambridge: Polity.

Habermas, J. (1991a) 'Peirce über Kommunikation', in J. Habermas, *Texte und Kontexte*. Frankfurt: Suhrkamp, pp. 9–33.

Habermas, J. (1991b) 'Exkurs: Transzendenz von innen, Transzendenz ins Diesseits', in J. Habermas, *Texte und Kontexte*. Frankfurt: Suhrkamp, pp. 127–69.

Habermas, J. (1992) *Postmetaphysical Thinking*. Cambridge: Polity.

Habermas, J. (1993) *Justification and Application*. Cambridge: Polity.

Habermas, J. (1996 [1992]) *Between Facts and Norms*. Cambridge: Polity.

Habermas, J. (1998a [1996]) *The Inclusion of the Other*. Cambridge: Polity.

Habermas, J. (1998b) *On the Pragmatics of Communication*. Cambridge: Polity (edited by Maeve Cooke).

Habermas, J. (2001) *Zeit der Übergänge*. Frankfurt: Suhrkamp.

Habermas, J. (2002) 'Postscript', in M. Aboulafia, M. Bookman and C. Kemp (eds) *Habermas and Pragmatism*. London: Routledge, pp. 223–33.

Habermas, J. (2003 [1999]) *Truth and Justification*. Cambridge: Polity.

Habermas, J. (2005) *Zwischen Naturalismus und Religion*. Frankfurt: Suhrkamp.

Habermas, J. (2006) 'Political communication in the media society', *Communication Theory* 16: 411–26.

Habermas, J. and Luhmann, N. (1971) *Theorie der Gesellschaftung oder Sozialtechnologie*. Frankfurt: Suhrkamp.

Halton, E. (2005) 'Pragmatism', in G. Ritzer (ed.) *Encyclopedia of Social Theory*, Vol. II. Thousand Oaks, CA: Sage, pp. 595–99.

Hanssen, B. (2004) 'Critical Theory and poststructuralism', in F. Rush (ed.) *The Cambridge Companion to Critical Theory*. Cambridge: Cambridge University Press, pp. 280–309.

Hegel, G. W. F. (1967 [1821]) *Philosophy of Right*. London: Oxford University Press.

Heidegger, M. (1967 [1927]) *Being and Time*. Oxford: Blackwell.

Honneth, A. (1985) *Kritik der Macht*. Frankfurt: Suhrkamp.

Honneth, A. (1992) *Kampf um Anerkennung*. Frankfurt: Suhrkamp.

Honneth, A. (1999) 'Reply to Andreas Kalyvas, "Critical Theory at the crossroads"', *European Journal of Social Theory* 2(2): 249–52.

Honneth, A. (2000a) 'The possibility of a disclosing critique: the Dialectic of Enlightenment in light of current debates in social criticism', *Constellations* 7(1):116–27.

Honneth, A. (2000b) *Das Andere der Gerechtigkeit*. Frankfurt: Suhrkamp.

Honneth, A. (2001) *Leiden an Unbestimmtheit*. Stuttgart: Reclam.

Honneth, A. (2002a) 'An interview with Axel Honneth', interviewed by Anders Petersen and Rasmus Willig, *European Journal of Social Theory* 5(2): 265–77.

Honneth, A. (2002b) *Befreiung aus der Mündigkeit*. Frankfurt: Campus.

Honneth, A. (2003) 'The point of recognition', in N. Fraser and A. Honneth, *Redistribution or Recognition*. London: Verso, pp. 237–67.

Honneth, A. (2004a) 'A social pathology of reason: on the intellectual legacy of Critical Theory', in F. Rush (ed.) *The Cambridge Companion to Critical Theory*. Cambridge: Cambridge University Press, pp. 336–60.

Honneth, A. (2004b) 'Organized self-realization: some paradoxes of individualization', *European Journal of Social Theory* 7(4): 463–78.

Honneth, A. (2007a) 'Pathologies of the social: the past and present of social philosophy', in *Disrespect: The Normative Foundations of Critical Theory*. Cambridge: Polity, pp. 1–48.

Honneth, A. (2007b) 'The social dynamics of disrespect: on the location of Critical Theory today', in A. Honneth, *Disrespect: The Normative Foundations of Critical Theory*. Cambridge: Polity, pp. 63–79.

Honneth, A. (2007c) 'Rekonstruktive Gesellschafskritik unter genealogischem Vorbehalt', in A. Honneth, *Pathologien der Vernunft*. Frankfurt: Suhrkamp, pp. 57–69.

Honneth, A. (2007d) 'Eine soziale Pathologie der Vernunft', in A. Honneth, *Pathologien der Vernunft*. Frankfurt: Suhrkamp, pp. 28–56.

Honneth, A. (2007e) 'Idiosynkrasie als Erkenntnismittel: Gesellschafskritik im Zeitalter des normalisierten Intellektuellen', in A. Honneth, *Pathologien der Vernunft*. Frankfurt: Suhrkamp, pp. 219–34.

Honneth, A. (2007f) *Pathologien der Vernunft*. Frankfurt: Suhrkamp.

Honneth, A. (2008) *Reification*. Oxford: Oxford University Press.

Honneth, A. (2009a) 'Die Anerkennung ist ein Grundmechanismus sozialer Existenz: Gespräch mit Krassimir Stojanov', in M. Basaure, J. P. Reemtsma and R. Willig (eds) *Erneuerung der Kritik*. Frankfurt: Campus, pp. 1149–66.

Honneth, A. (2009b) 'Erbe und Erneuerung der Kritischen Theorie: Gespräch mit Internationalen Studiengruppe zur Kritischen Theorie', in M. Basaure, J. P. Reemtsma and R. Willig (eds) *Erneuerung der Kritik*. Frankfurt: Campus, pp. 49–81.

Honneth, A. (2009c) 'Das soziologische Defizit der Kritischen Theorie', in M. Basaure, J. P. Reemtsma and R. Willig (eds) *Erneuerung der Kritik*. Frankfurt: Campus, pp. 83–9.

Honneth, A. (2009d) 'Schwierigkeiten kapitalismuskritischer Zeitdiagnosen: Gespräch mit Christoph Lieber', in M. Basaure, J. P. Reemtsma and R. Willig (eds) *Erneuerung der Kritik*. Frankfurt: Campus, pp. 137–47.

Honneth, A. (2009e) 'Vorwort', in R. Celikates, *Kritik als soziale Praxis*. Frankfurt: Campus, pp. 8–13.

Honneth, A. and Saar, M. (2003) *Zwischenbilanz einer Rezeption: Frankfurter Foucault-Konferenz 2001*. Frankfurt: Suhrkamp.

Horkheimer, M. (1970 [1937]) *Traditionelle und kritische Theorie*. Frankfurt: Fischer.

Horkheimer, M. and Adorno, T. (1969 [1944]) *Dialektik der Aufklärung*. Frankfurt: Fischer.

Horkheimer, M. and Adorno, T. W. (1972 [1947]) *The Dialectic of Enlightenment*. New York: Herder and Herder.

Iser, M. (2008) *Empörung und Fortschritt*. Frankfurt: Campus.

Jaeggi, R. (2009) 'Was ist Ideologiekritik', in R. Jaeggi and Wesche, T. (eds) *Was ist Kritik?* Frankfurt: Suhrkamp, pp. 266–95.

James, W. (1978) *Pragmatism*. Cambridge, MA: Harvard University Press.

Joas, H. (1993) *Pragmatism and Social Theory*. Chicago: University of Chicago Press.

Kant, I. (1968 [1781]) *Critique of Pure Reason*. London: Macmillan.

Kant, I. (1956 [1788]) *Critique of Practical Reason*. Indianapolis: Bobbs-Merrill.

Kant, I. (1957a [1784–98]) *On History*. Indianapolis: Bobbs-Merrill.

Kant, I. (1957b [1795]) *Perpetual Peace*. Indianapolis: Bobbs-Merrill.

Kant, I. (1972 [1790]) *Critique of Judgement*. New York: Hafner.

Kant, I. (1996 [1798]) *Anthropology from a Pragmatic Point of View*. Carbondale: Southern Illinois Press.

Keat, R. and Urry, J. (1975) *Social Theory as Science*. London: Routledge & Kegan Paul.

Kelly, T. (2000) 'The unhappy liberal', *Constellations* 7(3): 372–81.

Kemp, S. (2003) 'Rethinking social criticism', *History of the Human Sciences* 16(4): 61–84.

Kierkegaard, S. (2001 [1846]) *A Literary Review*. London: Penguin.

Kierkegaard, S. (1980 [1849]) *The Sickness unto Death*. Princeton, NJ: Princeton University Press.

Kierkegaard, S. (1992 [1843]) *Either/Or*. London: Penguin.

Korsch, K. (1966 [1923]) *Marxismus und Philosophie*. Frankfurt: Europäische Verlagsanstalt.

Kousis, M. and Eder, K. (2001) 'EU policy-making, local action, and the emergence of institutions of collective action', in K. Eder and M. Kousis (eds) *Environmental Politics in Southern Europe*. Dordrecht: Kluwer, pp. 3–21.

Kuhlmann, W. (ed.) (1986) *Moralität und Sittlichkeit*. Frankfurt: Suhrkamp.

Löwith, K. (1964) *From Hegel to Nietzsche*. London: Constable.

Luhmann, N. (1995) *Social Systems*. Stanford, CA: Stanford University Press.

Lukács, G. (1968 [1923]) *History and Class Consciousness*. London: Merlin Press.

McCarthy, T. (1978) *The Critical Theory of Jürgen Habermas*. London: Hutchinson.

McCarthy, T. (1991) 'Complexity and democracy', in A. Honneth and H. Joas (eds) *Communicative Action*. Cambridge: Polity Press, pp. 119–39.

McCarthy, T. (1993 [1991]) *Ideals and Illusions*. Cambridge, MA: MIT Press.

McCarthy, T. (1994a) 'Philosophy and Critical Theory: A reprise', in D. C. Hoy and T. McCarthy, *Critical Theory*. Oxford: Blackwell, pp. 5–100.

McCarthy, T. (1994b) 'Rejoinder to David Hoy', in D. C. Hoy and T. McCarthy, *Critical Theory*. Oxford: Blackwell, pp. 217-48.

McCarthy, T. (2001a) 'Die politische Philosophie und das Problem der Rasse', in L. Wingert and K. Günther (eds) *Die Öffentlichkeit der Vernunft und die Vernunft der Öffentlichkeit: Festschrift für Jürgen Habermas*. Frankfurt: Suhrkamp, pp. 627–54.

McCarthy, T. (2001b) 'Critical Theory today: An interview with Thomas McCarthy', in W. Rehg and J. Bohman (eds) *Pluralism and the Pragmatic Turn: The Transformation of Critical Theory – Essays in Honor of Thomas McCarthy*. Cambridge, MA: MIT Press, pp. 413–29.

McCarthy, T. (2004) 'Political philosophy and racial injustice: from normative to critical theory', in S. Benhabib and N. Fraser (eds) *Pragmatism, Critique and Judgment*. Cambridge, MA: MIT Press, pp. 149–70.

Mannheim, K. (1972 [1936]) *Ideology and Utopia*. London: Routledge & Kegan Paul.

Marcuse, H. (1968) *One Dimensional Man*. London: Sphere.

Marcuse, H. (1969a [1955]) *Eros and Civilization*. London: Sphere.

Marcuse, H. (1969b) 'Repressive tolerance', in R. P. Wolff, B. Moore and H. Marcuse, *A Critique of Pure Tolerance*. London: Cape, pp. 95–137.

Marcuse, H. (1972 [1937]) *Negations*. Harmondsworth: Penguin.

Marcuse, H. (1973 [1941]) *Reason and Revolution*. London: Routledge & Kegan Paul.

Marx, K. (1963) *The Eighteenth Brumaire of Louis Bonaparte*. New York: International.

Marx, K. (1954 [1867]) *Capital*, Vol. I. London: Lawrence & Wishart.

Marx, K. (1967a [1843]) 'Toward the critique of Hegel's philosophy of law', in L. D. Easton and K. H. Guddat (eds) *Writings of the Young Marx on Philosophy and Society*. New York: Doubleday.

Marx, K. (1967b [1888]) 'Theses on Feuerbach', in L. D. Easton and K. H. Guddat (eds.) *Writings of the Young Marx on Philosophy and Society*. New York: Doubleday.

Marx, K. and Engels, F. (1969 [1846]) *The German Ideology*. New York: International.

Marx, K. and Engels, F. (1978 [1847]) *The Communist Manifesto*. Harmondsworth: Penguin.

Maton, K. (2003) 'Reflexivity, relationism, and research', *Space and Culture* 6(1): 52–56.

Mead, G. H. (1974 [1934]) *Mind, Self and Society*. Chicago: University of Chicago Press.

Mead, G. H. (1959) *The Philosophy of the Present*. La Salle, IL: Open Court.

Menke, C. (2000) 'Critique and self-reflection', *Constellations* 7(1): 100–115.

Miller, M. (1986) *Kollektive Lernprozesse*. Frankfurt: Suhrkamp.

Miller, M. (2002) 'Some theoretical aspects of systemic learning', *Sozialer Sinn* 3: 379–421.

Mills, C. W. (1940) 'Situated actions and vocabularies of motive', *American Sociological Review* 5: 904–13.

Mills, C. W. (1964) *Sociology and Pragmatism*. New York: Oxford University Press.

Mills, C. W. (1970 [1959]) *The Sociological Imagination*. Harmondsworth: Penguin.

Misgeld, D. (1977) 'Critical Theory and hermeneutics', in J. O'Neill (ed.) *On Critical Theory*. London: Heinemann, pp. 164–83.

Morrow, R. and Brown, D. (1994) *Critical Theory and Methodology*. London Sage.

Nietzsche, F. (1994[1887]) *On the Genealogy of Morality*. Cambridge: Cambridge University Press.

Øfsti, A. (2003) 'Apriori der idealen Kommunikationgesellschaft', in D. Böhler et al. (eds) *Reflexion und Verantwortung*. Frankfurt: Suhrkamp, pp. 197–219.

Outhwaite, W. (1987) *New Philosophies of Social Science*. London: Macmillan.

Outhwaite, W. (2000) 'Rekonstruktion und methodologischer Dualismus', in S. Müller-Doohm (ed.) *Das Interesse der Vernunft*. Frankfurt: Suhrkamp, pp. 218–41.

Parsons, T. (1977) *Social Systems and the Evolution of Action Theory*. New York: Free Press.

Peirce, C. S. (1960) *Collected Papers*, Vol. V. Cambridge, MA: Harvard University Press.

Peirce, C. S. (1958) *Collected Papers, Vol. VIII*. Cambridge, MA: Harvard University Press.

Pels, D. (2003) 'Unhastening science', *European Journal of Social Theory* 6(2): 209–31.

Pratschke, J. (2003) 'Realistic Models?', *Philosophica* 71: 13–38.

Projektgruppe Zivilisationspolitik (2009) *Aufbruch aus dem Patriarchat: Wege in eine neue Zivilisation?* Frankfurt: Lang.

Putnam, H. (1982) 'Why reason can't be naturalized', *Synthese* 52: 1–30.

Radnitzky, G. (1970) *Contemporary Schools of Metascience*. Gothenburg: Akademiforlaget.

Rawls, J. (1985 [1972]) *A Theory of Justice*. London: Oxford University Press.

Rawls, J. (1993) *Political Liberalism*. New York: Columbia University Press.

Rockmore, T. (2002) 'The epistemological promise of pragmatism', in M. Aboulafia, M. Bookman and C. Kemp (eds) *Habermas and Pragmatism*. London: Routledge, pp. 47–64.

Rorty, R. (1979) *Philosophy and the Mirror of Nature*. Princeton, NJ: Princeton University Press.

Rorty, R. (1982) *The Consequences of Pragmatism*. Minneapolis: University of Minnesota Press.

Rorty, R. (1989) *Contingency, Irony, and Solidarity*. Cambridge: Cambridge University Press.

Rosa, H. (2004) 'Four levels of self-interpretation: A paradigm for interpretative social philosophy and political criticism', *Philosophy and Social Criticism* 30(5–6): 619–720.

Rosa, H. (2009) 'Kritik der Zeitverhältnisse', in R. Jaeggi and Wesche, T. (eds) *Was ist Kritik?* Frankfurt: Suhrkamp, pp. 23–54.

Rousseau, J. J. (1966 [1762]) *The Social Contract and Discourses*. London: Dent.

Royce, J. (2001 [1913]) *The Problem of Christianity*. Washington, DC: Catholic University of America Press.

Rusch, G. (1999) 'Eine Kommunikationstheorie für kognitive Systeme', in G. Rusch and S. J. Schmidt (eds) *Konstruktivismus in der Medien- und Kommunikations-wissenschaft*. Frankfurt: Suhrkamp, pp. 150–84.

Saar, M. (2007) *Genealogie als Kritik*. Frankfurt: Campus.

Saar, M. (2009) 'Genealogische Kritik', in R. Jaeggi and Wesche, T. (eds) *Was ist Kritik?* Frankfurt: Suhrkamp, pp. 247–65.

Sandbothe, M. (ed.) (2000) *Die Renaissance des Pragmatismus*. Weilerswist: Velbrück Wissenschaft.

Sayer, A. (1992 [1984]) *Method in Social Science*. London: Routledge.

Sayer, A. (2000) *Realism and Social Science*. London: Sage.

Schmidt, S. J. (1999) 'Blickwechsel: Umrisse einer Medienepistemologie', in G. Rusch and S. J. Schmidt (eds) *Konstruktivismus in der Medien- und Kommunikationswissenschaft*. Frankfurt: Suhrkamp, pp. 119–45.

Schnädelbach, H. (1987) *Vernunft und Geschichte*. Frankfurt: Suhrkamp.

von Schomberg, R. (1992) 'Argumentation im Kontext wissenschaftlicher Kontroverse', in K.-O. Apel and M. Kettner (eds) *Zur Anwendung der Diskursethik in Politik, Recht und Wissenschaft*. Frankfurt: Suhrkamp, pp. 260–77.

Schulz, W. (1962) *J. G. Fichte*. Pfullingen: Neske.

Strydom, P. (1987) 'Collective learning', *Philosophy and Social Criticism* 13(3): 265–81.

Strydom, P. (1992) 'The ontogenetic fallacy', *Theory, Culture and Society* 9(3): 65–93.

Strydom, P. (1993) 'Sociocultural evolution or the social evolution of practical reason', *Praxis International* 13(3): 304–22.

Strydom, P. (1999) 'Triple contingency: the theoretical problem of the public in communication societies', *Philosophy and Social Criticism* 25(2): 1–25.

Strydom, P. (2000) *Discourse and Knowledge*. Liverpool: Liverpool University Press.

Strydom, P. (2001) 'The problem of triple contingency in Habermas', *Sociological Theory* 19(2): 165–86.

Strydom, P. (2002) *Risk, Environment and Society*. Buckingham: Open University Press.

Strydom, P. (2004) 'The "contest of the faculties" and cultures of time', unpublished lecture, Science Faculty Public Lecture Series, University College Cork, 3 February.

Strydom, P. (2006a) 'Intersubjectivity: Interactionist or discursive?', *Philosophy and Social Criticism* 32(2): 155–72.

Strydom, P. (2006b) 'Contemporary European cognitive social theory', in G. Delanty (ed.) *Handbook of Contemporary European Social Theory*. London: Routledge, pp. 218–29.

Strydom, P. (2007) 'Introduction: A cartography of contemporary cognitive social theory', *European Journal of Social Theory* 10(3): 399–56.

Strydom, P. (2008a) 'Philosophies of the social sciences', in C. Crothers (ed.) *Historical Developments and Theoretical Approaches in Sociology*, in *Encyclopedia of Life Support Systems* (EOLSS). Developed under the auspices of UNESCO. Oxford: Eolss Publishers, <www.eolss.net> accessed 11 November 2010.

Strydom, P. (2008b) 'Risk communication: World creation through collective learning under complex contingent conditions', *Journal of Risk Research* 11(1–2): 5–22.

Strydom, P. (2009a) *New Horizons of Critical Theory: Collective Learning and Triple Contingency*. Delhi: Shipra.

Strydom, P. (2009b) 'Social practices and cultural models: Outline of a cognitive sociological approach', unpublished paper, workshop on cognitive sociology/social epistemology/sociology of science/economics of scientific knowledge, Université de Provence, France, 18 March.

Strydom, P. (2009c) 'On normative commitment: Towards a social theory of mechanisms', unpublished paper, workshop on philosophy of social science, Université de Provence, France, 26 June.

Strydom, P. (2011) 'The cognitive and metacognitive dimensions of social and political theory', in G. Delanty and S. Turner (eds) *Handbook of Contemporary Social and Political Theory*. London: Routledge, pp. 328–38.

Taylor, C. (1986) 'Foucault on freedom and truth', in D. C. Hoy (ed.) *Foucault: A Critical Reader*. Oxford: Blackwell, pp. 69–102.

Thompson, J. (1981) *Critical Hermeneutics*. Cambridge: Cambridge University Press.

Touraine, A. (2000) *Can We Live Together?* Cambridge: Polity.

Trenz, H.-J. and Eder, K. (2004) 'The Democratizing Dynamics of a European Public Sphere', *European Journal of Social Theory* 7(1): 5–25.

Wacquant, L. (2004) 'Critical thought as solvent of doxa', *Constellations* 11(1): 97–101.

Walzer, M. (1987) *Interpretation and Social Criticism*. Cambridge, MA: Harvard University Press.

Walzer, M. (1988) *The Company of Critics*. New York: Basic Books.

Wellmer, A. (1971 [1969]) *Critical Theory of Society*. London: Heinemann.

Wellmer, A. (1986) *Ethik und Dialog*. Frankfurt: Suhrkamp.

Wellmer, A. (1998) 'Truth, contingency, and modernity', in A. Wellmer, *Endgames*. Cambridge, MA: MIT, pp. 137–54.

Wellmer, A. (2003) 'Der Streit um die Wahrheit: Pragmatismus ohne regulative Ideen', in D. Böhler, M. Kettner and G. Skirbekk (eds) *Reflexion und Verantwortung*. Frankfurt: Suhrkamp, pp. 143–70.

Index